The Politics of Religion in the Age of Mary, Queen of Scots

The Earl of Argyll and the Struggle for Britain and Ireland

Early modern historians have theorised about the nature of the new 'British' history for a generation. This study examines how British politics operated in practice during the age of Mary, Queen of Scots, and it explains how the crises of the mid sixteenth century moulded the future political shape of the British Isles.

A central figure in these struggles was the 5th earl of Argyll, chief of Clan Campbell and leading Lowland aristocrat, who was the most powerful magnate not only at the court of Queen Mary, his sister-in-law, but throughout the three kingdoms. His domination of the Western Highlands and Islands drew him into the complex politics of the north of Ireland, while his Protestant commitment involved him in Anglo–Scottish relations. During the British crises of 1559–60, 1565 and 1567–73 his actions also helped determine the Protestant allegiance of the British mainland and the political and religious complexion of Ireland. Argyll's career therefore demonstrates both the possibilities and the limitations of British history throughout the early modern period.

JANE DAWSON is John Laing Senior Lecturer in the History and Theology of the Reformation, University of Edinburgh.

Cambridge Studies in Early Modern British History

Series editors

ANTHONY FLETCHER
Victoria County History, Institute of Historical Research, University of London

JOHN GUY
Professor of Modern History, University of St. Andrews

JOHN MORRILL
*Professor of British and Irish History, University of Cambridge,
and Vice-Master of Selwyn College*

This is a series of monographs and studies covering many aspects of the history of the British Isles between the late fifteenth century and the early eighteenth century. It includes the work of established scholars and pioneering work by a new generation of scholars. It includes both reviews and revisions of major topics and books, which open up new historical terrain or which reveal startling new perspectives on familiar subjects. All the volumes set detailed research into our broader perspectives and the books are intended for the use of students as well as of their teachers.

For a list of titles in the series, see end of book.

THE POLITICS OF RELIGION IN THE AGE OF MARY, QUEEN OF SCOTS

The Earl of Argyll and the Struggle for Britain and Ireland

JANE E.A. DAWSON

University of Edinburgh

CAMBRIDGE
UNIVERSITY PRESS

PUBLISHED BY THE PRESS SYNDICATE OF THE UNIVERSITY OF CAMBRIDGE
The Pitt Building, Trumpington Street, Cambridge, United Kingdom

CAMBRIDGE UNIVERSITY PRESS
The Edinburgh Building, Cambridge CB2 2RU, UK
40 West 20th Street, New York, NY 10011-4211, USA
477 Williamstown Road, Port Melbourne, VIC 3207, Australia
Ruiz de Alarcón 13, 28014 Madrid, Spain
Dock House, The Waterfront, Cape Town 8001, South Africa

http://www.cambridge.org

© Jane E.A. Dawson 2002

First published 2002

Printed in the United Kingdom at the University Press, Cambridge

Typeface Sabon 10/12pt.   *System* LaTeX 2_ε [TB]

A catalogue record for this book is available from the British Library

Library of Congress Cataloguing in Publication data
Dawson, Jane E.A.
The politics of religion in the age of Mary, Queen of Scots : the Earl of Argyll and the struggle
for Britain and Ireland / Jane E.A. Dawson.
p.   cm. – (Cambridge studies in early modern British history)
Includes bibliographical references and index.
ISBN 0-521-80996-7
1. Argyll, Archibald Campbell, Earl of, 1530–1573.   2. Scotland – History – Mary Stuart,
1542–1567 – Biography.   3. Religion and politics – Great Britain – History – 16th century.
4. Religion and politics – Ireland – History – 16th century.   5. Mary, Queen of Scots,
1542–1587 – Contemporaries.   6. Great Britain – Politics and government – 1558–1603.
7. Ireland – Politics and government – 1558–1603.   8. Politicians – Great Britain – Biography.
9. Nobility – Scotland – Biography.   10. Campbell family.   I. Title.   II. Series.
DA787 .A74 D39   2002
941.105′092 – dc21   2001052679

ISBN 0 521 80996 7 hardback

For
Marian Dawson
and
in memory of
Norman Dawson

CONTENTS

FIGURES

ACKNOWLEDGEMENTS

It is a pleasure finally to have the opportunity to thank the numerous people and institutions who have helped me during the protracted gestation of this book. I am especially indebted to the 12th duke of Argyll for his enthusiastic encouragement of the project and for access to the Argyll Manuscripts at Inveraray; it is a particular regret that this book will appear after his unexpected death. I would like to thank the 13th duke for continuing his father's permissions. The earl of Moray was equally generous in allowing me to consult and cite from his family's archives. I am grateful to the National Gallery of Scotland and to the trustees of the Dunimarle Collection for permission to reproduce the drawing on the dust jacket. The staff of the National Archives of Scotland, the National Library of Scotland, the Public Record Office, the British Library, the Bodleian Library, the University libraries of St Andrews, Edinburgh and Cambridge have all been of great assistance to me. Grateful acknowledgement is made to the British Academy, the Leverhulme Trust and the Universities of Edinburgh and St Andrews for their financial support of different aspects of this project.

Nancy Bailey, Linda Dunbar and Anne Johnston have given immeasureable help over the research and production of this book. I am grateful to Fiona Macdonald, Martin Macgregor and Pam Ritchie who, as well as allowing me to consult their unpublished work, have provided much additional information and ideas. Stephen Alford, by generously sharing with me his unrivalled knowledge of William Cecil, greatly improved the balance of the book. I am especially indebted to my present and former colleagues in Ecclesiastical History, the Faculty of Divinity and the other history departments at Edinburgh, and to those in the School of History at St Andrews, who have been a permanent source of encouragement and strength. Over the years I have drawn heavily upon the immense knowledge and kindness of Alastair Campbell of Airds and of other historians of the Campbells and Highlands: David Sellar, Steve Boardman, Jean and Billy Munro, Nick MacLean-Bristol along with many others, especially those in Argyll. Keith Brown and Margaret Sanderson generously read the entire book in draft and offered helpful criticisms that have done much to improve the text, though all remaining errors are my own. Throughout my academic career, Geoffrey Barrow, Bruce Lenman and Donald Meek have been unstinting in their encouragement and support. John Morrill and John Guy gave the book their backing from its inception and, as two of the series editors, demonstrated exemplary patience awaiting its delivery and then improved it with their comments. The equally patient William Davies, supported by his colleagues at Cambridge University Press, has combined his accustomed professionalism with the light touch of an understanding editor. I am especially grateful to Hamish Scott who contributed so much to this book at every stage of its creation. Finally, my thanks go to many other friends who have helped me over the past dozen years, and who must forgive me for not mentioning them by name. The book is dedicated with love and gratitude to my parents.

ABBREVIATIONS

Alford, *Cecil*	S. Alford, *The Early Elizabethan Polity: William Cecil and the British Succession Crisis, 1558–1569* (Cambridge, 1998).
Argyll Inventory	*Argyll, An Inventory of the Ancient Monuments* (7 vols., RCAHMS, Edinburgh, 1971–92).
APS	*Acts of the Parliaments of Scotland* eds. T. Thomson and C. Innes (12 vols., Edinburgh, 1814–42).
AT	Argyll Transcripts, made by Niall Campbell, 10th duke of Argyll.
Bannatyne, *Memorials*	*Memorials of Transactions in Scotland 1569–72 by Richard Bannatyne* ed. R. Pitcairn (Bannatyne Club, 51, Edinburgh, 1836).
BL	British Library
Brady, *Chief Governors*	C. Brady, *The Chief Governors: The Rise and Fall of Reform Government in Tudor Ireland, 1536–1588* (Cambridge, 1994).
BUK	*'The Booke of the Universall Kirk of Scotland': Acts and Proceedings of the General Assemblies of the Kirk of Scotland* ed. T. Thomson (3 vols., Bannatyne Club, 81, Edinburgh, 1839–45).
Calderwood, *History*	D. Calderwood, *The History of the Kirk of Scotland* ed. T. Thomson (8 vols., Wodrow Society, Edinburgh, 1842–9).
Campbell Letters	*Campbell Letters, 1559–1583* ed. J.E.A. Dawson (SHS, 5th ser. 10, Edinburgh, 1997).
Carswell, *Foirm*	*Foirm Na N-Urrnuidheadh: John Carswell's Gaelic Translation of the Book of Common Order* ed. R.L. Thomson (Scottish Gaelic Text Society, Edinburgh, 1970).

Clan Campbell	*The Clan Campbell* eds. D. Campbell and H. Paton (8 vols., Edinburgh, 1913–22).
Coll. de Rebus Alban	*Collectanea de rebus Albanicis* (Iona Club, Edinburgh, 1847).
CSPSc	*Calendar of State Papers relating to Scotland and Mary, Queen of Scots, 1547–1603* eds. J. Bain *et al.* (13 vols., Edinburgh, 1898–1969).
CSP Sp	*Calendar of State Papers, Spanish* eds. R. Tyler *et al.* (13 vols., London, 1862–1954).
CSP Ireld	*Calendar of State Papers relating to Ireland* eds. H.C. Hamilton *et al.* (24 vols., London, 1860–1911).
CSP For	*Calendar of State Papers, Foreign Series, Edward, Mary and Elizabeth* eds. J. Stevenson *et al.* (25 vols., London, 1861–1950).
Dawson, 'Clan, Kin and Kirk'	J.E.A. Dawson, 'Clan, Kin and Kirk: The Campbells and the Scottish Reformation' in N.S. Amos, A. Pettegree and H. van Nierop, eds., *The Education of a Christian Society* (Aldershot, 1999), 211–42.
Dawson, 'Cecil'	J.E.A. Dawson, 'William Cecil and the British Dimension of Early Elizabethan Foreign Policy' *History*, 74 (1989), 196–216.
Dawson, 'The Emergence of the Highlands'	J.E.A. Dawson, 'The Gaidhealtachd and the Emergence of the Scottish Highlands' in B. Bradshaw and P. Roberts, eds., *British Identity and Consciousness* (Cambridge, 1998), 259–300.
Dawson, 'The Protestant Earl'	J.E.A. Dawson, 'The Protestant Earl and the Godly Gael: The Fifth Earl of Argyll (c. 1538–73) and the Scottish Reformation' in D. Wood, ed., *Life and Thought in the Northern Church c. 1100–c. 1700: Essays in Honour of Claire Cross* (Studies in Church History, Subsidia, 12, Woodbridge, Suffolk, 1999), 337–63.
Dawson, 'Two Kingdoms or Three?'	J.E.A. Dawson, 'Two Kingdoms or Three?: Ireland in Anglo-Scottish Relations in the Middle of the Sixteenth Century' in R. Mason, ed., *Scotland and England, 1286–1815* (Edinburgh, 1987), 113–38.

Diurnal	*A diurnal of remarkable occurrents that have passed within the country of Scotland since the death of King James the Fourth till the year MDLXXV* ed. T. Thomson (Bannatyne Club, 43, Edinburgh, 1833).
Donaldson, *Queen's Men*	G. Donaldson, *All the Queen's Men: Power and Politics in Mary Stewart's Scotland* (London, 1983).
Hayes-McCoy, *Scots Mercenary Forces*	G.A. Hayes-McCoy, *Scots Mercenary Forces in Ireland, 1565–1603* (Dublin, 1996 reprint of the 1937 edn).
Herries, *Memoirs*	*Historical Memoirs of the Reign of Mary, Queen of Scots by Lord Herries* ed. R. Pitcairn (Abbotsford Club, 6, Edinburgh, 1836).
Highland Papers	*Highland Papers* ed. J. Macphail (4 vols., SHS, 2nd ser. 5, 12, 20; 3rd ser. 22, Edinburgh, 1914–34).
Hill, *Fire and Sword*	J. Michael Hill, *Fire and Sword: Sorley Boy MacDonnell and the Rise of Clan Ian Mor 1538–90* (London, 1993).
HMC	*Reports of the Historical Manuscripts Commission*
Illustrations of the Reign of Queen Mary	*Selections from unpublished manuscripts . . . illustrating the reign of Queen Mary* ed. J. Stevenson (Maitland Club, 41, Edinburgh, 1837).
Keith, *History*	R. Keith, *History of the Affairs of Church and State in Scotland, from the Beginning of the Reformation to the Year 1568* eds. J.P. Lawson and C.J. Lyon (3 vols., Spottiswoode Society, 1, Edinburgh, 1844–50).
Knox, *History*	J. Knox, *The History of the Reformation in Scotland* ed. W.C. Dickinson (2 vols., London, 1949).
Knox, *Works*	*The Works of John Knox* ed. D. Laing (6 vols., Edinburgh, 1846–64).
Letters to Argyll Family	*Letters to the Argyll Family* ed. A. MacDonald (Maitland Club, 50, Edinburgh, 1839).
MacGregor, 'MacGregors'	M. MacGregor, 'A Political History of the MacGregors before 1571' (University of Edinburgh PhD thesis, 1989).

MacLean-Bristol, *Warriors and Priests*	N. MacLean-Bristol, *Warriors and Priests: The History of Clan MacLean, 1300–1570* (East Linton, 1995).
NLS	National Library of Scotland
NRA(S)	National Register of Archives, Scotland
PRO	Public Record Office
PSAS	*Proceedings of the Society of Antiquaries of Scotland*
RCAHMS	Royal Commission on the Ancient and Historical Monuments of Scotland
Records of Argyll	*Records of Argyll* ed. Lord Archibald Campbell (Edinburgh, 1885).
Reg. Hon. de Mort	*Registrum Honoris de Morton* eds. T. Thomson *et al.* (2 vols., Bannatyne Club, 94, Edinburgh, 1853).
RMS	*Registrum magni sigilii regum scotorum, Register of the Great Seal of Scotland* eds. J. Thomson *et al.* (11 vols., Edinburgh, 1882–1914).
Rose of Kilravock	*A Genealogical Deduction of the Family of Rose of Kilravock* ed. C. Innes (Spalding Club, 18, Edinburgh, 1848).
RPC	*Register of the Privy Council of Scotland* eds. J. Burton *et al.* (1st ser., 14 vols., Edinburgh, 1877–98).
RSCHS	*Records of the Scottish Church History Society*
RSS	*Registrum secreti sigilli regum scotorum, Register of the Privy Seal of Scotland* eds. M. Livingstone *et al.* (8 vols., Edinburgh, 1908–82).
Sadler	*The Letters and Papers of Sir Ralph Sadler* ed. A. Clifford (3 vols., Edinburgh, 1809).
SHR	*Scottish Historical Review*
SHS	Scottish History Society
TA	*Accounts of the Lord High Treasurer of Scotland* eds. T. Dickson *et al.* (12 vols., Edinburgh 1877–1970).
TGSI	*Transactions of the Gaelic Society of Inverness*
White, 'Tudor Plantations'	D.G. White, 'Tudor Plantations in Ireland before 1571' (2 vols., Trinity College, Dublin, PhD thesis, 1967).
Wormald, *Lords and Men*	J. Wormald, *Lords and Men in Scotland: Bonds of Manrent, 1442–1603* (Edinburgh, 1985).

1560: British policies and the British context

On 27 February 1560 in the town of Berwick, on the Anglo-Scottish border, a secret agreement was signed containing a range of unusual and profoundly important clauses. In the first place it constituted a diplomatic revolution. A group of Scots were abandoning their 'auld alliance' with France and embracing as allies their long-standing enemies, the English. The central purpose of the Treaty of Berwick was to furnish desperately needed English military aid to the Scottish Lords of the Congregation to prevent them being overrun by the French troops of Mary of Guise, Scotland's regent.[1] From a Scottish perspective, the language employed to describe this diplomatic revolution was equally remarkable. Though exchanging one dominant protector for another, the treaty had carefully avoided any threat to Scotland's independence, in particular making no mention of England's imperial claims that had played such a prominent part in previous Tudor incursions across the Border.[2]

Another unusual feature was that Elizabeth I of England concluded this formal alliance not with a fellow monarch, but rather with those Scots who were fighting against the regent and her daughter, the Scottish queen. In the volatile international situation of spring 1560, aiding rebellious subjects against their lawful rulers was a risky diplomatic gamble for the precarious Elizabethan regime. It also ran counter to all Elizabeth's political and personal instincts, yet the queen had been persuaded of its necessity by her chief adviser William Cecil, supported by her Privy Council.[3]

One highly significant aspect of the treaty was tucked away in a fleeting reference to the 5th earl of Argyll – one of the leading Lords of the Congregation and the dominant magnate in the West Highlands. He agreed to 'imploy his force and guid will wher he salbe requyred by the quenis

---

[1] See below pp. 96–101.
[2] Dawson, 'Two Kingdoms or Three?', 118–20; Dawson, 'Cecil', 207–8.
[3] For a perceptive study of the formation of English policy during this period, see Alford, *Cecil*, ch. 2.

majestie to reduce the north partis of yrland to the perfyt obedience of england'.[4] This short clause quietly, but completely, reversed English policy in Ireland. At a stroke it replaced England's hostility towards the presence of Scots there with a welcome for Scottish Gaels as valued, subsidised allies. The explicit link between Anglo-Scottish friendship and the Tudor subjugation of Ulster signalled a new departure for both the Scots and the English.

The diplomatic revolution and the novel Irish strategy were the obvious signs of a dramatic change in relations between the three kingdoms. They were products of a remarkable new three-sided approach, which embraced Ireland as well as Scotland and England, and heralded a new era of 'British politics'.[5] That British dimension flowed from the separate, but complementary, British policies pursued by the 5th earl of Argyll and William Cecil. Both were British politicians, but while the English minister's claim has been recognised, his Scottish ally's even greater credentials have been overlooked. Through their joint efforts in the Treaty of Berwick, the triangular approach was for the very first time given official countenance.

Such a momentous development was made possible by a series of changes within Europe and, more especially, within the three kingdoms of England, Ireland and Scotland. Together these changes produced a 'British context' within which the Berwick treaty could be agreed. The most important shift in the international scene was the signing of the Treaty of Câteau-Cambrésis in April 1559, ending the Habsburg–Valois warfare that had dominated European politics since the late fifteenth century. In its wake, the treaty brought peace to Scotland and England, respectively the allies of France and Spain. As a consequence of the peace settlement, European attention was redirected, shifting from the border between France and the Netherlands, the English Channel, and the British mainland, which had been the focal point of the struggle during the 1550s. Preoccupied with their own domestic and international concerns, the last thing either the Spanish or

---

[4] BL Cotton Calig. B 9 fo. 34. This clause was not included in *CSPSc*, I. 23–4 though it was summarised in *CSP For 1559–60*, 413–5, and see below.

[5] Finding an acceptable shorthand geographical description for the countries which formed the UK before the creation of Eire has proved difficult. Whilst accurate, the term 'Atlantic archipelago' is rather cumbersome so, for convenience, I have used the following as virtual synonyms: the islands of Britain; these islands; the British Isles, and the adjective, British. Without intending to imply any hidden imperial or other agenda, they describe the kingdoms of Ireland, Scotland, and England and Wales as they existed in the sixteenth century, following the definition of the British Isles in the *Oxford English Dictionary*: 'a geographical term for the islands comprising Great Britain and Ireland with all their offshore islands including the Isle of Man and the Channel Islands'. A discussion of some of the ways in which early modern politicians conceptualised these islands can be found in the concluding chapter.

the French king wanted in 1559–60 was for a British problem to restart the fighting.[6] The conclusion of European peace also gave Elizabeth the opportunity to introduce a Protestant ecclesiastical settlement into her realms. One immediate consequence was England's return to the diplomatic isolation that had followed Henry VIII's break with Rome. In 1559, it was conceivable that France and Spain, the two leading Catholic powers, might combine against the heretical Elizabethan regime. Although it did not materialise, the fear of a great Catholic conspiracy haunted England's statesmen for the rest of the reign and dominated their diplomatic outlook.

The peace treaty confirmed the English loss to France of Calais, the final trophy of the Lancastrian continental empire. This was a severe psychological blow, with repercussions for England's defence and for her self-perception. By removing her toehold inside France, it dragged her own southern border into the English Channel. Elizabeth's realm was now separated by the sea from the continental land mass and had become an island 'off' and not 'of' Europe. The entire Tudor state was contained within the Atlantic archipelago, which encouraged the development of an insular mentality and redefined England's defensive needs.[7] The new perspective placed particular emphasis upon the remaining land border with Scotland and the sea frontier between the two states, which ran through the North Channel.

England's geographical and political separation from Europe sharply focused attention upon events within the British mainland. In particular it highlighted Anglo-Scottish relations, which had been subject to a number of twists and turns during the first half of the sixteenth century. At the century's start, the marriage of James IV and Margaret Tudor had failed to end the long-running animosity between the two countries. The possibility of a dynastic alliance re-emerged in the 1540s, when Scotland's ruler was the child Mary and young Edward was heir, and later king, of England. However, the Scottish choice of a French husband and alliance for their queen led to renewed military confrontation in the 'Rough Wooing'. The propaganda that accompanied the English invasion was based upon the concept of a united, Protestant mainland of Britain. Such notions were even welcomed by some 'assured Scots' who, for financial and ideological reasons, supported an alliance with the 'auld enemy'.

---

[6] M.J. Rodríguez-Salgado, *The Changing Face of Empire: Charles V, Philip II and Habsburg Authority, 1551–9* (Cambridge, 1988), ch. 8.
[7] The Channel Islands provide the obvious exception, but the point concerns a shift in perception, as demonstrated in contemporary maps, e.g. P. Barber, 'A Tudor Mystery: Laurence Nowell's Map of England and Ireland', *Map Collector*, 22 (1983), 16–21; Dawson, 'Cecil', 197–8.

Despite the circulation of these British ideas, a union between the two kingdoms was not a serious political option. Instead, for the English the main result of their military campaigns was proof of an unpalatable truth. England could readily defeat the Scots, but could not hold Scotland permanently by force. Future English policy makers such as Cecil, who had participated personally in the 1548 campaign, concluded that alliance, not conquest, was the best way to eradicate the threat from the north. For the Scots, the long-term consequences of the Rough Wooing were the enduring association between the Scottish Protestant cause and English intervention, and the planting of the conviction that an English alliance could be of benefit for Scotland.[8]

In 1558, Anglo-Scottish relations were further complicated by two dynastic events. The first was the marriage of Mary, Queen of Scots to Francis, the French Dauphin, who was subsequently granted the Scottish crown matrimonial, creating a regnal union between the two kingdoms.[9] The realisation of her cherished dynastic goal allowed Mary of Guise much greater freedom to pursue her pro-French programme within Scottish domestic politics.[10] This, in turn, led several leading nobles to conclude that Scotland's incorporation into France had already begun. Believing its independence was threatened, these aristocrats were willing to consider an alliance with England to defend their kingdom. By the close of 1558, an Anglophile party had been resurrected within Scottish politics.

The second event to transform Anglo-Scottish relations was the death in November 1558 of Mary Tudor, England's Catholic queen. Elizabeth's accession installed Mary, Queen of Scots as the next heir in blood to the English throne. Scotland's queen thus became a central and immediate part of the English succession question. For those who believed that the divorce of Catherine of Aragon was invalid and that the illegitimate Elizabeth could not inherit the crown, Mary was presumed to be the lawful queen of England. This posed a direct threat to Elizabeth personally and to her kingdom, especially if the French king, Mary's father-in-law, chose to press her claim with any vigour.

The change of monarch in England had immediate consequences north of the Border. Her daughter's elevated position in the English succession altered Mary of Guise's approach in both domestic and international politics by providing her with a new dynastic goal: a united British mainland under

[8] M. Merriman, *The Rough Wooings: Mary, Queen of Scots, 1542–1551* (East Linton, 2000); G. Phillips, *The Anglo-Scots Wars, 1513–50* (Woodbridge, Suffolk, 1999).
[9] See below, ch. 3.
[10] I am grateful to Dr Pamela Ritchie for her help on the policy of Mary of Guise. See her thesis, 'Dynasticism and Diplomacy: The Political Career of Marie de Guise in Scotland, 1548–60' (University of St Andrews PhD thesis, 1999).

Franco-Scottish rule. At the same time, Elizabeth's accession and her Protestant settlement gave new heart to Scottish reformers in their own struggle for religious recognition. By the summer of 1559, the Scottish Protestants had moved into outright rebellion. Past association and present necessity led them to seek aid from their southern neighbour. Their pleas were answered at Berwick.[11]

The inclusion in that treaty of a provision for co-operation in Ireland was unprecedented. Previous diplomatic exchanges on the subject had been hostile, and during the preceding two years the English had conducted a campaign to expel all Scots from Ireland.[12] Since the thirteenth century, mercenaries from the Western Isles had been employed by the Irish Gaelic chiefs on permanent or seasonal contracts. These professional soldiers upheld the chiefs' authority and independence and encouraged the increasing militarisation of the Irish lordships. Over the next three centuries, the presence of these gallowglass and redshank mercenaries had helped prevent the English conquering or remodelling Irish Gaelic society.

The flourishing mercenary trade was one dimension of the strong interconnexion between Gaelic Ireland and Gaelic Scotland. The two communities were united by their common language and culture and by their shared identity as Gaels. In the majority of circumstances, Gaeldom ignored the official boundaries between the Stewart and Tudor kingdoms, focusing instead upon its own cultural and social unity. The separate political worlds of the Gaelic regions were different from the national politics revolving around their monarchs, which characterised the kingdoms of England and Scotland. Within Gaeldom, political power was diffuse, being shared between a group of independent chiefs, each able to exercise sovereign powers within their areas of influence. Although sharing the same social structure and values, Gaelic politics did not possess a common focus. There was no unifying centre of authority, not even the limited coherence previously provided by a Lord of the Isles or High King of Ireland. Politics within the Scottish Highlands and Islands and Gaelic Ireland had fragmented into a series of overlapping regional networks.

By the middle of the sixteenth century, the power of the earls of Argyll was offering a new unity and focus to the Gaelic communities on either side of the North Channel. Though firmly rooted in the Scottish mainland, Campbell power had spread from the Highlands into the Isles and into northern

---

[11] For a detailed discussion see pp. 96–101.
[12] 'Notes for Sussex' and 'A present remedy for the reformation of the north', 27 April 1556, *CSP Ireld*, I. 33–4 (11 and 13); Act 'against the bringing in of Scots, retaining of them and marrying with them' printed in *Irish History from Contemporary Sources, 1509–1610* ed. C. Maxwell (London, 1923), 298–9; for Sussex's 1558 expedition against the MacDonalds, see Dawson, 'Two Kingdoms or Three?', 117–8.

Ireland.[13] After the forfeiture of the Lord of the Isles in 1493, the earls of Argyll extended their influence over the Hebridean chiefs, thereby increasing their involvement in the mercenary trade with Ireland and the Western sea routes along which it travelled. This led to a greater awareness of, and interest in, Irish politics, especially in the north. With its close links to the Isles and the Scottish seaboard, Ulster had become part of the earls' political world. By 1555, the formal adoption into his affinity of O'Donnell, the ruler of Donegal, signalled that Argyll's political dominance had traversed the North Channel and was extending into the north of Ireland.

Geographical proximity maximised the ties between the Gaelic communities of Ulster, Kintyre and the southern Hebrides.[14] In the sixteenth century, these links were represented by the MacDonalds, who held lands on both sides of the North Channel, a mere day's sailing apart.[15] The southern branch of Clan Donald, whose forbears had been the Lords of the Isles, had expanded from their original Ulster settlement in the Glynnes of Antrim into the Route.[16] Though they were by far the most successful colonists in Ireland during the sixteenth century, they did not forsake their ancestral lands in Kintyre and Islay. Because of his Scottish origins and holdings, the MacDonald chief owed his allegiance to the Stewart crown. Within Ireland, his clansmen were regarded by both English and Irish communities as foreigners and unwelcome colonists. They were also assumed to pose a security threat. In Edward VI's reign, the MacDonalds had offered a base for a French invasion of Ireland, and as long as a Franco-Scottish alliance survived, the English believed they would act as a French fifth column. In the late 1550s, their chief, James MacDonald of Dunivaig and the Glens, was regarded with deep suspicion by the English.[17]

With so much of the country beyond its control, Ireland's vulnerability to foreign intervention became a permanent concern for the English authorities in Dublin and London. King Henry VIII's adoption of the title 'King of Ireland' in 1541 had underlined the problem that, despite the grandiose rhetoric, beyond the small area of the Pale, the English did not rule over the island nor its inhabitants. By 1556, with Sussex's appointment as chief

---

[13] See below p. 61.

[14] F. Macdonald, 'Ireland and Scotland: Historical Perspectives on the Gaelic Dimension, 1560–1760' (2 vols., University of Glasgow PhD thesis, 1994). I am grateful to Dr Macdonald for many helpful comments on the links between Scotland and Ireland.

[15] The MacDonalds could bring reinforcements in a few hours, if the tides were right, see below p. 135. The warning beacons on the Antrim hills were drawn on a map of Ulster c. 1602: D. Rixson, *The West Highland Galley* (East Linton, 1998), Plate 13, 208, n. 8.

[16] Hill, *Fire and Sword*, 14 (Map 2).

[17] For example Sidney to Privy Council, 8 February 1558, SP62/2, fos. 15–6; D. Potter, 'French Intrigue in Ireland during the reign of Henri II, 1547–1559', *International History Review*, 5 (1983), 159–80.

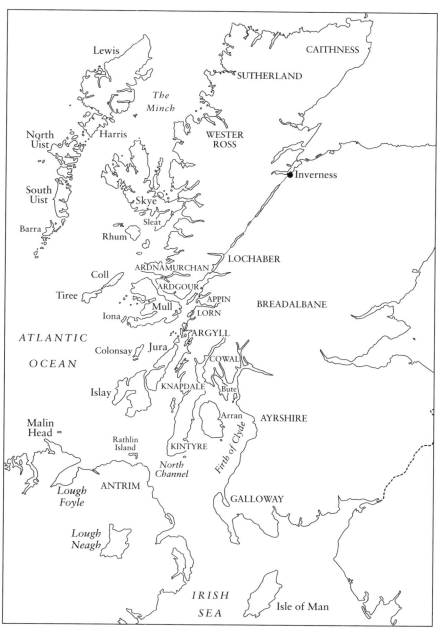

1. Map of the north-western seaboard

governor, schemes of plantation and conquest began to replace conciliation and consent as methods of extending English authority throughout Ireland. The goal of controlling the entire island became increasingly important, but in practice English rule remained fragile and patchy.[18] Dublin's authority was least effective in the north, dominated by two great Gaelic lords, the O'Neill ruling Tyrone and the O'Donnell holding sway in Donegal.[19] At the beginning of Elizabeth's reign, both Ulster chiefs were consolidating their positions. Having won his succession battle against Matthew, Baron of Dungannon, who had been supported by Dublin, Shane O'Neill was determined to keep English influence out of Ulster. Two years earlier, his rival Calvagh O'Donnell had forcibly replaced his own father in Tyrconnell. In that task he had been assisted by Argyll and had strengthened his ties with the earl through a Campbell marriage.[20]

As the major power in the West Highlands and Islands, Argyll was the dominant figure in the Gaelic world that straddled the North Channel. Within Ulster politics, he was involved with all three chiefs. Calvagh O'Donnell and James MacDonald were both members of his affinity. Relations were cooler with Shane O'Neill, who maintained a healthy respect for Argyll as an obstacle to his own plans to rule the north. The Irish clause in the Treaty of Berwick originated in the earl's personal experience of the situation in Ulster and was the first tentative expression of the British policy he was to develop during 1560.

That Irish clause and the other distinctive features of the Berwick treaty were only possible because a British context had been created by the convergence of these long- and short-term factors. The repercussions of European peace and the accession of Elizabeth combined with the situation in Ireland to propel this British context into policy making within mainland Britain. Two men understood that context more clearly than their contemporaries, seeing it as a marvellous opportunity rather than a threatening development. They seized the chance to devise and gain acceptance for their revolutionary British policies and in so doing created a form of British politics not seen before.

With neither 'British state' nor supranational British political system, the Atlantic archipelago contained a complex of polities which intersected, but

---

[18] For the major debate concerning Tudor policy towards Ireland during the sixteenth century, see B. Bradshaw, *The Irish Constitutional Revolution in the Sixteenth Century* (Cambridge, 1979); N. Canny, *The Elizabethan Conquest of Ireland: A Pattern Established 1565–76* (Hassocks, Sussex, 1976); C. Brady, *The Chief Governors: The Rise and Fall of Reform Government in Tudor Ireland, 1536–1588* (Cambridge, 1994); C. Lennon, *Sixteenth-Century Ireland: The Incomplete Conquest* (Dublin, 1994); S.G. Ellis, *Ireland in the Age of the Tudors, 1447–1603* (London, 1998).

[19] T.W. Moody, F.X. Martin and F.J. Byrne, eds., *A New History of Ireland III* (Oxford, 1978) III. 2–3, 15–16.

[20] See below pp. 23–5, 105–6.

did not combine. The policies of Argyll and Cecil made a conscious effort to connect the fragmented Gaelic politics of Ulster and the West Highlands, the Irish political arena of the Dublin administration, the political world of the English court and the national politics of Scotland. In 1560, British policy briefly held these separate political worlds together. Its slender thread was not strong enough to unify them nor was it able to weave together a single, inclusive British political system. It was spun by two men who emerged from contrasting political backgrounds. On a personal level, the co-operation of the Englishman and the Scottish Gael symbolised the policy of joint action they advocated.

As Elizabeth's chief adviser, Cecil operated within the political orbit of the Tudor state. His remit covered all aspects of the queen's rule, and he strove to formulate comprehensive policies to serve her interests both at home and abroad. In 1559 he was primarily concerned with two separate areas: Anglo-Scottish relations, particularly the threat from Mary, Queen of Scots, and Elizabethan policy within Ireland, especially as regards Ulster. Having received Argyll's offer of help in northern Ireland, Cecil was quick to make the connexion between his twin concerns. By weighing his options within the British context that emerged in 1559–60, he was able to develop a coherent British strategy, which dominated English political decision making during the critical early years of Elizabeth's reign. Later, both the aims of that British policy and its methods of implementation changed, yet Cecil never lost his capacity to impart a British dimension to his planning.[21]

By contrast, when he was formulating a British policy linking different political worlds, the 5th earl of Argyll had the advantage of personal experience. As part of the Gaelic world, which took no notice of the boundaries between the Stewart and Tudor realms, the earl was involved in events in Ulster as well as in the Western Isles. He was deeply embroiled in Scotland's national politics and its international dimension of relations with London. His Protestantism was the driving force behind his commitment to an English alliance. It was the plight of the Lords of the Congregation and their urgent need for English support that triggered his offer of assistance in Ulster. Whilst the 5th earl's triangular British policy grew out of his daily contact with the Gaelic political world, the catalyst was his involvement in Scottish politics and Anglo-Scottish relations.

The British policies of both Argyll and Cecil initially came together in the Berwick treaty. That first flowering rapidly became a plant in full bloom in the summer of 1560.[22] Their shared commitment to a Protestant Britain

---

[21] Alford, *Cecil*, chs. 1–2.
[22] Traditionally, the conclusion of the Wars of the Congregation and the Treaty of Edinburgh have been viewed as the major turning point in British and even imperial history.

was the foundation for a single, harmonious British policy. It was revealed
in two documents completed in July 1560. The first was Cecil's personal
diplomatic triumph, the Treaty of Edinburgh, which guaranteed Protestant
ascendancy in Scotland, cementing the Anglo-Scottish alliance and the diplomatic revolution it had produced. Alongside the treaty the 5th earl signed
a personal agreement with the English in which he promised a substantial contingent of Scottish troops and all his political authority to help the
English subdue Ulster.[23] The document could only have been negotiated by
one man. No other magnate could make an independent agreement with a
foreign monarch to provide an army to fight outside his own territories. The
5th earl of Argyll had the vision to create a British policy and, crucially, he
possessed the power to implement it.

F.W. Maitland in the *Cambridge Modern History*, wrote of 1560, 'a new nation, a British
nation was in the making' and 'the fate of the Protestant reformation was being decided,
and the creed of unborn millions in undiscovered lands was being determined', cited in
D. Armitage, *The Ideological Origins of the British Empire* (Cambridge, 2000), p. 67. More
recently, G. Donaldson, 'Foundations of Anglo-Scottish Union', in G. Donaldson, *Scottish
Church History* (Edinburgh, 1985), 137–63.

[23] For a full discussion, see below, pp. 107–8.

1

Argyll's life and character

In an age of personal monarchy and small, tightly-knit élites, personal rule lay at the heart of political power in the early modern period. The story of personalities and powers revealing the interplay of men and events forms the central narrative of its political history[1] and comes closest to the way in which contemporaries analysed their own world. The structures of government were important, but at each level of the political process it was the personal and kin networks that ensured they worked. This was particularly true of Scotland, where governmental institutions were less well developed than in other European states. Political biographies are essential in the study of sixteenth-century British history. Before 1603, there were no common political institutions covering all three kingdoms. In that sense, British politics had not yet arrived, though a handful of British policies and British politicians flourished. The political history of the Atlantic archipelago during the sixteenth century has to be written around these personalities and their actions.

The use of political biography also offers an escape from two concepts that have dominated modern historical writing and have bedevilled the writing of British history.[2] The first is state-centred history, which assumes that politics

---

[1] The general links between history and biography have been explored in T.C.W. Blanning and D. Cannadine, eds., *History and Biography: Essays in Honour of Derek Beales* (Cambridge, 1996) and in Professsor Beales' inaugural lecture on the subject reprinted on pp. 266–82. Diarmaid MacCulloch's outstanding study of *Archbishop Cranmer* (New Haven, CT, 1996) illustrates the way in which a biographical approach can transform English political and ecclesiastical history of the first half of the sixteenth century.

[2] The pioneer of the 'new' British history is Professor J.G.A. Pocock whose seminal articles, 'British History: A Plea for a New Subject', *Journal of Modern History*, 4 (1975), 601–28; 'The Limits and Divisions of British History', *American Historical Review*, 87 (1982), 311–86, sparked a lively debate and created a group of adherents for the new subject, myself included. It has taken some time for the subject to establish itself in print, with M. Nicholls, *The History of the Modern British Isles, 1529–1603* (London, 1999) being the first sixteenth-century textbook to appear. It was preceded by a series of collected essays, most notably R. Asch, ed., *Three Nations: a Common History?* (Bochum, 1992); S. Ellis and S. Barber, eds., *Conquest and Union: Fashioning of a British State 1485–1720* (London, 1995); A. Grant and K. Stringer,

and international relations can be explained exclusively in terms of the state and its institutions. Although the interaction between centre and localities has long been recognised, many of the underlying assumptions about the institutional nature of early modern politics remain. The second and related problem is the national approach that has divided British history into the separate compartments of Welsh, Irish, Scottish and English histories. Much effort has recently been expended on breaking down the barriers, but it has proved difficult to construct the new 'British' history. Many of these problems cease to exist when the subject is approached through the career of a single figure who moves across the boundaries of nation and state. Because of his highly unusual position within the British Isles and his career as a British politician, a political biography of Argyll offers an ideal opportunity to reveal the complexities and subtleties of the world of early modern British politics.

A study of the 5th earl has become possible because of the wealth of available evidence. Of central importance for understanding Argyll's thought and actions is the survival of a considerable quantity of his correspondence, comprising over 200 items. These letters demonstrate the huge range of Argyll's contacts and concerns, encompassing the local, regional, national and international spheres. Over half were previously unknown, forming part of the sixteenth-century correspondence discovered in the Breadalbane collection in the National Archives of Scotland. The Breadalbane correspondence as a whole opens a window into the worlds of Gaelic and Scottish politics, especially, but by no means exclusively, seen through the eyes of Clan Campbell and their chief, Argyll.[3]

The Argyll manuscripts at Inveraray Castle contain extensive records of his property and other legal and financial affairs, though few letters. At the start of the twentieth century, Duke Niall devoted much of his life to the collection of Campbell records, which he entered in his manuscript volumes of Argyll Transcripts. These have been extensively consulted and, where possible, checked against those originals held at Inveraray.[4] The Argyll manuscripts furnish a vast quantity of information about the day-to-day rule which the 5th earl exercised over the region of Argyll and the Western Highlands and provide a guide to his movements. The existence of so much sixteenth-century material within the Breadalbane and Inveraray collections

---

eds., *Uniting the Kingdom?: The Making of British History* (London, 1995); B. Bradshaw and J. Morrill, eds., *The British Problem, c. 1534–1707* (London, 1996); B. Bradshaw and P. Roberts, eds., *British Consciousness and Identity: The Making of Britain, 1533–1707* (Cambridge, 1998).

[3] See *Campbell Letters*, Introduction.

[4] Except where there is no AT listing or a full quotation has been included from the original, references have been given to the Argyll Transcripts. I am most grateful to the present duke of Argyll for permission to consult and cite from his muniments.

was not accidental. It reflects a general Campbell attitude towards the use and preservation of documentation. The quantity of surviving manuscript evidence has proved a hazard as well as an opportunity by delaying the completion of this study.

As well as the wealth of private documentation, Argyll's career left considerable traces within the public records of Scotland, England and Ireland, and the earl attracted comment in the memoirs and chronicles of the time. Less conventional sources also provided insights into the 5th earl's life. What set Argyll apart from his contemporary Scottish peers was being a member of the Gaelic-speaking community, the Gàidhealtachd. Unfortunately, apart from the 1555 treaty with Calvagh O'Donnell, no manuscript in Gaelic has survived which can be firmly linked to the 5th earl himself or his period. This is unremarkable because Gaelic was not the language normally employed for either correspondence or legal documents. However, the contemporary Gaelic poetry has given valuable evidence concerning Argyll and his court. The strong oral tradition within the Gàidhealtachd has furnished a number of stories, though the hazards of dating such material precisely has usually prevented a firm link being established with the 5th earl. Less acute dating difficulties were encountered in the use of material evidence. A number of buildings associated with Argyll remain, though nearly all are in ruins. Carnasserie castle, built by the 5th earl, in particular, yields many clues as to his lifestyle and outlook.[5]

Although there was no shortage of documentary evidence, there were some important gaps, most notably the absence of formal ecclesiastical records for the Highlands. This has made it difficult to reconstruct the full impact the 5th earl had upon the Reformation of the region.[6] Similarly, the lack of judicial records hides the great importance of Argyll's control over justice in the Highlands. Details concerning the earl's household were also unavailable because no accounts or lists of its members survived. However, it is the wealth of evidence, rather than the occasional gap, that is most striking. From this material, it has been possible to provide a remarkably detailed picture of the 5th earl's life, his mental world and his political activities.

In common with other rulers and nobles, the 5th earl was a public figure, making it hard to draw a sharp line to separate his public from his private life. For example, Argyll's marital difficulties could not remain a personal

---

[5] The task of interpreting such evidence has been greatly simplified by the splendid *Argyll, An Inventory of the Ancient Monuments* (hereafter *Argyll Inventory*) produced by the Royal Commission of the Ancient and Historical Monuments of Scotland (7 vols, Edinburgh, 1971–92).

[6] The existing evidence has been discussed in Dawson, 'Clan, Kin and Kirk'; Dawson, 'The Protestant Earl'; Dawson, 'Calvinism in the Gaidhealtachd in Scotland' in A. Pettegree, A. Duke and G. Lewis, eds., *Calvinism in Europe, 1540–1620* (Cambridge, 1994), 231–53.

problem, becoming instead a public, and even a political, issue. Nearly all the earl's actions as an adult had a significance within, and an effect upon, one or more of the political arenas in which he moved. For Argyll and his contemporaries, this merging of the two spheres was an inevitable consequence of the personal nature of political rule. Consequently, a ruler's personality was of crucial importance. The 5th earl's character and his mental world were formed by his upbringing and education during the 1540s and 1550s.[7] His adult life was dominated by his political activities and by his unhappy marriage.[8] Thanks largely to the survival of his letters, it has been possible to piece together a picture of Argyll's personality and his beliefs, which help reveal the man as well as the politician.

EDUCATION AND FORMATION

During his brief career from 1558 to 1573, the 5th earl played a crucial role in the mid-century upheavals within Scottish and British politics, which transformed the relationships between the three kingdoms. That role rested upon his position as both a Highland chief and a Scottish peer. These were responsibilities for which his education and training were intended to prepare him. In many respects, his childhood and adolescence were typical of the Scottish aristocracy into which he had been born. However, two formative experiences during his teenage years brought him a different perspective, enabling him to think in British and European terms and operate successfully within all three kingdoms of the Atlantic archipelago.

Archibald was twenty years old when he succeeded to the title of earl. He was a striking figure of a man, being very tall, strong and handsome. No portraits survive, but the 5th earl was 'lovely of face' with a fair complexion and brown hair, accounting for his Gaelic nickname 'Gilleasbuig Doun' or Brown Archibald.[9] He was a child of his father's first marriage to Helen Hamilton, the eldest daughter of James, 1st earl of Arran and sister of James Hamilton, later duke of Châtelherault. The duke was heir apparent to the Scottish throne and the Hamiltons were one of the most powerful and extensive aristocratic kindreds within Scotland. Archibald was born in 1538, nearly ten years after his parents' wedding. As their first and only surviving child, his arrival would have been a joy and a considerable relief: securing the succession was as crucial for a noble house as it was for a ruling dynasty.[10] Although his mother died two years later, leaving him with few recollections

---

[7] Discussed on pp. 14–26, below.   [8] Discussed in chs. 3–6 and pp. 27–35, below.
[9] To distinguish him from his father who was a redhead and nicknamed Archibald 'roy': *Records of Argyll*, 5.
[10] The 4th earl had married Helen Hamilton by 27 August 1529: AT, III. 220; *RMS*, III. 826–7.

of her, his respect for her memory and her lineage were reflected in the loyalty he displayed towards his maternal kin. As an adult, the 5th earl remained close to the Hamiltons, whom he treated as far more than political allies, with their unpopularity sometimes causing him political problems.

The 4th earl quickly remarried, taking as his second wife Margaret Graham, only daughter of William, 3rd earl of Menteith. Young Archibald would have attended the wedding on 21 April 1541 in the beautiful setting of the Priory of Inchmahome, on the Lake of Menteith. Within the next four years, his immediate family grew with the birth of three siblings, Colin, Margaret and Janet. Archibald was not especially close to his younger brother, probably because they spent so little time together as children after Colin was sent to Menteith to be fostered.[11] He did become attached to his sisters and to his illegitimate half-brother John, who was probably brought up in the 4th earl's household.[12] After his second wife died, the 4th earl married for a third time in 1545. His young bride was Katherine MacLean, daughter of the Highland chieftan Hector Mòr MacLean of Duart, with the wedding being celebrated by the bishop in his cathedral at Dunblane.[13] There were no surviving children from this last marriage, with Katherine outliving her husband and later becoming an important dimension of the 5th earl's Irish policies.[14] The third marriage sought to end the feud between the MacLeans and the Campbells.[15] The links between the two clans were further strengthened by the wedding of the 5th earl's sister Janet to Hector Og, son of Hector Mòr MacLean of Duart, which took place around the New Year of 1558.[16]

Throughout his childhood, Archibald was at the heart of an extended kin network, which spread out from the inner group of his parents and siblings to the close relatives in the house of Argyll and into the extended family of his Campbell kinsfolk. In addition, he was a valued member of his foster family, which Gaelic tradition regarded as closer even than blood kin. As was usual for the sons of Gaelic chiefs, Archibald was fostered away from his parental home. Following family tradition, he was placed in the household of one of the major Campbell cadet families, thus keeping the fostering within the clan and reinforcing the links between the main line and its subsidiary branches. Archibald was raised by Matilda Montgomery and

---

[11] Hence his Gaelic nickname 'Cailean Teach or Tealach', meaning Colin from Menteith, *Records of Argyll*, 5; *Highland Papers*, II. 102.
[12] John, later provost of Kilmun, who has erroneously been called the illegitimate son of the 5th earl, e.g. *Highland Papers*, II. 101–2.
[13] Maclean-Bristol, *Warriors and Priests*, 78–9, n. 29. Marriage contract 12 December 1545: AT, IV. 159.
[14] See below pp. 104–10 and pp. 155–65.
[15] As explicitly stated in the charter Archibald gave to his father and Countess Katherine, 23 January 1547: AT, IV. 164; 173; *HMC*, 4th, 477.
[16] 26 December 1557, confirmed 26 January 1558, AT, V. 80–1, 97–8; *RMS*, IV. 1240.

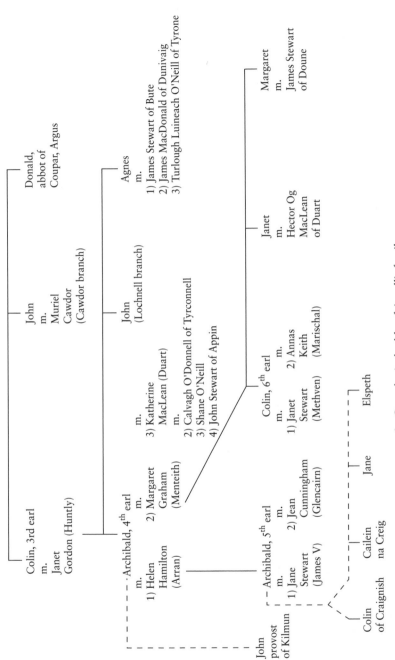

2. Genealogical table of Argyll's family

her husband Colin Campbell, 5th laird of Ardkinglas, who was his official curator or guardian.[17] Ardkinglas had lands in Cowal and his seat was the castle at Ardkinglas at the top of Loch Fyne, not far from the centre of Argyll power at Inveraray. As one of his main advisers, Ardkinglas frequently attended the 4th earl, allowing young Archibald easy access to his father and family.[18] Until his death in 1562, Ardkinglas remained one of Archibald's closest advisers. More distant, though still important, were the ties between Archibald and his godparents. The affection he continued to feel for his godmother, Agnes Leslie, did not diminish when they found themselves on different sides during the civil wars.[19]

One of the most significant relationships of Archibald's life began during his early years, when he encountered the cleric John Carswell. By 1549 at the latest, the future superintendent of Argyll had entered the 4th earl's service. Carswell knew Archibald well as a boy and may have acted as one of his tutors.[20] Little is known directly about Archibald's education, except that the Protestant convictions, which were so strong a part of his life and later policies, were rooted firmly in his upbringing. After his own conversion to the new faith, the 4th earl ensured that his family were raised as Protestants.[21] Carswell later praised Archibald for having read the Bible assiduously in his youth, learning from an early age to value its teaching more than the 'old-established customs' that had been followed by his ancestors.[22] Alongside his religious education, Archibald was taught to read and write in Scots and Latin. By the age of six he could sign his own name.[23] He could also read and

---

[17] For example 7 May 1554, GD112/23/1/5. At the death of Matilda Montgomery, the 4th earl claimed a 'bairn's part' of her estate, which indicates a fostering relationship, 4 September 1557, AT, V. 78; Dumbarton Protocol Book B 16/1/2 fo. 57v.

[18] Shown by the frequency with which Ardkinglas acted as a witness to the 4th earl's legal documents: AT, V. *passim*.

[19] Agnes Leslie was the daughter of the 4th earl of Rothes and wife of William Douglas of Lochleven. The 5th earl sent his special regards to his 'cumer' (godmother) when he wrote to William Douglas, 22 July 1570: *Reg Hon de Mort*, I. 59, and see below pp. 35–6, 184.

[20] Witness to contract, 8 March 1549, AT, IV. 200. Carswell was also closely associated with the 5th earl's foster family, later marrying Margaret, daughter of Campbell of Ardkinglas: Carswell, *Foirm*, 173, 178. There are interesting similarities between Carswell's handwriting and that of the 5th earl, which suggest that he might have taught Archibald to write, cf. GD112/39/16 and 17.

[21] The Family Pedigree of 1634 implied that the 4th earl was introduced to Protestant ideas when he was in France, possibly during 1536 when he accompanied James V to his wedding. It categorically stated that the 4th earl 'was instructed in the religion, came to Scotland a convert long before the Reformation . . . [and] caused his son Archibald . . . to be instructed in the religion': *Records of Argyll*, 7. Although no firm date for the 4th earl's conversion has been established, he certainly provided an evangelical education for his children.

[22] Carswell, *Foirm*, 175. For a full discussion of Carswell's dedicatory epistle, see D. Meek, 'The Reformation and Gaelic culture' in J. Kirk, ed., *The Church in the Highlands* (Edinburgh, 1998), 37–62.

[23] For example charter of 9 April 1544, AT, IV. 140–1.

write in Gaelic and was educated to appreciate that language's flourishing literary culture by the members of the MacEwan family, who served as bards to the earls of Argyll.[24]

In conjunction with his literary and religious formation, Archibald's education prepared him for his future role as clan chief and one of Scotland's foremost peers. This involved long hours of practising the noble arts of warfare and hunting and becoming an apprentice learning the administrative duties of 'lordship'. His early experiences were predominantly within the Gaelic culture and society of the Highlands but from the beginning the Scots language and Lowland practices were also present. Within Campbell households, the two cultures and languages co-existed and Archibald grew up equally at home with both. In 1542, at the tender age of four, Archibald was introduced to feudal grants. He became the 'fiar' or possessor of most of the lands held by the 4th earl, leaving his father with a life rent. On 13 November the little boy had been personally present to receive sasine of the Lordship of Lorn.[25] From that time onwards Archibald, assisted by his father and by his guardian Ardkinglas, was involved in the granting of charters. As the eldest son of the 4th earl, he was known as the Master of Argyll, and by 1554 had become Lord Lorne, the title held by the Argyll heir.[26]

From his earliest years he followed a peripatetic lifestyle, travelling extensively around the region of Argyll, learning about the heartland of Campbell power and meeting his clansmen. He visited the earl's Lowland residences such as Castle Campbell, seeing for himself the many different properties that formed part of the earldom. His training also prepared him for a role within national politics, and, as he grew older, he attended the royal court. He was welcomed there by his Hamilton uncle, the regent Arran, who was lavish in his gifts to his nephew. Archibald remained in Arran's household for extensive periods during 1549–50, gaining valuable experience. During these prolonged stays, the young Archibald became fully acquainted with James Hamilton, Arran's heir. His cousin was an exact contemporary, and they became firm friends and later close allies during the Reformation crisis.[27]

Arran's eventual loss of the regency in 1554 did not damage Argyll's links with the court. The queen dowager, who succeeded as regent, had been cultivating good relations with the Campbells for some time. Father

---

[24] 'The MacEwans', Appendix II in Carswell, *Foirm*, 183–6.

[25] *RMS*, III. 2811–6; AT, IV. 113, 116–9; sasine at Dunstaffnage AT, V. 17 (where misdated 1552: see AT, IV. 119, 121). Such a transfer of lands avoided feudal casualties at the time of succession and was a device used by the earls of Argyll throughout the sixteenth century and permitted by the crown, their feudal superior.

[26] For example *RMS*, IV. 139, 467, 944. When referring to the Argyll heir, Lorne is spelt with a final 'e'; when the geographical area is meant, the spelling is the more typical 'Lorn'.

[27] *TA*, IX. 261, 298–9, 306–7, 394, 428, 457. James was four or five years old in 1542: J. Durkan, 'James 3rd Earl of Arran: The Hidden Years' *SHR* 65 (1986), 154–66 at p. 155.

and son had both accompanied Mary of Guise on her progress to the north
of Scotland in 1552. Whilst staying in Aberdeen, Archibald fell ill and the
queen regent sent her own apothecary and paid for expensive remedies to
help him recover.[28] Mary's general concern to cultivate the Master of Argyll
can be seen in the generous pension paid by the crown throughout the 1550s,
which, in 1558, had risen to the princely sum of £525 annually. By that date,
Archibald had completed his noble training and gained the basic political
education at court needed by a young aristocrat who would one day take
his place at the centre of Scottish and Highland affairs.[29]

Three events during his mid-teens had a profound influence upon
Archibald's life and his future policies as earl. The first was his marriage
to Jane Stewart in April 1554; the second was the military expedition which
Archibald led to Ulster in the winter of 1555–6; and the third was his meeting with John Knox during his preaching tour to Scotland of 1555–6. They
represented the main concerns that would dominate the rest of Archibald's
life and career: the importance of his house and his honour, his commitment
to the Protestant faith, and his involvement in Irish and British affairs.

An advantageous marriage was an essential component in the successful
formation of any early modern nobleman. It was primarily a decision for
the house rather than the individual.[30] As one of their main methods of
integration within the national political elite, the earls of Argyll had pursued a consistent long-term strategy of marrying their sons into the Lowland
aristocracy. In 1542, the crown had granted the 4th earl the feudal right
of the marriage of his son and heir.[31] However, plans had been made for
a prestigious marriage in the first year of Archibald's life.[32] King James V
had agreed that Archibald should marry Jane, his illegitimate daughter by
Elizabeth, daughter of Sir John Beaton of Creich. Despite this arrangement,
in 1549 another pre-nuptial contract was signed betrothing Archibald to
Margaret, eldest daughter of George Gordon, 4th earl of Huntly.[33] Such
changes were not uncommon, especially when the prospective couple were
still children, and reflected the shifting patterns of aristocratic politics. By
1553, when Archibald was fifteen and of marriageable age, the choice of
partner had returned to Jane Stewart.[34] She was about four years older than

[28] £14 was paid to the queen's pottingar: *TA*, X. 102.
[29] *TA*, X. 130, 212, 233, 240, 291, 312, 331, 354.
[30] For a fuller discussion of noble marriage strategies, see *Campbell Letters*, 28–34.
[31] 18 October 1542: AT, IV. 114, 116.
[32] The date of 10 December 1538 was given for an initial agreement in the copy of the marriage
contract of 5 July 1553 now in the Moray Papers, NRA(S), 217, Box 15 No. 441. I am grateful
to the earl of Moray for permission to consult and cite from his muniments.
[33] 10 July 1549: AT, IV. 203.
[34] By canon law a man was thought fit to marry at fourteen years old, a woman at twelve,
and these ages were retained by Scots law after the Reformation: G.C.H. Paton, ed.,
An Introduction to Scottish Legal History (Stair Society, 20, Edinburgh, 1958), 92.

her future husband, having been raised in the royal household and serving as a maid of honour to Mary of Guise.[35] It was the queen dowager who took the leading role in the marriage contract of July 1553. That agreement also involved the duke of Châtelherault, as heir to the throne and senior male relative, and James V's other illegitimate sons, James Stewart, commendator prior of St Andrews; James, commendator prior of Kelso; Robert, commendator prior of Holyrood and John, commendator prior of Coldingham in the payment of Jane's tocher or dowry.[36]

The match brought Archibald into the immediate circle of the royal family. Even though they were illegitimate, James V's children had an honoured and secure place in the royal household and in the affection of Mary of Guise. When Mary, Queen of Scots returned to Scotland in 1561 she emulated her mother's example and gathered her half-brothers and sisters around her. She had a particular affection for Jane, who became one of her ladies in waiting and a close confidante.[37] At the time of Jane and Archibald's wedding in April 1554, the marriage alliance offered a prestigious husband and generous settlement for the bride, and a good dowry and political connexions for the groom and his family.[38] In the event, the marriage became a personal disaster for the couple and ended in a messy and acrimonious divorce. The breakdown and the lack of a legitimate heir were to have a profound impact upon the 5th earl for the rest of his life.

The second episode that shaped Archibald's future outlook and career took place in Ireland. Although the earls of Argyll had adopted the Lowland practice of male primogeniture to govern their own succession, within Gaelic society it remained essential for the heir to prove he was a worthy chief for his clansmen to follow. The traditional way to demonstrate his fitness to be MacCailein Mòr, the honorific Gaelic title for the head of Clan Campbell, was to lead his clansmen in battle.[39] An opportunity arose for Archibald in 1555. During the previous summer, the 4th earl had commanded a military

---

[35] For example *TA*, VI. 205, 262, 411, 416; VII. 101, 120–1, 319, 410. A. Thomas, '"Dragonis baith and dowis ay in double forme": Women at the Court of James V, 1513–42' in E. Ewan and M. Meikle, eds., *Women in Scotland, c 1100–c 1750* (East Linton, 1999) 83–94 at p. 87. I am grateful to Dr Andrea Thomas for information concerning Jean Stewart's childhood in the royal household.

[36] James V's illegitimate sons had been granted these monasteries *in commendam* as a way of funding their upbringing. The marriage contract, 1/5 July 1553, NRA(S) 217: Box 15 No. 441; AT, V. 25, 27; Hamilton Papers in *Miscellany of the Maitland Club IV* ed. J. Robertson (Maitland Club, 67, Edinburgh 1847), 200. Payments of the tocher, *Letters to Argyll Family*, 2; *Clan Campbell*, 6, 2; NRA(S), 217, Box 1 No. 130; P. Anderson, *Robert Stewart Earl of Orkney, 1533–93* (Edinburgh, 1982), 9, 169.

[37] Donaldson, *Queen's Men*, 58.

[38] The month of the marriage is taken from the divorce decree, 22 June 1573: CC8/2/6 fo. 121v, and see below, pp. 27–35.

[39] At the end of the seventeenth century, Martin Martin recorded that it was still necessary for potential chiefs to lead their men on a raid to prove their prowess, *A Description of the Western Islands of Scotland, c 1695* (Edinburgh, 1994; reprint of 1934 edn), 165.

expedition in the West Highlands against the MacDonalds of Clanranald. His son had probably used that successful campaign to convince his father he was ready for an independent command.[40] At the time, Calvagh O'Donnell of Tyrconnell or Donegal was in the middle of a bitter dispute with his own father Manus O'Donnell and was seeking military assistance to over-throw him and seize Donegal for himself.[41] Like many Ulster chiefs before him, he looked across the North Channel for his mercenaries and found the Campbells willing to negotiate. The subsequent agreement marked the first formal extension of Argyll's authority into Ulster. By accepting a prominent Irish chief into his affinity, the 4th earl extended the Campbell sphere of op-erations to include the north of Ireland. Archibald was immediately involved in this major development, which was to have such an impact upon his fu-ture. On 13 July 1555, having travelled to the Highlands for the purpose, Calvagh signed a bond with the 4th earl.[42] As a result, Archibald, Calvagh, a large number of Highland troops and some artillery sailed to Donegal, arriving on 1 November. Foreshadowing future alliances, the MacDonalds of Antrim, linked by marriage to the earl, formed part of the expedition. Employing a pincer movement with the Campbell soldiers and Calvagh on one side and their allies, the MacDonalds, on the other, the winter campaign was swiftly and successfully concluded. Manus O'Donnell was captured at the outset at Rossneagh, remaining in prison for the remainder of his life. His strongholds at Greencastle in Inishowen and Eanach castle near Derry, as well as his fine house at Lifford, were taken. Large numbers of casualties were slain and prisoners seized during the campaign, which laid waste sixty miles of Donegal countryside.

Leaving his clansmen to complete operations, Archibald returned home by 24 February 1556.[43] The key to the campaign's success had been the artillery Archibald brought with him, which was capable of demolishing castle walls. One cannon in particular impressed the Irish annalists who named it *Gonna Cam* or 'Crooked Gun'.[44] The use of the latest military

---

[40] *The Scottish Correspondence of Mary of Lorraine 1542/3–60* ed. A.I. Cameron (SHS, 3rd ser. 10, Edinburgh, 1927), 388–9; *Letters to Argyll Family*, 2–3.

[41] B. Bradshaw, 'Manus "the Magnificent" : O'Donnell as Renaissance Prince' in A. Cosgrove and D. MacCartney, eds., *Studies in Irish History Presented to R. Dudley Edwards* (Dublin, 1979), 15–36.

[42] The contract of 13 July 1555 exists in both a Gaelic and Scots version: AT, V. 39, 45–7; printed in J. Mackechnie, 'Treaty between Argyll and O'Donnell', *Scottish Gaelic Studies*, 7 (1953), 94–102; *Highland Papers*, IV. 212–6. It was renewed in 1560, see below, pp. 105–6.

[43] Lorne personally signed a charter in Stirling on 24 February: AT, V. 62. The Campbell troops remained in Ireland until St Brendan's Day (16 May).

[44] *The Annals of the Kingdom of Ireland by the Four Masters from the Earliest Period to the Year 1616* ed. J. Donovan (7 vols., Dublin, 1851), V. 1541; G.A. Hayes-McCoy, 'The Early History of the Gun in Ireland', *Journal of the Galway Archaeological and Historical Society*, 18 (1938–9), 43–65 at p. 65; G.A. Hayes-McCoy, *Irish Battles: A Military History of Ireland* (Belfast, 1989; reprint of 1937 edn), 76.

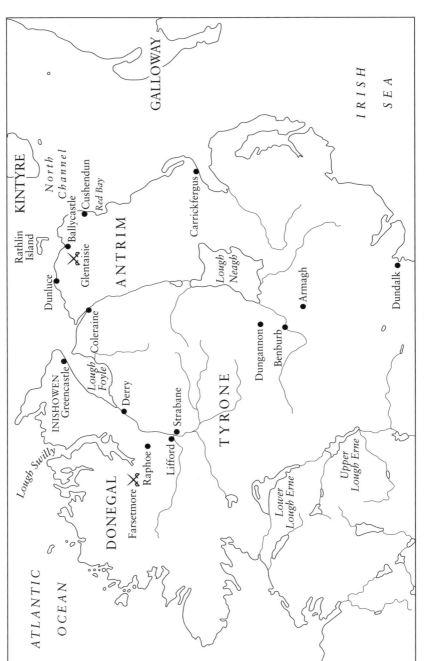

3. Map of Ulster

technology also caught the attention and created alarm among the English authorities in Dublin. They were convinced that because the expedition possessed expensive and sophisticated brass cannon, it must have the covert support of the Scottish government.[45] The English had little experience of Argyll's military capabilities and could neither comprehend the political independence he enjoyed nor the semi-sovereign nature of his power.[46] For his first serious command Archibald had been entrusted with a magnificent artillery train and he had deployed it and the rest of his forces with considerable skill. The Irish expedition had proved he could lead his clansmen in battle, thereby strengthening his authority within the clan. A reputation as a successful war leader brought him other clans' respect, needed to operate successfully within Gaelic society. His Donegal campaign provided Archibald with first-hand experience of the Ulster countryside and its politics. It marked the beginning of his long-term friendship with Calvagh O'Donnell and of his continuing interest in the Irish wing of the Gàidhealtachd. His expedition had also brought him into contact with the English presence in Ireland. In 1559, these experiences made it possible for the 5th earl to take the next step of adding an English dimension to the pre-existing link between Ireland and Scotland and thus creating a British policy.

Archibald's future career was equally profoundly influenced by the third episode in the mid-1550s. His first meeting with John Knox took place in October 1555. Lord Lorne, as Archibald was then known, along with his brother-in-law Lord James Stewart, commendator prior of St Andrews, and his cousin John Erskine, 6th Lord Erskine, went to listen to Knox. At this point in his clandestine preaching tour of Scotland, the reformer was staying at Calder House, Mid-Calder, outside Edinburgh. The three young nobles, already sympathetic to reforming ideas, were sufficiently impressed with the sermon and their subsequent conversation with Knox to urge him to start to evangelise publicly. Lorne wanted more positive and direct action to promote the Protestant cause, but could do little immediately because he spent most of the winter in Ulster. He had been back for two months when Knox decided to return to Geneva, in May 1556. This provoked a concerted attempt by members of Clan Campbell to persuade the reformer to remain

---

[45] They reasoned that 'the great pieces of ordnance of brass which being not wont to be the furniture of a common subject is the more like to have come from some other of greater power than themselves'. Sir Thomas Challoner's complaint to Mary of Guise in February 1556 SP 51/1 fo. 18. The English were only partially correct in their deduction. Although the brass cannon had probably been taken from the royal collection at Dumbarton castle as part of the 1554 Highland expedition (*TA*, X. xlvii–viii, 229, 287), they had not been sent to Ireland with Mary of Guise's authorisation. She had written to the 4th earl unsuccessfully countermanding the expedition and instructing Argyll to come to her: 8 and 9 October 1555, *TA*, X. 298; *HMC*, 6th, 614b.

[46] See below ch. 2.

in Scotland under its protection.[47] Knox would only stay a few extra days
at Castle Campbell, during which time he preached and possibly celebrated
communion, and in July he left for Geneva promising to return, if called.[48]

The 4th earl was strongly committed to the Protestant cause but, with his
health failing, it was his son who took the initiative.[49] Archibald was one
of the signatories of the letter of 10 March 1557, which requested Knox
to return to Scotland.[50] After much delay, confusion and misunderstanding
about his proposed role, the preacher remained on the Continent. This did
not prevent the Protestant nobles taking decisive action on their own. On
3 December 1557, they made their most challenging move to date by drawing
up the First Band. It contained a bold and uncompromising affirmation of the
Protestant cause, declaring that the nobles would renounce 'the congregation
of Sathan, with all the superstitions, abomination and idolatry therof' and
use 'our whole power, substance and our very lives' to maintain, nourish
and defend the 'whole Congregation of Christ'.[51] Following the order of
precedence in the Scottish aristocracy, the 4th earl was the first to sign,
followed by two other earls, Glencairn and Morton, then Lorne and finally
his cousin John, Lord Erskine. Having been endorsed by these leading nobles,
the bond was then circulated among other Scottish Protestants.[52]

The five lords had agreed a programme of action to accompany their declaration. Being the most prestigious and powerful, the house of Argyll took
the lead in implementing its provisions. John Douglas, a former Carmelite
friar, was brought into the earl's household where he preached publicly and
carried through reforming measures.[53] Such actions were a direct challenge

---

[47] Knox was brought by Robert Campbell of Kinzeancleuch, one of the leading Ayrshire Protestants, to visit the 4th earl and Lorne at Castle Campbell. Colin Campbell of Glenorchy, chief
of one of the main cadet branches, was also present and together the Campbells sought to
convince the preacher to stay.

[48] Knox, *History*, I. 123–4; S. Cruden, *Castle Campbell* (HMSO, Edinburgh, 1984), 19;
Dawson, 'The Protestant Earl', 339–40.

[49] With scant regard for humility, the Family Pedigree likens the 4th earl to David and
the 5th earl to Solomon who fulfilled his father's wish to build the Temple: *Records of
Argyll*, 7.

[50] Knox, *History*, I. 132.

[51] Knox, *History*, I. 136–7. Although the subject was religious, the First Band was phrased in
the language of bonds of maintenance. The five nobles took the ministers and all other Protestants as their dependents whom they would protect and support against the Catholic
clergy.

[52] Knox, *Works*, VI. 675, for facsimiles of the five noble signatures, no other signatures are
extant. The final signature was that of the nobleman Lord Erskine, later earl of Mar, and not,
as has previously been assumed, that of John Erskine of Dun, the Protestant laird and later
minister. The signature on the original (NLS Ch 902) is the same as that of Lord Erskine,
e.g. NLS MS 73 fos. 20–1, 29, 32–7.

[53] Knox, *History*, I. 125, 138; Keith, *History*, I. 152; see below pp. 43, 86–7. *The History of
the Church of Scotland. By John Spottiswood, Archbishop of St Andrews* eds. M. Napier

to the Scottish ecclesiastical hierarchy and close to open defiance of the regent.[54] They were the initial public steps along the road leading to the Wars of the Congregation. In the two years from his meeting with Knox to the implementation of the First Band, Archibald had moved from being a passive enquirer to an active leader of the Scottish Protestant movement. His dedication to the Protestant cause was further strengthened by his father's dying command to establish Protestantism within Scotland, at whatever cost to himself or his lineage.[55]

The years between 1555 and 1558 had changed Archibald from an untried adolescent to a twenty-year-old who had proved himself capable of military leadership and of taking political and religious initiatives. By the time the 4th earl died, in the middle of November 1558, Archibald was prepared for the demanding duties of a Scottish peer and Highland chief. He had already acquired the ideas and experiences that would mould his future policies. He knew his own mind and, having become the earl of Argyll, he wanted to put those new ideas into practice. His successes and failures can be followed in the analysis of his political career, which lasted for the next fifteen years until his untimely death in 1573.

Apart from an illness in 1554, he seems to have had a trouble-free childhood and grown into a strong and healthy adult. He was fortunate to avoid serious injury when he was involved in the military campaigns in Donegal, during the Wars of the Congregation and the civil wars. However, on the day of the battle of Langside he was afflicted by a seizure, possibly a minor stroke or heart attack, which prevented him commanding the queen's forces. Any incapacity he experienced was temporary and he was functioning normally a few weeks later.[56] This might have been the first signs of a problem that was diagnosed as 'the stone', the sixteenth-century term for a variety of ailments of the internal organs. This caused him considerable pain, and in September 1571 he was taken seriously ill. Though reported to be dying, Argyll appeared to make a full recovery. However, he had been sufficiently shaken by his brush with death to make immediate provision for his succession.[57] For

and M. Russell (3 vols., Bannatyne Club, Edinburgh, 1850), I. 186; J. Durkan, 'Heresy in Scotland, the Second Phase 1546–58', *RSCHS*, 24 (1992), 320–65 at pp. 352–3.
[54] Archbishop Hamilton's letter to the 4th earl, 28 March 1558, Knox, *History*, II. 246–54; Dawson, 'Clan, Kin and Kirk', 218–9.
[55] The Family Pedigree stated that the 4th earl 'has left in his testament and latter will that Archibald would overthrow the masse altho it should endanger his estate, God would build him up. This he enjoyns him under a heavy curse. This to be seen in his testament': *Records of Argyll*, 7. The 4th earl's will has not survived but Knox recorded a very similar injunction, 'that he should study to set forward the public and true preaching of the Evangel of Jesus Christ, and to suppress all superstition and idolatry, to the uttermost of his power': Knox, *History*, 138–9.
[56] See below, pp. 32, 155, 174.   [57] 9 October 1571, *CSPSc*, IV. 4.

the next two years the earl was as busy as ever, and there were no further reports of weakness, incapacity or illness.

His death was sudden and unexpected. The 5th earl was making a routine journey through mid-Argyll and stayed the night of 12 September 1573 at Barbreck. He had been well when he retired to bed but died before morning. It was assumed the 5th earl had died of a further attack of 'the stone', rather than poisoning, the common sixteenth-century suspicion after a sudden demise.[58] His brother, Colin, succeeded him as 6th earl. When they heard the news, he and his wife Annas Keith had been on their way to overwinter at Darnaway castle in Moray. They stopped at Dunnottar castle near Stonehaven, Annas' family home, and hurriedly rearranged their plans.[59] In Edinburgh, Regent Morton had reacted rather differently to Argyll's death. He broke into the 5th earl's room at Holyroodhouse and unceremoniously deposited all his belongings in the open street. This unseemly behaviour was viewed by the Campbells as offensive to the 5th earl's memory and insulting to the 6th earl.[60]

Argyll died at the height of his powers, when he was only 35 years old and had ruled as earl for a scant 15 years. He was buried alongside his predecessors at the collegiate church of Kilmun in Cowal. His tomb had no effigy, in accordance with his Reformed convictions, which included a desire to avoid ostentation, especially at death. Its Latin epitaph simply read, 'Archibald Campbell, earl of Argyll, an imitator of ancestral virtues and most worthy of such a family, a most resolute supporter of religious truth, died in the year 1573'. Those restrained and succinct Latin phrases expressed the essence of a humanist understanding of Protestant nobility and virtue, one of the models to which Argyll had aspired. A Latin poem written by John Johnston elaborating upon these sentiments was later carved on the plaque.[61] On the other side of the North Channel, the Gaelic community noted the passing of the 5th earl. The *Annals of the Four Masters*, which did not often trouble itself with foreigners, recorded the death of Macailein Mòr with the laconic comment, 'by no means the least distinguished of the Gaels of Scotland'.[62]

---

[58] Valentine Brown to Burghley, 4 October 1573, *CSP For 1572–74*, 427. Poison was suspected when the 4th earl of Atholl died suddenly in 1579 and an autopsy was undertaken, NLS MS 3157.

[59] Annas Keith to Hugh Rose of Kilravock, 1 November 1573, *Rose of Kilravock*, 263–4.

[60] This was the first of eight complaints the 6th earl made about Morton's behaviour towards him which led to a feud between the two men: n.d., AT, VI. 224–6.

[61] *Argyll Inventory*, 7, 178 and 547, n. 19; Johnston's poem was also printed in *Heroes ex omni historia scotica lectissimi* (Leiden, 1603), 36: see below pp. 46–7. I am grateful to my colleague Professor David Wright for his assistance in translating the poem and to Mr and Mrs Gilles of Kilmun and Ian Fisher of the RCAHMS for further details concerning the mausoleum and the inscription.

[62] *Annals of the Four Masters*, V. 1663.

MARRIAGE AND DIVORCE

The 5th earl's adult life was dominated by the failure of his marriage, which became a public as well as a personal tragedy.[63] From a relatively early stage, the couple had encountered difficulties. The countess enjoyed living in the Lowlands, certainly preferring it to the peripatetic lifestyle as wife of a magnate in the Western Highlands where she missed her friends and life within the court. After the sophisticated French ambience of the royal household, she might have judged the Gaelic culture of her husband's court in Argyll strange and even 'barbaric'.[64] Another source of friction was that the marriage was childless. The 'blame' for failing to produce an heir fell upon the countess because the 5th earl's illegitimate children proved he was not sterile. A clash of personalities exacerbated these underlying tensions. Lady Jane inherited the pride and stubborn wilfulness evident in James V's other children. She was not afraid to leave her husband and was sufficiently brave and determined to withstand menaces, captivity and relentless pressure. For his part, Argyll could be just as proud and intransigent, and he became deeply resentful of his wife's behaviour. His wife's defiance revealed a cruel and violent streak in his nature. On several occasions he ordered, or at least permitted, his clansmen and servants to imprison her and threaten her life.[65] By the end of the 1560s, there was too much bitterness between them for any amicable settlement to be reached.

Mutual hostility and recrimination were evident by 1560 when Lady Jane was accused of adultery, which might have provoked her imprisonment for a fortnight during that summer. According to later statements in court, one of Argyll's servants laid hands upon her and threatened her. At this juncture John Knox was invited to intervene and a reconciliation took place. When Mary, Queen of Scots returned in 1561, the countess of Argyll became a close companion of her royal half-sister and resided a great deal at court.[66] By spring 1563, the couple were at loggerheads again. The queen was in the difficult position of being on warm terms with both husband and wife and able to see the faults on each side. Mary strove hard to bring them

[63] David Sellar and I are preparing an extended discussion of the Argylls' divorce set in its legal and social context.
[64] For Lowland attitudes towards the Gàidhealtachd, see Dawson, 'The Emergence of the Highlands', 280–92.
[65] The details of Lady Jane's treatment were given in the legal pleadings in her later case concerning the divorce. Although no longer extant among the Court of Session papers (CS15), they survive in a late sixteenth-century copy made by Oliver Colt in his Legal Style Book, RH13/2 fos. 73v–77v. I am grateful to Dr Alan Borthwick for his assistance in tracing this manuscript.
[66] In 1566 the countess was receiving a pension of £150, *TA*, XI. 512. She was one of the very select group who were dining with the queen on the night of Riccio's murder: Keith, *History*, III. 266–7 and see below, p. 145.

back together. In an improbable alliance, she enlisted Knox's help in her marriage guidance plans. The queen and the preacher worked harmoniously together in an attempt to save the Argylls' marriage. Knox agreed that Mary should deal with her half-sister whilst he concentrated his attention upon the 5th earl. On 7 May he wrote an extremely sharp letter criticising Argyll for refusing to sleep with his wife. The preacher declared the earl's duty was to live with the countess, unless he could prove that she had committed adultery since their last reconciliation. He added that it made no difference that the countess's pride and stubbornness were driving Argyll to distraction. In addition, Knox had heard rumours that the 5th earl had taken a mistress. In his best prophetic style the minister thundered, 'every moment of that filthy pleasure shall turn to you in a year's displeasure; yea, it shall be the occasion and cause of everlasting damnation, unless speedily ye repent: and repent ye cannot, except that ye desist from that impiety'. Not surprisingly, Argyll found the letter's tone difficult to accept. However, as even Knox grudgingly admitted, in public he remained on his accustomed friendly terms with the reformer.[67]

Mary, Queen of Scots had chosen a softer approach. She was anxious that Argyll did not discover she had spoken to Knox because, 'I would be very sorry to offend him in that or any other thing'. Instead she sought to influence Lady Jane by warning her that royal patronage and favour would be withdrawn if, after a new reconciliation, 'she behave not herself so as she ought to do'. In a subtle move, the queen chose to go on progress to the Western Highlands that summer. This ensured that the couple had no choice but to unite to entertain her during her journey through Argyll to Inveraray castle. The successful progress was a happy and light-hearted journey, which probably also advanced the queen's agenda of a reconciliation.[68] The hope that the marriage would endure was expressed in stone at Carnasserie castle, built in the 1560s. The armorial panel carved directly above the main doorway displayed in its two halves the royal arms of the countess alongside those of the house of Argyll.[69]

The marital truce lasted four years; however, in August 1567 the countess left Dunoon and, by refusing to return to live with the earl, caused a complete breakdown of the marriage.[70] Her decision was connected to the loss of her secure place in the royal household, which had been dismantled following the queen's imprisonment and abdication in July and August 1567. The

---

[67] Knox, *History*, II. 74–6.

[68] T.A. Small, 'Queen Mary in the Counties of Dumbarton and Argyll', *SHR* 25 (1927), 13–19.

[69] *Argyll Inventory*, VII. 218; J.W. Bannerman, 'Two Early Post-Reformation Inscriptions in Argyll', *PSAS*, 105 (1972–4), 307–12; Dawson, 'The Protestant Earl', 337.

[70] The details of the separation were given in the decree of adherence, 28 January 1572, CC8/2/5, no pagination; and the divorce decree, 22 June 1573, CC8/2/6 fo. 121v.

precise order of events during that summer is unclear. Probably in July, Lady Jane had been imprisoned again, and her life was threatened by a Campbell laird. She then either escaped on foot or was allowed to leave to consult her friends. Whatever happened, she did not return. The 5th earl immediately sought an uncontested divorce on the grounds of his own infidelity, but the countess refused. Her half-brother, Moray, was bitterly opposed to the idea, which, along with the disagreement over Mary's abdication and the regency, created a rift between him and Argyll.[71]

The final separation caused serious problems for the 5th earl. The lack of a legitimate heir of his own body threatened the continuity of the house of Argyll and the stability of the whole of Clan Campbell, ensuring his marital difficulties could not remain a personal matter. His dilemma was particularly acute because the Campbells belonged to two different cultural worlds. Within Gaelic society, marriage customs had traditionally permitted greater flexibility over sexual relationships, including the institution of Celtic secular marriage, and there was no sharp division between legitimate and illegitimate offspring. A chief was expected to sire children from a variety of liaisons and, like most of his forbears and contemporaries, the 5th earl had fathered illegitimate offspring.[72] A chief's mistress, especially one of noble birth, was a recognised and respected member of his household. The sister of John Campbell of Cawdor, Jean or possibly Beatrix, was a noblewoman of considerable standing within the clan and was one of Argyll's mistresses.[73] She was the mother of Colin, called Cailein na Creig, and of Jane and probably also of Elspeth, Argyll's two natural daughters who were born in the early 1570s.[74] An earlier illegitimate son, also named Colin, had been born to his first mistress in 1557 or 1558 and was tutored by John Carswell.[75]

---

[71] Throckmorton to Queen Elizabeth, 22 August 1567, Keith, *History*, II. 746, and see below, p. 153.

[72] W.D.H. Sellar, 'Marriage, Divorce and Concubinage in Gaelic Scotland', *TGSI* 51 (1978–80), 464–93.

[73] She subsequently married Patrick Grant of Glenmoriston. In the legal pleadings Lady Jane alleged the earl had three mistresses, but only initials are given and the dates left blank in the manuscript, RH13/2 fo. 77r.

[74] These three natural children were mentioned in the 6th earl's will of 1584, *Letters to Argyll Family*, 65. Jane was noted as being particularly beautiful and was married to Angus Mackintosh of Dunnachten, contract 26 February 1586, mentioned in 18 May 1586, GD176/140. Jane's second marriage was to Donald Campbell of Ardnamurchan. See A. Campbell of Airds, *The Life and Troubled Times of Sir Donald Campbell of Ardnamurchan* (Society of West Highland and Island Historical Research, Inverness, 1991), 9–11. Elspeth became Lady Macfarlane and Cailein na Creig died without issue in 1606.

[75] RH13/2 fo. 77r. Colin received the castle and lands of Craignish in 1564 from his father, see 27 January 1584, GD112/1/249. He was legitimated on 4 July 1566, *RSS*, VII. 2926. He was probably the son who was fostered with Donald Gorm MacDonald of Sleat, see 21 April 1571, AT, VI. 160–2: see below, p. 207. In 1573 he was fifteen years old when he was suggested as a hostage to be held in England, 18 April 1573, *CSPSc*, IV. 549. There is confusion as

A relationship with a third mistress based in Argyll was only ended by the earl's second marriage in August 1573.[76]

None of the natural children could inherit the earldom. Unlike other Highland chiefs, the integration of the earls of Argyll into the Lowland aristocracy, and particularly their choice of Lowland brides, had made their adherence to primogeniture obligatory. With Lady Jane unable, or perhaps unwilling, to conceive his child, the 5th earl needed a legal divorce so that he could remarry and produce a legitimate heir. As Henry VIII had famously discovered before him, achieving that goal was not a straightforward matter. Each man had to resort to parliamentary statute as well as court cases to ensure remarriage and legitimate heirs.

In the decade after the Scottish Reformation of 1559–60, considerable confusion remained concerning the appropriate jurisdiction over divorce cases. Much of the business of the old ecclesiastical courts was transferred to the new secular commissary courts set up in 1564, which gave the Edinburgh court comprehensive jurisdiction over all divorce suits.[77] In addition, through its own disciplinary courts, the new Kirk dealt with cases of sexual misdemeanour and with the 'scandal' of marital breakdowns. It had adopted the view that the guilty party in a divorce suit, especially if the grounds were adultery, was not free to remarry.[78]

Since the countess had rejected a swift, uncontested divorce in 1567, it was difficult for the 5th earl and his legal advisers to know how to proceed. The problem concerned the grounds on which to seek a divorce. The earl could not cite the countess' adultery because the subsequent reconciliation removed

---

to whether this is the Colin (cf. *Records of Argyll*, 6), or whether there was a third Colin, the illegitimate son of the 4th earl, who married Katherine Campbell, the heiress of Barbreck, and became known as Colin of Barbreck or Craignish, 25 February 1578, GD111/4/6; 'The manuscript history of Craignish' in *Miscellany of the Scottish History Society IV* (SHS, 3rd ser. 9, Edinburgh, 1926), 222 and 270; 31 January 1577, *Clan Campbell*, VI. 32. I am grateful to Alastair Campbell of Airds for advice concerning the various Colins.

[76] RH13/2 fo. 77r.

[77] D. Smith, 'The Spiritual Jurisdiction, 1560–64', *RSCHS*, 25 (1993), 1–18; L. Leneman, *Alienated Affections: The Scottish Experience of Divorce and Separation, 1684–1830* (Edinburgh, 1998), 6–7.

[78] Although this was the practice in the church courts, doubts remained, e.g. the Thomson v. Philib divorce in St Andrews, *Register of the Minister, Elders and Deacons of the Christian Congregation of Saint Andrews...1559–1600* ed. D. Hay Fleming (2 vols., SHS, 1st ser. 4 and 7, Edinburgh, 1889–90), 302. The conviction of Nicol Sutherland at an assize in Elgin caused Regent Moray to raise the matter again in the General Assembly, March and July 1569 and March 1570, *BUK*, I. 140, 146, 197. For a discussion of the legal position, see Paton, ed., *An Introduction to Scottish Legal History*, chs. 7 and 8; W.D.H. Sellar, 'Marriage, Divorce and the Forbidden Degrees: Canon Law and Scots Law' in W.M. Osborough, ed., *Explorations in Law and History: Irish Legal History Society Discourses, 1988–1994* (Dublin, 1995), 59–82. I am grateful to David Sellar for his help on the legal aspects of the 5th earl's divorce.

it as a reason for divorce and no attempt was made to prove further infidelity. In addition, it was a dangerous course for Argyll to pursue in view of his own extra-marital liaisons, which could have been employed as a counter charge.[79] Since it would probably block his remarriage, being labelled the guilty party was to be avoided, if possible. Consequently, the earl's legal case concentrated upon the separation, though this would not necessarily lead to an action for divorce. Argyll wanted a ruling from the commissary court of Edinburgh giving civil legality to the divorce and guarding against challenges to the legitimacy of any future heir. Suing for a divorce on the grounds of non-adherence or separation took Argyll into uncharted legal waters.

Despite its proclamatory and abrasive style, Knox's intervention in 1563 had been informal and pastoral. The public knowledge and ensuing 'scandal' of the separation of the earl and his countess brought the matter to the official notice of the Kirk. In December 1567, the General Assembly summoned both parties to appear. The 5th earl blamed his wife for their separation but declared himself willing to submit to ecclesiastical discipline for moral offences 'slanderous to the Kirk'. The Assembly was showing leniency as well as political acumen when it directed the earl's close friend John Carswell, the superintendent of Argyll, to deal with him. It is not clear what the Assembly ordered for Lady Jane concerning the separation. Instead of investigating her departure from Dunoon, it censured her for acting as a surrogate godmother at the Roman Catholic baptism of James VI.[80]

With matters fully in the public domain, at the beginning of 1568 the earl sent a legal letter to his wife requesting her to return to Dunoon within fifteen days and promising to receive her back without conditions.[81] In the spring of 1569, two more letters were sent and when these failed the 5th earl approached the General Assembly.[82] On 8 July it directed the veteran super-intendent of Fife, John Winram, to visit the countess and urge her to rejoin her husband.[83] In the summer of 1570, there was a serious attempt by the two kin groups to negotiate a settlement. The countess' kinsman, John Stewart, 4th earl of Atholl, had discussions with Colin Campbell of Glenorchy, act-ing on Argyll's behalf.[84] By then, relations between the couple had become

---

[79] As they were in the later Court of Session case, RH 13/2 fo. 77r.

[80] The countess acted on behalf of Queen Elizabeth I: *BUK*, I. 114, 117.

[81] 19 and 20 January 1568, noted in the probation of the divorce case, 11 June 1573, CC/8/2/6 fo. 112r.

[82] Argyll's letter to the Assembly excusing his absence, 28 July 1567; Assembly's renewed request to attend, July 1570, *BUK*, I. 101, 178. The earl's letter of authorisation for Robert Montgomery, archdeacon of Argyll and his legal servant John Hutton, 27 June 1569, noted in CC/8/2/6 fo. 112v.

[83] *BUK*, I. 148–9.

[84] Letters from countess to Atholl and Atholl to Glenorchy, 25 June and 2 July 1570, *Campbell Letters*, 110–12 and see below, p. 32.

extremely bitter. In a letter to her cousin, the countess showed no surprise that Atholl's attempts to arbitrate had failed, adding, 'I lwikit for na bettir at that ongrait manis hand'. She warned Atholl that she would never change her mind and no true friend could ask her to do otherwise.[85] During that summer Lady Jane stayed with the countess of Mar at Stirling castle and was reported to be 'very angry and in great poverty'.[86] Undoubtedly, one of the obstacles to a settlement was the countess' control over her dower lands and the issue of her future income.[87] The 5th earl believed himself wronged and, as Glenorchy explained to Atholl in July 1570, the marriage had become 'ane great bardane onto him'.[88]

Argyll was under mounting pressure to secure the line by fathering a legitimate heir. He had to find a means of extracting himself from his existing marriage in such a way as to leave him free to remarry. At the beginning of 1572 there was a new urgency. Having been seriously ill the previous year, Argyll decided to settle family affairs by transferring his lands to his brother, who became Lord Lorne, the official heir to the earldom.[89] Colin, whose first marriage had proved childless, remarried in mid-January.[90] Although making these precautionary arrangements, the earl had not given up hope of securing a divorce and marrying again. At the end of January, his case was presented before Edinburgh's commissary court, and he obtained a decree commanding the countess to adhere to him.[91] When, predictably, she did not comply she was outlawed.[92]

Having reached an impasse in the secular courts, Argyll returned to the Kirk. Lady Jane was living in Edinburgh, and both private persuasion and public admonition in Leith and later in the Edinburgh and Holyrood churches were used to urge her to return to her husband.[93] The situation was complicated by the state of war in Edinburgh due to the occupation of the castle by Marian supporters, leaving the burgh without a proper ministry. At the start of 1573, the countess decided to enter the castle and was inside

---

[85] 2 July 1570, *Campbell Letters*, 111.

[86] Madam Peynes [?Pagès] to Mary, Queen of Scots, 15 August 1570, *CSPSc*, III. 314.

[87] The financial arrangements were the subject of a series of court cases after the 5th earl's death, see below, pp. 33–4.

[88] Atholl to Glenorchy, 28 June 1570, *Campbell Letters*, 110.

[89] 10 February 1572, AT, VI. 156, 174, 192–4; *RMS*, IV. 2013–18.

[90] To Dame Annas Keith, the widow of Regent Moray, 6 and 13 January 1572, AT, VI. 168; NRAS 217, Box 15, No. 344.

[91] 28 January 1572, CC8/2/5, no pagination.

[92] 23 February 1572, date and details given 11 and 22 June 1573, CC8/2/6 fos. 112r, 122r.

[93] Details of the involvement of John Spottiswood, superintendent of Lothian, the private mission of Gavin Hamilton, and the public proceedings of David Lindsay, minister of Leith and his kirk session in April 1572 followed by those of the Edinburgh church in January 1573 and John Brand, minister of Holyrood, and his kirk session in March and April 1573, in 11 and 22 June 1573, CC8/2/6 fos. 112r–113v, 122r–v.

its walls and out of touch when the final sentence of excommunication was passed on 26 April 1573.[94]

Neither the religious excommunication nor the civil outlawry advanced the earl's cause. He pressed the General Assembly in March 1573 to make an explicit ruling over separation as grounds for divorce. It had appointed a special commission of lawyers and ministers to investigate the issue, but they proved reluctant to pronounce, suggesting instead other Reformed churches in Europe be contacted for advice.[95] The 5th earl seemed little further forward and, probably with a touch of desperation, turned to another legislative body. Aided by his recent appointment as chancellor, Argyll's plea was given speedy redress by the estates gathered in Parliament. At the end of April, the first act they passed was 'anent thame that divertis fra utheris being joynit of befoir in lauchfull mariage'.[96] It made the interesting, but inaccurate, assertion that divorce on the grounds of non-adherence had been legal since the Reformation. The convoluted procedure to achieve such a divorce mirrored the process Argyll had already followed and was probably copied from the earl's experience.[97] Armed with the parliamentary act, the 5th earl returned to the commissary court and sought a divorce.[98] On 22 June 1573, the judges granted Argyll a divorce decree on grounds of separation, allowing the earl to remarry and stripping the countess of her tocher and her marriage portions.[99]

Shortly before these final legal stages, the siege of Edinburgh castle ended and Lady Jane was made a prisoner. One of her chief concerns was that she should not fall into Argyll's hands. Declaring her fear that he would kill her, she appealed directly to Queen Elizabeth.[100] In the event, Lady Jane travelled unmolested to Fife and was reported to be comfortable there.[101] Although not contesting any of the legal proceedings at the time, the countess later used the Court of Session to challenge the divorce decree and the roles played by the commissary court and Parliament. She did not win her case outright, but

---

[94] As a possible inducement for her to leave the castle the countess was relaxed from the horn, 11 June 1573, CC8/2/6 fos. 113r–v; John Brand's final letter of warning, 24 April 1573, *CSPSc*, IV. 500–1.

[95] Because the earl's other measures were successful, this was probably not attempted, *BUK*, I. 262–3.

[96] *APS*, III. 81–2.

[97] This point was part of the challenge that Lady Jane later made against the divorce decree and its whole legal basis: 15 January 1574, CS7/50 fos. 501r–502r; *Clan Campbell*, VIII. 58–9.

[98] 9 and 20 May, 5 and 11 June 1573, CC8/2/6 fos. 90v, 92v–93r, 108v, 111v–113v.

[99] CC8/2/6 fos. 121r–122v. For a discussion of the case, see J. Riddell, *Inquiry into the Law and Practice in Scottish Peerages* (Edinburgh, 1842), 546–55.

[100] Contemporary copy of the letter, n.d. GD24/5/152.

[101] Queen Elizabeth sharply told Morton that she had no desire to meddle in marital disputes about which she knew nothing: 9 June 1573, BL Cotton Calig. C IV, n. fo. 114; *CSPSc*, IV. 583; his reply 26 June 1573, *CSPSc*, IV. 593.

in 1576 the matter remained sufficiently in doubt for it to be referred back to Parliament, and a private agreement over the financial matters had to be concluded between the 6th earl of Argyll and the 5th earl's two wives.[102] For the remainder of her life, Lady Jane Stewart successfully retained her title of countess of Argyll, relict or widow of the 5th earl, and her will was proved under that name.[103]

Despite the time it had taken, the divorce achieved its main purpose, which was to free Argyll to remarry. This he did as quickly as possible by marrying Jean, daughter of his long-time friend and fellow Protestant, Alexander Cunningham, 4th earl of Glencairn. The pre-nuptial contract had been agreed on 8 March 1573, even before the divorce had been finalised, and the wedding was solemnised in the first week of August.[104] Unfortunately, the second marriage was over almost before it had begun. Within six weeks of his wedding the 5th earl was dead. The final sad twist came nearly nine months later when his posthumous son died at birth.[105]

The completion of Argyll's divorce brought immediate repercussions. The General Assembly was annoyed that its deliberations had been pre-empted by an Act of Parliament pushed through on the earl's behalf. It felt that the act, and probably also Argyll's own divorce, were 'aganes the ordour of the Kirk'.[106] The Assembly's displeasure was directed at the 5th earl's client, the hapless bishop of Dunkeld, who was censured for voting in Parliament in support of the act.[107] The Kirk's attitude was probably also influenced by disquiet about its own role in Argyll's divorce and remarriage. It had assisted the 5th earl in his case and had been lenient regarding his extramarital affairs.[108] The ecclesiastical courts appeared to be operating one rule for the nobility and another for commoners.

---

[102] 15 January, 5 March, 29 June 1574, CS7/50 fos. 501r–502r; CS7/53 fos. 153r–155r, 499v–500v; 5 and 18 March and November 1574 CS15/13 [Box]; 20 May 1575, CS15/17 [Box]; 10 March 1576, CS15/22 [Box]; *Clan Campbell*, VIII. 58–9, 68. There were a string of other cases related to the 5th earl's two wives and their marriage portions. For the decreet arbitral, 4 June 1576, CS7/63/2 fos. 243v–244v; 24 June 1577, GD16/41/42; *Clan Campbell*, VI. 35.

[103] 7 January 1588, *Letters to Argyll Family*, 71–8.

[104] Marriage contract 6–8 August 1573, RD1/12, fos. 365v–370r, *Clan Campbell*, VI. 25; charters to his wife, AT, VI. 204, 206, 208; *HMC*, IV. 484; *RSS*, VI. 2115. The tocher was 8,000 merks.

[105] Reported in Killigrew to Walsingham, 30 June 1574, *CSPSc*, V. 13.

[106] *The historie and cronicles of Scotland . . . by Robert Lindesay of Pitscottie* ed. A.J.G. Mackay (3 vols., Scottish Text Society, Old ser. 42–43, Edinburgh, 1899–1911), II. 301.

[107] 6 August 1573: *BUK*, I. 270.

[108] Pitscottie commented concerning the 5th earl's divorce, 'himselff being culpable', *The historie and cronicles of Scotland . . . by Robert Lindesay of Pitscottie*, II. 310. Argyll's adultery was common knowledge and provoked a reference in one of the bishop of Galloway's sermons in 1571, 17 June, *CSPSc*, III. 609–10.

The 5th earl paid a high price for resolving his marital difficulties. His reputation as a moral Protestant was severely damaged by his widely known adulteries and the rumours of cruelty suffered by the countess. The protracted process of marital breakdown, separation and divorce hung like a cloud over his adult life, encouraging the less attractive sides of his personality. It also deprived him of the support a noblewoman could provide, not simply in domestic affairs such as the smooth running of a household, but also within the arena of regional politics.[109] However, it was not the loss of domestic happiness or political support that weighed most heavily upon the 5th earl. The greatest consequence, and the one he probably felt most keenly, was not fulfilling the prime obligation to his lineage, that of fathering a legitimate successor. It was this duty to his house that drove Argyll to such protracted and extraordinary lengths to obtain his divorce and secure the chance to remarry.

CHARACTER AND BELIEFS

When describing the 5th earl's noble virtues, the author of the Family Pedigree singled out his courtesy, liberality and generosity of deed and spirit.[110] These qualities shine through Argyll's extensive correspondence. Though proud of his lineage and position, the earl was rarely stiff and formal. He tried to be open, friendly and even 'homely' with other people,[111] frequently adding a personal touch to his letters by scrawling a hasty postscript in his own hand to send special greetings or emphasise the main point.[112] He possessed a good sense of humour, enjoying a joke with friends.[113] For most of his life he maintained a positive and optimistic outlook, though, following his bouts of illness and after the frustrations of 1570, he became disillusioned and world-weary. Especially when he thought his honour had been impugned, Argyll could lose his temper, becoming 'sum pairt crabbit' as one Campbell laird phrased it.[114] During these brief tantrums, he could act or speak precipitantly but, once recovered, he was usually prepared to

---

[109] For example see Katherine Ruthven's contribution to the success of her husband, Colin Campbell of Glenorchy, *Campbell Letters*, 22–34.

[110] *Records of Argyll*, 6.

[111] For example Argyll to Cecil, 12 February 1562, SP52/7 fo. 33.

[112] For example Argyll to William Douglas of Lochleven, 22 July 1570, NLS MS 73 fo. 25v.

[113] For example his dry comment to Randolph about being willing to miss his summer's hunting in Argyll if that secured a meeting between Queen Elizabeth and Mary, Queen of Scots: 25 January 1562, SP52/7 fo. 19.

[114] John Campbell of Skipnish to Colin Campbell of Glenorchy, 13 October 1563, *Campbell Letters*, 14.

apologise.[115] Whilst he did not harbour personal grudges, he could be hard and unforgiving when he felt he or his principles had been betrayed.[116] His marital difficulties reveal most starkly the darker side of his character with a cruelty and bitterness alongside a stubborn determination to get his own way, if necessary by unscrupulous means.

The 5th earl was acutely conscious of his many obligations, which, at times, weighed heavily upon him. This made him particularly sensitive to criticism of the performance of his duties, especially that of protecting and defending those in his care. On occasions this led him to make extravagant declarations of support or to give promises to his clansmen or political allies that he could not easily keep. His instinctive approach was to be conciliatory, to search for consensus and to keep on good terms with as many people as possible. Sometimes this was carried too far and he became over-reassuring or too optimistic about finding a solution to an intractable problem. In attempting to please all sides, he could appear to be switching between positions or failing to provide a firm lead, especially noticeable when he was surviving in the political jungle of 1570. Friendship and the loyalty of friends to each other were extremely important to him, overriding most other considerations. By struggling to preserve all his connexions, including those with political opponents, he made his political life, and the choices he faced within it, much harder. During the civil wars, though all supported the King's Party, he remained on warm terms with his cousin the earl of Mar, his godmother Agnes Leslie and her husband William Douglas of Lochleven. His most spectacular failure was with the earl of Moray. Having been the closest of friends since their youth, the two men became bitterly alienated in 1567 over Mary's abdication and Argyll's wish for a divorce. Each man felt betrayed by the other.

The 5th earl had usually managed to separate the personal and political aspects of his most significant relationship, that with his monarch, Mary, Queen of Scots. On her return to Scotland, the young queen formed a deep affection for her brother-in-law. With the six-foot queen preferring the company of tall men, Argyll's great height was a considerable advantage. He became a member of the tight circle of family and friends whom Mary drew around her at court. Their profound disagreement over religion was not an obstacle to their friendship, and the queen found him easier, and possibly less censorious, company than her own half-brother Moray. As she had

---

[115] See the two letters from Argyll to Colin Campbell of Glenorchy, 23 August 1570, *Campbell Letters*, 145 and 146.

[116] For example over English policy in 1565 and his split with Moray in 1567, see below, p. 153.

explained to Knox in 1563, she wanted nothing to upset her relationship with Argyll. However, two years later, Mary's own remarriage caused a rift between them. When Argyll consistently refused to accept Darnley and went into rebellion, Mary, Queen of Scots was furious, once declaring she hated him.

Mary's attitude towards Argyll was changed by Darnley's behaviour, especially the king's involvement in the Riccio murder. From this point the queen regarded the 5th earl as a true friend and a good and dear brother. On the basis of their friendship, Mary sent a pathetic plea to Argyll to recognise her third marriage to Bothwell. In this instance, the 5th earl drew a sharp distinction between personal affection for Mary and loyalty to the Scottish crown and kingdom. He was willing to oppose Mary and Bothwell at Carberry, but was not prepared to allow the queen to be browbeaten into abdication. Mary's friend again became her political supporter. On her escape from Lochleven, Mary immediately appointed the 5th earl her lieutenant. He remained the leader of the Queen's Party for most of the civil wars. In her letters to him from her English prison, Mary's gratitude and affection were expressed in the intimate postscripts she added in her own hand. When he finally settled with the King's Party in 1571, the queen accepted that this was an unavoidable political decision rather than a personal betrayal. Despite frequently finding themselves politically at odds, Argyll and Mary did manage to preserve their friendship.

Throughout his political career, Argyll strove to uphold his principles, refusing to make concessions on matters he believed touched his honour, his duties to the Protestant faith or to the Scottish crown. However, his pursuit of principled ends was not incompatible with an enduring awareness of his self-interest. The main focus for his political ambition was the traditional noble aim of preserving and enhancing his house, and he appeared largely indifferent to private goals such as exercising political power for its own sake or amassing an individual fortune. After he had abandoned his British strategy in 1565, the earl found it difficult to formulate clear political objectives. Although certain about basic principles, his touch was less secure when deciding upon the day-to-day tactics of political life. His analysis of political problems tended to be simplistic and, particularly in his early years, idealistic, sometimes making him over-optimistic that simple solutions could be found and then implemented. Especially during the civil wars, his uncertainty about the best path to follow in the grey world of politics prevented him from offering a firm or decisive enough lead at certain critical junctures. With the exception of black-and-white issues or those on which he was sure in his own mind, such as his British strategy, he had a tendency to respond to, rather than direct, policy.

Lacking a feel or liking for political bargaining, the 5th earl was not an adept politician. Not relishing the minutiae of diplomatic negotiation, he was happy to pass that task to an experienced practitioner, such as William Maitland of Lethington. When faced with a particularly difficult or complex problem, sometimes he vacillated or procrastinated, perhaps taking too literally one of the family mottoes, 'I byd my tyme'.[117] During the latter stages of the civil wars, he gained a reputation for faithlessness. Rather than springing from devious or unscrupulous motives, his behaviour in such difficult times probably owed more to his hesitant uncertainties, cruelly satirised as foolishness by his enemies. To guide him with tactical decisions, he relied upon his close friends and advisers and could be heavily influenced by them. Aware of his strengths and weaknesses as a politician, Argyll preferred to act as part of a team. During the Reformation crisis and the Wars of the Congregation, he worked alongside his two great Protestant friends and contemporaries, his brother-in-law Lord James Stewart and his cousin James, earl of Arran. After the Protestant success of 1560 and Arran's eclipse with the onset of his madness in 1562, William Maitland of Lethington joined Argyll and Lord James to form the triumvirate that guided Scottish policy until 1565. Although Maitland stayed loyal to the queen over the Darnley marriage, the 5th earl's partnership with Moray was further strengthened by their joint rebellion during the Chase-about Raid, continuing until the rupture of 1567.

Argyll was left isolated during the civil wars, with most of his former Protestant friends and allies on the opposite side. The Roman Catholicism and regional rivalry between their two houses prevented any closeness between him and the earl of Huntly, the other main leader of the Queen's Party. For the same reasons, relations with the earl of Atholl remained cool. Though allied to the Hamiltons, the 5th earl did not strike up a close partnership with either of his maternal uncles. He found no leadership from the ineffective duke of Châtelherault, who headed the house, and probably did not fully trust John, archbishop of St Andrews, the political mastermind behind the Hamiltons. By giving his confidence to Robert, 5th Lord Boyd, another longtime, Protestant ally, Argyll demonstrated that the common religious bond was an essential ingredient in these partnerships. Though prepared to ally and remain on good personal terms with Roman Catholic nobles, the 5th earl only placed his complete trust in fellow Protestants. Particularly during the latter stages of the civil wars, Boyd, a generation older than Argyll, exerted

---

[117] From the 5th earl's arms recorded in 1566 in Forman's Manuscript, NLS Adv. MS 31.4.2 fo. 28; G. Harvey Johnston, *The Heraldry of the Campbells* (Inveraray, 1977; reprint of 1920 edn), 20. This motto was eventually adopted by the Loudoun branch of the family with the earls settling for *Ne obliviscaris* or 'Lest we forget', as their motto.

considerable influence over him. The two men were lampooned for being an inseparable, and rather foolish, couple.

In addition to these political partners, Argyll constantly sought advice from his council of kinsmen and dependents. Throughout his rule as chief of Clan Campbell, he sought consensus and agreement for his policies. This was not always forthcoming and at times Argyll was forced by his kinsmen to change policy when they felt he was damaging their interests. In 1569, his clan demanded he come to terms with Regent Moray, and Argyll had to bow to this pressure, possibly welcoming the opportunity to shift onto others the responsibility for an unpalatable decision. On regional matters, he was often willing to defer to the council's advice, especially concerning the MacGregor feud, and even be persuaded to act against his inclinations. The search for harmony within his clan and affinity did not prevent the 5th earl displaying greater ruthlessness when dealing with outsiders. Just after the MacGregor feud had been settled in 1565, Argyll callously recommended to Glenorchy that the MacGregors should be deployed in the most dangerous positions in battle in the expectation that many of them would be killed.[118] The earl could be very offhand concerning the fate of those captured in raids, as when he requested Glenorchy to 'keip vnpwt downe' one of MacGregor's servants.[119] He had few qualms about sacrificing others, in order to safeguard Campbell interests. He suggested to Glenorchy that, rather than risk his own dependents, 'broken' men, who had no lands or goods to lose, should be employed in a revenge raid.[120]

Such a callous and calculating attitude was less evident in his personal life, except with regard to his first wife. In this instance, he did stop short of her long-term imprisonment or murder, which some of his more ruthless clansmen appeared to have suggested. As John Knox was not slow to remind him, his treatment of Lady Jane and the keeping of mistresses fell a long way short of the moral standards required to match his Protestant profession. In this area of his life, the 5th earl adhered to the sexual morality of his aristocratic and Gaelic culture rather than that of his new faith. With the considerable exception of his first marriage, the 5th earl encountered no difficulties in his relationships with women. He was on amicable terms with the regent Mary of Guise, and enjoyed a warm friendship with her daughter Mary, Queen of Scots. Argyll bestowed upon another relation by marriage a similar level of affection. Katherine Ruthven, Lady Glenorchy, was older than the 5th earl who, ignoring the fact that they were only distantly related, addressed her as his loving aunt, occasionally calling her 'Kate', which was highly unusual in an age when Christian names were rarely employed, even among intimate

[118] 5 July 1565, *Campbell Letters*, 41.   [119] 28 August 1565, *Campbell Letters*, 47.
[120] 7 April 1566, GD112/39/6/8.

friends.[121] He treated Katherine as the equal of her husband, being prepared to discuss any issue with her, knowing Katherine and Colin routinely read each other's correspondence.[122] Although Colin was his kinsman, the 5th earl's letters to Lady Glenorchy were distinctly warmer in tone than those sent to her husband.[123] In particular, Argyll's most effusive declarations of support for the house of Glenorchy were written in the first instance to Katherine rather than Colin, the Campbell chief.[124]

A matrix of fundamental attitudes and beliefs underpinned Argyll's public and private conduct. The earl's correspondence offers an unrivalled insight into this conceptual world: those habits of thought and unspoken assumptions that are usually beyond the reach of the sixteenth-century historian. Many of Argyll's beliefs were shared by his fellow aristocrats in Scotland, Britain and throughout Europe. They comprised the mental landscape of the early modern European nobility in which medieval chivalric values were amalgamated with the classical virtues inculcated by a humanist education.[125] For the Scottish and Gaelic nobilities these assumptions were normally articulated in the language of kinship, honour and loyalty.[126] But they could as readily be expressed through the humanist concepts of service to God, country, parents and friends.[127] For the 5th earl the variety of emphases found within the Gàidhealtachd, Scotland and Europe, merged into a single system of noble values. He was proud to be part of a common culture that united him to the whole European nobility.

In common with other nobles, Argyll thought primarily in collective rather than individual terms. He was conscious of being part of a continuous lineage, embracing both his ancestors and his successors. As well as stretching

---

[121] For example 'luiffing ant', 19 March 1565, *Campbell Letters*, 37; 'Kayt', 16 December 1570, 20 May 1571, GD112/39/11/21 and 13/3. Argyll was concerned when Katherine fell ill and strongly advised her husband, Colin Campbell of Glenorchy, to secure the best medical help possible, 15 November 1572, GD112/39/14/11.

[122] 2 October 1570, GD112/39/11/1.

[123] Compare the letters written on the same day to Katherine and Colin, 29 January, 1 February, 19 March 1565; 24 July, 3 October 1570, *Campbell Letters*, 28–31, 37, 119, 170.

[124] For example 1 February 1565, *Campbell Letters*, 31. The one exception to the earl's friendly letters was when he upbraided Katherine for what he felt was a grave lapse in hospitality. However, in that letter the sense of sorrow and incredulity over what had happened were as pronounced as his anger: 30 May 1570, *Campbell Letters*, 94.

[125] R.A. Mason, 'Chivalry and Citizenship: Aspects of National Identity in Renaissance Scotland' in R.A. Mason, *Kingship and Commonweal: Political Thought in Renaissance and Reformation Scotland* (East Linton, 1998), ch. 3.

[126] For a discussion of these noble values, see *Campbell Letters*, 8–14. An illuminating study of the Scottish nobility has recently opened up this subject, K. M. Brown, *Noble Society in Scotland: Wealth, Family and Culture from Reformation to Revolution* (Edinburgh, 2000).

[127] For examples in the 5th earl's Latin epitaph, see above, p. 26, and below, p. 46, and for William Cecil's mental world, see Alford, *Cecil*, 22; D. Allan, *Philosophy and Politicis in Later Stuart Scotland: Neo-Stoicism, Culture and Ideology in an Age of Crisis* (East Linton, 2000).

back into the past and forward into the future, Argyll's kin existed in the present. His concept of living kin spread out in concentric circles encompassing his family, house, clan and surname, relations by marriage, allies and dependants and with the wider affinity occupying the outer circle. Kinship was assessed according to a hierarchy of significance and obligation, with relationships derived from lineage and blood taking precedence over those acquired through marriage alliances or bonds. At the core of his concentric circles of kindred was Argyll's 'house', the earl's dynastic family and lineage. This extended beyond his immediate family to other blood relatives. The earl's first duty was to defend the welfare of his own house. A blood relationship to Argyll conferred access to his protection and other privileges, which could be invoked many years after the original connexion. Within the Gàidhealtachd, a foster family was regarded as closer than blood kin, and the spiritual kinship created in godparenting formed a similar, if less intimate, bond which in legal terms was the equivalent of consanguinity.[128] Argyll's obligations extended to those joined by marriage alliances to his house. This group merged with his wider affinity and those with whom he had created an artificial kinship through bonds of friendship and manrent.[129]

Fulfilling one's duties and obligations to the kin-group was the means by which a noble's honour was maintained and enhanced. In addition to furnishing the essential rhetoric of noble life, the concept of honour required certain deeds. Argyll's honour had an individual dimension that depended upon his personal conduct and adherence to the code of noble behaviour. At its heart lay his integrity, encapsulated in his 'word of honour', which, when challenged, had to be defended with his life. In the heated atmosphere of charge and counter-charge in 1569 over complicity in Darnley's murder, Argyll and Huntly challenged their accusers, Regent Moray and Maitland of Lethington, to 'defend the same be law of armes as our awin proper honor'. By consenting to fight with Lethington, though he was 'nouther of quality nor bloode equal unto us', they waived the convention of only challenging one's peers.[130]

In early modern Scotland, individual honour formed part of the collective honour of the house, and to take or threaten the life of a nobleman's kinsman was to insult him and his kindred. It was the satisfaction of the kin-group, rather than the individual, which was crucial for the settlement of any blood

---

[128] The relationship between godparent and godchild was included within the forbidden degrees of consanguinity for marriage, Sellar, 'Marriage, Divorce and the Forbidden Degrees', 76.

[129] For a full discussion of Argyll's affinity, see below pp. 81–2.

[130] The protestation of the earls of Huntly and Argyll, January 1569, Keith, *History*, 293–4. The duel did not take place, see below pp. 176–7.

feud. Argyll's position as head of a lineage involved him in a number of feuds where he acted on behalf of his clan and surname. He could also be asked to act for distant relations, as when he represented the maternal kin of Neil Montgomery of Lainshaw.[131] Even if a life had not been taken, the insult remained. It was the dishonour, far more than the minimal damage inflicted, that was at issue when the Campbell laird of Glenlyon was attacked in 1570. Glenorchy, Atholl and Maitland all reminded the earl that such action against one of Argyll's blood must be revenged, to reinforce the message that no one could attack his clansmen with impunity.[132]

Defending one's kin merged into a more general duty of supporting and protecting one's dependents, termed 'keeping kindness'. This encompassed the reciprocal relationships of Scotland's hierarchical society, in which loyalty and service were rewarded by good lordship. The 'kindness' that the earl owed did not require supporting his affinity irrespective of the circumstances: only for actions that were just and honourable.[133] If there were conflicting obligations, the lines between kinsmen and outsiders, friends and enemies became difficult to draw. As a result of the size and extent of his kin and dependents, the 5th earl was frequently connected to both sides in a dispute, when the wisest course was to try to arbitrate. The broad concept of 'standing' a good friend to someone meant upholding their interests and honour, not automatically doing what they wanted. This permitted sufficient flexibility for the 5th earl, and other nobles, to stand by their friends whilst still steering an honourable course through the rivalries and disputes that characterised regional and national politics.

Argyll adopted the same approach to all levels of politics, believing that the concepts of kin and honour, loyalty and service were applicable to each of them and making no distinction between public and private life. In his view, they applied equally to international politics, and in 1568 he urged the English queen to act as a good friend would do towards Mary, Queen of Scots, thereby upholding her princely honour and her duty to a royal kinswoman.[134] Such ideas established the framework for the 5th earl's political world and the rhetoric for his actions. Argyll started with his fundamental concern for the welfare of his house and clan. Broadening out

<hr/>

[131] 10 February 1561, GD8/167 and 170; W. Fraser, *Memorials of the Montgomeries, Earls of Eglinton* (2 vols., Edinburgh, 1859), II. 155–9; J. Wormald, 'Bloodfeud, Kindred and Government in Early Modern Scotland' *Past and Present*, 87 (1980), 54–97 at pp. 70, 76. The relationship between Argyll and Montgomery was distant: Helen Campbell, daughter of the 1st earl of Argyll had married Hugh Montgomery, 1st earl of Eglinton in 1478, but it had been renewed by a bond between the families, 5 September 1548: Wormald, *Lords and Men*, 184 [Argyll 32].
[132] 7 and 10 June 1570, *Campbell Letters*, 96, 99–100.
[133] 18 August 1570, *Campbell Letters*, 140.
[134] 24 August 1568, BL Cotton Calig. C1 n.f. 209 and see below, p. 193.

from his kindred, he sought to rule his region or 'country' with justice, being a 'good lord' to all his affinity and receiving their service and loyalty in return. At the national level, he gave his political loyalty to the Scottish crown and commonweal, and a personal loyalty to his royal sister-in-law. These were conventional aristocratic aspirations, which Argyll shared with the majority of the Scottish nobility. During his career, the earl strove hard to remain within this framework, but such broad themes could neither provide him with the precise policies he needed to pursue in day-to-day politics, nor resolve the conflicting loyalties they occasionally produced.

His commitment to the Protestant cause provided one clear goal for which he was prepared to sacrifice his other obligations. This overriding religious duty profoundly affected his actions within the local, regional, national and international political arenas. Throughout his life, the 5th earl gave unwavering support to the Protestant cause, though at times he fell foul of some clerical leaders, such as John Knox, over his political stance and sexual behaviour. His personal religious convictions had been reinforced by the emotional impact of his father's deathbed command to promote true religion at whatever cost. The first stage was the creation of a Protestant Kirk in Scotland: the building of the Lord's Temple which, like the Old Testament King David, the 4th earl had longed to perform, but was compelled to leave to his son.[135] It was achieved by force through the Wars of the Congregation, followed by the legislation of the Parliament of August 1560. The new church had then to be established, and Argyll actively supported its work, especially within the Highlands. Thanks to his efforts and those of his close friend John Carswell, the superintendent of Argyll and the first Protestant bishop of the Isles, Gaelic Protestantism became firmly rooted in that region.[136] With understandable family pride, the Pedigree of 1634 lauded the role played by the 5th earl, whom 'the Lord made a glorious instrument of the Reformation of the Scottish Kirk, wrought by him principally'.[137]

The 5th earl also viewed his religious duty within a British and European context. A shared loyalty to the Protestant cause became the basis for his friendships with men such as William Cecil and Adam Loftus, archbishop of Armagh. Argyll believed that British Protestants should be united in the aim of strengthening and spreading their faith throughout the three kingdoms.

---

[135] *Records of Argyll*, 7; Knox, *History*, I. 138.
[136] For a full discussion of the Highland Reformation and the 5th earl's Protestant activities, see J. Kirk, *Patterns of Reform* (Edinburgh, 1989), chs. 7, 8 and 12; Dawson, 'The Protestant Earl'; Dawson, 'Clan, Kin and Kirk'; and Dawson, 'Calvinism in the Gaidhealtachd'.
[137] It also referred to George Buchanan's designation of the 5th earl as the *author instaurandae religionis*. The anonymous author of the Pedigree assumed that this part of Argyll's career was so well known, especially to the future marquis of Argyll, it was not necessary to detail it: *Records of Argyll*, 5–6.

In 1559, the goal of a common religion offered the foundation upon which Argyll's co-operation with England and his British policy could be constructed. For the next six years the 5th earl blithely assumed that support for Protestantism and amity with England were inseparable goals. After a harsh lesson in power politics during 1565, he was forced to change his mind.[138] Argyll chose to interpret Queen Elizabeth's behaviour over the Chase-about Raid as a betrayal of the Protestant cause. In his over-pessimistic view, the bridge linking Protestantism and the English alliance had been cut and could not be rebuilt. From 1566 he de-coupled the two elements, abandoning his previous policy of co-operation. His British strategies became less idealistic and more calculating. Relations with England and Ireland were relegated to a subordinate position and used to further the 5th earl's regional and national objectives. Above all, they no longer had as their ultimate aim the creation of a Protestant Britain. Henceforth, Argyll's religious goals were restricted to Scotland, especially the Highlands.

The support of Protestantism by military means during 1559–60 and 1565 brought Argyll's estates close to bankruptcy. Although prepared to pay such a price, his financial predicament left him open to clan pressure when non-religious principles were at stake, such as in 1569. In view of the strain upon his resources, the 5th earl had to struggle to preserve the welfare of his house and that of his clan. He was acutely conscious of being the trustee of a corporate inheritance stretching across the generations and giving him an obligation to protect what his forbears had gained and enhance it for his own heirs. This was such a fundamental duty that it could not be compromised, even for a close kinsman. Such a suggestion was enough to make Argyll extremely angry. When Colin Campbell asked to buy the feudal superiority over his territorial designation, the lands of Glen Orchy, the 5th earl was so incensed he could barely trust himself to reply. Argyll assured Colin that he could never grant away the patrimony his ancestors had struggled so hard to win, 'I belief that my foirbearis gait it [Glen Orchy] nocht so lychtly . . . For suirlie be ye assurit that howlang that I leif that I will nocht give you the said superieorietie. For I thynk me worthy of the samin suppois it ware better nor it is for I thynk to keip that thyng that my foirbearis haid.'[139] Despite this outburst, the 5th earl was unstinting in his support for Glenorchy's many other acquisitions. Provided it did not clash with other clan members or his wider affinity, he lent his backing to all Campbell operations, thereby assisting the general expansion of Clan Campbell power.

Argyll's obligations extended beyond the confines of his house and clan to the widest extent of his affinity. If he did not publicly maintain his followers,

---

[138] See below, ch. 4.   [139] 11 October 1563, *Campbell Letters*, 13.

his affinity would disintegrate and he would be dishonoured. Once the 5th earl had taken someone into his service, he was bound to support and maintain him, as he succinctly explained, he 'man do for him'.[140] One of his duties was to see to the ordering or 'dress' of his 'country'. Like a medieval king, Argyll believed that the administration of justice and the preservation of public order were the essence of good rule. Assuming they flowed best from his personal presence, the earl became concerned when other activities led to protracted absences from Argyll and the Western Highlands.[141] Being present to oversee the region's administration and arbitrate its disputes was part of the mutual obligations between a lord and his dependents.[142] As long as he performed his duties as overlord, the 5th earl could expect to receive the loyalty of his clan, his affinity and the rest of the political community of the region.

Argyll's own loyalty to Mary, Queen of Scots rested upon a similar assumption of reciprocity.[143] His obedience and service were conditional upon her fulfilling her responsibilities to Scotland's crown and commonweal. Like other rebels before him, in 1559–60 and 1565 Argyll proclaimed he was acting as a good subject. To justify the seeming paradox of being a rebel and a loyal subject, the earl employed the common distinction between his duty to the commonweal of Scotland and that to the person of the monarch.[144] Before her return in 1561, he had pledged himself to Mary, Queen of Scots against all other living persons, assuring her of his support in those actions 'that may stand with the glorye of God, wele of your hyenes realme and nautrall people thairof'.[145] Should the queen's policies threaten any of those three fundamentals, his obedience to the monarch's person was temporarily suspended and he would strive to preserve true religion, the welfare of the kingdom and the people, if necessary by force. During the Wars of the Congregation, he perceived a threat to two of these fundamental causes: the Protestant faith and Scotland's political independence. He therefore believed he was right to fight against royal forces.[146] Similarly, in 1565 he thought that the Kirk and the Protestant cause throughout Britain were in danger. He justified that rebellion with a radical summary of the right of resistance: they were fighting 'that we may first have God and thane our prince in God,

---

[140] 11 May 1562, *Campbell Letters*, 5; see below, ch. 2.
[141] For example 26 August 1559, *Campbell Letters*, 2; 8 November 1572, GD/112/39/14/9; 7 November 1560, *CSPSc*, I. 492.
[142] For example 9 July 1565, *Campbell Letters*, 43.
[143] For example declaration in letter to Elizabeth, 24 August 1568, BL Cotton Calig. C1 n.f. 209.
[144] J.H. Burns, *The True Law of Kingship: Concepts of Monarchy in Early Modern Scotland* (Oxford, 1996); Mason, *Kingship and the Commonweal*, and see below, p. 141.
[145] Instructions to his brother, 10 March 1561, Argyll MSS Bundle 62.
[146] See below pp. 92, 97–8.

wnder God and be Godis lawis'. Although seeking to present his cause in its most advantageous light, this did express the 5th earl's political priorities and Protestant commitment.[147]

Although endorsing resistance in defence of religion and the commonweal, Argyll retained a deep respect for the Scottish monarchy. In his mind the removal of a reigning queen was altogether different from resisting her policies. The 5th earl could not condone the treatment Mary, Queen of Scots received in the summer of 1567. Despite her foolish actions, she remained his and Scotland's queen. With the major problem, Bothwell, already removed, there was no reason to bully her into abdication. Despite the settlements with the regent, the Queen's Party continued to regard Mary as the legitimate ruler of the kingdom, even after her flight and imprisonment in England. Argyll sharply reminded Glenorchy in 1570 that lawful authority within the realm emanated from the queen's majesty and was not to be confused with that claimed by the King's Party.[148] In 1571 the hard practicalities of the situation made Argyll change his stance and finally accept the authority of the young King James and his regents. Although criticised by others for his capitulation, he consoled himself by believing that he had defending the queen's cause for as long as it was viable to do so.

The 5th earl's short career did not bring the realisation of the political goals he set himself at its start but, for him, that was not the sole consideration. His political conduct had been dictated by four fundamental duties: to defend Protestantism; to defend his house, clan and affinity; to defend his 'country'; and to defend his queen and kingdom. Pursuing these aims was more important than their eventual success or failure. As has been pointed out, noble achievement did not hinge upon a project's success: 'honour was established, not primarily by the skill with which events and situations were manipulated with a view to a successful outcome . . . but by the determined "steadfastness" with which they were confronted'.[149] For the 5th earl, the crucial test was faithfully fulfilling the four duties and, by this standard, he maintained his honour. The Latin poem on his grave judged Argyll's life in precisely these categories. It highlighted the worthy inheritance that enabled him to emulate the virtues of his Campbell ancestors and the race of Alba from which they came. The 5th earl had brought glory to his family by practising such traditional noble values. However, far greater glory had flowed from his commitment to Protestantism and his willingness to suffer,

---

[147] 5th earl to Loftus, 18 November 1565, SP63/15 fo. 172v. For ideas on resistance, see R.A. Mason, ed., *John Knox and the British Reformations* (Aldershot, 1998), chs 7 and 8.

[148] 19 October 1570, GD112/39/11/11.

[149] M. James, 'English Politics and the Concept of Honour' in M. James, *Society, Politics and Culture* (Cambridge, 1986), 308–415 at pp. 316 and 370.

or even to die, for the faith. The eulogy concluded that, as a shining example of the old order and as one who had warmly welcomed the new order, the 5th earl had indeed been doubly blessed.[150]

[150] This is a free interpretation, rather than an attempt at translation, of the sentiments expressed in Johnston's poem which reads:

> Gens Albina, vetus, gemina incunabula Regni
> Quae posuit (fuerant nam duo regna priùs:)
> Illa viris armisque potens totque aucta tropæis,
> Quæ dominos rerum tot dedit una Deos;
> Hæc et avos, atavosque dedit. Loca prisca tenemus,
> Tecta, Lares, mores, et decora alta ducum.
> Sufficeretque vetus nobis ea gloria: verùm
> Major ad ignoti nos vehit astra Poli.
> Adscriptique Dei jam sancta in federa cives,
> Magnanimi audemus pro Pietate mori.
> Gens quæ jura priùs dederat, nunc accipit. Ergo
> Bis felix: quæ dat, quæ nova, jura capit.

John Johnson, *Heroes ex omni historia scotica lectissimi* (Leiden, 1603), 36; and see above n. 61.

2

Semi-sovereign prince

Argyll held a unique position within the islands of Britain. Though at first sight appearing similar to other members of the early modern European aristocracy, he replicated and in certain ways surpassed the power of some contemporary ruling sovereigns. He was the most powerful nobleman in the sixteenth-century Atlantic archipelago with a substantial independent military and naval force at his disposal. What made Argyll distinctive was the unusual nature of his power and not solely its quantity. Whilst remaining a loyal subject of the Scottish crown, the earl wielded semi-sovereign authority within his own 'country'. This unusual status allowed him to operate successfully in the complex of polities and cultures that existed in the islands of Britain.

To the Gaelic poets, Argyll was 'King of the Gael', while a Scots commentator summarised his status as 'regal within himself'.[1] The 5th earl was a semi-sovereign prince who maintained his own court through which he ruled the heartland of Argyll and the Western Highlands and Islands. He held the temporal sword in his hand and could wield it as he chose, as one of his subordinate chiefs had reminded him.[2] The earl had no hesitation in exercising regalian rights, issuing proclamations and letters of legitimation, granting licences to travel, giving marriage dispensations and in practice ennobling his subordinates.[3] In his correspondence, the 5th earl employed the language

[1] For example 'An Duannag Ullamh' in *Bàrdachd Ghàidhlig: Gaelic Poetry 1550–1900* ed. W. Watson (3rd edn, Inverness, 1976), 259–62, cited in W. Gillies, 'Some Aspects of Campbell History', *TGSI*, 50 (1976–8), 256–95 at p. 260. Alexander Hay's description of the Scottish nobility, c. 1577, *Estimate of the Scottish Nobility* ed. C. Rogers (Grampian Club, 6, London, 1873), 8.
[2] Glenorchy to Argyll, c. 3–7 August 1570, *Campbell Letters*, 128.
[3] For example creating a chief for Clan MacIver 10 August 1564, AT, VI. 50 and see below p. 66; proclamation, Glenorchy to Argyll, 14 August 1570, *Campbell Letters*, 135; letter of legitimation, 17 June 1577, *Highland Papers*, IV. 216–8; Dougal MacDougall's licence to go to Lewis, see Argyll to Glenorchy, 20 November 1564, GD112/39/3/10; dispensation for marriage within the forbidden degrees, 11 October 1559, in *Liber officialis sancti Andree*, ed. J. H. Forbes, Lord Medwyn (Abbotsford Club, 25, Edinburgh, 1845), 169–70.

and terminology that modern historians associate exclusively with royalty, using the royal 'we' and referring to 'our awin proper persone'.[4] In addition to these indications of regal status, Argyll possessed sovereign attributes normally reserved for a state, such as participating in international diplomacy, raising large military forces, levying taxation and administering justice.[5]

The 5th earl's power and position rested securely upon his extensive estates and jurisdictions and the strength of his clan and affinity. What set him apart from his fellow Scottish magnates was the degree of political independence he enjoyed and the effective invulnerability of his authority. These qualities were most evident in his military power and in his control over the judicial system within the West Highlands. Inside his own country, he was untouchable, secure even from the displeasure of a Scottish monarch. When in rebellion in 1565, he remained virtually impregnable within Argyll, even though his fellow rebel lords had been forced to flee into exile. Despite their triumph, the Scottish king and queen were unable to challenge him in his Highland base. Such immunity from royal reprisal or interference and an exclusive control over his region made Argyll unique in Scotland. Other peers controlled autonomous provincial lordships, but they were vulnerable to royal disfavour. The immense power that the earl of Huntly exercised throughout the north-east of the kingdom made him Argyll's equal. However, when he opposed the crown in 1562, Mary, Queen of Scots, defeated him, forfeiting him for treason and placing much of his 'country' under the control of her half-brother Moray. The 5th earl was the only peer who could defy the Scottish monarch with relative impunity.

For most of the early modern period, the Stewart monarchs accepted Argyll's semi-sovereign authority within the Highlands with equanimity. They were prepared to enhance it, permitting royal authority in the region to be channelled exclusively through the earls. In practice, royal power in the Western Highlands belonged to the Campbells and became indistinguishable from Campbell power. Perhaps the crown's acceptance was a tacit recognition of the hard political truth that, should they wish to do so, the rulers of Scotland would find it difficult to challenge that control. Royal acquiescence was made easier by two considerations. The first was that Argyll's heartland lay in the Highlands away from the Lowland centres of power. The second and decisive factor was the Campbells' commitment to the Scottish realm and their loyalty to its ruling dynasty. The long record of Campbell service

---

[4] For example Argyll to Glenorchy, 16 September 1571, GD112/39/13/9.
[5] Jean Bodin offered the most famous and influential contemporary discussion of the marks of sovereignty. His theory tied sovereign power to the state. For a discussion of the different styles of sovereignty in Europe, see G.C. Gibbs, R. Oresko and H.M. Scott, eds., *Royal and Republican Sovereignty in Early Modern Europe* (Cambridge, 1997).

prevented the Stewart monarchs objecting to the exercise of sovereign powers or regarding Argyll's independent power as a serious threat. They never treated Clan Campbell with the hostility and suspicion earlier directed at the MacDonald Lords of the Isles. Royal trust was well placed, for at no stage did Argyll contemplate resurrecting the Lordship, abolished in 1493, into an independent principality under Campbell rule. The idea of a separate Gaelic state, even if it existed in sixteenth-century minds, did not form part of his agenda.

The position Argyll enjoyed in Scotland could be paralleled within the multiple and composite monarchies of sixteenth-century Europe. The constitutional arrangements of the Holy Roman Empire recognised the independence and sovereign powers of its princes, while at the same time assuming their allegiance to the emperor and the imperial institutions. In a similar way the complicated political structure of the Netherlands protected the privileges and freedoms of its nobility. In the empire, the Netherlands, Italy and, to a lesser extent, in their Spanish kingdoms, the Habsburgs worked with princes who acknowledged their suzerainty, yet continued to possess their own sovereign powers. During the sixteenth century, a group of princes, such as members of the houses of Lorraine, Savoy or Gonzaga, entered the service of the king of France. They were sovereigns in their own right who had chosen to serve the French monarch, but were technically not his subjects and, therefore, held the special status of *princes étrangers* within France. They occupied high positions at court and held considerable power and influence within French political life.[6] Within sixteenth-century Europe, it was normal for such working relationships to exist without either party seeing any incongruity in the situation. In a European context, the Stewarts' acceptance of Argyll as a semi-sovereign prince was unremarkable.

The Tudor state was out of step with this European norm because it was unwilling to countenance theoretically independent princes within its bounds. Over the centuries, a watchful English crown had reduced the might of the aristocracy in England and Wales. The final surviving separate jurisdictions within the realm were casualties of Thomas Cromwell's revolution in government of the 1530s. When the Tudor monarchs chose to exert their authority, even the power wielded by Border magnates, such as the Percies or the Dacres, crumbled. The dominance of the English crown over its subjects became an accepted fact of political life and ideology in England and Wales. It was enshrined in the 'imperial' theories invoked by the Henrician royal supremacy and supported by the 'common law' mentality of English legislators and administrators.

---

[6] S. Hodson, '*Princes étrangers* at the French Court in the Seventeenth Century', *The Court Historian*, 3.1 (1998), 24–8.

Such a unitary doctrine of sovereignty created conceptual and political problems when the Tudor state strove to govern Ireland. The declaration made in 1541 that royal authority extended over the entire island did not alter political realities there one jot. The Irish Gaelic chiefs remained the independent sovereign princes they had been before the Act of Parliament. They did not relinquish their powers nor accept the English political system, though some chiefs chose to swear an oath of loyalty to the English crown as part of a bargaining process. This awkward reality ran counter to the English belief that sovereign powers could only be exercised by the crown. Such a mismatch between practice and theory severely hampered the formulation of Tudor policy towards Ireland.

In an effort to make the English in Ireland comprehend the position of the Irish Gaelic chiefs, Agnes Campbell, wife of the O'Neill, turned instinctively to the Scottish example of a semi-sovereign prince. As the daughter of the 3rd earl and the 5th earl's aunt, Lady Agnes knew the power of the earls of Argyll. She described the combination of sovereign powers and an amicable relationship with the Scottish crown, which her English listeners found so difficult to understand, by explaining that the Scottish earls, 'challenged as much *jura regalia* and other sovereignties as he [*sic*] could, and yet contented themselves to submit their causes to laws of the realme, and themselves to the king's pleasure'.[7] In a nutshell, that was how and why this juxtaposition of independence and loyalty worked in Scotland.

MILITARY STRENGTH

The military strength the 5th earl possessed was a fundamental source of his power and its most visible manifestation. He commanded the largest independent military force in the British Isles, outnumbered only by the Scottish and English monarchies. Argyll could call upon a sizeable army, a fleet, an artillery train, and possessed most of the important castles of the Western Highlands. Although his shortage of cavalry and arquebusiers placed him at a disadvantage in a full-scale battle in the Lowlands, this was not a handicap when fighting in the Highlands or in northern Ireland. Argyll's military capability gave him a voice within the politics of the British Isles that could not easily be ignored.

The earl's main asset was the number of troops he was able to raise. Given the militarised nature of the Scottish clan system, these men had experience of Highland forays and battles and were the ruthless Gaelic swordsmen so

---

[7] Letter from Sir Henry Sidney to Sir Francis Walsingham, cited in G. Hill, *An Historical Account of the MacDonnells of Antrim* (Belfast, 1978; reprint of 1873 edn), 157.

feared in the Lowlands.[8] Many of them had gone on mercenary expeditions to Ireland as gallowglasses or redshanks.[9] The numbers Argyll could raise varied according to the situation and the duration of service expected. Gathering 1,000 or 1,500 men was a routine matter for him.[10] He offered Queen Elizabeth 3,000 soldiers and could raise 5,000 for a concerted effort. In a real emergency, 12–15,000 men, including raw levies, could be mobilised from the Highlands.[11]

This was a small force in European terms, where the shift from cavalry to infantry and the expansion of armies was already under way by the middle of the sixteenth century. In the relatively unsophisticated military world of the British Isles, 5,000 men were of great significance and 15,000 formidable. The sheer number far exceeded other private forces within the British Isles and rivalled the royal armies of England and Scotland. The Scottish host summoned from the entire kingdom produced c. 20,000 men, with roughly a quarter supplied by the earls of Argyll. At one of the largest musters ever achieved, c. 22–23,000 Scotsmen assembled for the battle of Pinkie in 1547. The English invading force that faced it had between 15,300 and 19,000 troops.[12] Special national efforts and full-scale war produced such large numbers, on other occasions English and Scottish armies were smaller. In the early 1560s, the English army in Ulster contained about 1,500 soldiers.[13] Similarly, the Scottish forces that faced each other at Langside in 1568 together totalled 10,000.

Independent military power on this scale was highly unusual by the mid-sixteenth century. The Tudor monarchs had been careful not to allow English

---

[8] Described in 1565 as 'the bloody Iryshe crew, that who so they take they helples downe hewe', *Satirical Poems of the Time of the Reformation* ed. J. Cranston (2 vols., Scottish Text Society, Old ser. 20 and 24, Edinburgh, 1891–93), I. 19–20, lines 494–5.

[9] The two terms reflect the duration of the mercenary service, with the redshanks fighting for a single season and the gallowglasses hired on for long periods and often settling in Ireland. For a general discussion, see G.A. Hayes-McCoy, *Scots Mercenary Forces in Ireland, 1565–1603* (Dublin, 1996; reprint of 1937 edn).

[10] For example the troops regularly raised in connexion with the MacGregor feud, *Campbell Letters*, 43–7.

[11] The numbers come from a variety of sources for the period 1540–79: *CSPSc*, I. 9, 63, 100, 370, 480; II. 152, 393–4, 406, 516; IV. 220; Calderwood, *History*, II. 468; III. 424. 5 July 1565, Argyll to Glenorchy, *Campbell Letters*, 41. The 4th earl of Argyll was reported to have 12,000 Highlanders before the battle of Solway Moss, 19 November 1542: *Hamilton Papers*, ed. J. Bain (2 vols., Edinburgh, 1890), I, lxxiii. In 1548 he brought 15,000 Highland troops to join D'Esse's 5,000 men: G. Phillips, *The Anglo-Scots War, 1513–50* (Woodbridge, Suffolk, 1999), 236–7. They compare with the 10,000 men raised by the Lords of the Isles, of which 6,600 were chosen, for the Harlaw campaign in 1411: *Acts of the Lords of the Isles, 1336–1493* eds. J. Munro and R.W. Munro (SHS, 4th ser. 22, Edinburgh 1986), xli.

[12] D. Caldwell, 'The Battle of Pinkie' in N. Macdougall, ed., *Scotland and War AD79–1918* (Edinburgh, 1991), 61–94 at pp. 67–8, 73.

[13] C. Falls, *Elizabeth's Irish Wars* (London, 1950), 47.

nobles either to gather their own private forces or gain control over royal armies. Such an ingrained suspicion of a potentially rival military power severely hampered those nobles who had to implement royal policy in Ireland and on the Scottish borders.[14] Within Ireland, the chief governors faced the forces of the independent Gaelic chiefs. In 1562, the English estimated that Shane O'Neill, the most powerful Gaelic chief in Ulster, could mobilise around 1,200 troops, with some additions if he called upon his allies and armed his peasants.[15] Within Scotland, the earl of Huntly could easily raise a similar number with the advantage of being able to field more horsemen, drawn from the fertile estates of the north-east. Whilst cavalry were more effective, he lagged behind Argyll in the overall size of his forces. A snapshot of the relative strengths of the Scottish magnates can be seen in 1567. The Queen's Party agreed that the Hamiltons, the earls of Huntly and Crawford, and Lord Herries – all major aristocratic families – should each provide 1,000 men, with Lords Fleming and Livingstone bringing some horsemen; Argyll was to bring 5,000 troops.[16]

The earl's military strength did not rest on numbers alone. He had under his control a quantity of artillery, including some large brass cannon. Early modern governments tried to maintain a monopoly over such guns, and the possession of these weapons by a leading magnate was unusual enough to provoke comment. After the Donegal expedition of 1555–6, the English were swift to point out to the Scottish regent that such guns were not normally possessed by a noble. They assumed that no government would willingly permit its subjects to use this type of artillery in an independent manner.[17] However, in 1560 the English were willing to pay for the 5th earl's military assistance in Ulster by agreeing to provide him with cannon and demi-cannon.[18] If Argyll had received these guns, he would have increased his technological superiority over other Highland chiefs.[19] The artillery posed a permanent threat

---

[14] Lord Dacre's ability to raise four to five thousand Borderers provoked comment in 1523: S.G. Ellis, *Tudor Frontiers and Noble Power: The Making of the British State* (Oxford, 1995), 101.

[15] The estimate was probably made around December 1562, Bodleian Lib., Carte MS No. 530 fo. 282. Shane O'Neill was the first Irishman to arm his peasants, Sidney to Leicester, 1 March 1566, cited in White, 'Tudor Plantations', II. 186. I am grateful to the Librarian of Trinity College, Dublin, for permission to consult and quote from this thesis. For the way in which the constant warfare against the English militarised Irish society, see K. Simms, 'Warfare in the Medieval Gaelic Lordships' *Irish Sword*, 12 (1975–6), 98–108; K. Simms, *From Kings to Warlords* (Woodbridge, Suffolk, 1987).

[16] *CSPSc*, II. 393–4.

[17] SP51/1, fo. 18; G.A. Hayes-McCoy, 'The Early History of the gun in Ireland', *Journal of the Galway Archaeological and Historical Society*, 18 (1938–9), 43–65, and see above, pp. 21–3.

[18] 19 July 1560 agreement, SP63/2, fo. 58, and see below, p. 107.

[19] The potential for domination of the Western Highlands and Islands had been demonstrated in 1554 when the 4th earl had subdued John MacDonald of Clanranald by firing on the walls

to the security of their castles and tower-houses.[20] Though their employ-
ment was limited within the Highlands, the simple possession of cannons
was menacing.[21] Argyll was able to employ his guns in the Lowlands, for
example bringing them to the siege of Edinburgh castle in 1573, where they
occupied a whole section of the battery.[22] Their value can be seen in the
care and attention paid to the transport by sea and land of one of the earl's
cannon which he loaned to Arran in 1560.[23]

An additional advantage of the 5th earl's naval power was the ability to
transport men and, occasionally, artillery. That power was based upon the
fleet of galleys drawn from the West Highlands and Islands. During the medieval period, the Highland galley had developed from its ancestor, the Viking
longship, into an efficient and versatile vessel. With its shallow draft and its
combination of sail and oars, it possessed exceptional manoeuvrability, essential in the difficult coastal waters, sea lochs and estuaries of the Scottish
and Irish littorals. Galleys could fight at sea, though they could not match
the armed ships of the Scottish or English navies. Their prime functions were
to provide speed and surprise for an attacking force or offer a quick retreat,
in most conditions being able to outrun other vessels.[24] Argyll's galley fleet
acted as both an offensive and a defensive weapon, and its reinforcement
during a crisis was deemed to be a prudent move.[25] At times it provoked
fear, especially in Ireland. In 1568, the Dublin Privy Council prohibited the
export of timber boards from Wexford and Carrickfergus in an ineffectual
attempt to slow down or prevent the 5th earl constructing extra galleys.[26]

Although appreciating the importance and versatility of sea power, the
Campbells were essentially a land-based clan who used the sea. This made
them different from their fifteenth-century predecessors, the Lords of the
Isles, whose territories had been united by the sea-lanes and who dominated the Hebridean waters and the North Channel. Donald Dubh, the
last claimant to the Lordship, mustered 180 galleys in 1545 when he sailed
4,000 men to Ireland.[27] Though not able to match those numbers, Argyll

of Castle Tioram: *TA*, X. xlvii–viii, 229, 287; N. Tranter, *The Fortified House in Scotland*
(5 vols., Edinburgh, 1962–70), V. 116.

[20] For a fuller discussion of the use of artillery, see J.E.A. Dawson, 'Argyll: The Enduring
Heartland', *SHR*, 74 (1995), 75–98 at pp. 92–3.

[21] Huntly reputedly kept a cannon at the door of his castle at Strathbogie to terrify the Highlanders who entered: Randolph to Cecil, 30 September 1562, *CSPSc*, I. 654.

[22] *Diurnal*, 331.   [23] *CSPSc*, I. 480–1.

[24] D. Rixson, *The West Highland Galley* (Edinburgh, 1998), ch. 3; J.E.A. Dawson, 'The Origins
of the "Road to the Isles": Trade, Communications and Campbell Power in Early Modern
Scotland' in R.A. Mason and N. Macdougall, eds., *People and Power in Scotland: Essays in
Honour of T.C. Smout* (Edinburgh, 1992), 74–103 at p. 92.

[25] See Glenorchy to 'Gossip' [Carrick], 13 February 1566, *Campbell Letters*, 79.

[26] 28 August 1568 SP63/25, fo. 150.

[27] *Acts of the Lords of the Isles*, xli; Lord Archibald Campbell, *Argyllshire Galleys* (London,
1906).

could call upon a substantial galley fleet. Two families of shipwrights, the MacGille Chonaills and the MacLucais, were employed building galleys for the earls.[28] With elaborate descriptive flourishes, MacLean's bard celebrated the beauty and power of Argyll's galleys in one of his praise poems.[29] In addition to their personal fleet, the earls paid particular attention to enforcing the galley service due in many of their charters. The captain of Inveraray castle was obliged to supply one of the larger galleys, a birlinn of sixteen oars, whilst from 1368 the Campbells of Melfort had provided a galley of six to eight oars.[30] As well as ensuring a supply from his kin and dependents, Argyll could expect naval help from his allies, the MacDonalds and the MacLeans, who remained the foremost sea powers in the West Highlands and Islands. All the galleys and other ships that Argyll used could be gathered together in one of the best anchorages along the West Highland coast, within the sheltered bay on Loch Etive, under the protective eye of Dunstaffnage Castle.[31]

The 5th earl could call upon other ships to transport his men. As well as possessing the general authority of his royal office as Admiral of the West Seas, he made specific local arrangements.[32] At least one Campbell merchant family had been given money by the earl to fit out their ship, which would be available to their chief when necessary.[33] On a corporate level, a similar relationship existed between the 5th earl and the Ayrshire port of Irvine. Argyll had given the burgh his special protection in return for a supply of boats to serve in Scotland and Ireland.[34] In 1554 and 1559, Irvine's sister port of Ayr had provided and paid for merchant ships for the earl's military operations.[35] The burghs of Renfrew and Dumbarton, on either side of the Clyde estuary, were closely associated with the Campbells.

---

[28] A. Campbell of Airds and D. McWhannell, 'The MacGillechonnells – A Family of Hereditary Boatbuilders', *West Highland Notes and Queries*, ser. 2, 14 (July 1995), 3–9.

[29] J. MacInnes, 'West Highland Sea Power', *TGSI*, 48 (1972–4), 518–56 at pp. 527, 531; 'An Duanag Ullamh' in *Bàrdachd Ghàidhlig*, 259–62, lines 6887–910.

[30] 1 September 1573, AT, VI. 203; 22 September 1566, HMC, 4th, 473, 477.

[31] *Argyll Inventory*, II. 198. For a full discussion of sea power, see D. McWhannell, 'Ship Service and Indigenous Sea Power in the West of Scotland', *West Highland Notes and Queries*, ser. 3, 1 (2000), 3–18.

[32] There appears to have been a trial of strength over jurisdiction between Argyll, as Admiral of the West Seas, and the High Admiral of all Scotland, the earl of Bothwell, *Acta Curiae Admirallatus Scotiae, 1557–61* ed. T.C. Wade (Stair Society, 2, Edinburgh, 1937), xxiv, 10, 27, 46–7, 50, 56–60.

[33] 15 December 1561, AT, V. 161.

[34] Argyll's letter of protection, July 1572, *Muniments of the Royal Burgh of Irvine* (2 vols., Ayrshire and Wigtonshire Archaeological Association, 15, Edinburgh, 1890–91), I. 59–60; the boats were specified in the contract between Irvine and the 6th earl, 21 October 1580, cited in *The River Clyde and the Clyde Burghs* ed. J.D. Marwick (Scottish Burgh Records Society, 20, Edinburgh, 1909), 30–1.

[35] *Ayr Burgh Accounts, 1534–1624* ed. G.S. Pryde (SHS, 3rd ser. 28, Edinburgh, 1937), 122, 130.

As Dougal Campbell was 'admiral' of the Renfrewshire boats, they were available for the 5th earl.[36] There was a similar Campbell link to the Clyde herring fleet, with Campbell of Ardkinglas holding the herring concession for the whole of the Clyde.[37] It proved crucial in 1568 when, in a surprise move, several hundred herring boats transported 2,000 of Argyll's Highlanders up the Clyde to Glasgow.[38] Through his kin, dependents and allies, Argyll had at his command the maritime strength of most of the ports on the Clyde and the south-west coast.

Military and naval power were underpinned by Argyll's control over the main fortifications within his own region. The quantity and quality of the castles built within the Western Highlands far outstripped those to the north.[39] Many Campbell redoubts commanded strategically important sea-lanes or lochs, whilst others were dotted along the land routes which were developing in the early modern period.[40] The earls and most of the Campbell cadets had been enthusiastic castle builders or acquirers, especially the Glenorchy branch.[41] Although the MacLeans in Mull or the Lamonts in Cowal remained in possession of their own castles, during this period they posed no threat. The Campbells had achieved a defensive screen around their heartland, which not even the Scottish crown chose to challenge.[42] A further obstacle for a ruler seeking to force entry into the 5th earl's territory was that the crown's own strongholds were in Campbell hands, principally Carrick, Dunoon, Skipness, Tarbert, Castle Sween and Dunstaffnage. Outside the Highlands, the 5th earl used Castle Campbell in Clackmannanshire as his main Lowland residence. At the top of a steep and narrow glen it was almost impossible to storm. If it were besieged, the 5th earl could withdraw to Argyll, where he could remain in safety.[43]

LEGAL JURISDICTION

The possession of legal jurisdiction was one of the defining characteristics of nobility. Defending and, when possible, increasing this section of a family's

---

[36] 18 January 1571, AT, VI. 155.   [37] AT, V. 166.

[38] *CSPSc*, II. 516 and see below, p. 175.

[39] The north defined as the point of Ardnamurchan northwards: Dawson, 'Argyll: The Enduring Heartland', 88–93.

[40] Dawson, 'Road to the Isles', 88–91.

[41] The 7th laird was nicknamed Duncan of the seven castles, stretching from Barcaldine on the west coast to Balloch at the eastern end of Loch Tay.

[42] The traditional saying coined after the removal of Muriel of Cawdor to Argyll at the start of the sixteenth century that 'It is a far cry to Loch Awe' summed up the sense of total security to be found within the Campbell heartland.

[43] Castle Campbell only fell to General Monck's English troops and artillery in 1654: S. Cruden, *Castle Campbell* (HMSO, Edinburgh, 1984), 23.

heritage was an essential duty to one's house.[44] Hereditary jurisdiction over entire localities or categories of people reinforced aristocratic authority, with the administration of justice being valued as the main instrument of order within society. Holding courts was a lucrative business, providing much needed cash to ease the perennial liquidity problems of the aristocracy.

Among Argyll's greatest assets were the judicial powers granted by the crown, giving him control over the judicial system within the Western Highlands. In theory, there was a distinction between the royal and the feudal courts with a right of appeal to the central courts at Edinburgh.[45] In practice, recourse to the courts in the capital was minimal, and in the West Highlands and Islands justice in all its forms was mediated through the 5th earl.[46] He was able to cover loopholes in this legal net by granting special commissions in his capacity of justice-general of Scotland.[47] It was extremely difficult for any Highlander to defy the earl of Argyll in the law courts.[48] Through its ability to enforce its will through legal process, Clan Campbell increased its grip upon the region. In Argyllshire, the earl held all the important legal offices, such as sheriff or justiciar, and he had received a special general commission covering the Western Isles.[49] The lesser offices of deputes, coroners, bailies, clerks and sergeants were filled by Campbells or other dependents, who were responsible for the running of the sheriff, regality and baronial courts throughout the West Highlands.[50]

As justice-general for life, Argyll was the highest criminal law official in the kingdom with the authority to hold a justice-ayre anywhere in Scotland.[51]

---

[44] See above, pp. 41–2.

[45] To judge by the keeping of later records, the activities of the different courts were run together, with the justiciary court records being found in the sheriff court books, *The Justiciary Records of Argyll and the Isles, 1664–1742,* eds. J. Cameron and J. Imrie (2 vols., Stair Society, 12 and 25, Edinburgh, 1949 and 1969).

[46] In the legal cases concerning Campbells listed in the *Clan Campbell* volumes, for this period those based in the Lowlands far outnumber the Highlanders who comprise the majority of Campbells. A similar impression of the absence of Highland cases has been gained from a perusal of the central courts, the Court of Session (CS7) and the Edinburgh Commissary Court (CC8). I am preparing a large-scale study of Campbell power that will explore this, and other, topics.

[47] For example in 1564 a special commission was given to John Carswell, Campbell of Ardkinglas and Campbell of Inverliever to ensure that John Stewart of Appin delivered one of his clansmen who had defied the law to be imprisoned in the Campbell castle of Innischonnell: 25 May 1565, AT, VI. 25.

[48] As Lamont of Inveryne complained in the 1530s, Wormald, *Lords and Men,* 121–5.

[49] For the offices, see the charter *RMS,* III. 2816; IV. 2018. Although no official grant has survived for the 5th earl, his predecessors held such a commission and he was referred to as lieutenant of the whole Isles, Carswell, *Foirm* 173; AT, VI. 67.

[50] For example AT, V. 103, 105; VI. 7, 25, 168.

[51] The earls of Argyll held the office for life, not during good pleasure, on a hereditary basis until 1628 when it was resigned to the crown, W.D.H. Sellar, ed., *Stair Society Miscellany II* (Stair Society, 35, Edinburgh, 1984), 93–4; *Justiciary Records of Argyll,* I. viii–xiv.

Most of the regular work of the justiciary court in Edinburgh was under-taken by deputies who were a mixture of professional men of law, such as Thomas Bellenden and Thomas Craig, or lairds with legal experience, such as John Campbell of Lundie and Archibald Napier of Merchiston.[52] When the matter was politically sensitive, the 5th earl would sit as judge.[53] He also personally presided at some of the justice-ayres, which lasted for sev-eral weeks or even months.[54] The 5th earl could authorise special courts to be held for particular cases.[55] This proved most advantageous during the Campbells' feud against the MacGregors when, as justiciar, the 5th earl com-missioned Colin Campbell to try Gregor MacGregor of Glenstrae.[56] Argyll also exercised the right to appoint his deputies and take culprits' pledges, which other holders of royal commissions were denied.[57] He guarded such extensive authority jealously, obtaining in 1562 a royal letter revoking all previous appointments as justice depute.[58]

Although none of the records for the regality, sheriff or baronial courts within Argyll survive for this period, they were operating effectively. The sheriff court was held at Inveraray and probably also at Dunoon and Dunstaffnage.[59] In common with other courts, its minute book was used to record all manner of deeds.[60] Between 1528 and 1583, the earls, as hereditary sheriffs of Argyll, made no official returns to the Scottish Exchequer. Unchar-acteristically, the crown allowed this omission without any form of censure.[61]

---

[52] The lawyers did the main bulk of the work and were paid £40 a year by the Royal Treasurer: e.g. *TA*, XI. 256; XII. 61. The other deputes were listed in JC 1/11–12. For a discussion of these men, see J. Finlay, *Men of Law in Pre-Reformation Scotland* (East Linton, 2000).

[53] As in May 1563 when the archbishop of St Andrews and other bishops were tried for saying Mass (Knox, *History*, II. 76), or the earl of Bothwell's trials for treason 2 May 1565 (JC 1/12; *CSPSc*, II. 152), and for Darnley's murder, 12 April 1567 (*CSPSc*, II. 319–20).

[54] For example Aberdeen, 27 August–12 October 1562, *TA*, XI. 198, 207; Jedburgh, 9 October– 8 November 1566, *TA*, XII. 31; Dumbarton/Glasgow, 8 March–1 May 1568, *TA*, XII. 120. When the 5th earl was present at the justice-ayre he was paid £3 a day expenses for himself and his servants.

[55] For example the letter of appointment sent on 22 November 1560 to the laird of Wemyss and his son to try two thieves, printed in *Memorials of the Family of Wemyss of Wemyss* ed. W. Fraser (2 vols., Edinburgh, 1888), II. 197–8. Also see commission to Edmond Hay and Thomas Bannatyne, 16 August 1565, *Bamff Charters and Papers, 1232–1703* ed. J. Ramsay (Oxford, 1915), Nos. 70, 97–101.

[56] 29 March 1570: GD112/1/182.

[57] Compare the reprimand to the earl of Caithness who exceeded his powers: 19 May 1566, *RPC*, I. 459.

[58] 10 January 1562, AT, V. 155; printed in *Memoirs of John Napier of Merchiston* ed. Mark Napier (Edinburgh, 1834), 79–80.

[59] For example 11 November 1567, *Campbell Letters*, 90.

[60] For example references to contracts extracted by the clerk Duncan MacArthur from the sheriff court books: 24 January 1559, AT, V. 105; 3 April 1570, GD112/1/183.

[61] Such a massive time lapse was most unusual and none of the normal penalties were imposed, A. Murray, 'The Procedure of the Scottish Exchequer in the Early Sixteenth Century', *SHR*, 11 (1961), 89–117 at p. 98 and n. 7. The royal grant of the judicial offices of Loch Awe, Lorn, Knapdale and Kintyre gave the 4th earl half of the wards, marriages, reliefs and escheats:

In addition to the criminal courts, the new commissary courts in the West Highlands, covering the old ecclesiastical dioceses rather than the shires, were staffed by the earl's men.[62] At a lower level, the baronial courts ran smoothly and generated substantial profits of justice.[63] At the start of the century, the escheats and fines from the barony courts of Lorn amounted to over £450 a year.[64] By 1576, the winter sittings of the Mid-Lorn and Benderloch courts yielded £50 and £12 respectively in customary dues and escheats.[65] The income that the earl and his dependents derived from these judicial bodies was welcome, but their significance lay in the power the courts gave. With the Campbells controlling the judicial system of the West Highlands from the top to the bottom, even royal justice was in Argyll's hands.

CLAN CAMPBELL

The foundation of Argyll's authority and his ability to mobilise fighting men flowed from his status as chief of Clan Campbell, the most powerful and one of the largest of the Highland clans. To his clansmen the 5th earl was MacCailein Mòr, the son of Great Colin, the successor of a long and proud line of Campbell chiefs. The respect with which their chief was held in the Campbell heartland was so great that, according to John Major, 'the people swear by the hand of Callum More'.[66] Great or Big Colin, celebrated in the chief's designation as the founder of Campbell fortunes, had been killed in 1296. His family of Lochawe, later granted the earldom of Argyll, formed the main Campbell lineage, with most of the important cadets branching from it.[67]

13 November 1542, AT, IV. 108. A receipt from the treasurer Robert Richardson for 700 merks for these feudal casualties exists at Inveraray: 15 December 1564, Argyll MSS Bundle 1074.

[62] For the first reference to the books of the commissary court of Skye, 16 April 1573, *Coll. de Rebus Alban*, 7; *Atlas of Scottish History to 1707* eds. P. McNeill and H.L. MacQueen (Scottish Medievalists, Edinburgh, 1996), 381. In 1568 Archibald Cunningham first signed himself Commissar of Argyll, 29 February 1568: AT, VI. 122.

[63] Court Book for lands of Discher and Toyer, 11 November 1573–29 October 1576 and 10 May 1592–7, June 1599: GD112/17/2; Acts and Statutes of the Court, 1573–1620, GD112/17/3.

[64] Glenorchy obtained a royal letter ordering the earl of Argyll to pay him £151 a year which comprised Glenorchy's third share of the profits, 31 January 1506[?] GD112/2/107/4; the original grant was 18 December 1480, GD112/2/107/2.

[65] Held on 11 and 15 December, GD112/2/107/5. A third of the dues would go to the presiding bailie. See Argyll's agreement about keeping two thirds of the profits of the bailiary of Lochawe with the other third going to the bailie: 18 January 1570 AT, VI. 142.

[66] *Scotland before 1700 from Contemporary Documents* ed. P. Hume Brown (Edinburgh, 1893), 49.

[67] I am grateful to Alastair Campbell of Airds for all his help over Campbell genealogy and for his recent illuminating study, *A History of Clan Campbell I: From Origins to Flodden* (Edinburgh, 2000); see also, G. Harvey Johnston, *The Heraldry of the Campbells* (Inveraray, 1977; reprint of 1920 edn).

In theory the 5th earl and his clansmen were bound by their common blood into a single kin-group. The Campbells were often known as Clan O'Duibne, indicating their common descent from Duibne, later amalgamated with the Fenian hero Diarmaid O'Duibne.[68] The unifying myth of kinship was at the heart of the clan system within the Scottish Gàidhealtachd, and similar notions were associated with the 'surname' in Lowland culture. As a kindred that straddled both cultures, the Campbells amalgamated the two concepts. In his correspondence, the 5th earl tended to employ the term 'clan' in its restricted sense of the clan hierarchy, and 'surname' to cover anyone who called themselves Campbell: he was chief over them all. The ties of blood, from which the clan derived its theoretical unity, brought the mutual obligations of loyalty to the chief in return for his protection.[69] In practice, it was this fundamental bond of loyalty to a single chief that held the clan together, allowing it to absorb smaller kindreds into its ranks.[70]

What set Clan Campbell apart from other Scottish clans was its tenacious cohesion stemming from an awareness of being 'ws Campbellis'.[71] As a group, Campbells used their surname more often than other Gaelic kindreds. Within the sixteenth-century Gàidhealtachd, patronymics were the normal means of identifying individuals, with clan names or surnames employed primarily in dealings with Lowland institutions.[72] Because they were in regular contact with the Lowlands and utilised so many legal documents, the Campbells developed a sharper sense of their corporate identity, which was reinforced by the careful preservation of the clan's unity. Although a large kin-group, it did not fragment into distinct and antagonistic branches. All the Campbell cadets were prepared to acknowledge Argyll as their head and, on certain issues, act as a single unit in support of their chief. When he needed it, the 5th earl was able to call upon the entire clan's strength.

A second asset enjoyed by the Campbells was their ability to operate equally effectively in the Highlands and the Lowlands, a feat no other large clan achieved in this period.[73] From their base in Argyll, they had reached

---

[68] For a discussion of the different Campbell pedigrees, see below pp. 76–7.

[69] A short definition of the role of a Highland chief was given in the bond of manrent given by the MacGillekers to John Campbell of Glenorchy, 2 June 1547, GD112/1/64; *Black Book of Taymouth*, ed. C. Innes (Bannatyne Club, 100, Edinburgh, 1855), 185.

[70] R.A. Dodghson, ' "Pretense of blude and place of thair dwelling": The Nature of Highland Clans, 1500–1745' in R.A. Houston and I.D. Whyte, eds., *Scottish Society 1500–1800* (Cambridge, 1989); R.A. Dodghson, *From Chiefs to Landlords: Social and Economic Change in the Western Highlands and Islands c. 1493–1820* (Edinburgh, 1998), ch. 2; A.I. Macinnes, *Clanship, Commerce and the House of Stuart, 1603–1788* (East Linton, 1996), ch. 1.

[71] Campbell of Dalwany to Glenorchy, 28 August mid-1570s, *Campbell Letters*, 197. For Argyll's own sense of belonging to house, kin and clan, see above, pp. 40–7.

[72] Dawson, 'The Emergence of the Highlands', 260–1.

[73] This might reflect their origins in the 'British' kingdom of Strathclyde before they settled in Argyll, see W.D.H. Sellar, 'The Earliest Campbells: Norman, Briton or Gael?', *Scottish Studies*, 17 (1973), 109–25.

across the Clyde, building a secure enclave in Ayrshire. They also occupied territory in the frontier areas between the Lowlands and the central, eastern and northern Highlands. The Campbells were as much at home within the Scots as the Gaelic-speaking world and were adept at employing the methods and techniques of one culture within the other. One instance of such transference was the Campbells' use in their Highland dealings of the Lowland practice of written documentation. Clan Campbell had absorbed feudal forms with greater enthusiasm and thoroughness than other Highland clans. Despite later assertions, they were not alone in this practice, but they did excel in the management and exploitation of the written word.[74] Though the majority were native Gaelic speakers, Campbells were expected and encouraged to be literate in Scots. Even at relatively modest levels, Campbell lairds were more likely than other Highland chiefs to be able to sign their own names. This skill was combined with an overall respect for communication in all its forms. The Campbells wrote to each other, preserved their records and were prepared to travel within the Highlands and to the Lowlands, giving them an advantage over rival clans in legal or administrative matters.[75]

The Campbell heartland was in Argyll, surrounding the clan's original base at Loch Awe. From there it had expanded both north into Lorn and south into Knapdale and Cowal. By the time of the 5th earl, the clan's dominance throughout Argyll was complete. In the middle of the fifteenth century, the earls moved their primary residence from Innischonnel castle on the inland Loch Awe to Inveraray castle on Loch Fyne. This sea loch gave them access to the Clyde and the North Channel and the castle straddled the land routes through the shire and on to the Lowlands.[76] The Campbells of Glenorchy had spearheaded a push eastwards, settling in Breadalbane and seizing control over much of the Central Highlands.[77] Another group of Campbells, assisted by holding key ecclesiastical offices in the area, had settled farther east in Angus.[78] This created a virtually unbroken corridor of Campbell influence from the west to east coasts of Scotland. In the north, the Campbells of Cawdor had their base on the Moray Firth close to Inverness. The largest and most independent Campbell group had migrated

[74] For the charters of the MacDonalds, Lords of Isles, see *Acts of the Lords of the Isles*. In the middle of the seventeenth century, the MacDonald poet Iain Lom satirised the Campbells for hiding behind the protection of 'the sharp stroke of short pens', cited in Gillies, 'Campbell History', 267; *Campbell Letters*, 20–2.
[75] Dawson, 'Road to the Isles', 88–9; *Campbell Letters*, Introduction, 5–9.
[76] Campbell of Airds, *A History of Clan Campbell*, 136–7.
[77] For a fuller study of the expansion of the Glenorchy Campbells see MacGregor, 'MacGregors', chs. 2–3.
[78] Donald Campbell, great-uncle to the 5th earl, was abbot of Coupar Angus and later Alexander Campbell was bishop of Brechin: E.J. Cowan, 'The Angus Campbells and the Origin of the Campbell-Ogilvie Feud', *Scottish Studies*, 25 (1981), 25–38.

across the Clyde to Ayrshire, where they were especially strong in Kyle.[79] As well as acquiring lands, Campbells were trading as merchants, especially in the burghs of Ayr and Irvine, and were working in the legal and clerical professions.[80] Campbell women added an important dimension to clan expansion. Though married into other kindreds, they retained unusually strong links with their own clan. The mid-sixteenth century witnessed a remarkable group of Campbell women, renowned for their force of character and independence. The political influence and importance of women such as Agnes, Lady Kintyre or Katherine, countess of Crawford or Katherine, wife of William Murray, 10th laird of Tullibardine, increased the geographical reach and strength of Clan Campbell.[81] The clan also benefited from the talents and the loyalty which many wives gave their Campbell husbands. Katherine Ruthven was the most striking example of the impact an astute and able wife could have upon the political and social standing of her husband, Colin Campbell of Glenorchy.[82]

The 5th earl benefited from the expansion of his clan into so many regions of Scotland and of Scottish life, giving him a dominant position within the Highlands and an interest in large areas of the Lowlands. Outwith his Argyll heartland, he was involved in his clansmen's affairs in the frontier zones between the Lowlands and the southern, central and eastern Highlands, the north-east and Moray coast, Angus, and finally the Clyde estuary and the south-west of Scotland. The earl's Lowland estates straddled across Clackmannan, Stirlingshire, Kinross, Fife and Lothian. This left few shires within Scotland in which the 5th earl did not have a direct interest.

One reason why Campbell influence stretched its tentacles over so much of Scotland was its continuous expansion. The need to satisfy the land-hunger of newly formed cadet branches was the ultimate purpose, but that did not dictate expansion tactics. Clan Campbell's primary concern was to acquire power over an area, not merely occupy land. Whilst taking advantage of any opportunity, the Campbells did not grow by accumulating adjacent

---

[79] M.H.B. Sanderson, *Ayrshire and the Reformation: People and Change, 1490–1600* (East Linton, 1997), 2–3.

[80] For the range of Campbell occupations, see those who feature in *Clan Campbell*, 5 and the sixteenth-century Campbell testaments, CC8/8. For the Campbell clerical dynasties, see Dawson, 'Clan, Kin and Kirk', 211–42. They were even found in the 'oldest profession'; in 1564 Bessie Campbell was convicted of being an Edinburgh prostitute, *The Buik of the Canagait, 1564–7* ed. A. Calderwood, (Scottish Record Society, Old ser. 90, Edinburgh, 1961), 11 and 75.

[81] For Agnes, wife of James MacDonald of Dunivaig and later Turlough O'Neill, see below, pp. 163–5. In 1565 the countess of Crawford's marriage was regarded as the wealthiest match in Scotland: Keith, *History*, II. 272; for her part in the establishment of the Campbells in Angus, see Cowan, 'Angus Campbells'. For Lady Tullibardine, see *Campbell Letters*, 47–8, 59.

[82] See *Campbell Letters*, 22–34.

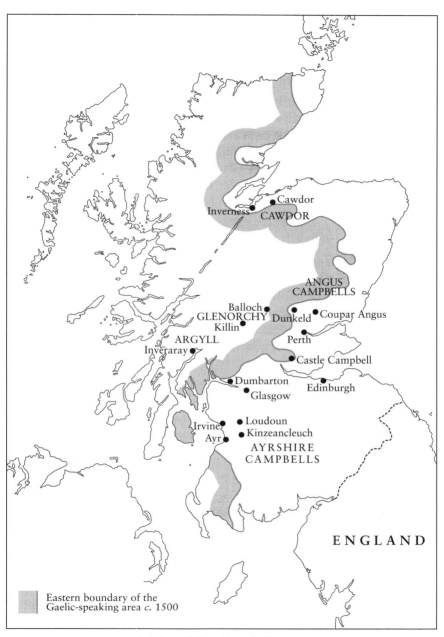

4. Map of Clan Campbell power

pieces of territory. Instead of filling out like a balloon, the clan chose to string itself out along the main land routes. This linear progression left some Campbell cadet branches surrounded by other kindreds. Their comparative isolation was an added incentive to keep in touch, remain united and be willing to assist fellow Campbells when in trouble. On a small scale, this can be seen where the Campbells of Craignish expanded down a single route from the west coast to Loch Awe. At the other end of the scale the march of the Glenorchy Campbells eastwards to Balloch at the east end of Loch Tay gave them control over a number of the key routes to the Lowlands.[83] By controlling communications and exploiting feudal land law, the Campbells could gain a dominant influence over the surrounding area. This allowed them two options: the first, perfected by the Glenorchy Campbells, was a slow squeeze upon their neighbours, obtaining other clans' lands through sale, exchange, debt repayment or eviction; the second possibility was the reduction of other kindreds to a subservient position, who ceased to pose a threat and instead entered Campbell service.[84]

Maintaining the unity of an expanding Clan Campbell was achieved through participation and consultation, with consent oiling the internal workings of the clan.[85] The representatives of the main Campbell kindreds met in Argyll's council and decided policy, reinforcing clan loyalty and cohesion.[86] Campbell internal government mirrored that of the Stewart monarchy, with the 5th earl acting as the head of his 'commonweal'. He involved the Campbell lairds in the running of his 'country' and consulted them on policy matters in the same way as the crown employed the Scottish aristocracy in ruling the realm. The Campbell council was probably copied from the 'Council of the Isles' and the more general Gaelic practice of associating a council of elders with a clan chief, rather than directly from Lowland models.[87] It varied in composition and size according to the gravity of the matter being discussed and the urgency of the situation. For routine matters or those that could not wait, the 5th earl sought advice from those in daily attendance. This inner council did not include every member of his household

---

[83] Dawson, 'Road to the Isles', 89–91.
[84] This happened to the MacNaughtons of Dunderarve, whose castle lay just a couple of miles from the earl's seat at Inveraray. A similar fate befell the MacDougalls of Dunollie, who had originally been Lords of Lorn: C.M. Macdonald, *The History of Argyll up to the Beginning of the Sixteenth Century* (Glasgow, 1950), chs. 10 and 12.
[85] Argyll to Glenorchy, 1 February 1565, *Campbell Letters*, 30.
[86] Glenorchy to Argyll, 5–8 November 1572, *Campbell Letters*, 196.
[87] It was less formal and structured than that of the Lord of the Isles, because there was no need to balance favours among different kindreds: *Acts of the Lords of the Isles*, xlvi–l; *Munro's Western Isles of Scotland and Genealogies of the Clans, 1549* ed. R.W. Munro (London, 1961), 95–110; J.W. Bannerman, 'The Lordship of the Isles' in J. Brown, ed., *Scottish Society in the Fifteenth Century* (London, 1977), 209–40 at pp. 221–8.

nor all those in close physical proximity to the earl.[88] For more serious concerns the main Campbell lairds regularly gathered to discuss policy and order the region.[89] In view of the distance from Argyll, the Ayrshire Campbells were only consulted for major decisions. If a Campbell chief could not attend the meeting, letters and messengers were sent to ascertain his views.[90] As well as Campbells, the 5th earl's council included clerics and members of the Gaelic learned orders as well as other Highland chiefs. As the English ambassador explained to Queen Elizabeth, the 5th earl would gather 'the principallest of his country . . . to take advice of them for his behaviour in these actions'.[91] Particularly when arbitrating Highland feuds, the 5th earl sought the united support of his council.[92] The broadest constituent group was gathered for matters, such as taxation, affecting the entire clan and region.[93]

Having been involved in conciliar decisions, the Campbell lairds held a collective responsibility to implement them. Whilst the 5th earl's personal presence was important, the daily running of business in the region was of necessity performed by others. Within the clan, there was a hierarchy of seniority headed by the chiefs of the cadet branches. The Ayrshire Campbells under Campbell of Loudoun remained semi-detached, running their own affairs in the south-west and not included in the administration of Argyll and the Highlands. By contrast, the Glenorchy and Cawdor Campbells remained involved in Argyll matters. Though based in Perthshire and Moray respectively, they had retained lands in Lorn. With their long-established territorial authority, the older cadet branches, such as the Campbells of Ardkinglas, Auchinbreck, Dunstaffnage, Duntrune and Strachur provided stability within Argyll. The Campbells managed their clan and the shire through a geographical division of duties and responsibilities. It was split into districts: Lorn, Cowal and

[88] John Campbell of Carrick, who was with Argyll most of the winter of 1565–6, complained to Glenorchy that, even though he was the 5th earl's kinsman, he was not part of this charmed inner circle, c. 2–10 December 1565, *Campbell Letters*, 69. A more formal version of the inner circle was attempted when a regency-style council for the minority of his son was created by the 6th earl in his will. The internal rivalries and jealousies of this body made it unworkable and led to the murder of Cawdor in 1592 which nearly split Clan Campbell apart, *Letters to Argyll Family*, 64–5; E.J. Cowan, ' "Fishers in drumlie waters": Clanship and Campbell Expansion in the Time of Gilleasbuig Grumach', *TGSI*, 4 (1984–6), 269–312.

[89] There were many references in the 5th earl's correspondence to the advice and counsel of his special friends, for example 24 January 1565, 16 September 1571, 3 November 1572, GD112/39/6/25; 13/9; 14/8.

[90] Much of the surviving correspondence in the Breadalbane collection between Argyll and Glenorchy was the product of such consultations and the circulation of information.

[91] 25 July 1567: Keith, *History*, II. 698.

[92] For example the MacDonald–MacLean feud, 15 September 1570, AT, VI. 150.

[93] For example the stents of 9 February 1559 and 12 April 1569, AT, V. 104; VI. 136. For a fuller discussion of taxation, see below, p. 72.

Mid-Argyll, with Knapdale sometimes being treated as a separate unit. With these districts corresponding to the crown's legal and administrative units, there ceased to be a clear distinction between Campbell and royal organisation. In terms of both power and administration, the Campbells absorbed royal institutions into their clan structure, weaving a seamless robe which the Stewart monarchs did not divide. The districts collected the taxes agreed by the earl's council with a similar system being used to raise troops.[94]

The 5th earl and his predecessors devolved authority and responsibility to their clan hierarchy. They assumed that strengthening the subordinate chiefs would increase the clan's power, just as a powerful national aristocracy aided royal rule. The earls encouraged the main branches to create noble houses in their own right, treating them with consideration and respect. In a weighty matter, such as the MacGregor feud, the 5th earl gave Colin Campbell of Glenorchy a free choice between alternative courses of action agreed by Argyll's council.[95] The courtesies were equally observed in routine business. The 5th earl left certain letters unsealed for their contents to be checked and approved by a Campbell chief, before being acted upon.[96] This willingness to acknowledge their independence helped dissuade cadet branches from breaking away and starting a separate clan, as happened in other Highland kindreds.[97]

By actively creating new chiefs, Argyll went much further than recognising cadet branches. Such an action was tantamount to assuming the power of ennoblement normally vested exclusively in a ruling sovereign. The 5th earl established and gave recognition to a new chief by formally transferring the allegiance and dues previously paid to him. In 1564, he made Iver MacIver of Lergachonzie chief of the Campbells of Asknish or the surname of MacIver.[98] On the basis of geographical proximity, similar transfers were made devolving responsibility from the earls to Campbell cadets. On condition that their new masters protected them, Argyll handed over the allegiance and services of subordinate kindred-groups. Being closer to his sphere of influence in the Central Highlands, two Balquhidder clans, the MacLarens and the MacIntyres, were granted by Argyll to Glenorchy.[99]

---

[94] In 1565 Lorn, Mid-Argyll and Cowal each provided 120 men to fight on a monthly rotation in the MacGregor feud, 5 April 1565, *Campbell Letters*, 39 and see *Campbell Letters*, 58–9.

[95] 24 and 25 January 1565 *Campbell Letters*, 27.

[96] 3 April 1565, GD112/39/2/15; 16 December 1570, GD112/39/11/21 enclosing GD112/2/117/1/45.

[97] Most obviously the splintering of Clan Donald, but also the splits within the MacLeods and the MacLeans.

[98] Argyll resigned to Iver the rights, the 'kindness' and the calps of the Campbells of Asknish, 10 August 1564, AT, VI. 50, the document survived in a 1792 copy, Argyll MSS Bundle 715.

[99] GD112/1/11/; 1/166; *Black Book of Taymouth*, 201–2, 211; AT, V. 129; VI. 86. The Glenorchy Campbells had been associated with Clan Tyre since the end of the fifteenth

The delegation of authority within Clan Campbell could leave overlapping boundaries bringing new problems, as happened with the MacGregor transfer. The superiority over the traditional MacGregor lands of Glenstrae was bought by Colin Campbell of Glenorchy in 1554.[100] It was intended that the MacGregors would continue to serve both the earl and the Glenorchy Campbells.[101] However, this arrangement ran into difficulties when the MacGregors, with Glenorchy's tacit approval, attacked the 5th earl's dependants, the MacTarlichs.[102] This provided the flashpoint for the start of the bitter feud between the Campbells and the MacGregors that had such disastrous consequences for Clan Gregor in the seventeenth century. During the feud, the question of whether the MacGregors were serving Glenorchy or the 5th earl remained a sensitive issue.[103]

However good its basic organisation, the clan was not immune from internal tensions and rivalries. One of Argyll's main tasks was to arbitrate in inter-Campbell disputes, preventing rivalries getting out of hand and punishing severely any feuding. At the end of 1567, the 5th earl acted decisively when there was trouble between two kindreds at the top end of Loch Awe. Dougal Campbell and his father Archibald Campbell of Inverawe were tried by a panel of Campbell lairds headed by the 5th earl for the crime of drowning members of Clan Arthur.[104] In this instance, as in the less deadly wrangle over lands in Lorn between two Campbells, the methods of private justice and arbitration were employed to handle the matter internally.[105] With the exception of disputes originating in the Lowlands and those among the

century. See the renewal of an old bond of manrent, 4 June 1556 GD112/24/1/2 fo. 15v; GD112/1/99; *Black Book of Taymouth*, 200–1. For a discussion of bonds of manrent, see below p. 82.

[100] Although there is no formal record, the grant of the MacGregor's bond of manrent was probably transferred at the same time as the land, 26 April 1554, GD112/2/81/5–6; GD112/75/19–20; *RMS*, IV. 944. The MacGregor chief had made a bond with the 4th earl 6 October 1544: AT, IV. 153; Wormald, *Lords and Men*, 183.

[101] For a full discussion of the close association of the MacGregors and the Campbells of Glenorchy and their joint expansion into Breadalbane, see MacGregor, 'MacGregors', ch. 3.

[102] Argyll to Glenorchy, 29 June 1562, *Campbell Letters*, 7.

[103] When discussing proposals for a settlement in 1565, the 5th earl told Glenorchy that, if the old arrangement of the MacGregors serving two masters was no longer acceptable, then they should only be Argyll's men, 5 July 1565, *Campbell Letters*, 41. The progress of the feud can be followed in the *Campbell Letters* and MacGregor, 'MacGregors', ch. 6.

[104] The MacArthurs were also of Campbell descent (despite the recent recognition of them as a separate clan); see *Highland Papers*, IV. 53–5. As well as providing the normal compensation to the dead men's kin, the Inverawe Campbells were stripped of the office which gave them jurisdiction over the MacArthurs. That office, of the 5th earl's bailie of both sides of Loch Awe, was subsequently granted to John MacArthur of Terivadich. Obligation by Campbells of Inverawe, 2 December 1567; letter of slains, 1569; grant of bailiary, 18 January 1570, AT, VI. 108, 132, 142.

[105] Dispute between John Campbell, commendator of Ardchattan and Alexander Campbell of Flienes, 21 June 1564, GD112/2/110/1.

Ayrshire Campbells, Clan Campbell rarely had recourse to the central courts to settle its quarrels.[106]

Clan unity and solidarity had a political dimension. The Campbells' practice was to decide in their council upon a policy and for the clan to follow it. During the turbulent reign of Mary, Queen of Scots, many Scottish kindreds found their members in opposing political camps. Complete Campbell solidarity could not be preserved, but the basic cement of kinship remained even at the battle of Langside, when Ayrshire Campbells were found on both sides. Robert Campbell of Kinzeancleuch, having fought bravely for Regent Moray, was granted the escheat of Matthew Campbell of Loudoun, who had been captured in the defeat of the Queen's Party. Without hesitation or seeking financial compensation, Kinzeancleuch returned all the forfeited goods to Loudoun, his friend and the head of his house.[107]

The power of a united Clan Campbell was greater than the sum of its constituent parts and, acting as a unit, it could exert great influence upon Scottish politics and life. It gave the earl of Argyll a huge reservoir of power: provided Clan Campbell remained strong and united, MacCailein Mòr was virtually impregnable.

LAND AND WEALTH

Campbell power rested upon its possession, exploitation and control of land. Land was the basic resource and creator of wealth in early modern Scotland, and owning land was a prerequisite for political power and social status. For early modern lineages it was more than an economic resource, being regarded as the foundation of all noble power. If it lost its land, a clan was reduced to a collection of 'broken men', the final fate of the MacGregors or 'the children of the mist', as they became known. From early in their rise to dominance, the Campbells had enthusiastically adopted the feudal forms of land tenure and the habit of documentation. However, a distinction should be made between tenurial arrangements and settlement patterns.[108] In the

---

[106] *Clan Campbell*, 6 and 8 and see p. 57 above. An exception was the case brought by Dougal Campbell, son of Inverawe, concerning the lands and office of serjeandry of Lismore, 14 May 1562: *Clan Campbell*, 8, 38.

[107] John Davidson, 'A Memorial of the Life of Two Worthye Christians, Robert Campbel, of the Kinyeancleugh, and his Wife Elizabeth Campbel' in C. Rogers, ed., *Three Scottish Reformers* (Grampian Club, 9, London, 1876), 100–31 at pp. 115–16; Dawson, 'Clan, Kin and Kirk', 225.

[108] The recent perceptive study of Balquhidder has demonstrated that it was possible to adhere to strict feudal forms and yet at the level of the township maintain the ancient inheritance and settlement patterns, J.H. Stewart, 'Highland Settlement Evolution in West Perthshire' (University of Newcastle-upon-Tyne PhD thesis, 1986), chs. 5 and 6.

Campbells' Highland properties they employed Lowland legal procedures whilst retaining the Gaelic social system, thereby combining the advantages of the clan system with those of feudal tenure. Tenants owed a variety of services to their lords, which were a mixture of feudal obligation, such as the military service stipulated in the formal charter, and Gaelic dues, such as a night's hospitality or 'cudeigh'.[109]

Its lands provided each noble house with a territorial designation and was the bedrock of its identity. In a real sense the 5th earl was Argyll, and to lose part of the territorial core he had inherited from his predecessors was to suffer dishonour. What mattered to the 5th earl was the feudal superiority rather than the economic exploitation of the land. He preserved his feudal rights and privileges with great care because they gave the control over territory and people that was the key to the successful expansion of Clan Campbell.[110] The row over Glen Orchy between the 5th earl and Colin Campbell of Glenorchy underlined the inseparable feudal connexion between land and jurisdiction.[111]

As feudal overlords, the Stewart monarchs permitted the earls of Argyll greater privileges than they deemed prudent for other tenants-in-chief.[112] The 5th earl's estates were unusual in their extent and concentration. The crown had permitted and encouraged the Campbells to accumulate large quantities of territory in the Highlands, where royal control was weakest.[113] Of greater importance than their spread was the legal jurisdiction granted in the consolidated regalities of Lorn, Loch Awe, Over-Cowal and Cowal.[114] Argyll's lands stretched from Loch Linnhe in the north, to the Clyde estuary

[109] For the 5th earl claiming his cudeigh or 'cuid-oidhche', literally 'a night's meat', John Stewart of Appin to Glenorchy, 24 September 1570, *Campbell Letters*, 164.

[110] For example in 1564 he granted a charter of ward and relief to the MacNaughtons of Dunderarve whilst specifically reserving the right of the marriage of John, the son and heir, 9 and 26 May 1564, AT, VI. 34, 44.

[111] The disputed property had given its name to Colin's house but remained in the hands of the earls of Argyll. There was never any doubt that the Campbells of Glenorchy would continue to hold the land from the 5th earl and his successors and that they in turn would lease it out to their tenants. What Colin sought, and the 5th earl so vehemently rejected, was to purchase the feudal superiority so that he could hold Glen Orchy directly from the crown, see above, p. 44.

[112] For example the earls of Argyll were permitted throughout the sixteenth century to pass over their lands, offices and jurisdictions to their heirs whilst retaining a life-interest, thereby eliminating the crown's levers of control through its rights of ward, marriage and non-entry at the death of a tenant-in-chief: see above, p. 18.

[113] For similar reasons, the earl of Atholl remained master of the consolidated block of territory in the Central Highlands comprising the ancient thanedom of Atholl.

[114] For the lands and jurisdictions which the 5th earl inherited 22 October 1542: *RMS*, III. 2811–16; J. Cameron, *James V* (East Linton, 1998), 248; and for those he passed to his successor, 10 February 1572, *RMS*, IV. 2013–18. See above pp. 56–9 for a discussion of the use of legal power.

and northern Kintyre in the south, and from the western seaboard to the Lennox and Menteith in the east. His north-eastern boundaries merged into the territory controlled by the Campbells of Glenorchy and thence into the Campbell west–east corridor across Scotland. The 5th earl had substantial holdings within the Lowlands, especially around Castle Campbell and in the former dioceses of Brechin and Dunkeld.

Control over land guaranteed the resources essential for the long-term security of one's house and facilitated expansion through the settlement of cadet branches. The bestowal of land was one of the main components of good lordship and the key to the continued loyalty of clansmen and other dependents. The 5th earl had the advantage that, when he had no land available to bestow, he could ask his clan chiefs to provide the lack.[115] Once settled, dependants had to be protected and maintained in the possession of their property.[116] This duty involved Argyll in many disputes when, as he phrased it, he defended the 'auld and iust possessioun of our frendis and kinsmen for quhome we man do'.[117]

The land produced men, especially in the Highlands, where loyal followers and clansmen would fight for their chief. This was achieved directly by granting out land and, indirectly, by using its produce to feed the men. Most of the 5th earl's rents were received in kind and gathered at specific storage points, which fitted the peripatetic lifestyle of the earl and his household, enabling them to consume the stores as they travelled through Argyll. The produce came in a variety of forms, including fish.[118] Most rents were paid in grain or meal from oats, malt, bere barley, rye and some wheat. The Highland pastoral economy produced large quantities of cattle and cheese rents. A snapshot of the half-yearly rents for some of the 5th earl's holdings and their estimated value is found among the debts owed at his death. The total rent for the first six months of 1573 was just under £1,400 Scots, around a tenth of which was in cash and with the grain bringing in slightly more than the rents in cattle and cheese.[119] These figures were conservatively

---

[115] Argyll to Colin Campbell of Glenorchy, 26 February 1566, GD112/39/6/3.

[116] For example the support the 5th earl offered to Ranald MacDonald of Keppoch, 31 May 1563, GD112/39/2/16.

[117] 29 June 1562, *Campbell Letters*, 7.

[118] For example the herring of Loch Fyne or the salmon to be provided for the earl's table, AT, IV. 196; V. 154.

[119] The total was £1,393 4s with £136 in money, £657 4s in meal and £600 in cattle and cheese. The will is printed in *Letters to Argyll Family*, 59–60 but the transcription errors with the roman numerals have been corrected from the original, CC8/8/4 fos. 160v–161r. The values ascribed to the different meal rents were less than the sale price on the open market, e.g. oatmeal was valued at 24s and was probably selling at £3–4, see *Atlas of Scottish History*, 326. All figures are in £ Scots which was worth approximately a quarter of £ sterling during this period.

costed and might have been kept artificially low. The lands of Argyll, Lorn and Cowal and the Lowland properties of Menstrie, Dollar and Muckart near Castle Campbell generated c. £3,000 Scots *per annum*. As these figures covering one part of his estates suggest, Argyll drew considerable wealth from his lands, which formed one element within his overall income. However, his estates did not make him the richest noble or ecclesiastic in the kingdom.[120]

Receiving little rent in cash, the 5th earl was restricted in how he could exploit his income. The lack of market centres within the Highlands and the problems of transportation meant selling produce was not a straightforward alternative.[121] Although the rents in kind could feed Argyll's troops in the Highlands, they could not cover the expenses of operating far from the home base. The earl's heavy and continuous military involvement, especially in the Lowlands, placed a strain upon his finances. His successor the 6th earl complained he had been left in serious debt with many lands alienated or held as security for loans.[122] Fifty years later, the author of the Family Pedigree detailed the long-term consequences of the 5th earl's enterprises, especially the support for Protestantism. He explained that Argyll had adopted two devices to raise money. The first was to sell the produce, 'putting the marts to merks, the boll of meal to ten shilling, the stone of cheese to two shilling'.[123] More seriously, the 5th earl had been forced to feu or lease his lands, which 'did mightily impoverish that great earldome that to this day [c. 1634] there

---

[120] The best figures available for comparison for the 1560s and 1570s come from Scottish ecclesiastical estates. The pre-Reformation church was by far the wealthiest landowner in Scotland, and the abbey at Arbroath was the richest foundation with a gross annual income in cash and kind of £13,000 with the Priory of St Andrews the next on the list with a rental of £10,600. Episcopal revenues did not reach these heights, though the primate, the archbishop of St Andrews, received about £6,000 a year: *The Books of Assumption of the Thirds of Benefices: Scottish Ecclesiastical Rentals at the Reformation* ed. J. Kirk (Records of Social and Economic History, New ser. 21, Oxford, 1995), xlvii, lvi. Noble incomes were probably much smaller, for between 1548 and 1553 the barony of Lochleven took in £1,740: M.H.B. Sanderson, *Scottish Rural Society in the Sixteenth Century* (Edinburgh, 1982), 29. For a comprehensive discussion of noble wealth, see K.M. Brown, *Noble Society in Scotland: Wealth, Family and Culture from Reformation to Revolution* (Edinburgh, 2000), Part I.

[121] As Professor G. Donaldson commented about the similar plight of the earl of Huntly, what could he 'do with his 1389 capons and 5284 eggs?': *Scotland: James V–James VII* (Edinburgh, 1978; reprint of 1965 edn), 7–8. For a general discussion of the transport and trade within the Western Highlands, see Dawson, 'Road to the Isles'.

[122] AT, VI. 224. One such debt which the 6th earl had to repay was the 4,000 merks which had been borrowed on 21 April 1570 from Lord Ogilvie on the security of the Farnwell lands in the diocese of Brechin, 11 November 1577, GD16/42/18; *Clan Campbell*, 6, 20; 8, 71.

[123] *Records of Argyll*, 6. If these really were the prices obtained they were well below market rates for the 1560s to 1570s and an indication that cash was needed quickly.

is nothing gotten from the vassals, tennents, but their small feu-duties'. As a result, the earl's rental had fallen and the clan had been forced to support their chief by special contributions.[124]

Taxation of the clan had been established by the time the 5th earl succeeded, and almost immediately the 1559 council of his kinsmen and friends agreed the onerous levy of 20s per markland to pay for the earl's trip to France with the crown matrimonial.[125] The 1569 tax was the clan's response to the parlous state of Argyll's finances caused by the civil wars with its explicitly stated aim to redeem the earl's alienated lands. The 5th earl had raised money for troops by offering lands as security for loans, but the full extent of his wadsetting has been difficult to assess.[126] He was, undoubtedly, extremely short of ready cash.[127] However, like most nobles, Argyll was more concerned to fulfil his noble duties than balance his books.

Another source of income was the 5th earl's jurisdictions. As feudal superior, Argyll collected the ward, relief and non-entry dues from his tenants when they succeeded to their lands.[128] For the major lordships, such as Glen Orchy, these could be substantial, amounting to 1,400 merks in 1539.[129] The processing of charters attracted fees, though these were sometimes waived as a favour to the recipient.[130] The holding of courts brought the profits of justice to which were added those flowing from the position of justice-general of Scotland. A more erratic source of wealth were gifts from the crown, including lands, marriages, wardships or escheats. After the Reformation, the 5th earl, in common with the rest of the Scottish nobility, was granted additional ecclesiastical properties and income. Outside of the Highlands, Argyll gained lands from the dioceses of Brechin and Dunkeld and the abbeys of Coupar

---

[124] Such complaints were frequently heard in the seventeenth century, see Brown, *Noble Society* ch. 4.

[125] The tax was probably not fully collected, as Argyll did not travel to France, AT, V. 104 and see below, p. 88. In 1565 Campbell of Ardkinglas mentioned to Glenorchy another stent to help with the 5th earl's debts: 25 January 1565, *Campbell Letters*, 27. Other nobles raised money from their kinsmen and dependents in the same way, see the 1565 subscription list for Alexander Ross of Balnagowan printed in *The Calendar of Fearn* ed. R. Adam (SHS, 5th ser. 4, Edinburgh, 1991), 243–4.

[126] For example he borrowed 1,100 merks in 1567 from Archibald Lyon, burgess of Glasgow on the lands of Rossmore in Rosneath, AT, VI. 87; and £606 13s 4d from the Edinburgh merchant Gilbert MacMurrych in 1570 on the lands of Panholls in Muckart, which was repaid two years later, AT, VI. 143, 193C.

[127] Poverty was one reason given for not making him Scottish regent in 1571. See below, p. 189.

[128] The earls kept a thorough record of their feudal casualties, though only one such book survives for c. 1527, GD103/2/49. I am grateful to Dr Stephen Boardman for bringing it to my attention and look forward to its publication.

[129] Paid by John Campbell of Glenorchy, GD112/2/111/2.

[130] For example the fee waived for the charters concerning the marriage of Glenorchy's daughter, 3 June 1570, GD112/39/7/7.

Angus and Culross.[131] More immediate rewards were obtained from the gift of an escheat, when someone was forfeited. It could either be exploited directly or sold, as the 5th earl did with the goods forfeited by Robert Crichton, former bishop of Dunkeld.[132]

His prolonged absences from court during the civil wars cut the flow of money from royal patronage and Argyll's central offices. Unlike some nobles, he was not heavily dependent upon such income.[133] Though the 5th earl had enough resources to function and retain the loyalty of his followers, he was forced to borrow when a steady supply of royal largesse dried up. By itself the deprivation did not dictate his policies, though it did create sufficient pressure in 1569 for his clan to demand a settlement with Regent Moray. The crown's failure to seize his Highland territories when he was in rebellion left the bulk of Argyll's income intact.[134] That security gave him a greater measure of economic independence than his relatively modest and cash-poor resources merited.

ARGYLL'S COURT

Argyll's power within the Highlands did not depend solely upon the material resources he could command. It was upheld by less tangible, but still powerful, means. To maintain a style fitting his pre-eminent status, the 5th earl kept a large household which operated as a court. Its prime functions were to support the Gaelic learned orders, who sustained the cultural life of the Gàidhealtachd, and provide lavish hospitality and access to their chief for his clansmen and dependants.

The 5th earl patronised both the different Gaelic learned orders and Lowland artists and craftsmen. As well as providing the professional and skilled services which he needed, the Gaelic *literati* gave cultural adornment and distinction to his court. The dominant literary family were the MacEwans, whose members were poets, bards and *sennachies* (or historians) for Argyll and probably ran a bardic school for the region.[135] Argyll's court

[131] For example *Books of Assumption*, 40, 292, 303, 355, 384–6, 389, 410.
[132] Gift of escheat to Argyll, 9 September 1571, *RSS* ,VI. 1276; debt of £240 owed at 5th earl's death by Sir James Hamilton for its purchase, *Letters to Argyll Family*, 60.
[133] Argyll's experience provided a contrast to the fate of the duke of Châtelherault and the Hamiltons, where the perquisites of office and especially their loss after 1567 played an important part in their fortunes. E. Finnie, 'The House of Hamilton: Patronage, Politics and the Church in the Reformation Period', *The Innes Review*, 36 (1985), 3–28 at pp. 6, 8, 21.
[134] During 1565–6 only Argyll's Lowland estates were seized, in sharp contrast to the fate of his fellow lords, see below p. 126.
[135] A. Matheson, 'The MacEwans' in Carswell, *Foirm*, 183–6; J.W. Bannerman, 'Literacy in the Highlands' in I. Cowan and D. Shaw, eds., *The Renaissance and Reformation in Scotland* (Edinburgh, 1982), 214–35 at pp. 227, 229; 29 January 1567, AT, VI. 94.

was part of the bardic 'circuit', being visited by Irish and Scottish poets of the *ollamh* or highest bardic grade.[136] They ensured that the best classical Gaelic poetry was available for the entertainment and edification of the earl and his household. The fifth earl's patronage of Scots literature and his Protestant commitment brought a fulsome dedication from the Lowland writer Robert Norvell, whose *The Meroure of an Christiane* was published in Edinburgh in 1561.[137] Musicians of all sorts were important members of his Highland court. The traditional dominance of the harp was giving way to the bagpipes, especially in a martial setting.[138] A branch of the great MacCrimmon piping family based in Balquhidder was associated with the Campbells of Glenorchy and possibly served the earl as well.[139] Medical skills were provided by the O'Conchobhair and MacLachlan families, who acted as Argyll's physicians and as general men of business within the Highlands.[140] Other hereditary families, such as the MacGille Chonaills, supplied the 5th earl's court with the artistic skills of wood and stone carving and metalwork.[141] Craftsmen from the Lowlands were imported to provide the latest European styles, especially for the decoration of the new castle at Carnasserie.[142]

Members of the learned orders attached to Argyll's court were trilingual, moving easily between Gaelic, Scots and Latin in their daily work and bridging the two cultures of Scotland by translating from Scots or Latin into Gaelic. Such an ability was essential if the key Protestant texts of the vernacular Bible and the liturgy were to reach the Gàidhealtachd. They could equally well use their skills in a reverse direction by providing for monoglot Gaelic speakers the written and legal documents required in Scots or Latin. Although the *literati* possessed the most polished and wide-ranging skills, the whole of Argyll's court reflected this bilingual approach. From the earl himself down through his household there was an assumption that all could operate in Scots as well as Gaelic. The court, like its ruler, belonged to both cultural worlds.

---

[136] W.J. Watson, 'Classic Gaelic Poetry of Panegyric in Scotland', *TGSI*, 29 (1914–9), 196–234; Bannerman, 'Literacy in the Highlands', 234.

[137] Dawson 'The Protestant Earl', 350–1.

[138] Argyll's troops were accompanied by the pipes at the battle of Pinkie (1547) and there was a harper in the earl's train at the battle of Glenlivet (1594).

[139] Bonds 17 April 1561, 29 November 1574, *Black Book of Taymouth*, 204; GD112/24/1/2 fo. 26r; Wormald, *Lords and Men*, 214, 217 (Breadalbane Nos. 36, 49).

[140] J.W. Bannerman, *The Beatons: A Medical Kindred in the Classical Gaelic Tradition* (Edinburgh, 1986), 144–9; J.W. Bannerman, 'The MacLachlans of Kilbride and their Manuscripts', *Scottish Studies*, 21 (1977), 1–34.

[141] For the MacGillechonaills who were shipbuilders and clerics, see n. 28 above. For the artistic tradition, see K. Steer and J. Bannerman, *Late Medieval Monumental Sculpture in the West Highlands* (RCAHMS, Edinburgh, 1977).

[142] See below pp. 77–9.

The Gaelic *literati* were the main image-makers for their society. At a simple level, their presence and the support given to their cultural attainments was a witness to Argyll's generosity and patronage of Highland culture, attributes expected of a Gaelic chief. In a more direct way, the poets and *sennachies* projected a specific image of their chief through their panegyric poetry and pedigrees. In the predominantly non-literate culture of the Gàidhealtachd, which set such store by the oral tradition, the vivid descriptions of the chiefs in the eulogies and satires shaped popular perceptions. Over time these word pictures became the fixed portraits of the chief and his clan. Those images were grafted onto the broader picture of the kin-group presented by its pedigree. The claiming of ancestors was of central importance within Gaelic society. A kin-group located itself through its pedigree, whilst a patronymic provided the main component of Gaelic personal identity. Pedigrees became a vital conceptual tool with which a clan could alter its standing. As a result, a clan's famous ancestors sometimes owed more to the social and political realities of the day than to accurate genealogy. The propaganda value of Gaelic poetry and pedigrees was incalculable: through them the reputation of a chief and his clan could be made, or marred.[143]

The Campbells were well aware of the importance of the images created by classical Gaelic poetry. A number of poems addressed to the earls written by the MacEwans or visiting poets survive, but only a fragment remains of a Campbell *duanaire*, or collection of poems.[144] The precise dating of these poems is difficult, and none can confidently be placed within the 5th earl's rule, though three were addressed to his father and probably composed during the 1550s.[145] The image projected in the poems remained constant and can be recognised in poems addressed to other earls of Argyll.[146] In addition

---

[143] W.D.H. Sellar, 'Highland Family Origins – Pedigree Making and Pedigree Faking' in L. Maclean, ed., *The Middle Ages in the Highlands* (Inverness Field Club, Inverness, 1981), 103–16; Dawson, 'The Emergence of the Highlands'. The hostile images of Clan Campbell created by the MacDonald poets of the seventeenth century have been sufficiently successful to survive to the present.

[144] Part of NLS Adv. 72.2.2. J. MacKechnie, ed., *Catalogue of Gaelic Manuscripts* (Boston, MA, 1973), I. 209–11, Nos. 2, 10, 13; B. O'Cuiv, *The Irish Bardic Duanaire or Poem-Book* (Dublin, 1973), 28.

[145] These three poems are 'Maith an chairt', printed in Watson, 'Classic Gaelic Poetry', 217–22; 'An Duanag Ullamh' printed in *Bàrdachd Ghàidhlig*, 259–62 ; and 'Dual ollamh do triall le toisg', NLS Adv. 72.2.2; MacKechnie, ed., *Catalogue of Gaelic Manuscripts*, 210, No. 10.

[146] For example the poem in the Book of the Dean of Lismore addressed to the 2nd earl before Flodden (1513) 'Ar Sliocht Gaodhal' printed in *Bàrdachd Albannach: Scottish Verse from the Book of the Dean of Lismore* ed. J.W. Watson (Scottish Gaelic Texts Society, 1, Edinburgh, 1937), 158–65; or the seventeenth-century poem, 'Triath na nGaoidheal' printed in *Scottish Gaelic Studies*, 3 (1931), 143–51. The Campbell poems are discussed in Gillies, 'Campbell History'; J. MacInnes, 'The Panegyric Code in Gaelic Poetry and its Historical Background', *TGSI*, 50 (1976–8), 435–98; D. Thomson, *An Introduction to Gaelic Poetry* (Edinburgh, 1990 reprint of 1974 edn), ch. 1.

to the normal lavish praise for a chief, the Campbell poems have several distinctive features. They declare that the earls of Argyll held the lordship and headship of the Gael, an unequivocal claim that the Campbells had replaced the MacDonalds as Lords of the Isles. They display an awareness, unusual within Gaelic poetry, of the wider Scottish and British dimension. Argyll was portrayed as ruling 'Galls', foreigners, as well as Gaels, and his power was seen to stretch throughout 'Alba' or Scotland. The same themes were replicated in the dedicatory epistle to the 5th earl of John Carswell's *Foirm*. Although mostly written in prose, it drew heavily upon the Gaelic poetical conventions and language.[147]

The pedigrees revealed a sharper British dimension. The Campbells claimed an almost bewildering variety of ancestors. In a rare display of reticence, the Campbells did not seek entrance into the most prestigious of the Irish Gaelic lineages, the Milesian genealogies. They did claim a place within professional Irish genealogies through their descent from Fergus Leithderg, the son of Nemed. Later, at a popular level, the old and probably authentic name of the Campbells as Clan Duibne or O'Duibne led to the adoption of the Feinian hero Diarmaid O'Duibne as an ancestor. Diarmaid's killing of the magical boar of Galban was connected to the boar's head, which had become part of the Campbell armorial crest.[148] These were respectable, but not exceptional, pedigrees for a leading Highland clan. The spectacular addition to the Gaelic pedigrees was the inclusion as an ancestor of King Arthur with its assertion of British descent.[149] The Campbell claim to descend from the heroic king himself and his son Myrddin was one that emphasised the British nature of their interests and ambitions. The Campbells also created a Norman French genealogy for themselves, which made them more acceptable to the Lowland aristocracy. This was based upon the acquisition of the 'p' in the middle of their name, which diverted attention from the original unflattering association with the Gaelic 'cam beul' or 'twisted mouth'.[150] Campbell could be equated with De Campo Bello or De Beauchamp allowing a Norman and French ancestry to be grafted on. The great variety and geographical spread of the Campbell pedigrees demonstrated that their interests and political

---

[147] For a full discussion of the Gaelic literary context of the epistle, see D. Meek, 'The Reformation and Gaelic Culture' in J. Kirk, ed., *The Church in the Highlands* (Edinburgh, 1998), 37–62 at pp. 43–55.

[148] First seen on the tomb of Sir Duncan Campbell of Inverawe (d. 1453) at Kilmun, *Argyll Inventory*, 7, 179. I am grateful to Dr Boardman for this observation.

[149] Sellar, 'Earliest Campbells'; W. Gillies, 'The Invention of Tradition, Highland-Style' in A. MacDonald, M. Lynch and I. Cowan, eds., *The Renaissance in Scotland* (Leiden, 1994), 144–56; W. Gillies, 'The "British" Genealogy of the Campbells', *Celtica*, 23 (1999), 82–95.

[150] The 'p' slipped into use during the fifteenth century.

ambitions spread far beyond the Gàidhealtachd.[151] Like their ancestors, the Campbells proclaimed that they were at home in all worlds.

As well as feeding hearts and minds with Gaelic culture, Argyll's court offered more mundane fare. One travelling bard rated Argyll's generous provision as second only to the hospitality of MacDonald of Glengarry among Scotland's noble households.[152] Within Gaelic society, a chief was expected to display his lordship through high feasting. The provision of food and drink on a massive scale for his followers was an essential stage within the Highland pastoral system, offering the most efficient method for a chief to return food resources to his clansmen and reinforce their loyalty.[153] Because Argyll and his household were peripatetic, the earl's entertainment was spread throughout the region, consuming his produce rents in the process. Traditional Gaelic hospitality dues, like cudeigh, fitted well into this system.

The earl's court moved around Argyll but his main base within the region was Inveraray castle on Loch Fyne, more an administrative centre than a permanent residence.[154] The previous Campbell headquarters at Innischonnell had been turned into a prison and was not often used by the earl as a residence. Carrick castle on Loch Goil regularly entertained the earl because it was the main staging post on the most frequently travelled route to the Lowlands and housed many of his charter chests. Dunoon castle on the Firth of Clyde, and close to the family mausoleum at Kilmun, was within easy reach of the Lowlands and often used. The 5th earl was fond of his hunting lodge at Garvie in Glendaruel in Cowal and stayed there whenever he could. He spent less time in northern Argyll, though he did use Dunstaffnage castle.

The only residence built for the 5th earl was Carnasserie castle.[155] It was a charming Renaissance-style tower-house set in the middle of Argyll which illustrated the peace and security the earl enjoyed within his heartland. The castle was constructed with spacious rooms and large windows, demonstrating that domestic comfort and not fortification was its main requirement.

---

[151] Sellar, 'Earliest Campbells', 121–2; S. Boardman, 'The Medieval Origin Legends of Clan Campbell' *Journal of the Clan Campbell Society (UK)*, 27 (2000), 5–7; Gillies, 'Campbell History', 276–85.

[152] Gillies, 'Campbell History', 263.

[153] R.A. Dodgshon, 'West Highland Chiefdoms: A Study of Redistributive Exchange' in R. Mitchison and P. Roebuck, eds., *Scotland and Ireland* (Edinburgh, 1988), 27–37; K. Simms, 'Guesting and Feasting in Gaelic Ireland', *Journal of the Royal Society of Antiquaries of Ireland*, 108 (1978), 67–100.

[154] The castle was pulled down in the mid-eighteenth century to make way for the present Inveraray castle: I. Lindsay and M. Cosh, *Inveraray and the Dukes of Argyll* (Edinburgh, 1977), 21–8.

[155] In an account written about 1630 it was described as 'builded be him [John Carswell] to the Earle of Argyll': *Macfarlane's Geographical Collections*, eds., A. Mitchell and J. Clark (3 vols., SHS, 1st ser. 51, 52 and 55, Edinburgh, 1906–8), II. 149.

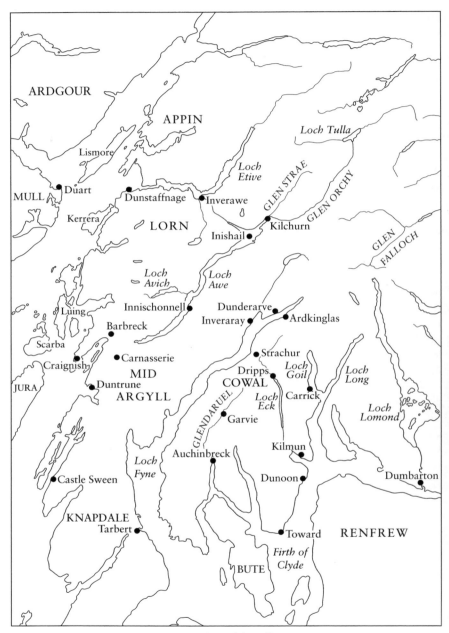

5. Map of Argyll

The residential accommodation was considerably more elegant and comfortable than the region's other castles. As the first such residence to be built within the West Highlands, Lowland masons, probably from Stirling, were imported to carve the fine exterior and interior decorations.[156] With the 5th earl permanently on the move, John Carswell, superintendent of Argyll, was given the castle as his main base. When he was in the Lowlands, the 5th earl spent much of his time at the spacious and magnificently furnished Castle Campbell in Clackmananshire.[157] Argyll also owned town houses in Edinburgh, Perth, Stirling and possibly Glasgow.[158] In addition, the residences of Argyll's clansmen and dependents were available whenever needed.[159] His journeys through his region were frequently by or across water, using galleys and ferries, upon which the earl had first call.[160]

The personnel of Argyll's household reflected his ability to live and move between the Highlands and Lowlands with his servitors being drawn from both the Gaelic and the Scots-speaking cultures of Scotland.[161] The line between Argyll's inner council and his household was blurred. His close friends and advisers, such as Colin and James Campbell of Ardkinglas, Dougal Campbell of Auchinbreck or Duncan Campbell of Duntrune frequently accompanied him. Other lairds, such as Donald Campbell of Auchinwilling, and Highland dependents, such as John Stewart of Bute, remained in daily attendance.[162] For legal and financial business, normally transacted in the Lowlands, the 5th earl employed notaries and general 'men of business' such as John Hutton, a St Andrews graduate, or John Graham of Ballindoran.[163]

---

[156] *Argyll Inventory*, VII. 214–26.

[157] N. Campbell, 'The Castle Campbell Inventory (1595)', *SHR*, 10 (1913), 299–315.

[158] Edinburgh house on the north side of the High Street, *Calendar of Laing Charters, 847–1837* ed. J. Anderson (2 vols., Edinburgh, 1899), I. 122, No. 458; Perth house between Meal Vennel and St John's Church, AT, V. 21; Stirling house of unknown location, though not the recently restored 'Argyll's Lodging' which was a seventeenth-century purchase, *HMC*, 4, 484.

[159] It was a serious breach of honour and hospitality if a suitable welcome were not forthcoming, e.g. the 5th earl's furious letter to Katherine Ruthven when the Glenorchy castle of Kilchurn (top of Loch Awe) was barred against him, 30 May 1570, *Campbell Letters*, 94.

[160] For example the ferry at Kilmun 21 September 1554, AT, V. 37 and see previous charters AT, II, ii. 597; III. 123.

[161] With no accounts surviving, little is known about the domestic servants who surrounded the earl, though there are passing references to some, such as Thomas Baillie, his master stabler: 6 June 1575, *Clan Campbell*, 8, 64. The extent of the household can be gauged from the list of servants and their wages recorded in the 1588 will of Annas Keith, the wife of the 6th earl: *Letters to the Argyll Family*, 86–7.

[162] Stewart agreed to be the 5th earl's household man, 16 December 1571, AT, VI. 170.

[163] Hutton graduated in 1540/1, *Early Records of the University of St Andrews* ed. J. Anderson (SHS, 3rd ser. 9, Edinburgh, 1926), 141, 143, 242; 12 February 1573, Argyll MSS Bundle 46. John Graham was first given the lands of Panholls for his services 9 July 1553: AT, V. 26, he was not a very successful shepherd on those lands, 1 November 1572, AT, VI. 169, 188, but kept them until 1583, 25 July 1583, *Clan Campbell*, 8, 92.

Though he had no heirs, the boys fostered or raised by the 5th earl, such as his nephew Lachlan MacLean of Duart, or his pages, such as Neil Campbell, formed part of his household alongside the earl's illegitimate children.[164] They were educated in Gaelic and Scots, as the 5th earl had been himself.

There was a strong link between the Argyll's household and the Reformed Kirk. Previous earls had followed the noble practice of placing younger or illegitimate sons in the church, where Campbell clerics played a role in clan expansion and later helped to staff the new Kirk. They also served in a variety of household, administrative or even military capacities.[165] Many of the members of the learned orders in Argyll's household followed a similar path, holding ecclesiastical benefices and then becoming Protestant ministers. They had formal literary training within the Gaelic tradition as well as, for some, a university education in the Lowlands. They served as clerics, notaries, advisers and, taking advantage of the diplomatic immunity bestowed by their status, as high-level negotiators and confidential messengers.[166]

John Carswell's own clerical career exemplified the close association with Argyll's household. He acted as notary, chaplain and possibly tutor to the 4th earl and his sons in the 1550s and educated the first of the 5th earl's illegitimate sons. In 1559 he was given his own estates and household by the 5th earl as a prelude to becoming the leader of the Kirk in the Highlands, officially recognised when he became superintendent of Argyll two years later. Drawing upon those clerics already serving the 5th earl, Carswell led a group of ministers who provided the manpower for spreading the Protestant message throughout the Western Highlands. Despite his elevated ecclesiastical position, he remained the earl's client, being given Carnasserie castle as his operational base, thus retaining a physical link with Argyll's own household. Carswell's great work of translation was undertaken under the patronage of the 5th earl. In 1567 he produced the first book ever printed in Gaelic, a translation of the *Book of Common Order*. In its dedicatory epistle, Carswell acknowledged that, without Argyll's military protection, financial

---

[164] For Lachlan MacLean, see N. MacLean-Bristol, *Murder under Trust: The Crimes and Death of Sir Lachlan Mor Maclean of Duart, 1558–1598* (East Linton, 1999); Neil Campbell, 16 December 1570, *Campbell Letters*, 187. The household probably also included Alexander Campbell, made bishop of Brechin in 1566, but young enough to be sent to Geneva to study in 1569: *Books of Assumption*, 388. One of Argyll's pages was killed during the Wars of the Congregation: Knox, *History*, I. 257 and below, p. 99.

[165] The 5th earl's half-brother John, provost of Kilmun also took troops to Ireland in 1570, see below, p. 203. Another John, natural son of John Campbell of Cawdor, commendator prior of Ardchattan and later bishop of the Isles, helped to administer northern Argyll for the 5th earl.

[166] For a general discussion of the link between Campbell households and the Kirk, see Dawson, 'Clan, Kin and Kirk', 229–37.

support and the security provided by his court, Protestantism would not have flourished in the Gàidhealtachd.[167]

Argyll's court offered a physical focus for his clansmen and affinity. As well as the lavish hospitality, it provided the setting for his council and the arbitration of disputes, bringing greater unity among his dependants. Non-Campbell members of his affinity were bound to him through ties of marriage and lordship. Marital kin frequently, but not invariably, became political allies. In search of national connexions, the earls of Argyll had pursued the strategy of marrying into the Lowland aristocracy. The 5th earl's mother Helen was the duke of Châtelherault's sister and, as the only child of this marriage, Argyll remained close to the Hamiltons, forming strong political associations with them. His father's other marriages brought alliances with the Grahams, earls of Menteith, and the MacLeans of Duart.[168] The 5th earl's own marriages conformed to the Lowland pattern. Through his first wife, Lady Jane, Archibald became the brother-in-law of his great friend and political partner Lord James Stewart and part of the circle of Stewart kin centred upon Mary, Queen of Scots. His second wife, Lady Jean Cunningham, was the daughter of his old friend and staunch Protestant ally the 4th earl of Glencairn. The kindred resulting from the marriages of preceding generations increased Argyll's affinity. The emotional appeal of kin ties remained a significant ingredient in Scottish politics, and at various times the 5th earl utilised his distant kinship to the earls of Mar, Atholl and Cassilis.

The marriages of the earls' daughters and younger sons were used for the purpose of strengthening the Highland affinity. Clan Campbell expansion owed much to alliances made by Campbell women. Lady Agnes, the daughter of the 3rd earl, had a colourful marital career. Her first marriage to James Stewart of Bute ended in annulment, and by 1554 she was the wife of James MacDonald of Dunivaig and the Glens. This kin tie underpinned the close cooperation between the 5th earl and MacDonald. After MacDonald's death and as part of the 5th earl's strategy within northern Ireland, Lady Agnes married Turlough O'Neill, the great Ulster chief, in 1569.[169] When younger sons were not placed in the church, their marriages helped expand Campbell power within the Highlands. The most spectacular example was John, son of the 2nd earl, who married Muriel, the heiress of Cawdor, creating the

---

[167] Carswell, *Foirm*, 173–82; D. Meek, 'The Reformation and Gaelic Culture' in J. Kirk, ed., *The Church in the Highlands* (Edinburgh, 1998), 37–62; Dawson, 'The Protestant Earl', 351–8.
[168] See above, pp. 14–15.   [169] See below, pp. 163–4.

powerful cadet branch of the Campbells of Cawdor. The marriages of the 5th earl's illegitimate children follow the pattern of Highland alliances, though they happened after his death.[170]

Alliances and allegiances were also created through bonds of manrent.[171] The 5th earl was sufficiently powerful not to need to make bonds to establish or enlarge his affinity. The only bond of friendship, made between equals, that Argyll entered was with the earl of Atholl, being used to end the disputes arising between two magnates with adjoining spheres of influence. During his rule, the 5th earl made approximately twenty bonds of manrent, between a superior and an inferior, with eighteen different individuals or kin-groups.[172] Most relate to specific problems, such as the complex settlement of the MacLeod inheritance, and reflect stages in a pre-existing relationship rather than the inclusion of a new member of the affinity.

One guide to the breadth of Argyll's affinity can be found in the other bonds made by his dependents containing a clause excepting the allegiance owed to the earl. Members of Clan Campbell and close dependents, like John Stewart of Appin, would naturally adopt such an exclusion.[173] The inclusion of this clause by most West Highland chiefs, some of whom have no record of a bond with Argyll, indicated how many saw themselves as his dependants.[174] The list of the earls' Highland allies provided by the Gaelic poets in their praise poems corroborates this picture. They mention the northern and southern branches of MacDonalds; all of the clans of the Western Isles, including the MacLeans; the MacLeods; the MacNeills and the MacKinnons. They also named O'Donnell of Tyrconnell and O'Neill of Tyrone, the Gaelic chiefs of

[170] See above, pp. 29–30.
[171] The seminal work on bonds is Wormald, *Lords and Men*. The bonds of the earls of Argyll are discussed on pp. 108–13 and listed in Appendix A, 177–98.
[172] Wormald, *Lords and Men*, 184–8, 196–7; (Argyll Nos. 33–49, 87–92). Two other bonds not found in *Lords and Men* are those of Patrick Robertson of Tullgavane, 21 July 1562, GD112/1/119, and the Burgh of Irvine, July 1572, *Muniments of the royal burgh of Irvine*, I. 59–60. A bond with the MacDoulkers of Balquhidder, before October 1563, was mentioned in the letters between the Argyll and Glenorchy, but has not survived, 1 and 4 October 1563, *Campbell Letters*, 11 and 12.
[173] In the bond of friendship made in the 5th earl's presence, Glenorchy and Duntrune tactfully excepted their allegiance to their chief, 23/24 December 1564 GD112/1/156–7; AT, VI. 51; *Black Book of Taymouth*, 210; Wormald, *Lords and Men*, 388 (Friendship 56). Stewart's bond with Glenorchy, 4 December 1570 GD112/1/192, *Black Book of Taymouth*, 215, Wormald, *Lords and Men*, 216 (Br 46).
[174] For example two branches of Clan Donald, the MacDonalds of Glencoe and Clanranald excepting their allegiance to Argyll, 6 May 1563 GD112/1/131, *Black Book of Taymouth*, 208; Wormald, *Lords and Men*, 215 (Br 41); John MacDonald of Clanranald's bond with Hugh Fraser of Lovat, 6 July 1572, GD112/1/848; Wormald, *Lords and Men*, 277 (Fraser 2). Clanranald had made a bond with the Argyll, 23 November 1571, AT, VI. 166, Wormald, *Lords and Men*, 187 (Arg 45).

Ulster, as Argyll's supporters and allies.[175] These names deliberately echo those listed as members of the council of the Lords of the Isles.[176] In the eyes of the Gaelic world, Argyll ruled the West Highlands and Islands, with his power stretching across the North Channel into the north of Ireland.

The relationships that bound Argyll's clients to him did not always leave traces. Like an iceberg, much of his affinity lies hidden. One reliable sign of membership was the 5th earl's willingness to act on someone's behalf, especially when they were in trouble. The earl himself summed up the reciprocal obligations that held his affinity together, 'sa lang as he dependis vpoun ws and vpoun na vther we cann do na less of our honor nor to assist him in honest and ressonable actionis seing he and his freindis ar redde to servfe ws at all tymis'.[177] This test reveals the social depth of Argyll's affinity, with the earl supporting all social levels from 'my frend and my servant', the powerful magnate James MacDonald of Dunivaig, lairds such as John Butter of Gormock, burgesses such as Andrew Ross of Nairn, smaller kin-groups such as the MacTarlichs of Ardeonaig to individuals like Patrick Robertson of Tullgavane.[178]

NATIONAL OFFICE AND INFLUENCE

One of the services the 5th earl performed for his affinity was to act as their champion and patron at the Scottish court. His personal presence was invaluable because he applied pressure to get a task completed, such as lobbying the queen to outlaw the MacGregors.[179] On more routine matters, he made it his business to ensure that the necessary authorisations were obtained or the correct procedures followed in the institutions of central government. For example, he personally oversaw the presentation of the sheriff's books and accounts to the Exchequer.[180] Sometimes court life delayed the transaction of business. In 1565, the 5th earl testily complained that he could not organise a commission because the court was forever banqueting.[181]

---

[175] From the poems, 'Maith an chairt' and 'An Duanag Ullamh'; MacInnes, 'The Panegyric Code in Gaelic Poetry', 448f.
[176] *Acts of the Lords of the Isles*, xlvii.
[177] Argyll to Glenorchy, 19 March 1565, GD112/39/3/26.
[178] MacDonald 18 November 1565 SP63/15 fo. 172; Butter, Mary, Queen of Scots to Argyll, 31 March 1566, *Letters to Argyll Family*, 5–6; Ross, 14 October 1562, *Rose of Kilravock*, 237; MacTarlichs, 27 June 1562, GD112/39/2/7; Patrick Robertson, 11 May 1562, *Campbell Letters*, 5.
[179] 28 March 1563, GD112/39/2/14.
[180] He angrily explained to Hugh Rose of Kilravock that the delay in sending the Nairn books meant it would have to wait until the next Exchequer sitting, 30 January and 30 September 1561: *Rose of Kilravock*, 232–2, 235.
[181] 6 March 1565, GD112/39/3/22.

Attending the monarch and court enabled nobles to gain royal patronage. Argyll had the advantage of his inherited office of Master of the Royal
Household to guarantee him access to court. During Mary, Queen of Scots'
personal rule, he was one of her inner circle of advisers and an active member of the Privy or Secret Council. Because so little Highland business was
dealt with in council or elsewhere in central government, Argyll appears
less involved in government than some of his fellow councillors.[182] With the
majority of his interests lying outside the government's effective jurisdiction,
instead of bringing them to the national stage, Argyll dealt with them himself.
During the civil wars, he stopped attending court and the council. Ceasing
to be a conduit for patronage and business at the centre had a damaging
effect upon his clan and affinity, something they sought to rectify in 1569 by
forcing the earl to settle with the regent. Though absence from Edinburgh
diminished Argyll's power, it did not cripple it. In many respects, the West
Highlands were an autonomous province inside the Scottish kingdom, and
the 5th earl could rule it with, or without, access to the centre.

Secure in his powerbase, Argyll demonstrated little interest in formal government posts. At the end of his life, he briefly held the chancellorship,
valued for the pre-eminence it bestowed as much as the office itself. Knowing it would hinder effective rule in the Highlands, he avoided any office of
state requiring constant attendance upon the monarch.[183] Argyll sought political power, his ambition formulated in the traditional terms of exercising
his ancient right and duty as a Scottish noble to give advice and counsel to
his monarch. Upon the national political stage, the 5th earl's goal was to
act as one of the chief advisers to Mary, Queen of Scots, helping direct her
policies. He held this position between 1561 and 1565, giving his counsel
at the level of policy making without becoming involved in the minutiae
of day-to-day administration. The 5th earl had no desire to be a Scottish
Cecil, nor to emulate the court positions of the French *princes étrangers*. As
a Scottish noble counsellor he did not need to maintain continuous attendance at court, but could give his advice during his frequent visits. Within the
relatively unsophisticated nature of Scottish political life, power remained
decentralised and regionalised. In the middle of the sixteenth century, except
for the regency, the offices on offer at the Scottish court were not substantial
enough to provide a rival source of political authority to that based on land
and men. As a group, Scottish aristocrats drew most of their power from

---

[182] The exceptions were the MacGregor feud and that between MacDonald of Dunivaig and
MacLean of Duart, see below, pp. 131–2, 159.

[183] After the 1603 union, Scottish nobles had to face a similar choice of being resident at a
distant court and not able to maintain personal rule over their regions or being absent from
the centre of political power.

their lands and affinities rather than court offices or clientage networks, far removed from a service nobility tied to the royal court, fighting for place and patronage in order to survive.

At the cost of spending many hours on horseback travelling between the Highlands and Lowlands, it was possible for Argyll to be both a national politician and an autonomous prince. The earl's unique position rested upon his powerbase, allowing him to stand outside the machinery of central government as well as be part of it. He could draw upon the resources and the men from his extensive estates, jurisdictions, clan and affinity to provide him with the political and military might to defend his autonomy even against the Scottish crown. In this he resembled the great supranational magnates of the medieval period more than the nobles of his own time.[184] The 5th earl thought and acted as a sovereign prince, and the awareness of his own power and status allowed him to move effortlessly onto the British stage.

[184] For the supranational magnates of medieval British Isles, see R. Frame, *The Political Development of the British Isles, 1100–1400* (Oxford, 1990).

3

The creation of a British policy: 1558–1560

Argyll's political career highlights the fact that, before 1603, British politics could only be found in the interstices between the overlapping political worlds of the Atlantic archipelago. The British strategies formulated by a few politicians sought to integrate those separate worlds into a comprehensive whole. However, without a political system at its heart, the story of British politics does not easily fit into a single, linear narrative. In addition to its fresh perspectives, the 'new' British history requires novel ways of writing.[1] A balance needs to be struck when uncovering the hidden drama of British politics during the sixteenth century. On the one hand, the British dimension of events should be highlighted and, on the other, the integrity of the political worlds in which they occur must be respected. In an attempt to achieve such a balance, the chronological narrative that follows (chapters 3–6) has been divided into three parallel sections. Each section focuses upon events in one of Argyll's political worlds, with the British dimension and the 5th earl himself binding the separate sections together. For the sake of narrative clarity, the order of the sections varies between chapters.[2] During his career as a British politician, Argyll moved constantly between the regional politics of the Gàidhealtachd, Scottish national affairs, and the triangular relationships of the English, Irish and Scottish realms, which formed part of the international arena of European diplomacy. He had daily experience of these three political worlds and used that to formulate his own British policy. His power, position and interests had placed him centre stage within British politics, and following his career allows the drama to unfold.

In his first two years as earl, Argyll found himself at the heart of one of the greatest crises in British history.[3] His semi-sovereign power and his Protestant beliefs ensured that he played a major role in the events of

---

[1] See above, pp. 11–12.
[2] The parallel chronology on pp. 220–9 provides a crosscheck of the interrelation of events.
[3] J. Morrill, 'The British Problem, c. 1534–1707' in B. Bradshaw and J. Morrill, eds., *The British Problem, c. 1534–1707: State Formation in the Atlantic Archipelago* (London, 1996), 1–38, at p. 22.

1559–60, when Scotland was caught up in a religious and political revolution which placed the country permanently on the Protestant side of the confessional divide. The Reformation struggle had an Anglo-Scottish dimension which produced a momentous diplomatic realignment, inaugurating the Anglo-Scottish alliance which led to the union of the crowns in 1603 and eventually the creation of the United Kingdom. From the perspective of the Gaelic political world, the crisis gave Argyll the opportunity to triangularize British politics by adding the Irish dimension into bilateral Anglo-Scottish relations. The enthusiastic support of William Cecil enabled the two men to secure official adoption for their joint British policy in the summer of 1560.

THE REFORMATION IN SCOTLAND

Argyll succeeded to his earldom in the middle of November 1558, around the time of Elizabeth's accession to the English throne. On his deathbed, and under the penalty of a curse, his father had insisted that his successor strive to overthrow the Mass and introduce Protestant worship throughout Scotland.[4] The young earl was now the country's most powerful Protestant noble. As he had demonstrated during the previous two years, he was willing to lead the active Protestant minority within Scotland in its campaign of escalating pressure for national change which accompanied the limited reform already being undertaken within noble households. His dilemma was how to proceed should Protestant pressure and persuasion not work. He would have to reconcile the use of force to achieve his father's command with his duty of loyalty to the Scottish crown and commonweal. The struggle for a Protestant Kirk introduced the 5th earl to international politics. The need of the Lords of the Congregation for English assistance drove Argyll to devise a British policy. Its adoption enabled the treaties of Berwick and Edinburgh to be concluded permitting the Scottish Protestants to seize control and introduce their reformation.

An opportunity for action immediately presented itself. After the 4th earl's burial in the family mausoleum at Kilmun, his son, with no time to settle affairs at home, left for Edinburgh to attend the Parliament held at the end of November 1558. As part of their campaign, the Protestants presented threatening petitions to the regent and Parliament demanding ecclesiastical reforms.[5] Although conciliatory noises were made, nothing was decided on

---

[4] *Records of Argyll*, 7; Knox, *History*, I. 138–9 and see above, pp. 23–5.
[5] Presented to the regent by James Sandilands of Calder, possibly on 20 November: Knox, *History*, I. 149–52. Letter and protestation to Parliament c. 5 December 1558, Knox, *History*, I. 154–8; M.H.B. Sanderson, *Ayrshire and the Reformation: People and Change, 1490–1600* (East Linton, 1997), 86–8.

religious matters. Mary of Guise concentrated upon persuading Parliament to vote the crown matrimonial for Mary, Queen of Scots' husband Francis.[6] This was a major triumph for the regent, which freed her from the necessity of making further political or religious concessions. The 5th earl and his friend, Lord James Stewart, had been chosen to carry the honours of Scotland to Francis, but it was not a prospect they relished. The selection of two key Protestant nobles to go to France was assumed to be a Catholic plot, which either threatened their lives or would use their absence to weaken the Protestant cause.[7] Travelling in suitable style would be expensive, and the 5th earl had called upon his kin and friends for financial support.[8] In the event, the French trip was not made. Although Elizabeth had succeeded to the English throne without incident on 17 November 1558, her claim was not recognised in France. Backed by Henry II, Francis and Mary, Queen of Scots had adopted the English arms and title, underlining their claim to the Tudor throne. With the greater prize of the English realm in view, the delivery of the Scottish crown matrimonial paled into insignificance, allowing Argyll's journey to be quietly aborted.

After the failure to secure religious change in Parliament, the Protestants fulfilled their threats to increase pressure upon the political and ecclesiastical authorities.[9] The posting of the 'Beggars Summons' on the doors of friaries on the first day of 1559 sounded a new and aggressive note. If the friars did not completely change their ways, they would be evicted on 'Flitting Friday', the annual day for the removal of tenants.[10] In a more constructive vein, the 5th earl granted substantial lands and castles to John Carswell, thereby furnishing the resources and local prestige the minister needed to spearhead a programme of ecclesiastical reform in the Highlands.[11] With this endowment, the 5th earl took another step on the road to reforming his region, proceeding with a local reformation 'without tarrying for any'. A similar forward policy was being pursued by some burghs, such as Dundee and Ayr, where reforms were introduced on the authority of the town council.[12]

---

[6] P. Ritchie, 'Dynasticism and Diplomacy: The Political Career of Marie de Guise in Scotland, 1548–60' (University of St Andrews PhD thesis, 1999), ch. 8.

[7] Calderwood, *History*, I. 422.

[8] 9 February 1559: AT, V. 104, and see below p. 104.

[9] J. Kirk, *Patterns of Reform* (Edinburgh, 1989), 100–1.

[10] Flitting Friday fell on 12 May: Knox, *History*, I. 139 n. 2; II. 255–6. G. Donaldson, 'Flitting Friday, The Beggars' Summons and Knox's Sermon at Perth', *SHR*, 39 (1960), 175–6.

[11] Dawson, 'Clan, Kin and Kirk', 230–4 and see above pp. 43, 80–1.

[12] For Ayr, which had the support of its Campbell sheriff, Sir Hew Campbell of Loudoun, see Sanderson, *Ayrshire and the Reformation*, ch. 7. For Dundee, see I. Flett, 'The Conflict of the Reformation and Democracy in the Geneva of Scotland' (University of St Andrews MPhil thesis, 1981). F.D. Bardgett, *Scotland Reformed: The Reformation in Angus and the Mearns* (Edinburgh, 1989), ch. 4; Kirk, *Patterns of Reform*, 13, 101–2.

Protestants still hoped that national church reform could be achieved by agreement and looked for doctrinal and liturgical changes from the provincial council meeting in Edinburgh during March and April. The previous councils of 1549 and 1552 had passed statutes to remove the worst clerical abuses, but their implementation had been hampered by the hierarchy's vested interest in the status quo. If Protestant aspirations were to be met in 1559, a major theological shift and radical practical changes were required.[13] However, the reform-minded clergy within the clerical establishment failed to persuade the church council to adopt such a programme. The position was made plain to Argyll when his own chaplain, John Douglas, was condemned as a heretic.[14] The last chance of compromise had gone and the clergy split into rival camps over how to celebrate Easter. The situation had reached crisis point. Protestant pressure had failed to propel the ecclesiastical authorities towards reform. Further reforming action would involve direct defiance of the crown as well as ecclesiastical authority. The regent was faced with an unattractive choice: repressing the burgeoning Protestant movement or granting them freedom of worship.

Perth provided the flashpoint that turned the crisis into a rebellion. Its provost, Patrick, 3rd Lord Ruthven, had already stoutly defended Protestant preaching in the burgh against the regent's criticism, and its minister was among those legally summoned for defying the proclamation forbidding preaching at Easter without licence.[15] Unlike previous summons, on this occasion the regent was determined to enforce obedience to royal authority.[16] She was ready to call the Protestants' bluff: they constantly reiterated that they remained obedient subjects, despite their actions against the church. The Protestants organised a massive show of strength for the preachers' 'day of law'. After negotiations, the preachers and their supporters dispersed,

---

[13] Sanderson, *Ayrshire and the Reformation*, 89. There had been some movements in that direction, as in the 'Twapenny Faith' and Hamilton's Catechism: *Statutes of the Scottish Church* ed. D. Patrick (SHS, 1st ser. 54, Edinburgh, 1907), 163–7; *The Bannatyne Miscellany III* ed. D. Laing (Bannatyne Club, 19, Edinburgh, 1855), 313–20; D. McRoberts, *Essays on the Scottish Reformation 1513–1625* (Glasgow, 1962).

[14] John Douglas under his alias of Grant: *Statutes of the Scottish Church*, 186.

[15] Knox, *History*, I. 159–60. Ruthven was at the centre of a strong circle of Perthshire nobles linked by marriage ties who supported reform, which included Colin Campbell of Glenorchy, see *Campbell Letters*, 40–41. Within Perth itself, Ruthven was supported by the craft guilds who were pushing for ecclesiastical change, similiar to those measures already in place in Dundee and Ayr: M.B. Verschuur, 'The Outbreak of the Scottish Reformation at Perth, 11 May 1559', *Scotia* (1987), 41–53; M.B. Verschuur, 'Perth and Reformation' (2 vols., University of Glasgow PhD thesis, 1985), II. ch. 8.

[16] Two prominent Protestants from the south-west, the earl of Glencairn and Sir Hew Campbell, sheriff of Ayr, went to the regent seeking a compromise, but were unsuccessful. However, it seems unlikely that the regent said the ministers would be banished, 'albeit they preached as truly as ever did St Paul', Knox, *History*, I. 159.

to discover that on 10 May the ministers had been outlawed for failing to answer their legal summons. The Protestants of Perth, Angus and the Mearns were furious at what they interpreted as a trick. In this tinder-box atmosphere on 11 May, the day before 'Flitting Friday' and the start of Whitsuntide, John Knox delivered his famous Perth sermon. The 5th earl, Lord James Stewart, Ruthven and other prominent Perth Protestants were present in St John's church to hear Knox.[17] When a priest attempted to say Mass at the end of the sermon, an iconoclastic riot broke out smashing church images and sweeping through the burgh destroying its friaries and monasteries.[18]

The 5th earl approved of such 'cleansing' of idolatrous images and the attack upon monastic life. Preferring less violent means to achieve the same end, shortly after the Perth riot he travelled to Coupar Angus Abbey, where he negotiated an extraordinary settlement with his great-uncle Abbot Donald Campbell.[19] The monastery was reformed along Protestant lines with Abbot Donald and his monks abandoning their monastic habits and ceasing to say Mass. All the altars and images were stripped from the interior and publicly burnt. Future services were to be based upon the Scriptures and conducted in Scots. In addition, the community agreed to implement Protestant reform throughout the abbey's lands, and promised military support and a vote in the next Parliament for national reform. In return the abbot and his monks would enjoy their property and continue their corporate existence, shorn of spiritual duties.[20] This exceptional agreement allowed the 5th earl to

---

[17] Argyll was mentioned in the eye-witness account of Oliver Tullidelph handed down in his family and recorded in J. Lawson, *The Book of Perth* (Edinburgh, 1847), 104.

[18] Knox, *History*, I. 162–3. The first move has traditionally been credited to William Stewart of Grandtully, a close friend of Colin Campbell of Glenorchy and his wife, Katherine Ruthven, sister of Lord Ruthven, *Red Book of Grandtully*, ed. W. Fraser (2 vols., Edinburgh, 1868), I. lxxv; *Campbell Letters*, 266.

[19] The abbey lies about ten miles northeast of Perth. Herries dates the Coupar changes immediately after Perth: 'The next storme fell upon Couper. Those people, upon notice of this busines at Perth, fell lykwayes upon there Church; which they spoyled and ransackt, and chased away the priests': Herries, *Memoirs*, 38.

[20] This was the only such agreement to have survived from the Scottish Reformation, AT, V. 115, printed in N. Campbell, 'Two Papers from the Argyll Charter Chest', *SHR*, 21 (1923–4), 142–3. The abbot's orthodoxy was in doubt before May 1559 and he had stopped wearing his monastic habit, which was given as one reason why the Pope was refusing to elect him to the bishopric of Brechin: John Row to Abbot Donald, 11 May 1559, Rome, printed in *Rental Book of the Cistercian Abbey of Cupar Angus*, ed. C. Rogers (2 vols., Grampian Club, 17, London, 1879–80), I. 108–9. Abbot Donald brought Dame Katherine Campbell, countess of Crawford, and her son, 5th Lord Ogilvy, into the Protestant camp: Bardgett, *Scotland Reformed*, 73–4. On 19 May from Berwick Sir James Croft reported that the abbot of Coupar Angus had adopted 'secular weed': CSPSc, I. 213. The Coupar agreement was possibly made at the same time as that between the 5th earl and his half-brother, John, provost of Kilmun, concerning the lands of the collegiate church at Kilmun, 12 May ?1559, AT, V. 120; misdated as 1450 in *The Bighouse Papers* ed. D Wimberley (Inverness, 1904), 23.

combine his roles as clan chief and religious activist, engineering a smooth transition at Coupar Angus from a monastic community to a non-religious legal corporation.[21]

Elsewhere confrontation seemed unavoidable. For the regent, the situation had moved from being a religious crisis to a rebellion. She viewed the Perth iconoclastic riot as a seditious challenge to her authority and directed the local nobility to provide troops to punish the disorder.[22] In response, the Congregation, as it became known, summoned its own troops.[23] In this volatile situation, Argyll's political inexperience showed. He found himself torn between his obedience to the crown and his Protestant commitment. With her considerable charm and powers of persuasion, Mary of Guise convinced the 5th earl, Lord James Stewart and Lord Ruthven, all three declared Protestants, to support her. Argyll had gone as far as promising that he would fight the Congregation if they would not compromise. On 24 May the regent sent the 5th earl, with Lord James and Lord Sempill, to Perth to discover if the burgh were being held against royal authority. The Angus and Fife lairds, who had arrived to support their Perth brethren, offered to open the gates, providing the religious changes remained and no persecution ensued. They persuaded their fellow Protestants, Argyll and Lord James, that they were not rebels.[24] The lords returned to the regent, and a settlement was agreed on 29 May to reopen the burgh and disband the troops on condition there would be no reprisals and no French soldiers stationed in or around Perth.[25] When the 5th earl and Lord James brought this agreement to Perth, they were accused of betraying the Protestant cause by Knox and the preacher John Willock, who had arrived from the south-west with the earl of Glencairn's reinforcements. Having explained themselves, they promised that, if the regent broke the agreement, they would leave her and join the Congregation.[26] Argyll was now in the dangerous position of having naively made promises to both sides.

Mary of Guise marched triumphantly into Perth the next day. During the boisterous entry, a soldier accidentally shot the thirteen-year-old son of a prominent Protestant laird.[27] The regent reintroduced Catholic worship and

---

[21] For the changes in land-holding at Coupar Angus, see M.H.B. Sanderson, *Scottish Rural Society in the Sixteenth Century* (Edinburgh, 1982), 89–94, 191–201.

[22] For example the summons to David, Lord Drummond, 17 May 1559, GD160/136/15.

[23] Especially from the south-west: Knox, *History*, I. 164–73.

[24] Knox, *History*, I. 173–6.   [25] Keith, *History*, I. 200.

[26] Knox, *History*, I. 177. The story that Argyll and Lord James had deliberately remained with the regent as insiders for the Congregation, seems a later gloss: Herries *Memoirs*, 38–9.

[27] Patrick Murray of Tibbermuir, a nephew of the Ruthvens. Knox reported that the regent commented it was a pity the father had not been killed: Knox, *History*, I. 179; *The History of Scotland by George Buchanan* ed. J. Aikman (4 vols., Edinburgh, 1827), II. 401; R.S. Fittis, *Ecclesiastical Annals of Perth* (Edinburgh, 1885), 88; *Campbell Letters*, 26, 53–4, 264.

removed Ruthven as provost, replacing him by the unpopular John Charteris of Kinfauns. On her departure, she garrisoned the burgh with four companies of Scotsmen in French pay. As a consequence, many Protestant sympathisers fled from Perth. These events forced the 5th earl to choose between the regent and the Congregation. He felt angry and dishonoured, believing the regent had duped him into securing an agreement she had always intended to break. When told that his soldiers must leave the burgh, he bitterly reminded Mary of Guise of the broken settlement terms and warned her he would depart as well.[28] Argyll left Perth secretly with the other Protestant nobles and, before going their separate ways, the 5th earl and Lord James made bonds with the Ayrshire and Perthshire Protestants.[29] It was a time of rapidly shifting allegiances, when it was difficult to know friend from enemy and, as one Frenchman wryly commented, those who were with the regent in the morning were with the opposite party before the midday meal.[30]

By aligning himself with the Congregation, Argyll had taken an irrevocable step into rebellion. Mary of Guise was furious at his defection, commanding him to return. The 5th earl replied on behalf of all the Protestant nobles, 'That with safe conscience they could not be partakers of so manifest tyranny as by her was committed, and of so great iniquity as they perceived devised by her and her ungodly Council the Prelates'.[31] He later wrote to the regent justifying his stance without reference to the religious controversy, concentrating upon the broken settlement terms, the introduction of soldiers in French pay, and the forcible change of the provost and burgh council.[32]

From this point, Argyll and his close friend Lord James assumed the leadership of the Congregation, guiding it through its critical first months. In the short term, the two nobles sought to consolidate their position and spread the ecclesiastical reforms over as much of Scotland as possible. The immediate target for their reforming zeal was the burgh of St Andrews, the ecclesiastical capital of the country, where Lord James was commendator of the priory. The two lords travelled with a small contingent of about fifty men

---

[28] 'A Historie of the Estate of Scotland from July 1558 to April 1560' in D. Laing, ed., *Miscellany of Wodrow Society I* (Wodrow Society, 11, Edinburgh, 1844), I. 59.
[29] 30 May 1559 bond between Argyll, Lord James, Glencairn, Boyd, Ochiltree and Matthew Campbell of Loudoun: Knox, *History*, I. 178–9; and 1 June 1559 bond between Argyll, Lord James, Ruthven, Menteith and William Murray of Tullibardine: Knox, *History*, I. 180.
[30] Villeparisis to Noailles, 14 June 1559, *Papiers d'état relatifs a l'histoire de l'écosse au 16ᵉ siècle* ed. A. Teulet (3 vols., Bannatyne Club, Edinburgh, 1852–60), I. 311.
[31] Knox, *History*, I. 180, the marginal note identifies the answer as coming from Argyll. In his letter to Anne Locke, 23 June 1559, Knox had commented that when the 5th earl and Lord James joined the Congregation, 'by their presence many hearts were erected from desperation', Knox, *Works* VI. 24–5.
[32] 15 June 1559, Knox, *History*, I. 187–8.

from their households, not anticipating opposition because they knew that the priory, the university and the burgh were receptive to religious change.[33] On learning that the archbishop of St Andrews was arriving that evening with French troops, 'to mak impediment of sic thingis as we wald sett fordwart to the glory of God', they wrote to Argyll's Perthshire kin to send troops with all speed.[34] The following day, Sunday 11 June, Knox preached in the parish church under the 5th earl's military protection because of the archbishop's threats to have him shot. After a rousing sermon on Christ's cleansing the Temple, images were stripped from the parish church of Holy Trinity, the cathedral and the university chapels. The St Andrews populace carried the 'idols' to the spot where the elderly Protestant Walter Miln had been martyred the previous year and ritually burnt them.[35] With the archbishop's withdrawal from the burgh leaving no organised resistance, the 5th earl and his men could conduct the iconoclasm in an orderly manner. In a calculated effort to intimidate the friars, viewed as the main threat to the Protestants, the houses of the observant Franciscans and Dominicans were completely destroyed.[36] The archbishop carried the news to the regent at Falkland Palace in central Fife, who immediately dispatched her soldiers and artillery to Cupar on the main road to St Andrews. With less than a hundred cavalry and a small infantry force, the 5th earl moved to intercept. Fortunately for Argyll, reinforcements arrived from the surrounding regions. Knox, celebrating divine intervention, proclaimed, 'God did so multiply our number, that it appeared as if men had rained from the clouds'.[37] These reinforcements persuaded the regent's commanders to negotiate a truce, signed on the Garliebank overlooking Cupar.[38]

After these early successes, the Congregation went on the offensive.[39] Perth was besieged with the help of troops sent by Argyll's relations, the earl of Menteith and Colin Campbell of Glenorchy.[40] After a short bombardment,

---

[33] 'Historie', *Wodrow Miscellany*, I. 59; J.E.A. Dawson, ' "The Face of Ane Perfyt Reformed Kyrk": St Andrews and the early Scottish Reformation' in J. Kirk, ed., *Humanism and Reform: The Church in Europe, England and Scotland, 1400–1642* (Studies in Church History, Subsidia 8, Oxford, 1991), 413–35 at pp. 414–6.

[34] Argyll and Lord James to Menteith, Ruthven, Murray of Tullibardine and Campbell of Glenorchy, 10 June 1559, *Campbell Letters*, 1.

[35] 'Historie', *Wodrow Miscellany*, I. 60.

[36] Knox, *History*, I. 181–2; Dawson, 'Ane Perfyt Reformed Kyrk', 416–8.

[37] Knox, *History*, I. 183. Lothian, Perthshire, Fife and the burghs of Dundee, St Andrews and Cupar sent their contingents.

[38] Knox, *History*, I. 185–6.

[39] Around this time the abbey of Lindores, which lay about 8 miles northwest of Cupar, was reformed. This was probably a breach of the truce that had forbidden further reformations: Knox to Anne Locke, 23 June 1559, Knox, *Works*, VI. 26; Knox, *History*, 186 n.

[40] Summoned on 10 June, see above n. 34. Kirkcaldy lists those who relieved Perth, in 1 July 1559, *CSPSc*, I. 220.

the garrison surrendered and the Congregation triumphantly entered the
burgh. The men from Dundee and Perth, fuelled by their hatred of its abbot,
Patrick Hepburn, bishop of Moray, departed for the nearby abbey of Scone.
The violence generated by their image-breaking spread, only contained by
the timely arrival of the 5th earl and Lord James. Forestalling the destruction
of the church and bishop's palace, they persuaded the men to leave, though
troops returned and burnt the abbey the following day, when their restraining
presence was withdrawn.[41] During the previous night, the two friends departed post-haste for Stirling to prevent it being occupied by French troops.
Having won that race, they seized the burgh and reformed it.[42] With the
strategically important Stirling securely in their hands, on 29 June the Congregation felt confident enough to take Edinburgh, where the iconoclasm
was repeated.[43]

The move to Edinburgh precipitated a national struggle between the regent and the Congregation which was accompanied by an escalating war of
words.[44] Mary of Guise believed she would triumph if she could only detach
the 5th earl and Lord James from the Congregation. Certain her political
acumen and charm could win them, she tried to get the two nobles to talk to
her in person. The other Congregation leaders were suspicious, refusing to
allow Argyll and Lord James to negotiate on their own, especially after the
regent's adviser's comment, 'That ere Michaelmas day, they two should leave
their heads'.[45] These 'young plants', as Knox called them, were the driving
force behind the Congregation. They had steered the revolt through its early
phase as a religious uprising, changing it into a national rebellion. In order to
survive, the rebels needed external aid and that would alter the complexion
of the revolt. In the summer of 1559, Argyll and Lord James began the task of
securing English help for their cause (see next section). During the next year
the Wars of the Congregation developed into a national and international
conflict in which military considerations took priority over religious ones.

The story of the Scottish Reformation, in its restricted sense, did not re-
sume until the fighting was over. After the peace treaty of July 1560, ecclesiastical reform returned to the top of the agenda. Hopes centred upon the

---

[41] Knox, *History*, I. 190–1.   [42] Keith, *History*, I. 211.

[43] One report suggested that the Black and Grey Friars were attacked by the Edinburgh towns-
folk before the Congregation arrived: 'Historie', *Wodrow Miscellany*, I. 61. Others name the
5th earl, Ruthven, Glencairn and Lord James, as destroying the friaries: *Diurnal*, 53; Knox,
History, I. 192. Kirkcaldy to Percy, 1 July 1559, *CSPSc*, I. 219–20; John Lesley cited in
D. Hay Fleming, *The Reformation in Scotland* (London, 1910), 377–8; McRoberts, *Essays
on the Scottish Reformation*, 434.

[44] For example the regent's proclamation of 1 July, stressing the rebellious nature of the revolt,
was countered by the Congregation's open letter of 2 July which reiterated their political
obedience but asserted the need to remove idolatry from the realm, Knox, *History*, I. 193–5.

[45] Knox, *History*, I. 196–7.

Parliament called for the following month.[46] Argyll worked hard to max-
imise support for Protestant legislation. He ensured as many kinsmen as
possible attended Parliament, with seven Campbell lairds led by Loudoun,
the chief of the Ayrshire branch from the south-west, and Glenorchy travelling down from Breadalbane. Abbot Donald of Coupar Angus honoured his
agreement by voting for reform along with John Campbell, bishop elect of
the Isles.[47] The 5th earl lobbied furiously to sway those nobles with doubts
about the Protestant measures.[48] He threatened to 'give over kindness' to his
cousin, the earl of Cassilis, probably causing that earl to absent himself from
the vote.[49] During the Parliament, the 5th earl's uncle, Archbishop Hamilton,
and the bishops of Dunkeld and Dunblane failed to provide the decisive
leadership the conservative side so badly needed.[50] Argyll had applied pressure to the bishops of Dunkeld and Dunblane, ordering their cathedrals to be
'cleansed',[51] and imprisoning William Chisholm of Dunblane for six weeks
the previous winter at Castle Campbell, which might have tempered his outright opposition.[52] Thanks to the efforts of Argyll and his fellow Protestants,
the Scots Confession of Faith was adopted and acts were passed abolishing
papal authority and the Mass.[53] Mindful of the nobles' close connections
with the benefice holders and the fragile political situation, the Parliament
did not attempt wholesale reform of the old ecclesiastical institution, allowing the existing structure to survive, deprived of its spiritual functions. The
First Book of Discipline, under discussion since April, provided the blueprint
for the new organisation of the Protestant Kirk. It was not laid before the
August Parliament but reviewed by a convention of estates six months later.

---

[46] It was authorised by Mary, Queen of Scots as part of the concessions to the Scots in the Treaty
of Edinburgh. For the two parties in the Reformation Parliament, Donaldson, *Queen's Men*,
36–44; and a discussion of the parliament, J. Goodare, 'The Scottish Parliamentary Records,
1560–1603', *Historical Records*, 72 (1999), 248–55.

[47] They were part of an exceptionally large contingent of lairds who attended this Parliament.
Donaldson, *Queen's Men*, 37, 163–4.

[48] This had been a continuous process, e.g. 28 May 1560, *Two Missions of Jacques de la Brosse*
ed. G. Dickinson (SHS, 3rd ser. 36, Edinburgh, 1942), 169.

[49] Cassilis was not listed in the sederunt, but there were conflicting reports as to whether he
was absent or voted against the bills: Randolph to Cecil, 25 August 1560, *CSPSc*, I. 471;
Donaldson, *Queen's Men*, 44.

[50] Donaldson, *Queen's Men*, 44.

[51] Argyll, Lord James and Ruthven to lairds of Arnetully and Kinvaid directing them to remove
the images from Dunkeld, 12 August 1560, printed in *Chronicles of the Families of Atholl
and Tullibardine* ed. John, 7th duke of Atholl (5 vols., Edinburgh, 1908), I. 35–6; McRoberts,
Essays on the Scottish Reformation, 442. The same letter referring to Dunblane cathedral
printed in A. Barty, *History of Dunblane Cathedral* (Stirling, 1995), 64.

[52] 'Report by de la Brosse and d'Oysel on Conditions in Scotland, 1559–60' ed. G. Dickinson
in *Miscellany of the Scottish History Society, IX* (SHS, 3rd ser. 50, Edinburgh, 1958), 103.

[53] W.I.P. Hazlitt, 'The Scots Confession 1560: Context, Complexion and Critique', *Archiv für
Reformationsgeschichte*, 78 (1987), 287–320.

Although Argyll supported it, many nobles felt its financial demands were too great, and it failed to secure full approval.[54] This did not prevent the new Kirk organizing itself throughout the kingdom. When the 5th earl attended the first General Assembly in December 1560 he knew he had fulfilled his father's injunction. The Mass had been abolished and Protestant worship was spreading. Without his enthusiastic leadership, his military contribution and his vital role in bringing English aid, the Scottish reformation of 1559–60 would not have succeeded.

THE FORGING OF THE ANGLO-SCOTTISH ALLIANCE

At the end of May 1559, when they formally joined the Lords of the Congregation, Argyll and Lord James became rebels. If their uprising were to succeed, the Protestants needed external assistance, which could only come from England. From the start of the crisis, William Cecil had been kept informed by Sir James Croft at Berwick.[55] Argyll and Lord James opened communications with the English in the middle of June.[56] Having been encouraged by Cecil's messages, they wrote to the secretary and the queen explaining their motivation and seeking help.[57] After an auspicious start to their campaign, the Congregation ran into difficulties, being forced to withdraw from Edinburgh and retreat to Stirling. The stunning news of Henry II's death in July after a jousting accident made them fearful that the new French king would give priority to the suppression of rebellion within his wife's realm.[58] At the same time, a discouraging letter arrived from Cecil reminding the Scots that England could not lightly risk another war and criticising them for not being firm enough against the French.[59] The 5th earl and Lord

[54] *The First Book of Discipline* ed. J.K. Cameron (Edinburgh, 1972).
[55] Croft and Northumberland were dealing with the Scottish aspects of the Treaty of Câteau-Cambrésis, April 1559 onwards: *CSPSc*, I. 210f. For a full discussion of Cecil's role, see S. Alford, 'Knox, Cecil and the British Dimension of the Scottish Reformation', in R. Mason, ed., *John Knox and the British Reformations* (Aldershot, 1999), 201–19.
[56] On 22 June there was a secret discussion between the Argyll, Lord James and Kirkcaldy of Grange and they agreed to a letter sent from Maitland of Lethington to Sir Henry Percy, 28 June 1559, *CSPSc*, I. 217–8. Cecil's memo of 18 July noted the great offers made by Argyll and Lord James, *CSP For 1558–9*, 386. William Kirkcaldy of Grange had been writing to Cecil from 23 June, *CSPSc*, I. 216–7.
[57] 19 July 1559, *CSPSc*, I. 226–8; full texts in Knox, *Works*, VI. 40–4. Cecil's letter to Percy 4 July, *CSPSc*, I. 222; Knox, *Works*, VI. 38–40. Knox was acting as scribe and adviser to the Lords and was later sent to negotiate directly with the English on Lindisfarne, 30 July, Instructions, *CSPSc*, I. 237–8.
[58] Henry died on 10 July and the news reached Scotland around the end of the month: Knox, *History*, I. 193, 199, 297.
[59] Cecil's letter was written after the matter had been discussed by the Privy Council, 28 July 1559, *CSPSc*, I. 234. A more encouraging letter from the Privy Council had been drafted but not sent, *CSPSc*, I. 234–5; Alford, *Cecil*, 57, 61.

James were bitterly disappointed. They were puzzled and angry that the secretary had failed to send a clear answer about English assistance, criticised their past performance, raised queries about the future, and given them irrelevant or impractical advice.[60] Although offering a vigorous defence, Argyll and Lord James realised that the Congregation's tactics had to change. They reorganized the military effort, changed the propaganda, erected a great council headed by the duke of Châtelherault, and deposed the regent. This package of measures was designed to secure English aid and steady the Congregation's rocky campaign.

In August 1559, the Congregation needed to regroup after its ignominious retreat from Edinburgh. The fundamental problem was how to keep adequate forces in the field for a prolonged period. The feudal-style levies mustered men effectively, but could only keep them for a month, unless they were paid to stay longer. The 5th earl with his reservoir of manpower could rotate his troops, but that reduced numbers. The regent was aware of these limitations. Her army, with its core of professional French troops, had the choice of seeking a decisive engagement or waiting in its fortified bases until the Congregation's soldiers returned home.[61] The Lords of the Congregation returned to their regions to reorganize their forces, to be ready at an hour's notice throughout the autumn and winter. As the main contributor of men, Argyll would signal the start of operations when he was ready.[62]

At the end of August, the 5th earl held a council in Lorn with the chiefs of the Isles.[63] He confirmed their support for the rebellion and the military mobilisation and probably discussed with James MacDonald of Dunivaig and the other chiefs his British policy of offering to aid the English in Ulster. Instead of urging the Highlanders to defend true religion, he employed arguments indicating the new direction of the Congregation's propaganda, warning, 'that the France ar cumin in and sutin down in this realm to occupy it and to put furtht the inhabitantis tharoff, and siklik to occupy all uther menis rowmes pece and pece, and to put away the blud of the nobilite'. He concluded his case by reminding them of the fate of Brittany, absorbed by the French crown earlier in the century.[64]

[60] 6 August to Croft and 13 August to Cecil, *CSPSc*, I. 240; 242–3; also Knox's letters, Knox, *Works*, VI. 67–70. Cecil had recommended the example of Denmark as a model of how to reform the Catholic clergy, but, as the 5th earl and Lord James pointed out, both Denmark and England had the backing of royal authority when religious changes were being enforced which was very different from the current situation in Scotland.
[61] Knox explained this point to Cecil in his letter of 15 August 1559: Knox, *Works*, VI. 67–70.
[62] Archbishop Hamilton to the regent, 29 September 1559, *The Scottish Correspondence of Mary of Lorraine, 1542/3–60* ed. A.I. Cameron (SHS, 3rd ser. 10, Edinburgh, 1927), 426–8.
[63] Argyll and Lord James to Colin Campbell of Glenorchy, *Campbell Letters*, 2.
[64] Hamilton to the regent, 29 September 1559, *Scottish Correspondence of Mary of Lorraine*, 427.

This patriotic argument was not solely a matter of expediency, but reflected Argyll's convictions about Scottish independence and the rightful role of the aristocracy within the commonweal. The new emphasis upon expelling the French was found in the Congregation's letter to the Scottish nobility at the end of August 1559. From this point onwards their propaganda focused upon the threat from France.[65] By shifting to a constitutional and patriotic justification for rebellion, the Congregation broadened its appeal to those Scots unpersuaded by religious arguments. In addition it chimed with the line of reasoning urged by Cecil to make aiding rebels more palatable to Queen Elizabeth.

In his speech to the Hebridean chiefs, Argyll asserted the traditional right of the higher nobility to participate in royal government. Although probably seeing little need for the formality, he supported the establishment of a great council, thereby satisfying Cecil's desire to regularise the Congregation's constitutional position.[66] Correct legal form was preserved by the Keeper of the Privy Seal, the 5th earl's great uncle. Abbot Donald issued writs under the seal authorising the Congregation's activities.[67] The 5th earl played a key role in securing the co-operation of the heir to the Scottish throne, the duke of Châtelherault. On a visit to Hamilton Castle in the middle of August when the news of Arran's escape from France had just arrived, he almost persuaded his uncle to join the Congregation. However, Châtelherault would not risk an open declaration because his other son, David Hamilton, remained in a French prison. When the Protestant Arran returned to Scotland, he rapidly changed his father's mind.[68] Employing the head of the Hamiltons as a constitutional figurehead satisfied the English desire for a veneer of legitimacy, but was a mixed blessing for the Congregation. It allowed the regent to suggest that the Hamiltons were seeking the Scottish crown for themselves.[69]

[65] After 28 August 1559: Knox, *History*, I. 219–26. For an examination of the different languages used by the Congregation, see R.A. Mason, 'Covenant and Commonweal: The Language of Politics in Reformation Scotland' in N. Macdougall, ed., *Church, Politics and Society: Scotland, 1408–1929* (Edinburgh, 1983), 97–126; R.A. Mason, *Kingship and the Commonweal: Political Thought in Renaissance and Reformation Scotland* (East Linton, 1998), ch. 5; J.H. Burns, *The True Law of Kingship: Concepts of Monarchy in Early Modern Scotland* (Oxford, 1996), chs. 4 and 5.
[66] For a discussion of Cecil's constitutional thinking, especially the role of the council, see Alford, *Cecil*, ch. 1.
[67] For example proclamations 29 November and 14 December 1559: Keith, *History*, I. 246–8; Bardgett, *Scotland Reformed*, 54, 75.
[68] Knox, *History*, I. 229–30; Arran to Cecil, 20 September (not December) 1559: CSPSc, I. 276–7.
[69] For example the regent's proclamation and Congregation's replies, end of September and start of October 1559: Knox, *History*, I. 235–49. On 10 November an investigation was begun into the treasonable activities of the duke and his allies which became the 'Report by de la Brosse and d'Oysel', 85–125.

With their constitutional arrangements in place, the Congregation repudi-ated the authority of Mary of Guise.[70] They made a formal declaration on 21 October suspending the regent, prudently not replacing her by the duke.[71] The 5th earl was delighted to be working with Arran, his cousin and child-hood friend, in a common cause. Together with Lord James, they formed a formidable team, about whose 'vertu' the English ambassador, Thomas Randolph, waxed eloquent, declaring, 'I profesce before God, I could never se but mervileus tokens of singular wysdome and godlines.'[72] In the autumn of 1559, Argyll and Arran, impatient with formalities, galvanised the Congrega-tion into action, including dispatching Maitland of Lethington to England.[73]

By the time Maitland left Scotland, the Congregation's fortunes were at their lowest ebb. Lack of cash to pay the soldiers led to a mutiny, and in the ensuing riot a boy from the 5th earl's household was killed. Argyll had to ex-ert all his authority to restrain his Highlanders from seeking revenge. Taking advantage of the confusion, the French sallied out from Leith creating a rout, which the 5th earl stemmed by rallying his men within Edinburgh's Nether Bow.[74] This reverse persuaded the Congregation to abandon Edinburgh. Al-though Knox's rousing sermon in Stirling gave them new heart, Argyll and his fellow Lords decided to scale down military operations. In November, the Congregation sent most of its troops home, retaining bases in St Andrews and Glasgow. Their hopes now rested entirely on the success of the English negotiations.

The question of intervention in Scotland was brought to a head by Maitland's arrival at the English court in early December. He carried Argyll's firm offer of help for the English in Ulster.[75] Convinced that military

---

[70] From the earliest contacts, Cecil had been dropping hints about a possible deposition which had not entered Argyll's calculations: 'We have maid no mention of any change in Authoritie, neyther yet hath any such thing entered our hartes, except that extream necessitie compell us thereto.' 19 July 1559, Knox, *Works*, VI. 42; *CSPSc*, I. 226–7. Cecil might have meant the removal of Mary, Queen of Scots rather than her mother, but the Scots were discussing the regent.

[71] Knox, *History*, I. 249–55. For the deposition arguments, see Burns, *The True Law of King-ship*, ch. 5. Memories of the duke's tenure as regent from 1543 to 1554 were fresh in Scottish minds.

[72] Randolph to Killigrew, 15 April 1560, *CSPSc*, I. 362–3.

[73] As Randolph commented to Croft and Sadler, the two men 'desire to be dooyng', 22 October 1559, Sadler, II. 47–50. Arran had had discussions with Cecil on his way home, probably on the matters in Cecil's memo, 31 August 1559, printed in Alford, *Cecil*, Appendix I. 223–4; discussed, 59–64. 24 September 1559, *CSPSc*, I. 252. Maitland's departure was delayed, possibly until the regent's suspension had been accomplished. New instructions, 10 November 1559, BL Add. MS 32,091, fo. 174; *CSPSc*, I. 263.

[74] Knox, *History*, I. 257, 260.

[75] The wording in the Treaty of Berwick suggests that this was probably the same formula that Argyll had sent with Maitland. There were no changes or emendations of this clause in Cecil's draft of the treaty and it was very similar to the words used in Norfolk's instructions

intervention was essential, Cecil had to battle to persuade his fellow councillors and Elizabeth of the wisdom of such a policy.[76] At the start of the new
year, Cecil won the debate, and an English fleet was dispatched forthwith,
arriving off Fife Ness on 22 January 1560.[77] Its sighting proved a turning
point in the Congregation's military fortunes. When the French forces, who
had been closing on the St Andrews base, realised the ships were English,
they beat a hasty retreat to Leith.[78]

Careful negotiations were needed to secure a full treaty, bringing an English
army. Having focused exclusively upon England's security to persuade the
queen and council to accept intervention, Cecil introduced broader arguments into the debate over terms. In particular, he employed Argyll's offer
of aid in Ireland to sweeten the burden of aiding the Scots. His close ally,
Sir Nicholas Throckmorton, the English ambassador in Paris, made the
case to the queen by deploying arguments about Ireland to emphasise the
international significance of intervention in Scotland.[79] By then Elizabeth
had accepted the 5th earl's scheme and included it as a settled fact in her
instructions to the duke of Norfolk on 15 February 1560, calmly asserting, 'We have no doubt but the Erle of Argile will be redy to doo his
best herin, having alreddy gyven a signification of his good will and purpose thereunto.'[80] Having worked out the framework with Cecil, Maitland
and his team travelled to Berwick to finalise details with Norfolk.[81] The
Congregation sent Lord James and Ruthven to sign on Châtelherault's behalf, and the treaty was ratified by Elizabeth in March.[82] Mindful of her

of 15 February, see below n. 80; BL Cotton Calig. B IX, fos. 35r–36v and Hatfield House,
Cecil Papers 152, fos. 56r–58r; I am grateful to Dr Alford for his assistance on this point.

[76] The Privy Council met on 27 December and debated the issue, presenting its views to the
queen the following day. There was a split over whether intervention at that time was the best
policy particularly in view of the European situation. Initially, Elizabeth refused to intervene
and only did so when she was convinced that it would counter the threat to her own position
and to English security: Alford, *Cecil*, 64–73; Dawson, 'Cecil', 205–7.

[77] T. Glasgow 'The Navy in the First Elizabethan Undeclared War', *Mariners Mirror*, 54 (1968),
23–37.

[78] Knox *History*, I. 281; William Douglas of Lochleven later recorded that the arrival of the
ships was the first time he forgave the English for killing his father at the battle of Pinkie:
M.H.B. Sanderson, *Mary Stewart's People: Life in Mary Stewart's Scotland* (Edinburgh,
1987), 57.

[79] 'If they [the French] be driven thence [from Scotland], Scotland is like to be friendly, and
French practices with Ireland die withall, when the Queen shall have commodity to order
some policy and to reduce the people and country to more service and profit than she
now has them, or her predecessors every had.' 20 February 1560, *CSP For 1559–60*, 389.
Throckmorton also used the example of Brittany.

[80] *Collection of state papers...left by William Cecil, Lord Burghley* eds. S. Hayes and
W. Murdin (2 vols., London, 1740–59), I. 242–4 at p. 244; *CSP For 1559–60*, 361–2.

[81] Cecil's annotated draft, BL Cotton Calig. B IX, fo. 34; Alford, *Cecil*, 74; text of treaty ratified
at Leith on 10 May 1560, printed in Knox, *History*, I. 303–7; *CSP For 1559–60*, 413–5.

[82] Instructions, 10 February 1560, Knox, *History*, I. 308–10.

sensibilities, the alliance was framed in the language of protection, the defence of the Scots' ancient rights and liberties and the unity of the British mainland.[83]

The Congregation had finally obtained its goal of English military assistance. Even with the wholehearted support of Secretary Cecil, it had been a close thing. In contrast to previous English imperial policies, the Scots' plight was not exploited by demanding castles or other Scottish bases. Cecil envisaged a limited intervention and a speedy withdrawal from Scotland, which would please the parsimonious Elizabeth. Despite the security arguments used in council, Cecil viewed the military expedition as a golden opportunity to transform Anglo-Scottish relations. An amicable alliance with Scotland was the cornerstone of a wider British strategy. Argyll's offer provided the perfect solution to the problem of seeking some recompense for English intervention which did not threaten Scottish independence or raise fears of English imperialism.

Whatever Cecil's long-term goal, most of the Privy Council remained suspicious of the Scots as allies, requiring guarantees of good faith. At every stage in the negotiations the Scots gave assurances they would not desert to the French. Noble hostages had been demanded, including the 5th earl's nephew, Alexander Campbell, and until they arrived the English army would not cross the border.[84] The English sought reassurance from those nobles who had not yet joined the Congregation, especially the earl of Huntly.[85] The greatest concern was the military campaign. The Scots offered 5,000 soldiers, but, without English money, they could only stay in the field for twenty days.[86] With England shouldering most of the financial and military burden, the queen's council was consoled by Argyll's offer of future benefits in Ireland.

The English army arrived in Scotland at the beginning of April and met the Congregation's troops at Prestonpans.[87] The Scots reorganised their army to supply 1,200 men for the duration of the campaign. In addition, Argyll offered an extra 1,000 men for thirty days, should they be required.[88] The hope of a speedy victory disappeared when Leith resisted capture and had

---

[83] 'Juste and due preservation of bothe these Kingdoms, thus conteynid in one Ile as in a little worlde by it selfe ... [which are] knytt in one continent Ilonde to gether at the creation of the worlde and severed notoriously from all the reste of the same worlde.' March 1560, BL Egerton 1818, fo. 9v; cited in Alford, *Cecil*, 74–5.
[84] Ruthven's letter to Cecil asking that his son Archibald, aged fourteen, be sent to Cambridge, 28 February 1560, *CSPSc*, I. 325; Knox, *History*, I. 310; list of hostages, *CSPSc*, I. 344–5.
[85] Huntly's letters to Elizabeth, Cecil and Maitland, 7 March 1560, *CSPSc*, I. 329.
[86] Norfolk to Cecil and Privy Council enclosing answers by Scots Lords, 29 February 1560, *CSPSc*, I. 325–7 and 10 February instructions, see above n. 82.
[87] Grey to Norfolk, 4 April 1560, *CSPSc*, I. 346; Knox, *History*, I. 311–2.
[88] Killigrew to Cecil, 20 April 1560, *CSPSc*, I. 370.

to be besieged.[89] Despite military failure, the success of the Anglo-Scottish campaign was achieved when Mary of Guise died and the worsening religious conflict in France persuaded the French to settle.[90] The seriously ill regent had retired to Edinburgh castle where, in the first week of June, she sent for the 5th earl. Along with several other Lords of the Congregation, he attended her deathbed and made his peace with the queen dowager.[91] Knox rejoiced in the departure of his enemy, but Argyll had retained his respect and affection for Mary of Guise, even though they had fought on opposite sides.

The French and the English ambassadors, having been conducting shadow negotiations for several months, could now discuss terms. In view of its importance for his British strategy, William Cecil travelled to Edinburgh in June.[92] The Treaty of Edinburgh, signed on 6 July 1560, was one of his greatest triumphs. Officially, it was a peace treaty between England and France to which was attached a separate document of 'Concessions' from the Scottish king and queen to their subjects. The package provided for the withdrawal of both English and French troops, making no attempt to reverse the Protestant changes already made, and treating the Lords of the Congregation as the present and future government of Scotland. On the Scottish side, Maitland laboured to persuade his countrymen to agree to the concessions Cecil had won and not wreck the entire process by pressing for more.[93]

The British dimension of the treaty was revealed in Cecil's own descriptions, rather than its formal clauses. Significantly, a treaty summary and the latest news were immediately dispatched to the Lord Lieutenant in Ireland.[94] Two of Cecil's key gains were particularly important to the 5th earl. In the first place the treaty had opened the door for a religious settlement for Scotland in which the French would not interfere. It had also provided long-term guarantees for the higher nobility's place in government, underwritten by the English queen by means of an Anglo-Scottish alliance. Following Cecil's plan, a council of twelve was proposed, with safeguards over their selection, to be linked to the three estates. In addition, the chief offices of state and justice were reserved for Scottish subjects. These provisions satisfied

---

[89] Description of siege of Leith, *Missions of de la Brosse*, 51–179; Knox, *History*, I. 312–22.
[90] In particular, the Tumult of Amboise in March 1560: R. Knecht, *Catherine de' Medici* (London, 1998), ch. 4.
[91] *Missions of de la Brosse*, 175–7; Randolph to Cecil, 7–8 June 1560, *CSPSc*, I. 421–2; Knox, *History*, I. 321. Mary of Guise died in the middle of the night 10–11 June and Argyll's kinsman, Sir John Campbell of Lundie, and the earl Marischal were made her executors, *Diurnal*, 276–7.
[92] Alford, *Cecil*, 80–5.
[93] M. Loughlin, 'The Career of Maitland of Lethington c. 1526–1573' (University of Edinburgh PhD thesis, 1991), 55.
[94] Cecil and Wotton to Elizabeth, 6 and 8 July; 'Note of theffect of the principall matters' sent to Sussex, 12 July; Leicester to Sussex, 11 July 1560, Alford, *Cecil*, 83–6.

Argyll's desire for a Protestant Scotland and aristocratic rule within the commonweal. During his visit to Edinburgh, Cecil struck up a friendship with Argyll, describing him to the queen as 'a goodly gentleman of person, and universally honoured here of all Scotland'. Together they discussed the 5th earl's Ulster plans in great detail.[95] Although starting from different premises, the two men's British strategies converged in July 1560. They had joined forces to remove the French from the British Isles and facilitate the reform of the Scottish church, thereby uniting the two kingdoms in a common faith. They now worked out a plan to incorporate Ireland into this new British dimension.

In the summer of 1560, Argyll found himself at the heart of Scottish and British politics. The experience of success gained through the Treaty of Edinburgh, the submission of his Ulster proposals and the Protestant legislation of the Parliament had matured him. When writing to Cecil, Randolph expressed astonishment at Argyll's character and achievements. Despite the earl's youth and his Gaelic background and upbringing, which the English ambassador regarded as a handicap, the 5th earl was greatly 'affectioned' to God and his country. Randolph, impressed by Argyll's political conduct, thought he was 'so earnest, constant, bold and frank in his talk with the greatest, so upright in conscience' that the only person who bore comparison with the earl was Lord James. The English ambassador concluded his paen of praise, 'Ther is only he [Argyll] and one more [Lord James] that deservethe immortall fame! Your honour had some proffe of them bothe at your beinge her. I knowe not wich passethe other.'[96]

Argyll and his fellow lords had impressed Cecil with their desire for as close friendship with England as possible. During the summer and autumn of 1560, the Anglophiles brought forward a previous suggestion for a marriage alliance to increase the strength and permanence of the amity. They proposed the earl of Arran should marry the English queen. Being Arran's cousin and close friend, Argyll was particularly attracted by the idea, pushing the matter vigorously at a late night meeting on 15 August with the English ambassador.[97] He signed, and probably helped draft, the letter to Elizabeth commending the match by stressing its benefits to all the islands of Britain, especially Ireland. Such arguments might have wooed Cecil, but held little appeal for his royal mistress. Both the matter, and the indiscreet manner in which the marriage proposal had been made, guaranteed Elizabeth would reject it. She waited until 8 December 1560 before sending a polite, but

[95] Cecil to Elizabeth, 19 June 1560, *CSPSc*, I. 426–7.   [96] 25 August 1560, *CSPSc*, I. 469.
[97] Argyll was the first of the Scottish earls to sign the marriage proposal, 16/18 August; he was reported to be very 'affectioned' to the matter, Randolph to Cecil, 19 August 1560, *CSPSc*, I. 465–7.

definite, refusal.[98] Although by then expected, it was a blow to Argyll and his fellow Anglophiles. Believing the 'amity' rested upon the secure foundations of a shared Protestant faith, they assumed that the diplomatic revolution of 1560, turning England from old enemy to new friend, was permanent.

BRITISH POLICY IN ULSTER

Immediately after his accession in November 1558, Argyll left his region to attend Parliament before having a chance to settle into his new role as clan chief and leader of the West Highlands. On his return, he found himself in the invidious position of having to ask for his clansmen's help to pay for the proposed French trip. The clan council agreed on 9 February 1559 to a tax of twenty shillings per markland to be paid by everyone dependent upon the earl. In return, Argyll agreed to tax his own property and free the signatories from their military service during the period of his absence.[99] Calling the council gave the new earl an opportunity to listen to the advice of the men who had run the Argyll heartland for his father and consult them about future policy. In particular, the council probably ratified the new reforming role planned for the Protestant minister, John Carswell, who took part in their deliberations.[100]

In the political hiatus that followed the inconclusive Scottish Parliament at the end of 1558, the 5th earl could give more attention to his regional commitments. At the start of 1559, Argyll attended carefully to local business. He travelled to Lochgoil in Cowal to bestow the office of its sergeant and a week later was in mid-Argyll giving sasine to his baillie in Ardskeodnish.[101] Such attention to detail was vital to maintain the loyalty of his dependents. In the troubled times of the following year his people turned instinctively to him.[102] The reformation crisis that exploded in May 1559 kept the 5th earl away from the Highlands for longer than he wished, providing a tempting opportunity for the regent to make trouble. Shortly after Argyll's 'desertion', in June Mary of Guise sought to detach the earl's ally, James MacDonald of Dunivaig, by selling him the wardship and marriage of the Highland heiress,

---

[98] *CSP For 1560–1*, 433–6; *CSPSc*, I. 495–6.   [99] AT, V. 104.

[100] Carswell signed the tax agreement and helped those unable to sign for themselves, AT, V. 104. He had been granted a series of charters, 1 February 1559 AT, V. 105; see above p. 88.

[101] At 2 p.m. on 16 February 1559, Argyll received the resignation of Dougal MacKellar of Glaslaid in favour of his kinsman, Duncan: AT, V. 103. On 22 February 1559, he was at Achachrone and then Roscalzie giving sasine to Duncan Campbell of Duntrune: AT, V. 104.

[102] A Cowal couple accepted Argyll's own authority, instead of a formal clerical dispensation, as sufficient warrant to proceed with their marriage within the forbidden degrees, 11 October 1559, *Liber officialis sancti Andree* ed. J.H. Forbes, Lord Medwyn (Abbotsford Club, 25, Edinburgh, 1845), 169–70; and see above, p. 48.

Mary MacLeod.[103] The ploy failed with the 5th earl and MacDonald coming to an arrangement concerning the wardship and sealing it with a bond.[104] The other major claimant to the MacLeod inheritance, Tormod MacLeod of Dunvegan, had given his bond to Argyll, who had recently ransomed him from French captivity.[105] With all the major clans in the Isles involved, the 5th earl had successfully prevented the disputed MacLeod inheritance from flaring up whilst he was fighting in the Lowlands.[106] At the end of August, he called a council of Islesmen to settle other outstanding matters and to persuade the chiefs to support the Congregation. Although redshanks were not suited to Lowland warfare, many Highlanders served with Argyll, including 700 men sent by James MacDonald.[107]

As early as the summer of 1559, the 5th earl was reviewing his options within a British idiom. He had probably discussed his proposal to help the English in Ulster with MacDonald during the summer and consulted his friend and ally, Calvagh O'Donnell. With his overlordship in Donegal being challenged by his brother Hugh, backed by Shane O'Neill of neighbouring Tyrone, Calvagh strengthened his existing alliance with the 5th earl. At the beginning of 1560, he married Katherine MacLean, the 4th earl's widow.[108] Though the dowager countess of Argyll was renowned for her beauty and education, her new husband was equally attracted by her dowry of redshanks, for which he was prepared to forgo his wife's Scottish lands.[109]

---

[103] 27 June 1559, *Coll. de Rebus Alban*, 141–3. A similar motive might have caused the granting of a royal charter to Hector MacLean of Coll, 28 June 1559, *RMS*, IV. 1352. Sadler and Croft reported to Cecil, 'the Regent by her policie, devised to stirre James McDonell and others of the Scottish Irishrie, against the Erle of Argyle, to the intent the said Erle might be so occupied at home in the defence of his country as he should have no tyme to attend this mater', 8 September 1559, *CSP For 1558–9*, 542 printed in *State Papers and Letters of Sir Ralph Sadler* ed. A. Clifford (2 vols. London, 1809), I. 430–1.

[104] In the bond the Argyll agreed to maintain MacDonald in the MacLeod wardship and MacDonald promised to resist an invasion of Frenchmen, Wormald, *Lords and Men*, 184–5. Probably mistakenly, it was dated 25 July 1560 (instead of 1559), by which time the fighting against the French had ended. A second bond, also dated 25 July 1560, exists in which Argyll agreed to renounce the bailliary of south Kintyre, AT, V. 147. MacDonald received the lands in Kintyre 24 September 1562, *RSS*, V, i. 1112, and the bailliary, 2 January 1564, *RMS*, IV. 1491. The originals of the bonds could not be located among the Argyll MSS.

[105] 1 or 14 March 1560, AT, V. 130, 137, 141; printed in *Coll. de Rebus Alban*, 91–2; Wormald, *Lords and Men*, 184. One account said that Argyll had also saved Tormod from assassination in Glasgow.

[106] For a full account of Mary MacLeod's inheritance, see I.F. Grant, *The MacLeods: The History of a Clan 1200–1956* (London, 1959), 97–131.

[107] For the 5th earl's arguments, 29 September 1559, Hamilton to regent, see above pp. 97–8. MacDonald's men, Sadler and Croft to Cecil, 25 October 1559, Sadler, II. 55–8.

[108] Katherine was married by 8 March, see below, n. 110; in his letter to Cecil, Maitland spoke of Katherine being lately married to O'Donnell, 10 April 1560, *CSPSc*, I. 353.

[109] MacLean-Bristol, *Warriors and Priests*, 178–9. Her judgement and abilities had made a considerable impression upon the English officials in Ireland who described her as 'very

Katherine and up to 2,000 Scottish soldiers arrived in Ireland around the end of February.[110] The 1555 treaty was renewed, with O'Donnell agreeing to pay Argyll a substantial tribute estimated at £100 sterling.[111] The 5th earl's bonds with MacDonald and O'Donnell gave him the right to uphold their interests in northern Ireland, thereby drawing him further into the complex politics of Ulster.

It was natural for Argyll to make the link between this section of his Gaelic political world and the Anglo-Scottish negotiations he had begun on behalf of the Congregation. Such a triangular approach flowed from the unity of his personal experience in all three worlds. Once his offer of assistance in Ulster had been made, Cecil seized it as the ideal way to sweeten the Treaty of Berwick. With his comprehensive knowledge of English policy for the entire Tudor state, the secretary grasped the potential of Argyll's assistance for the settlement of Ireland. He recognised it would entail a reversal of current Irish policy. In characteristic fashion, Cecil drew up a memorandum for the queen on the Ulster situation, including suggestions of how the 5th earl could be employed.[112] It formed part of an Irish policy review undertaken whilst the Lord Lieutenant was at court to receive new instructions.[113] With Sussex's main concern being the rise of Shane O'Neill's power in Tyrone, the alignment of his neighbours, O'Donnell in Donegal and the MacDonalds in Antrim, was of critical importance. Their support, or at least benevolent neutrality, was essential before any move could be made against Shane. Control over Ulster was assumed to be the key to the stability of the Irish kingdom.

Argyll's proposal offered a new approach to the three Ulster kindreds, the O'Neills, the O'Donnells and the MacDonalds. Although the Berwick treaty had referred to the 5th earl's military assistance, that was temporarily set aside. Cecil's memo listed areas in which Argyll could utilise his influence. The first was upon his fellow Scots. In 1558, Sorley Boy, James MacDonald's youngest brother, had become captain of the Route and resident leader of

sober, wyse and no lesse sottell, beyng not unlernyd in the Latyn tong, speckyth good French, and is sayd som lytell Italyone, (besydes that she is a natural Scote)', SP63/3, fo. 207r.

[110] Fitzwilliam to Sussex, 8 March 1560, SP63/2, fo. 17r.

[111] AT, V. 45, 47 where the treaty is dated 1560 but with the day and month left blank, which would suggest a date after 25 March, see above p. 21 for 1555 treaty. As well as the tribute, it was estimated that the countess' Scottish lands were also worth £100 sterling and that O'Donnell was unpopular among his own kinsmen because he had conceded too much to Argyll. Calvagh 'had neither estimacion, wealth, obedyence or love of his people and kynred but contrarywyse vilipended and hated amongs them, partly for that when he toke to wyfe the Conties of Argyle, he dyd gyve to therle of Argyle that now is, for his ayde and freindshippe one hundred pounds, sterling, yearlye by way of tribute, besides the remission of the said Countesses revenuewe in Scotlande': Cusake to Dudley, 9 June 1564, SP63/3 fo. 7v.

[112] 2 April 1560, NLS Adv. MS 33.1.1, I. No. 2.

[113] For an extended discussion of Sussex's viceroyalty, Brady, *Chief Governors*, ch. 3.

the Macdonalds within Antrim. He was negotiating with Sussex to reach a settlement officially recognising the MacDonald presence in Antrim.[114] Cecil noted that Argyll could ensure James maintained pressure upon his brother to make and honour an agreement. The 5th earl could also persuade O'Donnell to become a 'faithfull and true subject' to the English queen.[115]

Further developments had to await the successful completion of English intervention in Scotland and the return of Sussex to Ireland. After Cecil had negotiated the Treaty of Edinburgh in July 1560, he worked out the details of the Ulster plans with Argyll. The formal set of proposals which Argyll submitted on 19 July were far more ambitious than the tentative suggestions of the April memo, amounting to a military contract to hire the 5th earl's soldiers. Even to consider such a proposal was a remarkable volte-face for an English government, which three years before had legislated to expel all Scots from Ireland. Argyll's contract offered three options. In the first case the earl would lead a maximum of 3,000 'hieland men of weir' to fight O'Neill and other rebels. Once on Irish soil, the English would pay them, at a rate to be negotiated. The second possibility was that 1,200 men would be sent under the same arrangements except the earl would not accompany them. The final option was for 1,000 men to garrison forts within Ulster for as long as required.[116] Argyll was guaranteed safe havens and a castle on the Ulster coast to serve as a permanent place of safety and secure anchorage for his forces. He was permitted to collect the Gaelic military dues or *buannacht* previously uplifted by O'Neill and other rebels. In return he was promised 300 arquebusiers and large cannon, at the queen's expense, whenever he needed them in the Western Isles. The clause that Argyll's troops should keep the lands of obdurate Ulster rebels was deleted. The English queen and her government had accepted most of this revolutionary contract but they balked at the prospect of Campbells settling permanently in Ulster.[117]

The military agreement was accompanied by a memo with more detail than its April predecessor. It identified Shane O'Neill as the most powerful man in Ulster who was 'plane disobedient' to the queen. Unless Elizabeth recognised his claim to the earldom of Tyrone, he would have to be subdued by force. Accepting Shane's demands would undercut the policy of surrender and regrant within Ireland which had incorporated Gaelic chiefs into the English social and legal system. The titles of nobility granted by the English crown had been given on condition that the chiefs adopted the laws of feudal

[114] For example the offers of Sorley Boy with Cecil's notes, 9 May 1560, SP63/2 fos. 30r–31r; Hill, *Fire and Sword*, 53–5.
[115] The memo was sent to Scotland and received a favourable response from Argyll, Maitland to Cecil, 10 April 1560, *CSPSc*, I. 353.
[116] SP63/2 fo. 60v.   [117] SP63/2 fo. 58r–v.

inheritance, particularly male primogeniture. In the past, the English had declared Shane to be a bastard. Recognising him as earl of Tyrone at this juncture would reverse that decision and undermine the rules on which it was based. As the memo succinctly explained, the English queen could not put aside the 'linall discens of ye bluide' and endorse the 'auld custoum of the erishemen of Ireland that the eldest and maist active of the surname suld succeid'. It concluded that military measures against Shane were the only option.

The English hoped to use peaceful means to subdue the other Ulster chiefs. O'Donnell was classified as being neither a rebel nor fully obedient. It was noted that his brother Hugh was fighting both Calvagh and the English. However, with Argyll's persuasion it was assumed that both men, along with their dependents, the O'Boyles of western Donegal, would settle with the English government. Similarly, the 5th earl would pressurise the MacDonalds to finalise terms with the Lord Lieutenant or, if that failed, force them to comply. Once the main players had been brought to obedience, the lesser rebels would submit.[118]

Argyll's proposals offered a comprehensive scheme covering the north of Ireland from the west to east coasts. It formed part of an ambitious attempt to bring Ulster under English control and prevent it destabilising the rest of Ireland. The re-invigoration of Irish policy was expected to follow Sussex's return to the kingdom.[119] Cecil and Elizabeth were optimistic and wrote enthusiastically to Sussex about the 5th earl's plans and his willingness to co-operate.[120] The English queen wrote personally to Argyll thanking him for his 'peculiar good will' towards her.[121]

News of Argyll's offers reached Shane O'Neill, making him sufficiently alarmed to dispatch a special messenger. Writing in Gaelic to his fellow chief, O'Neill suggested an alliance, proudly asserting he was the best ally Argyll could find in Ireland. Shane offered generous terms to wed the earl's sister. He disarmingly explained that his present relationship with MacDonald's daughter or other women presented no impediment to his

---

[118] The lesser chiefs can probably be identified as Maguire, Magennis, MacMahon, O'Hanlon, O'Cahan, O'Donnell of the Bann, Savages and Turlough Luineach O'Neill: SP63/2 fo. 60r. For a map of the lordships, see T.W. Moody, F.X. Martin and F.J. Byrne, eds., *A New History of Ireland III* (Oxford, 1978), 2–3.

[119] Sussex returned in June 1560, instructions and 11 September report,*Calendar of the Carew Manuscripts Preserved in the Archiepiscopal Library at Lambeth 1515–1624* ed. J. Brewer et al. (6 vols., London, 1867–73), I. 291–6, 300–4; S.G. Ellis, *Ireland in the Age of the Tudors, 1447–1603* (London, 1998), 274–6.

[120] Elizabeth to Sussex (drafted by Cecil) which referred to previous letters, now lost, 15 August 1560, SP63/2 fo. 63r.

[121] 4 September 1560, *CSPSc*, I. 477 and *Letters to Argyll Family*, 4 (where the damaged copy is misdated 4 August).

proposed marriage.[122] Shane assumed that the 5th earl's grip over the Islesmen was sufficiently strong to guarantee safe passage through Mac-Donald territory for his messengers and that the earl could handle any repercussions from the rejection of MacDonald's daughter. Once allies, O'Neill boasted to Argyll, they would divide Ulster's wealth between them.

The 5th earl was not to be tempted by these generous offers. His involvement in Ulster was the key link in his British policy requiring co-operation with his English allies, so he was not interested in selling his friendship and military might to the highest bidder. O'Neill's messenger arrived in Edinburgh on 16 August, nearly a month after he set out. He had travelled most of the way by foot and had to pawn his saffron shirt to raise money. Argyll supplied fresh clothes and kept him in his household, drinking whisky and milk in the chimney nook, hoping his hospitality might bring the messenger 'to God or more civility'. The 5th earl rejected the marriage alliance out of hand because of 'the ungodlynes of the person, and the worthynes of hys syster'.[123] He delayed his reply to Shane to give time to consult with the English, writing straight to Cecil and enclosing O'Neill's letter with a Scots translation.[124] Informing Cecil that he had not heard from Sussex about the timing and details of his Irish expedition, he offered to resolve any queries by going in person to meet the Lord Lieutenant in Ireland.

The 5th earl, anxious to return to Argyll to prepare for his Irish campaign, left Edinburgh on 24 August. On his way, he made a sweep through the eastern and central Highlands sorting out potential problems. Having stopped at Perth to meet Atholl and Lord James to discuss Huntly's suspicious activities, he visited Colin Campbell of Glenorchy at Balloch castle.[125] Whilst there he wrote a letter to his agent in Moray, Hugh Rose of Kilravock, concerning a difficulty created in Nairn by his clansmen, Alexander Campbell of Fliens.[126] Back in Argyll he arbitrated the disputes between the MacLeods and MacLeans.[127] Such a clearing up of regional affairs was part of the preparations before a prolonged absence campaigning in Ulster. At the same time the earl reasserted his authority over Hector Mòr MacLean and his son Hector Og, the earl's brother-in-law. They gave Argyll their bond, agreeing

---

[122] This was probably Catherine the daughter of James MacDonald, see 22 January 1563 *CSPSc*, I. 678. Shane's marital affairs were complex: F. Macdonald, 'Ireland and Scotland: Historical Perspectives on the Gaelic Dimension, 1560–1760' (2 vols., University of Glasgow PhD thesis, 1994), I. 48.

[123] Randolph to Cecil, 25 August 1560, *CSPSc*, I. 469.

[124] 20 August 1560 *CSPSc*, I. 468; the translation of O'Neill's letter (later dated 19 July 1560): SP63/2 fo. 57r. The Gaelic original which was also sent to Cecil was probably returned as requested and has not survived.

[125] See below, p. 116.

[126] 5 September 1560, *Rose of Kilravock*, 230.

[127] 15 September 1560, AT, V. 147.

to repudiate the contract made that summer with James MacDonald and promising never again to enter a contract without Argyll's express permission.[128] The 5th earl was demonstrating that he would not tolerate his dependents taking an independent line. The offending contract, most probably concerned with supplying redshanks to Ulster, suggests he was tightening his control over the Irish mercenary trade. By the autumn of 1560, the 5th earl had a firm grip over the Western Highlands and Isles, and his region was ready to mount a military expedition to Ulster. It was an audacious programme following so soon after the end of the Wars of the Congregation. Since his accession, the 5th earl had led the Scottish Protestants to victory. Through his British policy, he had secured English intervention, thereby laying the foundations of the Anglo-Scottish amity. In partnership with Cecil, he was now contemplating bringing Ireland into the new unity within the islands of Britain.

---

[128] On this condition Argyll forgave their previous offence: 8 October 1560, AT, V. 148.

4

The collapse of amity: 1561–1565

In British politics, the period 1561–5 revolved around the return of Mary, Queen of Scots to rule her native land, with Shane O'Neill's rise providing a sub-theme. In Scotland, Mary's initial acceptance of the Protestant settlement and the Anglophile policies of Argyll, Moray and Maitland brought little upheaval to the country. Within the Gaelic world, Argyll served a hard political apprenticeship through the frustrations and disappointments of his dealings with the Dublin administration. During 1565, the situation in Ulster was transformed by O'Neill's crushing defeat of the MacDonalds, which threatened to remove the Scots from the north of Ireland altogether. It disrupted Gaelic politics on both sides of the North Channel destabilising Ireland and upsetting the British strategies. From the Anglo-Scottish viewpoint, Mary's return raised the question of her second marriage, the issue that dominated relations between the two mainland kingdoms. The Scottish queen's eventual choice of Darnley provoked the British crisis of the Chase-about Raid. It marked the turning point in the 5th earl's attitude towards amity with England, signalling the end of his British policy.

The contrast between Argyll's hopes in 1561 and his situation at the end of 1565 could not have been more stark. The prospects for peace and friendship with England were dazzling at the beginning of the decade. English intervention in the Wars of the Congregation had freed Scotland from French domination and opened the door for the reformation of the Scottish church. It appeared as if, under the guidance of the Lords of the Congregation, a Protestant realm could look forward to harmonious relations with its southern neighbour based upon a shared faith. In the distant future, after the 5th earl's contribution in Ulster had helped civilise and reform Ireland, that kingdom might join the united Protestant mainland. By December 1565 these hopes were dashed. The 5th earl found himself the sole remaining rebel defying the Scottish king and queen, and relations with England were so frosty that war seemed imminent. As a result, the resurgence of Roman Catholicism within Scotland appeared likely. In Argyll's jaundiced view, his English allies had deserted him and his fellow Protestants in their hour of need. To make matters worse, the MacDonalds and the O'Donnells, his Ulster dependants, were defeated and dispossessed, leaving Shane O'Neill triumphant. The three planks of his British policy, Protestantism, Anglo-Scottish amity, and co-operation in Ulster, had been smashed and Cecil seemed to have entirely abandoned an integrated strategy. Under the pressure of the events of 1565, the English secretary had jettisoned their joint British policy for the sake of Elizabeth's and England's security. Withdrawing inside his own political world, Cecil tried to sever the triangular interconnexions between England, Scotland and Ireland and keep apart the politics of the three countries.

MARY'S PERSONAL RULE

The summer of 1560 had witnessed the triumph of the Lords of the Congregation, bringing their leaders Argyll, Arran, Lord James and Maitland of Lethington to power. Protestantism had been officially adopted in the Reformation Parliament, and the new Kirk was taking the opportunity to establish itself throughout the country. It had been a young man's revolution, with Argyll, Arran and Lord James still in their early twenties, and they could contemplate an almost indefinite period of rule within Scotland. With Mary now queen of France, it was assumed she would remain in her adopted country for the rest of her life, only making an occasional visit to her northern kingdom. The French acceptance of the Treaty of Edinburgh and their preoccupation with domestic religious problems seemed to guarantee that, in the short term at least, Scotland would be left to its own devices.

All this changed on 5 December 1560 when Francis II unexpectedly died of an ear infection, aged seventeen. The news reached Scotland about a fortnight later, immediately putting in question the hold upon power of Argyll and his friends and the religious reforms they were implementing.[1] The 5th earl rushed back to Edinburgh from the Highlands, where he had been awaiting news from Ireland. Once it was known that Mary, Queen of Scots would be returning to Scotland, the Lords had to decide how to react. After considerable discussion, the Congregation sent Lord James to visit his half-sister and persuade her to accept the changes the past year had brought. They were aware that their opponents had sent diametrically opposed advice to the queen.[2] In addition to the official mission, Argyll dispatched a

---

[1] John Knox received the news from an informant in France and it was confirmed in a letter from Lord Grey of Wilton who was in Berwick, Knox, *History*, I. 351. James Sandilands, Lord St John, returned to Edinburgh from France on 19 December with additional confirmation.

[2] John Leslie was sent from the Catholic and conservative nobles in Scotland, especially the 4th earl of Huntly: M. Lynch, ed., *Mary Stewart: queen in Three Kingdoms* (Oxford, 1988), 54.

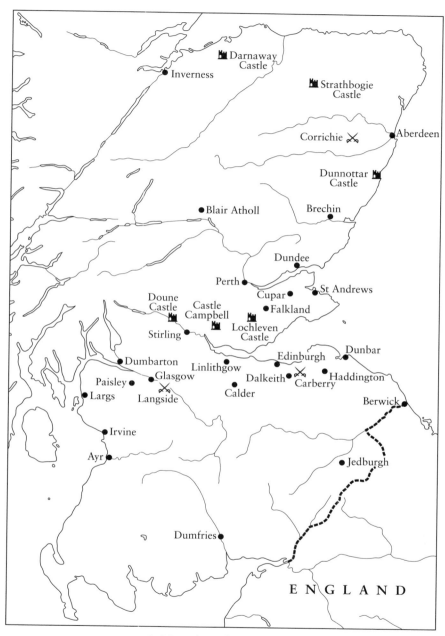

6. Map of Lowland Scotland

personal representative to the queen.[3] His younger brother Colin Campbell
of Boquhan joined Lord James' delegation armed with the 5th earl's letters and verbal messages. The earl sought to convince the queen that he
was her loyal subject, despite appearances during the Reformation crisis and
hostile reports.[4] In the final set of instructions for his brother, he assured
Mary that if anyone pressured her over her remarriage or anything else
'further then became subiectes to suit thair souverane', he would maintain
her 'just liberty' with his life and those of his dependents. This promise of
service extended to any case that 'may stand with the glorye of God, wele
of your hyenes realme and nautrall people thairof'.[5] Whatever or whoever
was meant, the 5th earl wanted to impress the queen with his loyalty and
devotion.[6]

Lord James personally presented his version of events to Mary, convincing
her to accept the status quo in Scotland. The queen returned to her kingdom in August 1561, arriving at Leith on the 19th, earlier than had been
expected. The 5th earl and other nobles, being caught in their regions, were
not present at the queen's initial welcome.[7] He arrived to be confirmed as one
of Mary's councillors on 6 September.[8] Although including Huntly and other
opponents, the composition of her council indicated that the young queen
intended keeping Argyll, Lord James and Maitland as her chief advisers and
continuing their Protestant and Anglophile policies.

These three remained at the heart of Mary's government until the Darnley
crisis of 1565. Drawing upon his extensive powerbase, the 5th earl gave the
triumvirate its political weight. Maitland possessed the best political and
diplomatic skills, but as a laird and career courtier his position rested upon

---

[3] He was not the only noble to feel that their involement with the Congregation necessitated
an extra declaration of obedience and service; William Murray of Tullibardine wrote directly
to the queen, 12 June 1561, BL Add. MS 19, 401 fo. 64.
[4] Argyll to Mary, Queen of Scots, 22 February 1561, BL Add. MS 19,401 fo. 56; copy with
marginal differences in Argyll MSS Bundle 62.
[5] After receiving the letter from the queen to her council, 12 January and 26 February 1561,
CSPSc, I. 506–7; 520, Argyll wrote a second letter on 8 March in which he could emphasise
that he had fulfilled the commands she had sent with the messenger, Robert Leslie, 8 and
10 March, Argyll MSS Bundle 62.
[6] The reference to Mary's remarriage probably alluded to the suggestion that the Scottish queen
wed the earl of Arran, who had so recently been rejected as a suitor by Elizabeth. The 5th earl
had been a firm supporter of his cousin's previous suit and might have felt it prudent to distance
himself from any hint of forcing Mary into the match. Arran's behaviour when Mary returned
and rejected the marriage grew increasingly strange, leading to his confinement in 1562 as a
madman.
[7] Contrary to Calderwood, *History*, II. 142, who placed the 5th earl, Lord James and Erskine at
Mary's arrival, Argyll was in Achallader on 24 August 1561, GD170/1/41; AT, V. 165. Huntly
was also caught unawares and rushed to court on a relay of sixteen post horses, Randolph
to Throckmorton, 26 August 1561, *CSPSc*, I. 548.
[8] *RPC*, I. 157.

his abilities, not his power. Although a royal bastard and raised to the peerage in 1562, Lord James lacked a strong regional network of dependents and was not a powerful noble in his own right. He was a good courtier but, according to Sir James Melville's critical assessment, not an adroit politician, being 'like an unskilful player in a tennis-court running after the ball; whereas an expert player would see and discern where the ball would light'.[9] Maitland and, to a lesser extent, Lord James oversaw the day-to-day running of affairs whilst the overall strategy for the triumvirate was probably the work of Argyll and Maitland.[10]

The queen's return raised the question of her personal religious stance. Since Francis' death, the issue had provoked hot debate among Scottish Protestants. When he saw her in France, Lord James had offered Mary a guarantee that she could practise her faith within her own household. The matter was tested on 24 August, the first Sunday after her return, when Mass was sung in the Queen's Chapel at Holyrood. A group of protesters attempting to storm the chapel were prevented by Lord James holding the door against them and smuggling the priest back to his room, much to the fury of John Knox.[11] The following day the queen issued a proclamation endorsing the religious situation she had found upon her arrival and calling for calm.[12] This uneasy compromise was the basis for Mary's religious policy until 1565. She accepted the existence of the new Kirk and gave it financial support.[13] In return, the queen retained her private Mass and her freedom to play the religious card in international diplomacy. Whatever his personal dislike of Roman Catholic worship, the 5th earl accepted this compromise and, unlike Arran, made no formal protest against the proclamation.[14] However, the agreement with Mary covered her private Mass and was not a licence for Roman Catholic services to continue when she was absent. Argyll and Lord James dramatically enforced this point on 14 September at Stirling Castle when, although Mary was not in residence, the Chapel Royal clergy started singing High Mass. The two nobles stopped the service, marching into the choir and beating the priests, some of whom left with 'broken heads and bloody ears'.[15] Despite such direct action, a split developed between the Protestant nobles at court, who reluctantly accepted the necessity of Mary's private Mass, and those who insisted no compromise with idolatry

[9] *The Memoirs of Sir James Melville of Halhill* ed. G. Donaldson (London, 1969), 27, 84–5. For a more positive view, see M. Lee, *James Stewart, Earl of Moray* (Westport, CT, 1953).
[10] For the other members of Mary's government, see Donaldson, *Queens' Men*, ch. 4.
[11] Knox, *History*, II. 8.   [12] 25 August 1561, *RPC*, I. 266.
[13] For the 'thirds of benefices' scheme, see *Accounts of the Collectors of Thirds of Benefices, 1561–1572* ed. G. Donaldson (SHS, 3rd ser. 42, Edinburgh, 1949).
[14] Knox, *History*, II. 10–11.
[15] Randolph to Cecil, 24 September 1561, BL Cotton Calig. B 10 fo. 184r; *CSPSc*, I. 555.

was possible.[16] One such precise Protestant was Argyll's kinsman, Robert
Campbell of Kinzeancleuch, who warned Lord Ochiltree not to fall under
the court's spell like the other nobles. Robert would have left his own chief
in no doubt about his disapproval of such conciliation.[17]

Mary's commitment to the personnel and policies of her Protestant and
Anglophile nobles was demonstrated in her treatment in 1562 of Huntly, the
pre-eminent Roman Catholic earl. It was her most decisive action to date,
setting the tone for her personal rule. The Gordons and the Campbells were
traditional regional rivals, competing for influence in the northern parts of
the Highlands. Although in the end giving his backing to the Congregation,
Huntly had retained his Roman Catholic faith. As early as September 1560,
Argyll and Lord James had been suspicious of his plans and made a bond
with Atholl against him.[18] Any immediate danger had been averted by the
queen's pointed rejection of Huntly's offer to receive her in Aberdeen on
her return to Scotland and bring her kingdom back to the Catholic fold by
force.[19] The earl's attempts to dissuade Mary from her Anglophile policy
were equally unsuccessful and, as a result, he stopped attending the council
in the spring of 1562.[20] Earlier that year, the queen had created Lord James
earl of Moray, but kept the grant secret. The earldom of Moray having been
in Gordon hands since 1549, Lord James' elevation was a blow to Huntly,
and it is not clear how, or if, the queen intended to compensate him. Publicly,
for his wedding to Annas Keith on 8 February, Lord James was made earl
of Mar.[21] Huntly's own behaviour did not endear him to Mary, and her
critical attitude was probably encouraged by Lord James and Argyll. For
both personal and political reasons they wanted Gordon power reduced.

---

[16] Despite the rift over tactics and his sharp letter of advice on marital matters, the 5th earl
remained on reasonable terms with Knox, even when Lord James and the preacher stopped
speaking to each other for eighteen months following their row at the end of May 1563:
Knox, *History*, II. 77–8.

[17] Dawson, 'Clan, Kin and Kirk', 224.

[18] The bond was made on 1 September but has not survived; 7 and 23 September 1560,
Randolph to Cecil, *CSPSc*, I. 478, 482; Lord James to Cecil, 4 September, *CSPSc*, I. 899.
Atholl was married to Elizabeth, Huntly's daughter. He had also remained a Roman Catholic,
so the bond was unlikely to have had a religious purpose. Atholl wrote to Argyll and Erskine
telling them that Huntly had made him offers he would find it difficult to resist, Randolph
to Throckmorton, 28 April 1561, BL Add. MS 35,830 fo. 84.

[19] Lynch, ed., *Mary Stewart*, 54. Lord James had later challenged Huntly's boast that at Mary's
command he could set up the Mass in three shires, 24 September 1561, *CSPSc*, I. 555.

[20] Huntly had been employed by the French to try to prevent the meeting between Mary and
Elizabeth, see below, p. 137. There is a gap in the council records between Huntly's last
attendance, 28 February, *RPC*, I. 204, and 19 May when the queens' meeting was approved,
RPC, I. 206, so it is not clear precisely when Huntly ceased to attend; Lynch, ed., *Mary
Stewart*, 59.

[21] *Diurnal*, 70–1; Randolph to Cecil, 12 February 1562, *CSPSc*, I. 603; Lee, *James Stewart*,
97–8.

The postponement of Mary's meeting with Elizabeth, which itself would have delighted Huntly, was the occasion of his downfall. The Scottish queen was now free to undertake the long-planned progress to the north-east. One of the aims of the progress was to demonstrate royal justice so, as justice-general, Argyll arranged a justice-ayre in Aberdeen at which Huntly's third son, Sir John Gordon of Deskford, twice failed to appear.[22] From the beginning of the progress Mary demonstrated her displeasure at the cavalier behaviour of the Gordons. On her journey north, she had pointedly refused to visit Huntly in his splendid castle at Strathbogie.[23] The earl was permitted to entertain Argyll and the English ambassador for two nights.[24] However, Randolph's reports that the Gordon chief was in a suitably obedient frame of mind were contradicted by Huntly's actions. On 30 August, he greeted Mary at Old Aberdeen with an excessive retinue of 1,500 men, not the hundred he had been permitted.[25] The following day the queen was incensed by Deskford's non-appearance before the law court. Ten days later came a grave insult, when the keeper of Inverness Castle refused to yield to the queen until he had the permission of Huntly's heir, Lord Gordon. Mary gathered local troops, took the castle the following day and hanged its captain. At this point she announced in public that her half-brother was the new earl of Moray.[26] Huntly hoped to ride out his disgrace by blaming his two sons. However, the failed attempt to attack or kidnap Mary as she crossed the River Spey belied his protestations of loyalty. Huntly's behaviour left him no sympathisers among the council, which set him an ultimatum. He was outlawed on 17 October and, when there was a call for troops, Argyll went to collect men from his own region. The battle of Corrichie, just outside Aberdeen, was fought sooner than planned, with the 5th earl failing to return in time. On 28 October, the Gordon chief was decisively defeated by Moray's royal army. He then suffered a stroke and died shortly after his capture.

The queen, who felt the rebellion was a threat to her person as well as her authority, wanted the Gordons severely punished. A number of those taken on the field were executed, including Deskford. His elder brother, Lord Gordon, was sentenced to death along with Sutherland, the other Gordon

---

[22] The court sat in Aberdeen from 27 August to 12 October 1562, *TA*, XI. 198, 207. Sir John had been summoned to the justice court on 31 August when he was ordered to ward in Stirling and again on 10 September when he was ordered to surrender the disputed land on pain of treason: *RPC*, I. 218–9.

[23] On 31 August Randolph still thought that her council would persuade Mary to change her mind, Randolph to Cecil, *CSPSc*, I. 649.

[24] Randolph mentioned this visit in his later letter, 18 September 1562, *CSPSc*, I. 651.

[25] *APS*, II. 572.

[26] 18 September 1562, Randolph to Cecil *CSPSc*, I. 651. Huntly sought in vain for compensation for the loss of Moray and assistance with the expenses of attending court: 24 and 30 September 1562, Randolph to Cecil, *CSPSc*, I. 652, 654–5.

earl, though both men were spared.[27] The 1563 Parliament witnessed the
legal conclusion to the rebellion. On 28 May, in a grisly scene enacted before
the queen, Huntly's embalmed body was propped on its feet to be accused,
stripped of his heraldic arms and, along with a dozen of his kinsmen, forfeited for treason.[28] Other Gordons were escheated and they did not receive
their remission until February 1567.[29] By Scottish standards, this was exceptionally harsh punishment and it hit the house of Huntly particularly hard.
Stripped of their dominating influence, there was a power vacuum in the
north-east and a re-alignment within the regional politics of the northern
Highlands. Royal authority in general and Parliament in particular had been
used to destroy the might of the Gordons. Such treatment was vividly recalled by other Scottish aristocrats in the aftermath of the Chase-about Raid
of 1565 when the fear of similar forfeitures provided an incentive to agree
to Riccio's murder.

Though provoked and made worse by his own arrogance and ineptitude,
Huntly's downfall fitted neatly into the political plans of Argyll and Moray.
It decisively shifted the balance of power within the council in their favour as
well as bringing substantial personal gains. The queen and her half-brother
emerged much stronger from the episode. Huntly's behaviour had made it
impossible to avoid a direct confrontation and Mary had been unanimously
supported by her council. For his part, Lord James had been careful to act in
his capacity as the queen's lieutenant and play down his major gains.[30] These
had massive potential, because his new earldom provided the opportunity to
fill the vacuum whilst the north-east was free from Gordon dominance. Curiously, the earl of Moray did not pursue this goal with much vigour, nor did
the queen try to impose direct royal control over the area. As a consequence,
the local network of Gordon dependants survived intact, awaiting the family's return to favour.[31] Though not an immediate beneficiary, the 5th earl
gained from the eclipse of Gordon power because, for several years, his main
rival for control of the north parts of the Highlands had been removed.

The Scottish queen gave further proof of implementing the pro-Protestant
policy of the triumvirate when the destruction of the greatest Roman Catholic
magnate in the kingdom was followed by the humbling of the Scottish
primate. Mary, enforcing her royal proclamation against public Roman
Catholic worship, proved that the clerical hierarchy were not exempt when

[27] During the rebellion Lord Gordon had remained with his father-in-law, the duke of
Châtelherault.
[28] *Diurnal*, 76; Randolph to Cecil, 3 June 1563, *CSPSc*, II. 10.
[29] 26 February 1567, *RSS*, V. ii, 3298.
[30] Moray was granted the escheat of the customs of the burghs of Elgin and Forres which
Huntly had just forfeited, 19 October, *RSS*, V. i, 1128.
[31] Lynch, ed., *Mary Stewart*, 64–5.

the archbishop of St Andrews and other bishops were charged with saying Mass and hearing auricular confession. Their trial on 19 May 1563 was presided over by the 5th earl. After the bishops' plea of clerical immunity had been discounted, a guilty verdict was inevitable, and Argyll sentenced the defendants to imprisonment.[32] When the clergy came before the bar of the court, the earl's staunchly Protestant client, Robert Norvell, mocked the archbishop by carrying before him a steel hammer in place of his processional cross.[33]

As a mark of the high regard and great trust in which she held the 5th earl, in the summer of 1563 the queen went on progress to the west, travelling into Argyll and staying at Inveraray.[34] In contrast to the rebellion encountered the previous year, this was a light-hearted journey. The idea of visiting the Highlands excited Mary. With her fondness for dressing up, she decided to adopt Highland attire, and Lady Agnes Campbell duly obliged by giving the queen a 'marvileus fayer' Highland costume. The prospect of donning a saffron shirt and plaid and travelling in the Highlands was too much for the English ambassador, who escaped by securing a temporary recall to England.[35] As well as allowing Mary great fun playing the Highland lady and enjoying the good hunting in Cowal, the progress performed its more serious side of transporting the queen and her government into the different parts of her realm. Mary was able to meet her subjects, granting them charters in person, as received by Ewir Campbell of Strachur when she stayed in his house in Cowal.[36]

In retrospect, this idyllic summer of 1563 marked the high point of Argyll's influence and favour. The following year brought a major readjustment of national politics with the return to Scotland of Matthew Stewart, 4th earl of Lennox. With the triumvirate's successes in 1562 and 1563, the other Scottish nobles were more willing to welcome back Lennox to offer a political counterweight. A bitter opponent of the Regent Arran and keen Anglophile during the Rough Wooing, the 4th earl and Margaret Douglas, his formidable wife, had remained in exile in England for twenty years. Lennox's suit to

[32] *Ancient Criminal Trials in Scotland* ed. R. Pitcairn (3 vols., Bannatyne Club, 42, Edinburgh, 1833), I. 427–30.

[33] Knox, *History*, II. 76. For Norvell see above p. 74.

[34] E. Furgol, 'The Scottish Itinerary of Mary, Queen of Scots, 1542–8, 1561–8', *PSAS*, 117 (1987), 219–31 and fiche C1–D6; T.A. Small, 'Queen Mary in the Counties of Dumbarton and Argyll', *SHR* 25 (1927), 13–19. A subsidiary purpose of the progress was an attempt to reconcile the earl and his wife, see above p. 28.

[35] Randolph to Cecil, 13 June 1563, *CSPSc*, II. 13. Wearing different dress as a symbol of moving from one culture to another was well known in Ireland where the Burkes, Gaelic chiefs and earls of Clanrickard changed their attire each time they crossed the River Shannon.

[36] At Dripps (Invernoaden) at the north end of Loch Eck, 27 and 30 July 1563, AT, VI. 16; *RMS*, IV. 1478–9.

return to Scotland had been pressed upon Mary by his Stewart relatives. It
also received support from Elizabeth and the English government. Despite
having been a favourite of Mary Tudor and maintaining her strong Roman
Catholic allegiance, the countess of Lennox retained a powerful position
within the Elizabethan court, which helped her to lobby constantly on her
husband's behalf. Knowing he was a firm advocate of the Anglo-Scottish
alliance, the English Privy Council either ignored or failed to appreciate the
effect his return would have upon their existing allies within Scotland. Mary,
Queen of Scots, agreed to the requests for Lennox's return, and the 4th earl
arrived in Scotland in September 1564.

The two families who had gained most from Lennox's exile were the
Hamiltons and the Campbells. With their main rival gone, the Hamiltons had
been able to dominate Glasgow and the west of Scotland. The long absence
of the Stewart earl had allowed the earls of Argyll to expand their influence into the Lennox, especially the area around Loch Lomond. Through
bonds of manrent, the 5th earl had taken over former Lennox clients, such
as the Buchanans, and he had no intention of relinquishing them.[37] Since
Mary's return, the Hamiltons had been gradually losing political influence.
The madness of Arran had cast a paralysing gloom over his father, the duke,
who was convinced that the rehabilitation of the Lennox Stewarts was a
plot to undermine his house. As soon as Lennox was back, the 5th earl
wrote to reassure his uncle, who was refusing to attend court to face his old
rival.[38] When the Privy Council formally agreed to the restoration, Argyll
had argued that consideration be given to those at odds with the Stewart
earl.[39] A conciliatory letter was sent to the duke seeking a compromise. In
addition, on 7 October, Argyll and Moray met privately with Morton at his
castle at Dalkeith to discuss the issue.[40] Lennox's restoration was formally
proclaimed in Edinburgh on 16 October, and in token of their personal reconciliation the 5th earl and Lennox rode side by side up the High Street.[41]
In the following settlement, Argyll agreed to relinquish his lands and offices
within the Lennox. However, the main loss fell upon the Hamiltons. After
three days of bitter wrangling and under pressure from his nephew, the duke
finally settled on 28 October. His capitulation marked a cessation of hostilities, not peace, between two deeply antagonistic kin-groups.[42] The final

[37] Argyll to Glenorchy, 11 March 1565, GD112/39/3/24.
[38] In a quick note in his own hand, 19 September 1564, NLS MS 73 fo. 12r; *Reg. Hon. de Mort*, I. 11.
[39] Anon. Scottish report, 28 September 1564, *CSPSc*, II. 77; there are no records of this meeting in *RPC*.
[40] Argyll to Glenorchy, 8 October 1564, *Campbell Letters*, 23.
[41] News from Scotland, 16 October 1564, *CSPSc*, II. 83.
[42] *RPC*, I. 290; Randolph to Cecil, 31 October and 3 November 1564, *CSPSc*, II. 90–1.

stage of the process took place in the December Parliament, when the legality of Lennox's banishment in 1545 by the Regent Arran (now the duke) was debated. As a gesture of solidarity with his uncle, the 5th earl absented himself, though he returned for the act detailing the land settlement, which ensured that the Lennox Stewarts recovered their regional powerbase in the west of Scotland, both north and south of the Clyde. The generous restoration of their lands, especially those in the Lennox, allowed the 4th earl to rebuild his affinity with great speed. On his return, the 4th earl had been welcomed back into the heart of Scottish politics where, resting upon his regional power, he could exert his traditional influence.

Most of the nobility, including the triumvirate, believed that the extremely sensitive episode of Lennox's return had been handled well. By gracefully relinquishing his previous gains, the 5th earl had made the best of a difficult situation. He probably assessed that the reduction of his influence on his southern borders, inevitable once Lennox's exile ended, was the price for stability within Scottish national politics and a necessary sacrifice for his British policy. In the winter of 1564, Lennox was a keen supporter of the preservation of amity with England and of the Protestant settlement and, by adding his weight, appeared to strengthen the triumvirate's policies. At the same time, Argyll would have had some reservations. He had seen his maternal kin forced to give up lucrative lands and offices with little compensation and, worse still, publicly humiliated. Though the duke had acquiesced under pressure, he was bitterly resentful of the Lennox Stewarts. His reversal of fortunes left him in a lethargic gloom, politically isolated from his fellow nobles. His self-aggrandisement as regent twenty years earlier had left little residual sympathy for his present plight.

What no one had foreseen in the winter of 1564–5 was the upheaval within Scottish politics brought about by the return of Lord Henry Darnley, Lennox's heir. Since coming home, Lennox had lobbied for his son to join him, presenting it as little more than a way of ensuring a smooth succession to his newly recovered lands. Queen Elizabeth gave her permission, and Darnley travelled to Scotland in February 1565.[43] Due to a series of changes in Anglo-Scottish relations, Darnley's presence in Scotland acquired an entirely different significance. Mary began to regard him as a serious suitor and by April had made up her mind to marry him. The prospect of the wedding of two major claimants to the English succession placed Anglo-Scottish relations under great strain.[44] When it was clear the match would not have Elizabeth's blessing, the Scottish queen abandoned her previous policy of

---

[43] Lynch, ed., *Mary Stewart*, 132–4. For a full discussion see S. Adams, 'The Release of Lord Darnley' in Lynch, ed., *Mary Stewart*, 123–53.
[44] See below, pp. 140–1.

amity. The marriage to Darnley also threatened the Protestant settlement, the second plank of that established policy associated with the triumvirate of Argyll, Moray and Maitland.

The sudden prospect of a Darnley marriage turned Scottish politics on its head. Within the space of a few weeks, the triumvirate's policies had been rejected and the political influence of Argyll and Moray had collapsed. In its place, a Lennox party at court materialised, created by Darnley's future elevation to royal estate, bringing with it the prospect of unrivalled access to the crown's patronage. Formed around the nucleus of Stewart kinsmen and former clients, the party attracted the enemies of the triumvirate. It posed a serious threat to the 5th earl, having many members with specific grievances against him, such as the Perthshire group led by the other Stewart earl, Atholl, and the Lennox kinsman, Ruthven, alongside the ambitious William Murray of Tullibardine, who in various ways had disliked the Campbell handling of the MacGregor feud. Even Argyll's brother-in-law Stewart of Doune was drawn into the new network.[45] The return from hiding in France of the staunchly anti-English earl of Bothwell and the partial restoration of George Gordon made 5th earl of Huntly in October 1565, brought Argyll's old enemies back into royal favour. Even Morton and Erskine, former friends and colleagues, were offered substantial concessions for their co-operation with Lennox.[46] As a career courtier, Maitland had little choice but to remain with his royal mistress and seek to change policy from within. With breathtaking speed, the Lennox party had left the 5th earl and Moray politically isolated.

The unnerving awareness of losing influence and control was present as early as March, when the 5th earl grumbled he could not conduct any business at court because of the succession of royal banquets.[47] Determined his dependants within the Lennox should not desert his service at this critical juncture, he made extra efforts to protect his affinity, exerting himself to keep the Buchanans contented.[48] Rumours were rife, speculating, even at

[45] Atholl, who was Argyll's rival in the Central Highlands, was reported to be always in Lennox's company, Randolph to Cecil, 24 October 1564, *CSPSc*, II. 85; Ruthven's first wife, Janet Douglas, had been the sister of the countess of Lennox and this connection ensured his support for Lennox and later for Darnley in the Riccio murder, see his apology, 30 April 1566, Keith, *History*, III. 260. He was critical of the 5th earl over his handling of the MacGregor feud which had caused such problems for Colin Campbell of Glenorchy, his brother-in-law: Ruthven to Grey Colin, 21 March 1565, *Campbell Letters*, 38. Murray and Stewart were two of those knighted at Darnley's elevation to the earldom of Ross in May 1565, Lynch, ed., *Mary Stewart*, 157–9, and had also suffered during the MacGregor feud, *Campbell Letters*, 49–52.
[46] Donaldson, *Queen's Men*, 74–5.   [47] 6 March 1565, GD112/39/3/22.
[48] Argyll to Glenorchy, 11 March 1565, GD112/39/3/24; Glenorchy's angry reply, 16 March 1565, *Campbell Letters*, 36.

this early stage, as to whether Darnley would wed the queen.[49] In this tense atmosphere, the 5th earl turned to two Roman Catholic earls in the south-west who were suffering from the rise of the Lennox Stewarts and were former Hamilton allies. He made a bond with Eglinton and was working for a marriage alliance with Cassilis. He also held a crisis meeting with Moray and the duke.[50] As well as undermining Hamilton regional power, a Darnley marriage would deprive the duke of his place in the Scottish succession. Never the most decisive of men, by the spring of 1565 he was so battered by his bad fortune that he was content to follow wherever his nephew led.

The dilemma facing Argyll and Moray was how to respond to the rise of Darnley and the Lennox party. Like all sixteenth-century politicians whose policies had been rejected and whose power and influence with the monarch had evaporated, few options remained. The matter was complicated by hav-ing to choose on which policy to fight, whether to rescue the English alliance or make their first concern the protection of the Kirk. They also needed to safeguard their powerbases. Argyll had to counter the regional threats posed by a resurgent Lennox affinity within Perthshire, Stirlingshire and the Lennox. The more vulnerable Moray had to retain the national influence from which his political power derived. Such diverse objectives called for conflicting tactics to be pursued. Throughout 1565, Argyll and Moray were fatally handicapped in their handling of affairs by their failure to decide their priorities.

During the late spring of 1565, the religious threat posed by the Darnley marriage received most attention. Busy in the Highlands with the MacGregor feud, Argyll was absent from court for most of April. When summoned, he came to Stirling and spoke to the queen about the Palm Sunday riot in Edinburgh, which had nearly killed a Roman Catholic priest.[51] Mary wanted to punish the capital and stamp out any signs of Protestant militancy. Argyll and the other Protestants were afraid the queen was using the incident to undermine the entire ecclesiastical settlement.[52] In this tense situation, the

---

[49] Randolph to Cecil, 17 March 1565, *CSPSc*, II, 136.

[50] The bond has not survived but Randolph wrote to Cecil 'My Lord Argile has taken into his defence in all his just actions the Earl of Montgomery, alias Eglintoun', and he outlined the moves to wed Cassilis to the duke's daughter or to the wealthy widow, Katherine Campbell, Countess of Crawfurd, and reported the meeting between the duke, Moray and Argyll, 20 March 1565, Keith, *History*, II. 272.

[51] Summons 21 April 1565, *TA*, XI. 361; Alexander Clerk to Randolph, 29 April 1565, *CSPSc*, II. 448. 'Randolph's Phantasy' suggested that the uproar was too great for Argyll to remain at court, *Satirical Poems of the Time of the Reformation* ed. J. Cranston (2 vols., Scottish Text Society, Old ser. 20 and 24, Edinburgh, 1891–93), I. 10, l. 178.

[52] M. Lynch, *Edinburgh and the Reformation* (Edinburgh, 1981), 107–10; J.E.A. Dawson, 'Mary, Queen of Scots, Lord Darnley and Anglo-Scottish Relations in 1565', *International History Review*, 8 (1986), 1–24 at p. 11.

earl of Bothwell's trial for treason at the start of May gave Argyll and Moray an excuse for a demonstration of Protestant strength in the capital. Bothwell and Moray were old antagonists and Argyll had never been on good terms with the earl.[53] As justice-general, the 5th earl presided at the trial, though Bothwell failed to appear, deciding to return to the safety of France.[54] On 1 May, around 6,000 men made a peaceful, if menacing, point to the queen, who was at Stirling. The gathering of leading Protestants was used to discuss the danger to the Kirk. Articles were drawn up for presentation to the queen demanding an end to every Mass, including her household devotions, the rigorous enforcement of the laws against Roman Catholic worship, and Protestant preaching without hindrance, such as the silencing of a preacher in Dunblane.[55] Mary, knowing that many prominent and committed Protestants, such as Ruthven, supported her and the Darnley marriage, was able to ignore such religious muscle-flexing. She countered the cry of 'religion in danger' by offering concessions without acceding to the articles.[56] The English ambassador had been impressed by the way in which the 5th earl above all others had defended religion and the safety of his house. However, in spite of his sincere belief that Protestantism was threatened, Argyll could not convince the majority of his co-religionists.[57] Whilst he agreed the Kirk was in danger, John Knox did not advocate armed resistance, preferring to employ the spiritual weapons of repentance and prayer. With many Protestants refusing to support a rebellion for religion in 1565, only a section of the 'party of revolution' of 1559–60 was mobilised in the Chase-about Raid.[58]

One reason for the lack of Protestant solidarity was the confusion over the main objective. The early May negotiations had offered religious guarantees in return for accepting the marriage, but Moray refused to sign the agreement because it would destroy the English alliance.[59] With some justification, fellow Protestants accused Argyll and Moray of sacrificing the Kirk's best interests for the sake of amity with England. The two earls realised that, if

[53] Moray wrote to his dependants urging them to attend, for example the laird of Tulliallan, 12 April 1565, GD15/829.

[54] Randolph reported that Mary had refused to allow a full condemnation, 3 May 1565, CSPSc, II. 153.

[55] Knox, History, II. 144. A week later, after Moray had taken these articles to court, a false rumour circulated in Edinburgh that Mary had accepted them, which provoked rejoicing until the truth was known, 11 May 1565, CSPSc, II. 158. The articles were later incorporated into the supplication made to the queen from the General Assembly in June 1565, BUK, I. 59–60; Knox, History, II. 148–53.

[56] She summoned the superintendents of Fife, Lothian and Angus promising to continue supporting the Kirk and agreeing to listen to Erskine of Dun preaching, Knox, History, II. 147. She also issued a proclamation giving further assurances to the Kirk, 12 July 1565, CSPSc, II. 182.

[57] Randolph to Cecil, 21 May 1565, SP52/10fo. 133v.

[58] Donaldson, Queen's Men, ch. 4.

[59] Knox, History, II. 145; Randolph to Cecil, 8 May 1565, CSPSc, II. 155–6.

English friendship were to be preserved, the marriage itself must be stopped. However, this was a high-risk strategy because the queen was publicly committed to the match, on 15 May creating Darnley earl of Ross, a prelude to the title, reserved for Scottish royalty, of duke of Albany on 20 July. The situation was critical by the time Argyll was finally able to leave his region at the end of June.[60] He met Moray and Robert, 5th Lord Boyd, at Sir William Douglas' castle at Lochleven to discuss tactics.[61] The queen had neatly outmanoeuvred their previous strategy of demanding religious concessions. Their only option appeared to be the capture of the bridegroom, and a plot to kidnap Darnley and deposit him over the border in England was probably hatched at Lochleven.[62] On hearing rumours of plots and assuming she was personally in danger, the queen decided to complete the marriage as soon as possible. Henry was proclaimed king and, without waiting for the requested papal dispensation, the wedding was celebrated at the end of July. As a public snub to Argyll, two days after her marriage Mary granted Atholl the revenues of Coupar Angus abbey, previously held by the 5th earl.[63]

The die had been cast. Argyll and Moray had been manoeuvred into rebellion, and from this point the 5th earl ran his own military campaign, primarily directed against Atholl, one of Lennox's chief allies.[64] Argyll's men made raids into the Atholl heartland and the Strathearn lands of some supporters. In view of the serious situation, the 5th earl had pushed Glenorchy into a settlement with the MacGregors.[65] By freeing himself from the MacGregor feud and adding their men to his fighting force, Argyll inflicted serious damage upon Atholl and the Lennox.[66] At the same time, his regional standing was sufficient to negate the queen's attempt to bribe Highland clans to fight against the Campbells. Despite proclamations sent throughout the region, few men mustered to support Atholl, the queen's lieutenant.[67] The royal forces attempted a pincer movement against Argyll with Atholl driving across

---

[60] To complicate matters the 5th earl, in the middle of a campaign against the MacGregors, had just heard the news from Ireland of James MacDonald's crushing defeat by Shane O'Neill, 11 May 1565, GD112/39/4/6; see below, p. 135.

[61] Argyll and Moray to Randolph, 1 July 1565, BL Cotton Calig. B 9 fo. 245; printed in *Illustrations of the Reign of Queen Mary*, 118.

[62] There were a variety of allegations of plots and counter-plots to kill or kidnap the various principals, 17 July 1565, *RPC*, I. 340; Donaldson, *Queen's Men*, 71.

[63] 31 July *RSS*, V. i, 2229, 2284.

[64] In early July there had been an attempt to stop the fighting in the Central Highlands, Glenorchy to Argyll, 9 July 1565, *Campbell Letters*, 43; Randolph to Cecil, 7 July 1565, *CSPSc*, II. 179.

[65] *Campbell Letters*, 41–9.

[66] Argyll to Glenorchy, 7 September GD112/39/4/21; Knox, *History*, II. 154; Randolph to Cecil, 9 and 19–20 September 1565, *CSPSc*, II. 205, 210.

[67] *RPC*, I. 355–9; *TA*, XI. 402–3; D. Gregory, *History of the Western Highlands and Isles of Scotland* (London, 1881), 202; Ranald Og MacDonald of Keppoch to Glenorchy, c. 26 September 1565, *Campbell Letters*, 52.

Perthshire whilst Lennox sailed up the Clyde into Cowal.[68] The 5th earl seized the initiative by attacking in the north and east, and Lennox's southern attack collapsed.[69] In military terms, the 5th earl was safe within Argyll, for not even a royal summons could be delivered there.[70] The one prize the queen secured was Castle Campbell in Clackmananshire, which the earl did not defend. It was handed over to Countess Jane who had remained in the queen's household throughout her estranged husband's rebellion.[71]

Beyond the Highlands, Argyll could not mount an offensive against the queen's forces until the other lords were ready. There had been a muted response to their claim that the Kirk was in danger and tyranny threatened.[72] With few joining the rebels' cause, Mary moved swiftly against Moray's base in Fife and then the south-west where the rebel lords had gathered. In the aptly named Chase-about Raid, the queen, sporting a steel cap and riding with a pistol in her saddle holster, drove the rebels before her. Having waited in vain for military help from Elizabeth I, by mid-October the rebel lords could delay no longer and crossed the Border into exile.

The 5th earl was left in Argyll, expecting the queen's forces to be massed against him. Nothing happened; having chased the other lords into England, Mary was content to seal the 5th earl within his region.[73] Argyll's military contest with the crown ended in stalemate. He had repelled the royal forces and inflicted heavy damage upon the queen's supporters, but could not prevent his friends and allies being driven into exile. As late as November he still hoped that English aid could be sent to him in his secure Argyll base.[74] The rebellion had been a disaster for the lords and the policies that had been pursued since Mary's return in 1561.

THE FAILURE OF BRITISH POLICY IN ULSTER

In 1560, through the Treaties of Berwick and Edinburgh, the triangular British connection linking the Anglo-Scottish alliance to Argyll's intervention in Ulster had been firmly established. From that date the 5th earl regarded

---

[68] Argyll to Glenorchy, 17 September 1565, GD112/39/4/24.

[69] Lennox had commanded the sheriffs in the west to disarm the rebels and ordered troops to gather near Dumbarton to prevent Argyll coming towards Glasgow. He later tried to assemble boats to attack Cowal, 20 September and 15 October 1565, W. Fraser, *The Lennox* (2 vols., Edinburgh, 1874), II. 264–6.

[70] Johnie Brand, the messenger who carried the summons, spent 156 days in prison in Innischonnell: *TA*, XI. lxxvi, 495; J.E.A. Dawson, 'The Fifth Earl of Argyll, Gaelic Lordship and Political Power in Sixteenth-Century Scotland', *SHR*, 67 (1988), 1–27 at p. 1.

[71] Escheat, 12 February 1566, *RSS*, V. ii, 2620; *TA*, XII. 133–4.

[72] Proclamations, 1 September, *CSPSc*, II. 200–1; general letter, 12 September 1565, *Campbell Letters*, 50.

[73] By stopping supplies, 3 November, *RPC*, I. 388–9.   [74] See below, pp. 141–2.

Ireland as the main arena in which he could contribute towards the amity with England and the eventual goal of a united Protestant British Isles. The 5th earl had worked out his plan with Cecil who, as Elizabeth's chief adviser, oversaw the policies for the entire Tudor state. He also remained in contact on Irish affairs with Thomas Randolph, the English ambassador in Edinburgh, who was equally supportive of the British policy. However, the kingdom of Ireland presented a major problem in governance within the queen's domains. Power, policy formation and its implementation were split uneasily between London and Dublin. Unwittingly, Argyll found his Irish initiatives subject to the convoluted political manoeuvrings that created English policy in Ireland. The 5th earl, having formed the alliance with his friend Cecil, from 1560 found he had to deal with Thomas Radcliffe, 3rd earl of Sussex, the Lord Lieutenant, who viewed him with hostility as a foreigner and a potential rival for Irish glory. What Argyll had thought was a simple triangular arrangement turned out to be a square, with Dublin vigorously fighting its own corner.

During the next four years, the 5th earl became increasingly frustrated as he met with covert opposition and direct obstruction from the English administration in Ireland. On several occasions having thought he had succeeded, Argyll discovered he had not after all brokered an agreement ensuring English acceptance of the MacDonald colony in Antrim. Similarly, although securing O'Donnell's co-operation with their plans, the English gave little help to the Donegal chief when he was captured by Shane O'Neill. Despite his own military preparations and readiness, Argyll was never asked to join the English campaigns against O'Neill. Instead, he watched the Ulster chief's power increase, especially after the crushing defeats of the O'Donnells and MacDonalds. The battle of Glentaisie in 1565 destabilised the Gaelic world on both sides of the North Channel. By then, Argyll's pursuit of a policy of co-operation with the English in Ulster had brought ruin to his Irish dependants and frustration and disappointment for himself. The immediate consequence of English failure to pursue his British policy was the harm it did within his Gaelic political world and his own affinity. It was little surprise that, in the winter of 1565 and after the fiasco of the Chase-about raid, the 5th earl rejected his former British policy in Ulster.

At the end of August 1560, the 5th earl had been eager to mount his expedition to Ulster to complete the implementation of the joint British policy. He returned to his region, gathered his men and waited for precise instructions from the earl of Sussex in Ireland.[75] Having had no news, he wrote a puzzled letter to Randolph a month later asking him to inform Cecil, who believed

---

[75] Argyll to Cecil, 20 August 1560, *CSPSc*, I. 468 and see above, pp. 109–10.

the Lord Lieutenant had already been in contact.[76] By November, Argyll, upset by Sussex's silence, complained he had been ready for over six weeks: 'I marvell verie myche I here not from hym consideringe bothe the necessitie of the cawse and also that lyke oportunitie wyll not serve of longe tyme.'[77] An embarrassed Randolph did not know how to excuse Sussex's behaviour, which was verging on the insulting.[78] As both he and Maitland told Cecil, Argyll had kept his promise whilst the Lord Lieutenant had broken the bargain. With English credibility in Scotland undermined by Sussex's failure to communicate, the ambassador implored Cecil, 'wolde God he [Argyll] myght receave some suche worde, that he myght be assured what he might do being so well wyllinge to set furthe all the Quenes Majestie's godlie purposes to the uttermoste of hys power'.[79] The English secretary appreciated that an important opportunity was slipping by in Ulster and Anglo-Scottish friendship was being damaged. Annoyed by Sussex's cavalier behaviour, Cecil administered a stiff rebuke in the summer of 1561.[80] Whilst he had integrated the British dimension to his strategic thinking, Cecil found implementing a British policy in Ireland a difficult task.

Sussex was not a convert to the British idiom, seeing the Ulster situation exclusively in Irish terms, without regard for Scottish consequences. The troublesome province of Ulster was a domestic problem of the kingdom of Ireland to be solved by its own governors. An unwilling partner from the outset, he did not want to share the glory of defeating O'Neill, especially not with a Scottish Highlander. Like many other English officials in Ireland, Sussex was reluctant to revise his hostile attitude towards the Gaelic Scots.[81] He did not want Argyll and his redshanks in Ulster and would have preferred the total expulsion of the MacDonalds from the north of Ireland. In his view, English interests were best served by keeping Scottish and Irish Gaels as far apart as possible. Such attitudes made Sussex unwilling to pay the price of Argyll's assistance in Ulster, which was the acceptance of the MacDonald

---

[76] 30 September 1560, SP52/5 fo. 89; and reference to a missing letter from Argyll to Randolph, 3 October 1560, *CSPSc*, I. 487.

[77] 7 November 1560, SP52/5 fo. 113; *CSPSc*, I. 492.

[78] 15 November 1560, *CSPSc*, I. 491–2.

[79] Maitland and Randolph to Cecil, 6 February 1561, SP52/6 fo. 35v; *CSPSc*, I. 510; 513–4.

[80] 'The erle of Argile hath remayned in redyness all this yere to herken whan yow wold send to hym for ayde. And as I perceyve he imagyneth that your Lordship alloweth not his offer of friendshipp. It wer well doone that he shuld not conceyve mistrust', 21 August 1561, BL Cotton Titus B 13 fo. 54v. I am grateful to Dr Alford for this reference, also see, Alford, *Cecil*, 87.

[81] For example 'The opinion of the earl of Sussex', 11 September 1560, *Calendar of the Carew Manuscripts Preserved in the Archiepiscopal Library at Lambeth 1515–1624* ed. J. Brewer et al. (6 vols., London, 1867–73), I. 302. For the intricacies of Irish policy making in this period, see C. Brady, *Shane O'Neill* (Dundalk, 1996), 37, 45–7; Brady, *Chief Governors*, ch. 3.

settlements and support for O'Donnell in Donegal. However, with few troops under his command and a tight budget, he had initially acquiesced to the scheme. The delay in receiving royal authorisation was a godsend, allowing him to abandon a campaign against O'Neill for the 1560 season. By not communicating with him at all, Sussex, in a graceless and provocative manner, avoided having to summon the 5th earl's military assistance.

Sussex's one grudging concession to the Argyll-Cecil scheme was to reopen negotiations with the MacDonalds. In the spring of 1561, the main issue to be resolved was the nationality and allegiance of the MacDonalds, who were subjects of the Scottish crown and foreigners in Ireland.[82] In English eyes, they ought to become subjects of Queen Elizabeth, accept English laws and customs and, crucially, obey English orders about relations with their neighbours. In return the MacDonalds sought a formally recognised title to the land they had gained through the Bisset inheritance in the previous century and the much larger tract of territory they had subsequently conquered and colonised in the Route and Glynnes of Antrim. If it secured his position as captain of the Route and leader of the MacDonalds in Ireland, Sorley Boy would become an English subject. As a consequence, the MacDonald brothers were prepared to formalise the separation of their Irish and Scottish territories. After the negotiations, William Hutchison, one of Sussex's gentlemen, sent to finalise the settlement went first to see Argyll, then to James MacDonald, and finally to Calvagh O'Donnell.[83] His mission included checking upon the British strategy in Ulster, ensuring Argyll, MacDonald and O'Donnell would co-ordinate their actions with the English attack upon O'Neill planned for summer 1561.[84] At this point Argyll's disappointment of the autumn of 1560 looked like a temporary setback. His Irish initiative seemed close to realisation, fulfilling the joint plans he had crafted with Cecil and vindicating the British dimension of their policy making.

Negotiations with Calvagh O'Donnell, Argyll's other dependent in Ulster, were moving well. He was to be granted the title of earl of Tyrconnell in a surrender and regrant agreement. In the forthcoming military campaign, O'Donnell was scheduled to attack Shane from the west. But O'Neill struck first, capturing O'Donnell and his wife Katherine and overrunning Donegal. Rumours that the former countess of Argyll had betrayed her husband

[82] Indenture between Queen Elizabeth and James MacDonald, 21 January 1561, SP63/3 fo. 9; *HMC Salisbury*, 13, 57; memos on Ireland, 13 March 1561, SP63/3 fos. 78 and 80.
[83] Sussex's letter was mentioned in Hutchison's instructions but has not survived, 27 April 1561, SP63/3 fos. 161r–2r and 163; Cecil's letter was dated 2 April but was sent on 27 April with Hutchison, SP63/3 fo. 138.
[84] Instructions to Sussex on his return to Ireland, 24 May 1561, SP63/3 fos. 192r–6v. It was rumoured that MacDonald had prepared 3,000 troops for action before Hutchison went to Scotland: Fitzwilliam to Cecil, 30 May 1561, SP63/3 fo. 207v.

seemed to be substantiated when she became Shane's mistress and bore him several sons.[85] Resentment in Donegal over Calvagh's marriage and his payment of tribute to the 5th earl help to explain why Katherine was blamed for the couple's capture. In Scotland, a different story circulated, that O'Neill was keeping the pregnant Katherine chained.[86]

Argyll was anxious to assist his dependant O'Donnell and Katherine, his former stepmother. However, Calvagh's son Con, who had taken control in Donegal, did not request help, which increased the difficulties of mounting a rescue attempt. Argyll assumed the English were best placed to negotiate their release as part of a wider settlement with Shane, especially after Sussex's disastrous Ulster campaign.[87] O'Neill's celebrated visit to London in January 1562 provided an ideal opportunity to secure O'Donnell's release.[88] The 5th earl wrote to Cecil and sent messages via Randolph, urging it be included in O'Neill's settlement.[89] When the English did nothing for Calvagh and Katherine, Argyll lost patience and opened negotiations with Shane. During his English visit, O'Neill had sent his compliments to Argyll.[90] Taking this cue, the 5th earl organized a coalition between Katherine's MacLean kinsmen and James MacDonald, offering Shane £300 sterling and 400 men for the release of Katherine and O'Donnell.[91] The parties agreed and Calvagh was subsequently freed, though Katherine chose to remain with O'Neill, eventually marrying him in the summer of 1565.[92] Argyll's efforts as a 'good lord'

---

[85] Fitzwilliam to Cecil and to Sussex, 30 May 1561, SP63/3 fo. 207r, 209r; Hayes-McCoy, *Scots Mercenary Forces*, 150–2, 194–6, 199–202, 238, 377. Katherine had been unhappy and had been expected back in Scotland to see the 5th earl at the end of 1560, less than a year after her marriage with Calvagh: Randolph to Cecil, 23 December 1560, *CSPSc*, I. 499.

[86] Randolph to Cecil, 24 December 1564, *CSPSc*, II. 110. For Calvagh's tribute, see pp. 105–6.

[87] It had provoked Cecil's sharp comment to Sussex 'for God sake my good Lord bestyrr yow and recover this mishapp as yow maye', 21 August 1561, BL Cotton Titus B 13 fo. 54r; I owe this reference to Dr Alford.

[88] J. Hogan, 'Shane O'Neill Comes to the Court of Elizabeth' in S. Pender, ed., *Essays and Studies Presented to Professor Tadhg Ua Domnachadha (Torna)* (Cork, 1947), 154–70; C. Brady, 'Shane O'Neill Departs from the Court of Elizabeth: Irish, English and Scottish Perspectives and the Paralysis of Policy, July 1559 to April 1562' in S.J. Connelly, ed., *Kingdoms United?: Great Britain and Ireland since 1500* (Dublin, 1999), 13–28.

[89] 12 February 1562, SP52/7 fo. 33; *CSPSc*, I. 603–4; Randolph to Cecil, 31 March, 7 April and 26 May 1562, *CSPSc*, I. 612, 615, 626.

[90] 31 March 1562, *CSPSc*, I. 612.

[91] Sussex to queen, 29 September 1562, SP63/7 fo. 61v; Hill, *Fire and Sword*, 68.

[92] Fitzwilliam to Cecil, 23 August 1565, SP63/14 fo. 164v; Randolph to Cecil 4 September and 13 October 1565, *CSPSc*, II 213, 223. Hector Mòr MacLean of Duart (Katherine's father), his son, Hector Og, and other Hebridean chiefs went to Ireland for the marriage. They returned at the end of October or start of November, Argyll to Glenorchy, 17 October 1565, GD112/39/5/3; Campbell of Carrick [Gossip] to Glenorchy, c. 11–16 November 1565, *Campbell Letters*, 65. The marriage did not last because O'Neill had 'put away Odonnells wief' by April 1566 in search of a more advantageous match, Sidney to Privy Council, SP63/17 fo. 31v; see below, p. 157.

to O'Donnell and Katherine had produced a satisfactory solution, though not perhaps the one he would have chosen. By contrast, the English had displayed little consideration for their new allies.

Although they had co-operated over Katherine's ransom, the MacLeans and the MacDonalds had a long-running feud over lands on Islay in the southern Hebrides. At the start of 1562, when James MacDonald and Hector Mòr MacLean of Duart fell out over a man's murder, Argyll called a Highland council, but he could not engineer a full reconciliation between the two chiefs.[93] The feud re-ignited eight months later when MacDonald received a royal grant of Islay lands including areas of the Rhinns in the north of the island where MacLean had been acting as baillie.[94] Raiding and counter-raiding began and the wider kindreds became involved when the northern branch of Clan Donald, led by Donald Gormeson MacDonald of Sleat, attacked lands in Mull, Tiree and Coll, irrespective of which MacLean branch held them.[95]

Despite exhortations, accompanied by the distribution of favours, the 5th earl could not bring the protagonists together.[96] The feud ran so deep that, at the wedding of Argyll's sister at Castle Campbell in January 1563, James MacDonald would not attend because the MacLeans would be present.[97] By the end of that year, the 5th earl sought to end the Islay feud by using the Privy Council's legal powers.[98] On New Year's Day 1565, both chiefs were commanded to remain in Edinburgh to hear a final judgement.[99] In that settlement, Argyll stood caution for both his dependants, MacDonald

---

[93] Randolph to Cecil, 15 January; Willock to Randolph, 30 January 1562, *CSPSc*, I. 593, 598–9.

[94] 24 September 1562, *RPC*, V. i, 1112; MacLean-Bristol, *Warriors and Priests*, 147.

[95] Remission for the raid, 7 December 1562, *RSS*, V. i, 1160; N. MacLean-Bristol, *Murder under Trust: The Crimes and Death of Sir Lachlan Mor Maclean of Duart, 1558–1598* (East Linton, 1999), 46–53.

[96] The favours to MacDonald included Argyll's resignation of the baillary of south Kintyre and securing its regrant for MacDonald, 2 January 1563, *RMS*, IV. 1491; assistance in the Privy Council concerning the agreement over Uist lands between MacDonald's dependants James and Farquhar MacAlistair of Sceirhow: 13 July 1563, *RPC*, I. 242; *RMS*, IV. 1474; AT, VI. 7; and the Argyll's licence to MacDonald to sell lands in Ardnamurchan held in ward from Argyll: 16 January 1564 or 1565, AT, VI. 28.

[97] Randolph to Cecil, 22 January 1563, *CSPSc*, I. 678.

[98] 14 December 1563 and 20 April 1564, *RPC*, I. 251, 272. In the winter of 1564–5 Argyll employed the Privy Council to settle other feuds among his network of clients including the internal divisions within the MacLeans, between Duart and Coll; a similar split within Clan Cameron; the disputes between Campbell of Glenorchy and Menzies of Weem; and the raiding of MacDonald of Keppoch, *RPC*, I. 291–4, 302, 311, 314, 322.

[99] *RPC*, I. 311. MacDonald was in the capital with Argyll discussing Irish matters, Randolph to Cecil, 24 December 1564, *CSPSc*, II. 110. He and his wife Lady Agnes received a royal charter for lands in Rathlin and Kintyre, 1 and 23 December 1564, *RSS*, V. i, 1840, 1879, and James had agreed to compensate some Ayr merchants for stealing from their ships, 21 December 1564, *RPC*, I. 306.

on a £10,000 surety and MacLean's second son, John, as a pledge of good behaviour.[100] The 5th earl maintained the truce in Islay for the rest of his life, though warfare returned in the final quarter of the century.[101]

An important safety valve and external outlet for these clans' martial instincts was available in the Irish mercenary trade. Because the two kindreds provided the majority of the redshanks, the MacDonald–MacLean feud had a direct effect upon Ulster politics. By preventing enough troops from aiding him during the 1564 summer season, it undermined Sorley Boy's position in Antrim, making him seek new sources of supply. Without his brother James' knowledge, Sorley hired Gregor MacGregor of Glenstrae and his clansmen for a season. The MacGregors saw military service in Ireland as a way out of an impossible situation. They were at feud with the Campbells, especially the Glenorchy branch of the clan.[102] Argyll, who was co-ordinating the Campbell effort, employed the Privy Council's authority to legalise Campbell actions, thereby driving the MacGregors to desperation, instead of a settlement.[103] Though he had dropped hints to the MacGregors about leaving the country, the 5th earl was not privy to the mercenary contract.[104] When James MacDonald heard the MacGregors had been hired, he quickly apologised to Glenorchy.[105] At the end of their contract, he blocked their access to MacDonald transport which, with other Scottish ships also denied them, forced the MacGregors to use the English base at Carrickfergus.[106] A bedraggled and impoverished group of MacGregors, having landed in Carrick and been refused entry into the burgh of Ayr, finally found their way home.[107] Although chastened by his Irish experience, the MacGregor chief was unable to negotiate the end of the Campbell feud which dragged on until the summer of 1565.[108] The MacGregors' season in Ulster demonstrated the

---

[100] 13 January and 13 March 1565, *RPC*, I. 314, 322.

[101] See below pp. 159, 205–7; for a full discussion see MacLean-Bristol, *Murder under trust*; W. D. Lamont, *The Early History of Islay* (Dundee, 1970; reprint of 1966 edn), 43–50. For trouble in Gigha, see below, p. 159.

[102] See MacGregor, 'MacGregors', and *Campbell Letters*, 55–9.

[103] He had obtained commissions of fire and sword against the MacGregors, *RPC*, I. 248–50, 256–8; Argyll to Glenorchy and reply, 1 and 4 October 1563, *Campbell Letters*, 11 and 12.

[104] Gregor MacGregor told Glenorchy that he left Scotland at Argyll's command believing that it would help settle the feud, c. 25 November 1564, *Campbell Letters*, 25.

[105] 6 June 1564, *Campbell Letters*, 20.

[106] Lady Agnes, MacDonald's wife, made sure Glenorchy was warned when the MacGregors left Ireland, 11 September 1564, *Campbell Letters*, 22. The Scottish Privy Council had issued a command preventing boats from the west coast from transporting the MacGregors, 13–21 August 1564, GD112/1/150–1; printed in Fraser, *Lennox*, II. 427–8; MacGregor, 'MacGregors', 335–6.

[107] Argyll to Glenorchy, 8 October 1564, *Campbell Letters*, 23; Randolph to Cecil, 24 October 1564, *CSPSc*, II. 88.

[108] Argyll to Glenorchy, 25 November 1564, GD112/39/3/11; Gregor MacGregor to Katherine Ruthven and to Glenorchy, before 25 November, c. 25 November and 2 December 1564, *Campbell Letters*, 24–26, 42–44.

separation as well as the interconnexion between the two spheres of Gaelic politics. Though linked by the mercenary trade, Ulster and the Highlands followed distinct political paths. Even James MacDonald, who straddled the North Channel, could not keep abreast of every development.

Having overrun Donegal, Shane O'Neill was growing in strength. Within Ulster, the MacDonalds were the sole barrier in his path, with little option but to preserve their neutrality.[109] They felt doubly insecure because their 1561 negotiations with the English had not delivered a final settlement nor the letters patent for their lands. Their pessimistic conclusion that O'Neill's superficial submission in London heralded a return to an anti-Scots policy seemed confirmed when the English queen complained to Mary, Queen of Scots about James MacDonald's raids in Ulster.[110] During 1562–3 nothing had been achieved in the endless negotiations between Sussex and James or Sorley Boy.[111] After Argyll's prompting, a further effort was made to bring together the English and the MacDonalds when Captain William Piers, the Carrickfergus commander, was dispatched to Kintyre.[112] Randolph had been sent the English proposals directly and, on Argyll's arrival in the Scottish capital, held a conference in which the earl and MacDonald promised to oppose Shane.[113] Argyll advised MacDonald to accept the tough English terms on condition they demonstrated their good faith by punishing Andrew Brereton, who had murdered two MacDonalds.[114] In his glowing report to Sussex, Randolph highlighted the 5th earl's role in concluding the business: 'I have ever founde a friendly goodwill in my Lord of Argile towardes our nacioun and a myndfull minde of our sovereign's benefites towardes this countrey in ther distresses.'[115] Although the decision had been made in Scotland, it needed to be finalised in Ireland. After delays due to bad weather, Captain Piers and MacDonald crossed to Antrim, consulted Sorley Boy and signed the articles.[116] However, James was wary of giving Piers specific commitments to fight O'Neill.[117] Back in Kintyre James wrote a reassuring letter to Randolph,

[109] Hill, *Fire and Sword*, 62f. [110] December 1561, *CSPSc*, I. 572.

[111] In self-defence Sorley had made an agreement with O'Neill in the summer of 1562, because it was clear that, should O'Neill attack him, the English would not assist: Hill, *Fire and Sword*, 66–71.

[112] Instructions, 10 December 1562, *CSP Ireld*, I. 211 [56].

[113] Randolph to Cecil, 22 January, 31 January and 6 February 1563, *CSPSc*, I. 678, 681–3.

[114] Brereton, an official in Ireland, was the object of a MacDonald blood feud. Whilst entertaining them at Ardglass, Brereton had broken the laws of hospitality and killed Alastair MacRanald Boye and his brother Gillesbuig, MacDonalds of Lecale: see Irish Council to Privy Council, 20 May 1551, *CSP Ireld*, I. 113; Sussex to Privy Council, 24 April 1563, *CSP Ireld*, I. 216; Hill, *Fire and Sword*, 38; G. Hill, *An Historical Account of the MacDonnells of Antrim* (Belfast, 1978; reprint of 1873 edn), 131–2, n. 29.

[115] N.d. (sent c. 6 February received 15 May 1563), SP63/8 fo. 98; *CSP Ireld*, I. 218 [461].

[116] At Red Bay on 7 April 1563, SP63/8 fos. 66r–7v; MacDonald to Sussex 4 April 1563, *CSP Ireld*, I. 214 [27].

[117] Piers reported to Sussex that 'I found him very far off', 11 April 1563, SP63/8 fo. 65r–v.

explaining everything had been concluded and promising to fulfil his side of the bargain, provided the English honoured their side.[118] Argyll was pleased with the outcome, believing the MacDonalds had been accepted by the English government in Ireland who would henceforth treat them as proper subjects and Ulster allies.[119] To the 5th earl, the MacDonald settlement was an excellent example of how a British strategy could solve a problem that had bedevilled Ulster politics.

Unfortunately, Captain Piers made a different assessment of his mission. In common with most of the English administration in Ireland, he remained deeply sceptical about the value of the Ulster Scots. His post at Carrickfergus had given him contact with, but little love for, the MacDonalds, and his mission in 1563 had not improved his opinion.[120] Piers' report was virulently anti-Scottish, including comments upon the rivalries within Highland politics that affected Ulster. In addition, he presented a separate paper with a proposal to colonise the province.[121] These ideas led to a change in English policy, influencing the subsequent instructions for Sir Henry Sidney which declared that the Scots were the most malicious and dangerous men in Ireland and should be expelled.[122] Such a sentiment sounded the death knell for Argyll's British policy in Ulster and, by attempting to keep Ireland and Scotland separate, explicitly denied a British dimension to policy making. Sidney's instructions were a programme for reforming the kingdom of Ireland, which sought to exclude every aspect of Scottish participation.[123] The English change of policy in Ireland was neither communicated to Argyll nor to the ambassador in Edinburgh. Its formulation did not stop the endless round of MacDonald negotiations. With its position too weak openly to repudiate the powerful Gaelic Scots, the Irish administration continued the diplomatic charade of talking to James and Sorley Boy.

Ironically, in 1565 the Ulster situation was transformed by O'Neill's Antrim campaign, rather than the new English initiative.[124] Shane took Sorley Boy by surprise, defeating him on 29 April at Knockboy in the southern

---

[118] 16 April 1563, *CSPSc*, II 7.
[119] The 5th earl kept Randolph supplied with news: Randolph to Cecil, 10 April 1563, *CSPSc*, II. 6.
[120] For example Piers had led the 1558 expedition against the MacDonalds, *CSP Ireld*, I. 152 [10] and he had reported MacDonald's slanders against the queen, 28 April 1561, SP63/3 fos. 171r–2v.
[121] N.d. SP63/9 fos. 179r–80v and fos. 181r–4v. These reports were calendared as one item under 1563, *CSP Ireld*, I. 228 [83], but probably belong to March 1565, D. G. White, 'The Tudor Plantations in Ireland before 1571' (2 vols., Trinity College, Dublin, PhD thesis, 1967), II. 163–7. I am grateful to the Librarian of Trinity College, Dublin, for permission to consult this thesis; Hill, *Fire and Sword*, 73–4.
[122] 20 May 1565, SP63/13 fo. 110r.
[123] On the battle over Irish policy at the English court, see Brady, *Chief Governors*; ch. 4.
[124] For a full discussion, see Hill, *Fire and Sword*, 77–99.

Glynnes.[125] Seeing the MacDonald distress beacons burning across the North Channel, James immediately sailed from Kintyre, leaving his brother, Alastair Og, to gather their forces. James arrived in time, but Alastair's reinforcements came too late for the battle.[126] As a result, Shane was victorious at Glentaisie, just south of Ballycastle, capturing both James and Sorley Boy.[127] This defeat shattered the military power of the Antrim MacDonalds, giving O'Neill complete dominance over Ulster. News of the disaster reached the 5th earl the following week, and Randolph shrewdly commented that the 5th earl would 'want a good friend at need'.[128] Expecting trouble in the Lowlands and fighting the MacGregors throughout the central Highlands, Argyll could not immediately send military assistance.[129] He wrote to O'Neill offering a ransom for the MacDonald chief, before he heard James had died of his wounds on 6 July.[130]

In the summer of 1565, Shane was more concerned about Argyll's reaction to his Ulster campaign than the English response. He therefore needed to discover precisely what the 5th earl was planning in relation to Ireland, and, in his quest for accurate information, he forged two letters. The first was addressed to Argyll and dated 4 August, purporting to come from the Irish Privy Council. It explained that Mary MacDonald, the dowager countess of Tyrone, had informed the council that the 5th earl was coming to Ireland or sending Lady Agnes to rescue her husband and restore O'Donnell. It requested details of the Scottish attack on Shane so that Sussex could mount a simultaneous campaign.[131] Realising it was a ruse by O'Neill to discover

---

[125] Robert Flemyng, Mayor of Drogheda to Cecil, 28 February 1565, SP63/12, fo. 109; Hill, *Fire and Sword*, 88–9.

[126] The time interval (about twenty-four hours) between James and Alastair sailing from Kintyre was the result of the particular tide conditions in the waters of Moyle that affect that crossing, see W. Clark, 'Tides in the Water of Moyle', *The Kintyre Antiquarian and Natural History Magazine*, 43 (Spring 1998), 9–11.

[127] Fitzwilliam to Cecil, 16 and 18 May 1565, SP63/13 fos. 96, 107 (18 June report); for a full description of the battle also known as Glenshesk, see Hill, *Fire and Sword*, 90–4.

[128] Randolph to Cecil, 11 May 1565, *CSPSc*, II. 157; Argyll to Glenorchy, 11 May, GD112/39/4/6.

[129] See above p. 125. Lady Agnes Campbell did take a force to Ireland to attempt a rescue, Randolph to Cecil, 4 September 1565, *CSPSc*, II. 203.

[130] Reference to letters from Argyll and other chiefs of the Western Isles made in O'Neill to Elizabeth, SP63/14 fos. 112r–3r. The Irish Privy Council attempted to get O'Neill to hand over his prisoners, but without success, see Privy Council to Arnold and to O'Neill, 22 June 1565, SP63/13 fo. 162r–v, 174r–5r. Shane kept James' death a secret for as long as he could, O'Neill to Irish Privy Council, 25 August 1565, SP63/14 fos. 188r–9r. Randolph had heard the news of James' death, confirmed by 2 September, *CSPSc*, II. 201. Fitzwilliam reported James' death without regret, adding, 'whos eares and lewde practysis I wolde also laye buryed with him', 23 August 1565, SP63/14 fo. 166r.

[131] Irish Privy Council to Argyll (forgery), 4 August 1565, SP63/15 fo. 176. The writing and the spelling in the letter are of a Scottish secretary hand, though there was an attempt to

his intentions, the 5th earl sent such an ambiguous reply that no one could deduce his plans.[132] The following month he enclosed the forgery in his letter to Adam Loftus, archbishop of Armagh.[133] A second forged letter was delivered to Loftus, supposedly written on 27 September by Argyll and his uncle, the duke, seeking to discover plans against O'Neill.[134] The counterfeit contained information about the Chase-about Raid and a sortie made by four Drogheda men sent by O'Neill to prey upon Loch Fyne in Argyll and upon the duke's Clyde properties. The detailed information about Scotland's politics and geography had probably been provided by Sorley Boy or O'Neill's other Scottish captives. Whilst packed with convincing detail, insufficient care had been taken to make the signatures look authentic or employ the correct styles and addresses.[135]

The forgeries were composed (and have survived) because Argyll and Loftus were in regular contact in the autumn of 1565.[136] The 5th earl used his connections with the archbishop and the Irish Privy Council to persuade Elizabeth to intervene in the Chase-about Raid. Sharing a common faith with Loftus and the new Irish Deputy, Sir Henry Sidney, he sought to exploit their sympathy for the plight of their co-religionists in Scotland. Argyll hoped

make the signatures look authentic. The names correspond to members of the Irish Privy Council, i.e. Sir Nicholas Arnold, Adam Loftus, the archbishop of Armagh, George Stanley, Sir Francis Agard, John Plunket and two others not identified.

[132] The 5th earl had been alerted by the peculiar behaviour of the messenger and the fact that, although written in English, the letter did not possess the correct forms of greeting normally employed in such correspondence, Randolph to Cecil, 4 September 1565, *CSPSc*, II. 203. It is possible that O'Neill wanted the forgeries to be detected: Brady, *Shane O'Neill*, 60.

[133] Loftus managed to trace the false messenger, and he was arrested at Dundalk and imprisoned in Dublin castle. Loftus enclosed the counterfeit and genuine letters in his packet to Leicester and Cecil, 13 December 1565, SP63/15 fos. 168, 170. He also included his earlier letter to Leicester discussing the forgeries, delayed by the lack of a ship, 20 November 1565, SP63/15 fo. 115.

[134] SP63/15 fos. 117v–8r. The letter was more scruffy than the 4 August one, having one line inked out. It was written in English but with a more Irish than Scottish hand. The signatures were not close to those normally employed by either the duke or the 5th earl and included the Irish form 'Arsybell Argall' which had only been employed in the Gaelic version of the 1555 contract with Calvagh O'Donnell, see above, p. 21. A second counterfeit letter addressed to the earl of Sussex has not survived.

[135] These forgeries were produced by people not instinctively familiar with the Anglophone world of written correspondence. Ulster *literati* could write letters in English as well as Gaelic and Latin, but they did not possess the deep familiarity that the Scottish learned orders had acquired by being embedded in a Scots-speaking environment, D. Meek, 'The Scots-Gaelic Scribes of Late Medieval Perthshire: An Overview of the Orthography and Contents of the Book of the Dean of Lismore' in J. McClure and M. Spiller, eds., *Brycht Lanterns: Essays on the Language and Literature of Medieval and Renaissance Scotland* (Aberdeen, 1989), 387–404.

[136] Loftus letter to Argyll of 21 October, now lost, was probably carried by John Douglas who returned with the three letters Argyll wrote to Loftus on 18 November: SP63/15 fos. 172–4. See below, pp. 141–2.

that, as in 1560, his offers of assistance within Ulster would be welcome as future recompense for English intervention in the northern kingdom. When he wrote to the archbishop, the 5th earl hoped an appeal to a British policy, grounded in the shared goal of a united Protestant British Isles, might still bring results.

THE FRACTURING OF ANGLO-SCOTTISH FRIENDSHIP

Although disappointed by the failure of the Arran marriage proposal, Argyll believed the amity between Scotland and England had put down deep roots. The first test of the new Anglo-Scottish alliance, forged in 1560, came with the return of Mary, Queen of Scots to Scotland the following year. With Mary accepting the advice of Argyll, Lord James and Maitland, there was no disruption to the policy of friendship with England. However, the continuity of personnel and policy at the Scottish court disguised a shift in the basis of amity. The main priority of Mary's foreign policy was to secure recognition of her place in the English succession. Friendship with England had become a means to that end, rather than an end in itself. Amity would last as long as it worked towards her goal. By contrast, the Anglophiles had built their policy upon a shared religion and a common security for the British mainland. At the start of Mary' personal reign, these different interpretations of the purpose of Anglo-Scottish friendship remained submerged as all parties pursued the same strategy. However, diversity of aims had the potential to destabilise the triumvirate's power, for if their policy failed to resolve the succession question, the queen could dispense with them and with the amity.

If she could discuss the issue with Elizabeth face to face, Mary was convinced the English succession could be settled. News that a meeting between the two queens was to take place in the summer of 1562 reached the 5th earl in January of that year. He was delighted, expecting the meeting to bring solid results 'quhilk I hoip in God it sall, to the glorie of his name, the confort of all thair subiectis, and tranquillite of thair realmis'.[137] His high hopes, along with those of his sovereign, were dashed when Elizabeth cancelled the York meeting because of the outbreak of the religious wars in France. In the subsequent negotiations, the succession became more closely tied to Mary's marriage. The English line which gradually emerged suggested that the best way for Mary to enhance her cause was to marry a husband whom the English queen deemed 'suitable'. As a magnate with many other duties, Argyll was not directly involved in the diplomatic missions or

---

[137] Argyll to Randolph, 25 January 1562, SP52/7 fo. 19; *CSPSc*, I. 594.

correspondence flowing between the Scottish and English courts from 1561 to 1565. The daily management of Mary's foreign policy was the province of his partners, Moray and Maitland, who kept him informed and relied upon his political support.[138]

The 5th earl's attitude towards the Scottish queen's marriage amalgamated two considerations. On the one hand, he wanted any match to cement the amity, though he did not share Mary's obsession with the English succession. On the other, he believed that, as befitted her royal station, Mary should have a choice in the matter, which he had declared himself willing to protect.[139] In a light-hearted discussion of the subject in the winter of 1563, Mary informed him that the English ambassador 'wolde have me marie in England'. He quipped, 'Is the Quene of Englande become a man?' Having been asked which Englishman she should marry, Argyll replied she should choose whom she liked, provided she could find a sufficiently noble man in England. To Mary's comment that this would displease the duke, the 5th earl countered, 'Yf yt please God, and good for your majesties countrie ... what recke whoe wer dyspleased.' Randolph, for whom this scene had been played, reported that Argyll had told him plainly his preferred English candidate.[140] As the 'official' English candidate, the 5th earl supported the suit of Robert Dudley, earl of Leicester, which, in 1564 Randolph could declare, 'no man approves it better'.[141]

Whilst Moray and Maitland were occupied with the diplomatic business of Anglo-Scottish negotiations, Argyll's chief contribution to the amity lay in Ireland. Alongside his Ulster role, he assisted the English in a range of smaller ways, such as the release of an English pirate, George Butsyde.[142] He was held captive by James MacDonald, who was loath to release him because of his unparalleled knowledge of the coasts between Scotland and Ireland. After pressure from Argyll and the payment of a ransom, Butsyde was freed in December 1562, eighteen months after his first petition. Six weeks later, in February 1563, Butsyde was sent by Randolph back to Kintyre with James MacDonald when he was negotiating with Captain Piers. The 5th earl regarded his admiral's duty to keep the western seas of Scotland

---

[138] Lee, *James Stewart*, ch. 5; M. Loughlin, 'The Career of Maitland of Lethington c. 1526–1573' (University of Edinburgh PhD thesis, 1991); Alford, *Cecil*, chs. 3–5.

[139] See above, p. 114.

[140] Randolph to Cecil, 31 December 1563, *CSPSc*, II. 32–3.

[141] Randolph to Cecil, 24 December 1564, *CSPSc*, II. 110.

[142] The negotiations for Butsyde's release, 2 September, 22 September 1561; 15, 25, 30 January; 7 April; 26 May; 8 July; 3, 16 December 1562, *CSPSc*, I. 549, 554, 556, 593–4, 599, 615, 638, 670, 672. Randolph to Cecil, 6 February 1563, *CSPSc*, I. 682. Butsyde knew Argyll personally because in 1548 he had been with the 4th earl as part of the ransom of Sir Ralph Bagenal: Thomas Hedley to Randolph, 22 September 1561, *CSPSc*, I. 554; also see 23 July 1548, *CSP Ireld*, I. 83 [58ii].

free of pirates as a particular service he could offer Elizabeth.[143] In 1562, he rescued some English pirates and sent them home.[144] After their narrow escape from execution, the pirate captains Fetiplace and Johnston remained in Kintyre, where they wrote to the English Privy Council seeking pardon in return for kidnapping James MacDonald or any other chief from the Isles. The council ordered them to report to Sussex so they could act against Shane O'Neill.[145] These men's knowledge of the coastal waters was invaluable to the Tudor government in its clandestine operations in the North Channel or around the Irish coast. Together with Argyll's geographical expertise on the Highlands, they probably made a major contribution to Cecil's map-making enterprises. The English secretary's strategic thinking about the islands of Britain and his policy making were heavily dependent upon his constant consultation of such maps. In this practical way, Argyll was reinforcing the British idiom of Cecil's policies.[146]

Although grateful for the 5th earl's many services, the English queen and council were less forthcoming when a reciprocal favour was requested. They turned a deaf ear to the 5th earl's pleas in favour of his friend Cormac O'Connor, who sought rehabilitation in Ireland.[147] Even the simple request for a licence to export three geldings took longer and required more reminders than it should have done for a valued friend of England.[148] The 5th earl must have felt by 1564 that in all levels of Anglo-Scottish relations the English did most of the taking and the Scots most of the giving. Whilst the rhetoric of friendship flowed freely, there were few English deeds to match the fine words.

---

[143] Argyll to Randolph, 25 January 1562, SP52/7 fo. 19.

[144] A mixed haul of Scottish, Irish and English pirates had been captured in the Western Isles and brought into Argyll's custody. The Scots were hanged but, as foreign nationals, the English and Irish were sent back to their countries: Randolph to Cecil, 15 July 1562, *CSPSc*, I. 640.

[145] 1 April 1563, *CSPSc*, II. 1; Sussex to Privy Council, 11 May 1563, *CSP Ireld*, I. 217. The dangers of Fetiplace's career caught up with him the following year when he died in a Spanish prison: Cuerton to Cecil, 14 March 1564, *CSPFor 1564–5*, 79.

[146] The expertise provided by the 5th earl and his contacts was probably the prime source for Lawrence Nowell's detailed maps of Scotland drawn for Cecil in these years and many of the later Irish maps he collected. For Laurence Nowell's maps of Scotland, drawn c. 1565 commissioned by Cecil, see F. MacLeod, ed., *Togail Tir: Marking Time, The Map of the Western Isles* (Stornoway, 1989), 22, 141; Alford, *Cecil*, 50–1. For Cecil's use of maps and the map he carried in his pocket, P. Barber, 'England II: Monarchs, Ministers and Maps, 1550–1625' in D. Buisseret, ed., *Monarchs, Ministers and Maps* (Chicago, 1992), 57–98. For the link between Cecil's maps and his British policy, Dawson, 'Cecil', 197–8.

[147] Cormac was O'Connor's fourth son who had spent nine years in Scotland as a child. As well as sending messages via Randolph, e.g 6 February 1561, Argyll wrote a special letter to Cecil, 5 October 1561, *CSPSc*, I. 513, 557; and another to Loftus, 18 November 1565, SP63/15 fo. 178.

[148] *CSPSc*, II. 33, 51, 59, 69, 64, 75.

Elizabeth's sponsorship of Lennox's return to Scotland reinforced the impression of an unequal partnership. Argyll was prepared to accept the damage the earl's restoration caused to himself and his Hamilton kin on the assumption that it would contribute towards a settlement between the Scottish and English queens of the succession and marriage questions. The return to Scotland of Lennox's son Darnley destroyed these calculations. Although he had been ill for over a week, at the beginning of March 1565 Argyll rose from his sickbed to visit Randolph. Expressing his dislike of Darnley's return, he commented prophetically, 'the affections of women are uncertain'. Having confirmed he would continue to support the Leicester match, he added that if another suit were proposed he and his clients would have to provide for themselves.[149]

The position of the Anglophile party at the Scottish court was destroyed when Randolph presented to Mary Elizabeth's letter of 5 March, which changed the conditions to be met before a settlement over the English succession could be reached.[150] Argyll, Moray and Maitland were at a complete loss to know what the English had intended: there seemed to have been no prior consideration of the consequences of the letter.[151] Five years' work for the Anglo-Scottish amity was ruined by a bungled missive, leaving the triumvirate's policy in tatters. Their failure to guarantee the succession for Mary had been glaringly exposed by their own allies. Her hopes dashed, the Scottish queen turned to Lennox and his supporters. They persuaded the queen to utilise the threat of a Darnley marriage to extract concessions from the English. Seizing upon this new aggressive strategy, Mary sent Maitland to London. What started as a gambit in the diplomatic game rapidly turned into a fixed policy.

If the English had accepted Darnley as a suitable match, Anglo-Scottish amity might have been salvaged. When it became clear that Elizabeth would not countenance the marriage under any circumstances, the 5th earl and Moray lost any remaining leverage over Mary's policies. Once their contention that Mary's best chance of securing the English succession lay in friendship and co-operation with England had been exposed as a sham, their influence over policy disappeared. Rejecting the policy of amity, the Scottish queen dispensed with the triumvirate who had championed it since 1561. Having driven Argyll and Moray into rebellion, Mary cleverly used their well-known support for the English alliance against them. Linking it

---

[149] Randolph to Cecil 15 March 1565, *CSPSc*, II. 136.
[150] For a discussion of the importance of this letter, see Dawson, 'Mary, Queen of Scots, Lord Darnley and Anglo-Scottish Relations in 1565', 8–10. A different interpretation is offered by Adams 'The Release of Lord Darnley', 142–3.
[151] Randolph to Cecil 17 March 1565, *CSPSc*, II. 136–7.

once more to Scottish patriotism, she revived the traditional anti-English rhetoric.[152]

From the beginning of the Darnley crisis, messages of English support had reached the 5th earl and Moray. They were sent by Randolph, Throckmorton and Tamworth, the special ambassadors, and Borders' officials like Bedford, and were accompanied by encouraging noises from London. Money was forwarded, but no military assistance was forthcoming. In June and September, the English Privy Council discussed the options, deciding, in view of the international situation, that England could not risk intervention.[153] As a consequence, most of the rebel lords were forced to flee into exile in England. For the Anglophiles, the crisis of 1565 reversed the 1560 achievement of a united Protestant British mainland. By the end of the year, England and Scotland were on the brink of war.

In November, the 5th earl tried a final appeal for English support, writing to Archbishop Loftus, a member of the Dublin council. Argyll's hard-earned experience of the dysfunctional relationship between London and Dublin had perhaps shown him how to employ that political link to his advantage. He hoped to use the Dublin government to apply sufficient pressure upon the English queen and her Privy Council to change their minds. In his letters to Loftus, he made an emotive appeal to his co-religionist, reminding him that 'our religioun and unioun in fayth is ane sufficient knot of amite and acquentance betuix ws'. Not surprisingly, he emphasised the religious motivation of the Scottish rebellion, explaining, 'we can nocht get Christis religioun fullie stablishit nor papistre abrogatet conforme to hir Majestieis promis'. He was bold enough to compare the persecution he and his allies were suffering with the experience of the Old Testament prophets and even of Christ himself. The 5th earl also introduced the constitutional argument to justify taking up arms, employing the standard complaint that noblemen had been deprived of their right to advise their sovereign and assist in ruling the commonweal. Finally, he asserted the rebels were victims of unprovoked royal aggression, outlawed without cause with their lands, houses and families attacked. Argyll begged the archbishop to lobby Elizabeth on behalf of the exiled lords and to provide aid in the shape of warships carrying money for troops, artillery, arquebuses, gunpowder and bullets to Loch Fyne.[154] The verbal messages sent with John Douglas included the promise that, if aid materialised, the 5th earl would supply 4,000 men for a future Irish

---

[152] For example Mary's proclamation, 16 July 1565, Keith, *History*, II. 326–8. The English were quick to pick up the rhetoric, BL Cotton Calig. B 10 fo. 35.
[153] For a full account, see Alford, *Cecil*, ch. 5; Dawson, 'Mary, Queen of Scots, Lord Darnley and Anglo-Scottish Relations in 1565', 14–19.
[154] 18 November 1565, SP63/15 fo. 172r–v; second letter with similar request fo. 174.

campaign.[155] Hoping Elizabeth's mind could be changed, as in 1560, because he could offer future recompense, the 5th earl played the Irish card, only to discover it was a minor suit.[156] He miscalculated because Ireland was not a high enough priority for its affairs to tip the balance and bring a change to English policy. Though fearful the earl would join with O'Neill, Elizabeth was more frightened of Spanish intervention.[157] The international situation held the trump card. For his part, Cecil had decided to sacrifice his British policy for the sake of English security.

To the 5th earl, the English failure to help the rebel lords followed by the deliberate humiliation of Moray in London amounted to a betrayal of the ideal of Anglo-Scottish amity.[158] The bitter experiences of 1565 combined and confirmed by the long-term frustrations of dealing with the English in Ireland persuaded him to change his Ulster policies. Prior to 1565, Argyll's first reaction had been to assist English attempts to control the province in whichever ways he could. This was based upon the assumption that the English would accept the MacDonalds and the O'Donnells as part of a peaceful Ulster. It gradually became clear that the English were unwilling to settle with the MacDonalds and were not prepared to re-establish Calvagh O'Donnell in Donegal. English behaviour over the Chase-about Raid was the final and crucial disillusionment. After 1565, the 5th earl's assistance in Ulster became a negotiating counter in his dealings with the English government.

[155] Loftus to Leicester, 13 December 1565, SP63/15 fo. 170.
[156] In addition to the troops, Argyll promised Randolph that without Elizabeth's advice he would not make separate terms with Mary, though good conditions had been promised, Randolph to Cecil, 12 November 1565, SP52/11 fos. 195r–6v; *CSPSc*, II. 237–8.
[157] O'Neill was reported to have asked Argyll for troops, Randolph to Cecil, 12 October 1565, *CSPSc*, II 223; Bedford to Cecil, 1 and 5 November 1565, SP59/10fos. 160r–1r, 170r–1v; Randolph reminded the secretary that only the 5th earl could do anything to hinder or help Shane O'Neill in Ireland or in the Irishman's communications with the Scottish queen, Randolph to Cecil, 19 November 1565, *CSPSc*, II. 239.
[158] For Moray's public rebuke on 23 October by Elizabeth, see Dawson, 'Mary, Queen of Scots, Lord Darnley and Anglo-Scottish Relations in 1565', 20.

5

The reconfiguration of British politics: 1566–1568

Between 1566 and 1568, the politics of the British mainland were turned upside down by the disintegration of Mary's personal rule. The Scottish kingdom was rocked by the murders of Riccio and Darnley, the Bothwell marriage, Mary's enforced abdication, the defeat at Langside and finally her catastrophic flight into England. These events splintered Scottish national politics, leaving a divided country slipping into civil war. For Argyll they also brought the bitter split with Moray, his close friend and political partner. At the start of 1566, Mary, Queen of Scots was dominating mainland Britain and threatening the English queen. By 1568 she was a fugitive in England begging Elizabeth for assistance. This dramatic reversal of fortunes shifted the balance of power within the mainland, leading to a major re-alignment of British politics.

The immediate consequences of Argyll's abandonment of an integrated British policy were felt within the Gaelic political world. With the loss of the triangular British link, the 5th earl severed the automatic connexion between his Ulster policies and Anglo-Scottish amity. Instead of co-operating with the English in Ireland, he treated the Dublin and London administrations as a foreign power with whom he needed to bargain. Within Ulster, the idealism of Argyll's British policy was replaced by the pragmatic goal of maintaining his Gaelic dependants. In particular, by re-establishing MacDonald power, he sought to stabilise the North Channel area. He then masterminded a momentous Ulster alliance, binding together the MacDonalds, O'Neills and O'Donnells. This unlikely coalition was achieved through the classic aristocratic tactic of dynastic marriage, with the joint weddings of Lady Agnes and her daughter Finola to the O'Neill and O'Donnell chiefs. By altering the complexion of Ulster politics, these marriages laid the foundation for that province's successful resistance to Elizabethan conquest and for Tyrone's rebellion at the end of the reign. Instead of working for the integration and assimilation of Ireland into a united, Protestant British Isles, the 5th earl created the preconditions that made possible the Nine Years War. In that crisis of Elizabeth's declining years, Ireland was nearly lost to the English crown, thereby fragmenting the Tudor state. Though James VI did inherit all three kingdoms in 1603, the place of Ireland within them had been changed. By adopting his new approach in Ulster in 1566, Argyll helped re-configure sixteenth-century British politics.

THE DISINTEGRATION OF MARY'S RULE

The collapse of the rebellion and the departure into exile of his fellow rebel lords in October 1565 left Argyll isolated. Without English aid the cause could not be revived and, despite the 5th earl's Irish lobbying, this was not forthcoming. Meanwhile, the earl's uncle, the duke, his Hamiltons and many lesser rebels had already made their peace with Mary. Having inflicted considerable damage within Atholl and the Lennox, Argyll was in a strong bargaining position, if he chose to negotiate. The 5th earl was aware of the difficulties faced by his subordinate chief, Glenorchy, caught between loyalty to Clan Campbell and to Atholl, his neighbour, friend and kinsman, and facing a legal challenge from Murray of Tullibardine, who was high in royal favour. Having secretly met Grey Colin, Argyll gave him permission to make a private settlement with the crown if necessary.[1] Throughout December, the 5th earl was himself secretly negotiating with the court, insisting upon religious guarantees and the return of the exiled lords. Although this was the height of Mary's five-week 'Catholic interlude', it was not Argyll's Protestant demands but Darnley's antagonism towards him that was the main sticking-point.[2] The king, upset because he had not been consulted about the duke's remission, insisted there should be no more private deals. In late January 1566, Glenorchy, finally forced to attend court and making his own submission on relatively easy terms, discovered Argyll would not find the same leniency. Though he had many 'gwd wyllars' at court, few dared advance the earl's cause in the face of the king's opposition.[3] The feast of Candlemas at the start of February 1566 provided an opportunity for Catholic display and royal triumphalism. Having been presented with the French Order of St Michael, the king and his entourage 'swaggered up the High Street of Edinburgh boasting

---

[1] 7 November 1565, GD112/1/161. Although quick to rebuild relations with his Perthshire neighbours, Grey Colin did not rush to make his peace with the government: *Campbell Letters*, 49–52. The 5th earl was also angry with MacLean of Duart for negotiating without permission: see below, p. 156.

[2] For example Carrick to Glenorchy c. 7–10 and c. 12–24 December, *Campbell Letters*, 70 and 72. J. Goodare, 'Queen Mary's Catholic Interlude' in M. Lynch, ed., *Mary Stewart: Queen in Three Kingdoms* (Oxford, 1988), 154–70.

[3] Glenorchy to Carrick, 13 February 1566, *Campbell Letters*, 79. Glenorchy also reported the rumour that was circulating in Edinburgh that Argyll was building Highland galleys which were probably to be used in connexion with Ireland.

that they had restored the Mass to the whole realm'.[4] Argyll's hopes for himself and for Scottish Protestantism seemed further than ever from realisation.

The situation was changed by Darnley's own actions. Despite the chivalric honours, the young king felt excluded from full regal power, particularly by his wife's refusal to grant him the crown matrimonial. He wanted the title authorised at the forthcoming Parliament called in early March to forfeit the rebel lords. After the treatment of the Gordons in 1562–3, the prospect of a major forfeiture alarmed the exiles. It could also be construed as part of a wider attack upon the higher nobility's place in government, part of a new direction in Mary's style of governing. When viewed as a whole, the queen's success in the Chase-about Raid, her taking counsel from non-noble members of her personal household, especially foreigners such as David Riccio, and her pro-Catholic moves, assumed to be part of an international Catholic conspiracy, added up to a worrying trend for the Scottish aristocracy.[5] Consequently, those sympathetic to the exiles, such as Morton, Ruthven, Lindsay and Maitland, played upon Darnley's wounded pride. They argued that, if the rebels escaped forfeiture and returned to Scotland, they would back the king's bid for the crown matrimonial and support the elimination of Riccio. The resulting agreement was sealed in two bonds, one given by Darnley on 1 March in Edinburgh and the other by the exiled lords on 2 March at Newcastle. As part of his side of the bargain, Darnley signed a pardon for the 5th earl and all his dependants.[6] Despite standing to benefit from the deal, Argyll remained in his region, not signing the Newcastle bond, though his name was on it.[7]

As they had agreed, on 9 March in Holyrood Palace a group of nobles led by Darnley killed Riccio whilst he was dining with Mary in her apartments. With unnecessary brutality, they dragged her favourite from the pregnant queen's side and murdered him in front of her.[8] Displaying considerable courage and resourcefulness, Mary detached Darnley from his fellow conspirators and they escaped to Dunbar. Though she had overcome the immediate crisis, the queen was left with an abiding hatred of the murderers, including her husband. Unlike the exiled lords who arrived in the Scottish

---

[4] M. Lynch, 'Queen Mary's Triumph: The Baptismal Celebrations at Stirling in December 1566', *SHR*, 69 (1990), 1–21 at p. 3.

[5] Goodare, 'Queen Mary's Catholic Interlude', 164–6.

[6] The copy of the remission in the Boyd Papers was signed by the king alone, 6 March 1566, GD8/157; W. Fraser, *Memorials of the Montgomeries, Earls of Eglinton* (2 vols., Edinburgh, 1859), II. 200–1. The full remission, 21 March, *RSS*, V, ii. 2702; AT, VI. 77.

[7] The fifth earl could not have visited the English city. The bonds are printed in W. Fraser, *The Melvilles, Earls of Melville and the Leslies, Earls of Leven* (3 vols., Edinburgh, 1890), I. xxxiii–iv; III. 110–12; Wormald, *Lords and Men*, 405 (13 and 14); *CSPSc*, II. 260–1.

[8] One of those present at the supper party with the queen was the countess of Argyll and it was probably her quick thinking in catching the candles when the dinner table was overthrown that prevented a fire in the palace. See Ruthven's account, Keith, *History*, III. 266–7.

capital, as planned, shortly after the murder, Argyll did not reach the Lowlands until the third week of March.[9] Having received their remissions, the 5th earl and Moray were received into the queen's presence and the following month returned to their places on the council. A grand reconciliation of enemies was staged between Atholl, Bothwell and Huntly, and Argyll, Moray and Glencairn.[10] As a further gesture of goodwill, which annoyed Darnley, the mad earl of Arran was temporarily released from prison with Argyll acting as one of his sureties.[11]

The shock of the Riccio murder removed any residual antagonism Mary harboured against the 5th earl after the Chase-about Raid. On 31 March she wrote in a most conciliatory tone, requesting him to negotiate with O'Neill, signing the letter 'your richt gud sister' and adding a postscript in her own hand: 'Wat ever bis sayed bi sur off my gud mynd, and that ye sal persayve.'[12] Although initially refusing Argyll's request to pardon Robert Lord Boyd's part in the Riccio conspiracy, the queen relented. This move infuriated Darnley, who, in addition to the general repudiation of his fellow conspirators, had a personal feud against Boyd.[13] The 5th earl helped mitigate the punishment of his brother-in-law Stewart of Doune, another Riccio conspirator.[14] Aided by Atholl and Moray, Argyll also sought Maitland's restoration to royal favour, though the secretary had to wait several months for his return.[15] Even with the earls pleading their case, the queen refused to allow back the main participants in the Riccio murder. Ruthven died in Newcastle in the spring of 1566 and Morton was left in dire straits in exile.[16]

---

[9] Randolph to Cecil, 21 March 1566, *CSPSc*, II. 269–70; *Diurnal*, 95. Bedford informed Cecil that Argyll had not come to Edinburgh and he did not know the reason, 18 March 1566, SP59/11 fo. 123v.

[10] Argyll's remission, *RSS*, V, ii. 2702; AT, VI. 77. Moray's, *RSS*, V, ii. 2698. Drury to Cecil, 20 April 1566, SP59/11 fo. 154r–v; Randolph to Cecil, 25 April 1566, *CSPSc*, II. 276. The 5th earl attended Privy Council 30 April 1566, *RPC*, XIV [Add.] 19. Moray was in Dunoon with the 5th earl on 8 April, Moray to Glenorchy, GD112/39/6/9. Atholl's lands had been devasted by Argyll's troops; Bothwell blamed Moray and probably Argyll for his earlier imprisonment; Huntly was at feud with Moray after his father's rebellion and defeat at Corrichie, De Siva to Philip II, 11 May 1566, *CSP Sp, 1558–67*, 548–9.

[11] Along with other Hamiltons and Huntly, 26 April 1566, *RPC*, I. 452–3.

[12] *Letters to Argyll Family*, 5–6.

[13] Boyd's servants had killed one of Lennox's men. Curiously, Darnley blamed Moray instead of Argyll for Boyd's pardon, Drury to Cecil, 7 May 1566, SP52/11 fos. 188r–v.

[14] The reference to 'Argyll's brother' almost certainly means his brother-in-law Stewart of Doune rather than Colin Campbell of Boquhan, his half-brother and heir: Randolph to Cecil, 7 June 1566, *CSPSc*, II. 283–4.

[15] After the Riccio murder, Maitland had been sent to Atholl under house arrest, see his letters of April 1566, *Campbell Letters*, 85 and 86. Through the agency of the 5th earl, Moray and Bothwell, Maitland was reconciled with the queen in September: Maitland to Cecil, 20 September, *CSPSc*, II. 300.

[16] Randolph to Cecil, 13 May 1566, *CSPSc*, II. 278; Morton to Bedford, 24 May, *CSPSc*, II. 280–1 and see below, pp. 165–6.

Whatever his prior knowledge of the conspiracy, the 5th earl had not been involved in the actual murder of Riccio, and that distinction was of great importance to the queen. Throughout the summer of 1566, Mary showered Argyll and his supporters with favours. In May, she granted the vacant bishopric of Brechin to his kinsman, Alexander Campbell.[17] During her confinement in mid-June, she placed the 5th earl in the chamber next to her own and appointed him one of the regents should she die in childbirth.[18] In September, he was regranted the office of chamberlain of Bute and its forests given to Lennox during the Chase-about Raid.[19] The queen's favour intensified Darnley's hostility and confirmed the opinion of the Pope's agents that Argyll was one of their foremost enemies.[20] The earl spent much of the summer and autumn of 1566 in the queen's service, regularly attending the council and auditing the treasurer's accounts.[21] Wanting to display a united Protestant front with the ministers and elders, he made a point of attending the General Assembly in June 1566.[22] Mary might have used these occupations to dissuade or delay Argyll from his stated intention of travelling abroad.[23] During this period, his most onerous task was running the justice-ayre for five weeks in October and November, which the queen took in person to Jedburgh to suppress the lawlessness of the Borders.[24] Argyll's personal participation prevented him travelling to Ireland as he had originally intended.[25]

As a result of his continuous residence with the court, Argyll became more conscious of Mary's deep antagonism towards her husband. Their mutual dislike of Darnley strengthened his friendship with the queen and drew him closer to Huntly and even to Bothwell, a man he never liked. In October

[17] 6 May 1566, *RSS*, V, ii. 2806. Alexander's brother was James Campbell of Ardkinglas, who had been heavily involved in the Chase-about Raid and specifically named in Argyll's remission.

[18] Mary entered confinement on 3 June and gave birth on 19 June, Donaldson, *Queen's Men*, 93. Argyll was one of a large group who signed a bond to uphold the queen's will, June 1566, GD18/3105.

[19] 16 September 1566, *RSS*, V, ii. 3056 and 3059; AT, VI. 76 (misdated) and 83–4. Lennox's grant, 12 January 1566, *RSS*, V, ii. 2538.

[20] Bishop of Mondovi to cardinal of Alessandria, 21 August 1566, *Papal Negotiations with Mary, Queen of Scots during her Reign in Scotland 1561–7* ed. J.H. Pollen (SHS, 1st ser. 37, Edinburgh, 1901), 278.

[21] For example from his return to the council on 29 April to the end of 1566, *RPC*, I. 454–95; 27 June 1566 audit, *TA*, XI. 258.

[22] *BUK*, I. 77.

[23] Argyll received a licence to travel for three years, Morton to Forster c. 21 July 1566, *CSPSc*, I, i. 415.

[24] Argyll was paid his £3 daily rate for 9 October to 8 November 1566, *TA*, XII. 31. J. Small, 'Queen Mary at Jedburgh in 1566', *PSAS*, 3 (1881), 210–33.

[25] See below, p. 158.

1566, a bond, which has not survived, was made between two sets of former enemies, the 5th earl and Moray, with Huntly and Bothwell, including an agreement to bury old feuds and probably making general reference to the need to free the queen from her marriage.[26] A discussion about Darnley had later taken place at Craigmillar castle, just outside Edinburgh, where the court resided from 20 November until 7 December to allow the queen to recover from the illness contracted on her return journey from Jedburgh. Subsequently, the 'Craigmillar conference' became the subject of accusation and counter-accusation between the participants. Argyll's version described a December morning when Moray and Maitland arrived at his chamber so early they found him still in bed. The two visitors discussed their obligation to obtain the queen's pardon for the Riccio murderers as a prologue to Maitland's suggestion that the way to get Mary's consent was to help her divorce Darnley. With his own experience of marital difficulties, Argyll was sceptical, but Maitland assured him a way could be found, provided neither he nor Huntly took offence. When sent for, Huntly gave his support, and the four men went to Bothwell's room and secured his agreement. Finally, they all went as a delegation to Mary. Controversy surrounds this part of the conference. The queen was concerned that any divorce should be lawful and would not prejudice her son's right to inherit. In reply, Maitland made his much-quoted remark that Moray would look through his fingers, but say nothing.[27] At this point Argyll's account abruptly stopped, being later circulated in order to exonerate Mary whilst implicating Moray and Maitland in Darnley's murder.[28] Though by no means complete, it was probably accurate enough. In his version, Moray accepted there had been discussions at Craigmillar, but asserted they had not led, at least while he was present, to 'ony unlawfull or dishonourable end'. He also insisted he had not signed a bond there.[29]

Whatever had been decided at Craigmillar, the first proposal was implemented when the Riccio murderers were pardoned on Christmas Eve 1566 shortly after the prince's baptism. It was the occasion for a magnificent

---

[26] In his reply to Argyll's protestation, Moray gave the October date and denied the bond had anything to do with the murder of Darnley: Keith, *History*, III. 295; G. Donaldson, *The First Trial of Mary, Queen of Scots* (London, 1969), 33.

[27] Protestation, Keith, *History*, III. 291–3. Maitland was reported as saying, 'and albeite that my Lord of Murraye heir present be lytill les scrupulous for ane Protestant, nor your Grace is for ane Papist, I am assurit he will looke throw his fingeris thairto, and will behald our doeings, saying nathing to the same'. Although not without a wider meaning, it would appear from the context of the discussion and from the reference to Mary's Roman Catholicism that the main meaning here concerned accepting any form of divorce. Moray was known to be opposed to divorce as a solution to Argyll's marital problems.

[28] Donaldson, *First Trial*, 34–5.

[29] Keith, *History*, III. 294–5; Wormald, *Lords and Men*, 151.

spectacle upon the themes of reconciliation and heroic royal triumph, displayed in a tournament, a mock siege and a firework display. During the Roman Catholic service, the 5th earl and other Protestant nobles had remained outside the Chapel Royal. Acting on behalf of Queen Elizabeth as the prince's godmother, the countess of Argyll took a leading part in the Roman Catholic ceremony.[30] By virtue of his hereditary office as Master of the Household, dressed resplendently in red, the 5th earl played a central role in the feasting. Both he and the Roman Catholic Lord Seton carried white staffs, the traditional emblem of peace after a feud. They represented the banquet's key theme, the reconciliation of the Scottish nobility under benevolent Stewart rule.[31] However, the symbolism of the great Renaissance festival held at Stirling could not remove the most pressing problem facing Scottish national politics: the king himself.

On the fateful evening of 9 February 1567, Argyll went with the queen to visit the sick Darnley at Kirk o' Field. A few hours later, the house had been blown up and the king was found dead in the garden. With hints of multiple conspiracies, the precise details remain a mystery, but contemporaries were convinced of the earl of Bothwell's involvement. It is impossible to know Argyll's part in the murder plots, but, along with other members of Scotland's ruling elite, he had a strong motive. He disliked the king, was a regional rival of the Lennox Stewarts and wanted the 'problem' of the queen's husband removed.[32] In the aftermath of Darnley's murder, the 5th earl remained in Edinburgh trying to restore normality to government. In March, he was chosen to accompany the young prince James to the safety of Mar's care in Stirling castle.[33] Seeking to distance himself from the political mess and the rise of his old enemy, Bothwell, Moray decided to leave the country.[34] Argyll, though never working easily with the volatile earl himself, did not feel he had that option. In his capacity as justice-general, he had to preside at Bothwell's trial on Lennox's charge of murdering his son.[35] After the predictable acquittal, a Parliament was held. With the queen freely making

---

[30] Elizabeth had written to Countess Jane, 31 October 1566: *CSP For, 1566–82*, 142. Lynch, 'Queen Mary's Triumph', 1–21. Jane was in trouble with the General Assembly for her participation in this Catholic baptism: see above, p. 31.

[31] *Diurnal*, 103–4; Lynch, 'Queen Mary's Triumph', 10. As both Argyll and Seton were Masters of the Household, the staffs might also have been the batons of their office.

[32] J. Wormald, *Mary Queen of Scots: A Study in Failure* (London, 1988), 160–1.

[33] With the duke out of the country, Argyll and Huntly, the two highest ranking nobles, conveyed the prince, 19–20 March 1567: *Diurnal*, 107.

[34] Cecil commented to Sidney, 23 April 1567, 'Scotland is in a quamyre, no body semeth to stand still the most honest desyre to goo away. The worst tremble with the shakyng of ther conscience.' SP63/20 fo. 144r. I am grateful to Dr Alford for this reference.

[35] 12 April 1567, Herries, *Memoirs*, 86–7; *CSPSc*, II. 319–20. Calderwood wrote that Bothwell asked the 5th earl to start the criminal investigation: Calderwood, *History*, II. 347–8.

grants looking suspiciously like payments to nobles for their acquiescence in the king's death, the situation deteriorated.[36] On 19 April, the day Argyll was given lands previously held by Darnley, a bond was made at Ainslie's Tavern, Edinburgh.[37] It is not clear if, or when, Argyll added his signature, but a large section of the Scottish aristocracy signed, accepting Bothwell's innocence and promising to persuade the queen to marry him. The following day, the bond was presented to the queen, who ratified it, entrusting it to the 5th earl's keeping.[38]

If Argyll had reluctantly acquiesced to the provisions in the Ainslie Tavern bond, he refused to countenance Bothwell's abduction of Mary on 24 April. The probable rape of the queen and the enforced and irregular marriage that followed were the equivalent of a *coup d'état*. The following week in Stirling, the 5th earl, Atholl, Mar, Morton, Montrose and Murray of Tullibardine, opposing Bothwell's unilateral seizure of power, bound themselves to release the queen from captivity in Dunbar and to protect the prince.[39] On his arrival in his region to gather troops, the 5th earl was greeted by the news of Shane O'Neill's defeat at Farsetmore. Though the Ulster situation was distracting, his central dilemma was how to proceed once Mary had actually married Bothwell on 15 May.

The queen took the initiative herself by sending his friend, Lord Boyd, with a conciliatory letter urging the 5th earl to be reconciled with Bothwell and promising her steadfast friendship and sincere goodwill.[40] At the same time, Argyll was bombarded by letters from those organising resistance to Mary's new husband. By the start of June, Atholl was exasperated at the 5th earl's failure to travel east or even to respond to the five letters he had already sent.[41] At this critical juncture, Argyll appeared to have been paralysed by indecision, torn by conflicting loyalties, his personal and political obedience to the queen at odds with his duty to the Scottish commonweal and the need to remedy the mess created by Mary's marriage to Bothwell. Eventually,

---

[36] Wormald, *Mary Queen of Scots*, 162–3. Parliament formally restored Huntly and he was re-granted the lands of Mamore in Lochaber, which bordered upon Argyll's sphere of influence, 21 April, *RSS*, V, ii. 3459; AT, VI. 96.

[37] Argyll's grant, *RSS*, V, ii. 3432.

[38] *CSPSc*, II. 321–2; Calderwood, *History*, II. 352–5; Keith, *History*, II. 563–5; Wormald, *Lords and Men*, 406 [15]. The signatures vary in the different versions of the bond. Those printed by Calderwood and Keith have both Argyll's and Moray's signatures, though Moray was not in Scotland at the time. The sixteenth-century copy in the Leven and Melville papers, GD26/15/1, does not contain Argyll's signature.

[39] AT, VI. 102; Wormald, *Lords and Men*, 406 [16]. In his letter to Cecil, Melville mentioned two other bonds, one between Argyll and Atholl and the other between Argyll and Tullibardine: 7 May 1567, *CSPSc*, II. 326–7; Kirkcaldy to Bedford, 8 May 1567 *CSPSc*, II. 327–8.

[40] Instruction to Boyd, c. end May 1567, BL Add. MS 23,109 fo. 11.

[41] Stewart of Grandtully/Atholl to Glenorchy, 1 June 1567, *Campbell Letters*, 89.

he made his decision, travelling to the Lowlands to oppose Mary.[42] The two sides met in a bloodless encounter at Carberry, outside Edinburgh near Musselburgh, where Bothwell fled and Mary was taken prisoner. Returning with the captive queen, who faced a hostile reception from the capital's citizens, the confederate lords made a formal agreement on 16 June to revenge the king's death, and Mary was sent to imprisonment in Lochleven castle.[43]

At this point, Argyll became seriously concerned about the intentions of his fellow confederates. He had no qualms about freeing the queen from her husband in as efficient a manner as possible, through divorce or Bothwell's death. However, the prospect of Mary being kept in permanent captivity and forced to abdicate deeply troubled him. Knox, from his pulpit in St Giles, and others were even calling for the queen's execution for murder and adultery. The 5th earl was horrified by the prospect that a reigning queen should be discarded in such a fashion and could not support what the confederates were doing. Though showing several times in the past, and as recently as Carberry, that he would rebel against the monarch, he was not prepared to take the revolutionary steps of deposition and even tyrannicide. This decision marked a watershed in Argyll's political career, bringing an end to his long partnership with many Protestant nobles with whom he had shared the triumphs of 1560 and the defeat of 1565. Such a breach was part of the splintering of Scottish national politics at all levels that brought the civil wars.

Despite having struggled so hard before Carberry to work out his duty, this agonising decision did not take Argyll long. Within a week of that confrontation, the 5th earl had left the confederate lords and was talking to the Hamiltons about how to rescue or support the queen.[44] His defection caused consternation, with the confederates making strenuous efforts to persuade him to return. Though causing him to waver briefly, Glencairn, an old and valued friend, failed to convince Argyll of the wisdom of the confederates' actions. The 5th earl rode west, joining his Hamilton kinsmen at Dumbarton.[45] Together they bound themselves to free the queen.[46] To counter this threat, the arch-negotiator Maitland was dispatched from Edinburgh to speak to the

---

[42] His movements make it highly unlikely that Herries' story was true that Argyll was at Holyrood in the first week of June and secretly informed Mary and Bothwell there was a plot against them, thus giving them a chance to escape, Herries, *Memoirs*, 91.

[43] *RPC*, I. 521; *The Warrender Papers* ed. A.I. Cameron (2 vols., SHS, 3rd ser. 18–19, Edinburgh, 1931–32), I. 49.

[44] Du Croc to Charles IX, 21 June 1567, *CSPSc*, II. 335–6.

[45] Glencairn was sent on 27 June: *Diurnal*, 116. Keith, *History*, II. 775, n. 3. Throckmorton to Cecil, 1 July, *CSPSc*, II. 342–3.

[46] 29 June 1567, NLS MS 3657; *CSPSc*, II. 339. A very similar bond was made at Hamilton, but bears the unlikely date of 25 December 1567: Wormald, *Lords and Men*, 409 [19].

5th earl. Meeting at Doune castle, the seat of Argyll's brother-in-law, they discussed the situation for four days before travelling to Stirling to speak with their old friend and ally Mar.[47] This was a confused and uncertain time when, in Melville's graphic description, the situation was in as much of a mess as a Welshman's hose.[48] Under the pressure of Maitland's persuasion and grappling with details concerning the nature and terms of Mary's captive status, the 5th earl's clear, black-and-white rules merged into a difficult to distinguish grey, leaving him unsure which path to follow.

One aspect Argyll plainly understood was that Elizabeth's attitude to Scottish events was crucial. The disintegration of Mary's personal rule profoundly affected English interests. As well as the shock Elizabeth experienced witnessing the enforced abdication of a fellow queen, the charges against Mary threatened her claim to the English succession. In relation to England's security, the instability of Scottish politics jeopardised the peace of the British mainland. As the 5th earl recognised, these factors ensured that the English queen and government would become involved in the Scottish situation, though it was not clear which party they would support. Elizabeth had reasons to back both sides: one was defending a monarch against deposition and possible execution; the other had rid her of a rival. Before policy could be formulated, the English needed accurate information, so Sir Nicholas Throckmorton was sent on a special embassy to Scotland. Argyll sent secret messages to Throckmorton on 11 July, to discover the English attitude.[49] The ambassador, deducing Argyll and the Hamiltons were not being completely frank with each other about their different agendas, relayed the implausible rumour that the 5th earl was considering marrying the queen to his brother, Colin Campbell of Boquhan.[50] If the scheme existed outside rumour, it faced the obstacle that Mary was flatly refusing to divorce Bothwell. After Throckmorton's report, no more was heard of the scheme.

Meanwhile, Argyll had made progress with Maitland and Mar, but not enough to reach a settlement.[51] The 5th earl returned to the Highlands via Stirling and summoned a council of Highland chiefs.[52] At the time of Mary's abdication and the poorly attended coronation of James VI on 29 July, the

[47] 4 July: *Diurnal*, 117.   [48] Melville to Drury, 8 July, *CSPSc*, II. 347.
[49] Argyll to Throckmorton, and reply 11 and 14 July 1567, *CSPSc*, II. 352–3; printed in *Illustrations of the Reign of Queen Mary*, 196–7, 210–11.
[50] Argyll sent a copy of the Dumbarton bond to Throckmorton: Throckmorton to Elizabeth, 14 July and 9 August 1567, *CSPSc*, II. 349–52, 382–3.
[51] Throckmorton to Elizabeth, 25 July 1567, Keith, *History*, II. 694–700.
[52] Contract with Stewart of Doune in Stirling 12 July, NRA(S) 217 Box 1, No. 167; Charter at Strathlachlan, 20 July, AT, VI. 106; for council at the end of July, Keith, *History*, II. 698, and see above, p. 65.

earl deliberately distanced himself, politically and geographically, from the events.[53] He was also coping with his wife's departure.[54] In a final effort to get Argyll and the Hamiltons to accept the fait accompli, the confederate lords sent Melville to explain and excuse their actions.[55] Moray's return to Scotland on 11 August clarified the situation and had a significant effect upon his old friend Argyll. Having visited his half-sister at Lochleven and treated her to a two-day lecture on her faults, Moray wrote to the 5th earl carefully setting out the reasons why he was going to accept the regency.[56] In reply, the 5th earl urged him to delay his decision, but Moray went ahead with the proclamation of his regency on 22 August.[57] The haste over accepting the Regency and the reasons for it, coupled with tension over Argyll's attempt to divorce Moray's half-sister, caused a deep rift between the two men, who had been childhood friends and constant political allies for the previous decade.[58] In 1565, their different reactions to English behaviour had first edged them apart, with Argyll abandoning his automatic Anglophilia whilst Moray had come to rely more heavily upon his English allies. The sharp and painful break came in the summer of 1567 as the result of their diametrically opposed views on Mary's abdication and on Argyll's own divorce, ending the trust and sense of shared ideals which had characterised their close and warm friendship. In its place mutual suspicion flourished, with the 5th earl believing Moray was seeking political dominance or even aiming for the crown itself. Equally, with rumours circulating about a possible Campbell marriage for Mary, Moray doubted Argyll's motives.

Political realities more than past friendships forced the Queen's Party to make its peace with the new regent. After meetings in Glasgow and Hamilton, with accusations of bad faith directed against Argyll for remaining in contact with the King's Party, serious negotiations began in Edinburgh.[59] By the second week of September, Moray could inform his English allies that the Queen's Party had acknowledged the young king and his own regency.[60]

---

[53] Argyll's name was included in the regency council named in the abdication, which was only to operate in the absence of Moray: *RPC*, I. 540–1. He did have the courtesy to write to the General Assembly explaining he was prevented by the political situation from attending, but assuring the brethren of his continued support for God's cause: 28 July 1567, *BUK*, I. 101.

[54] See above, p. 29.   [55] Keith, *History*, II. 716–8.

[56] Throckmorton to Elizabeth, 20 August 1567; Keith, *History*, II. 734–41. Herries, *Memoirs*, 99–100. It is possible but unlikely that the two men met on 17 or 18 August as Throckmorton had predicted to Elizabeth, 14 August 1567, *CSPSc*, II. 382–3.

[57] This was probably the 'fair' letter Argyll sent to Moray, mentioned by Throckmorton, 22 August 1567, Keith, *History*, II. 745; regency, *RPC*, I. 548–50; Throckmorton to Elizabeth, 23 August, *CSPSc*, II. 386–8.

[58] Keith, *History*, II. 746, and see above, p. 36.   [59] Keith, *History*, II. 775–6.

[60] Moray to Cecil and to Throckmorton, 15 September 1567, *CSPSc*, II. 394–5; *Diurnal*, 121.

Conscious of the pressing need to return to the Highlands, the 5th earl left
the capital, not to return until the first Parliament of the regency in December
where he was elected one of the Lords of the Articles.[61] In the Parliament,
Argyll, along with Huntly and Herries, took the precaution of obtaining an
act preventing charges of negligence concerning the discharge of their public
duties.[62] The fear of old accusations being resurrected was not misplaced,
with Moray using the trial of some of Bothwell's servants for Darnley's
murder to embarrass the 5th earl and other former Queen's Party supporters.
When John Hay confessed there had been a bond between Bothwell, Huntly,
Argyll, Maitland, Balfour and others concerning Darnley's death, the named
nobles withdrew from Edinburgh, prompting the speculation that they were
guilty.[63] Following this dose of humiliation, Moray graciously accepted them
back into government, setting the 5th earl to work on his law and order campaign by holding a protracted justice-ayre in Glasgow.[64] Although working
alongside Moray, the old camaraderie had gone. Probably disillusioned and
weary of the in-fighting, Argyll proposed leaving for several years to tour
the Continent.[65]

Whatever his long-term plans, the 5th earl departed for Cowal at the end
of the justice-ayre, leaving Moray in Glasgow. By the time he had reached
Dunoon in the first week of May, Argyll would have heard of Mary's escape
from Lochleven.[66] Overnight, Mary's freedom changed Scottish politics. The
patched-up settlement between the regent and Argyll was finished. He immediately declared for the queen, heading an impressive list of nobles and
clergy who signed the Hamilton bond of 8 May.[67] With the queen in their
care, her supporters could for the first time fight to restore her to the throne.
Everyone realised it would mean civil war, so each side gathered troops as
fast as it could. Though Argyll raised a good contingent, there was insufficient time to mobilise large numbers. Deciding it was in their best interests
to risk an immediate encounter, on 13 May the two armies met at Langside,
just outside Glasgow.

[61] *Diurnal*, 122, 126.
[62] 29 December 1567, *CSPSc*, II. 573. The act ran from the previous 10 June, an interesting
choice of date prior to Carberry.
[63] *Diurnal*, 127–8.
[64] On 20 January Argyll's commission as justice-general was renewed, AT, VI. 122, and he was
auditing the treasurer's accounts again in the following month, *TA*, XII. 62. Justice-ayre,
8 March to 1 May, *TA*, XII. 120; *Diurnal*, 128.
[65] Licence for five years travel, 31 March 1568, *RSS*, VI. 216.
[66] Charter by Argyll and possibly a Campbell council 3 May 1568, AT, VI. 123 and 136. Moray
had the news and issued a proclamation from Glasgow on 3 May, BL Cotton Calig. C 1
n. fo. 77.
[67] Keith, *History*, II. 807–10; Wormald, *Lords and Men*, 407 [20]. A proclamation was also
issued, BL Royal MS 18 B 6 fo. 278. Calderwood, *History*, II. 405.

The crushing defeat at Langside is sometimes blamed upon Argyll, Mary's commander-in-chief.[68] Although the battle started well for the superior numbers of the queen's forces, the vanguard were caught in a confined position and started to flee, provoking a general flight. The 5th earl was taken ill at the onset of the fighting, causing serious disruption to the command structure, which, combined with the superior generalship of William Kirkcaldy of Grange, won the day for the regent's forces.[69] Of greater significance than its effect upon the battle, Argyll's illness prevented him exerting any influence upon its aftermath. In particular, the 5th earl was not involved in Mary's flight from the battlefield nor was he present to stop the panic or change her mind when she opted to flee the country. The Queen's Party had fought the battle without making contingency plans, probably underestimating Mary's fear of once again facing capture and imprisonment. Her decision to cross the Solway Firth to England was a catastrophic error of judgement. By removing the incalculable asset of her person, she destroyed any hope of long-term success for the Queen's Party. With no queen to restore, their primary objective could not be accomplished. Within England, Mary's presence had an immediate and long-lasting effect upon English domestic politics. For the mainland, it added the extra destabilising focus to British politics of the prisoner queen herself and increased the existing imbalance between the two kingdoms caused by her fall.[70]

SHANE'S DEATH AND THE ULSTER MARRIAGES

Within the Gaelic world of the Highlands, Argyll's authority had remained secure during the Chase-about Raid. The crown could not loosen its grip on the region, even when the 5th earl was in open rebellion. Mary, Queen of Scots had tried to entice Highland chiefs to her side and use them against the 5th earl. Despite extravagant promises of royal largesse, most stayed loyal to Argyll. A few negotiated with the queen, particularly in January 1566 when it appeared as though the 5th earl would not be received back into royal

---

[68] Royal commission appointing Argyll lieutenant of Mary's forces, 13 May 1568, AT, VI. 124; printed in W. Fraser, *The Lennox* (2 vols., Edinburgh, 1874), II. 437.

[69] One report spoke of the earl 'being overtaken of a suddane with an apoplexe', suggesting a mild stroke or heart attack: Calderwood, *History*, II. 414. The aspersion that Argyll fainted from fright seems unlikely because the earl had fought in many engagements with no sign of nerves: 16 May report on battle, CSPSc, II. 407; criticism of the earl, Keith, *History*, II. 811. Possibly Argyll found he could not face fighting his old friend Moray: Wormald, *Mary Queen of Scots*, 173.

[70] R.B. Wernham, 'The British Question, 1559–69' in R.B. Wernham, ed., *New Cambridge Modern History III: The Counter Reformation and Price Revolution 1559–1610* (Cambridge, 1968), 209–33.

favour. With John Stewart of Appin's inflated promise to bring the Islesmen to fight for the queen coming to nothing, the sole contribution to Mary's cause was the information Stewart forwarded to Atholl.[71] Having returned to favour after the Riccio murder, the 5th earl and his Campbell kin punished the waverers and reasserted their authority over their affinities. On 8 May, Hector Mòr MacLean, while lying sick in Duart, sent an abject apology to Argyll for negotiating with the king and queen.[72] A few days later, Stewart of Appin gave an obligation to keep the peace and accept the council's decisions in his dispute with the 5th earl.[73] Donald Cameron of Lochiel apologised to Colin Campbell of Glenorchy for any offence he had caused, declaring he would remain true to his bond.[74]

Within the wider reaches of Gaelic politics, Argyll's most pressing problem was how to help the MacDonalds recover from their chief's death and defeat in Ulster. After their abortive Irish expedition, James' widow Lady Agnes and her sons sought the 5th earl's assistance. Alastair Og, James' younger brother, having assumed the leadership of Clan Donald South tried to re-establish its presence in Antrim and negotiate with O'Neill over the release of Sorley Boy. The same cause motivated the 5th earl to reopen talks with the Ulster chief. Much to Shane's relief, Argyll's priority in the winter of 1565 was to secure Sorley Boy's ransom. During the Chase-about Raid, the Irish chief had offered the earl his help. According to John Douglas' report, Argyll 'hath confessid him self to be much beholding to Shane, in that he offrid hym relief hear [Ireland] in the tyme of his banishement for which cause he saith he meaneth to visit hym this sommer'.[75] The 5th earl, comparing the assistance offered in his time of trouble by Shane, his erstwhile enemy, with the refusal of help from his English allies, changed his alignment accordingly.

In the spring of 1566, the English were seriously worried by the possibility of an alliance between Argyll and O'Neill. The Irish chief was taking a more independent and aggressive line than before, which Cecil believed was the result of his Scottish contacts, as he told Sir Thomas Smith, 'we have cause to feare that Oneyles boldnes is fedd out of Scotland'.[76] Elizabeth was incensed against O'Neill and was unrealistically demanding Sidney engineer

---

[71] Stewart of Appin, Cameron of Lochiel, MacRanald of Keppoch and an ambassador from MacLean of Duart (probably Hector Og MacLean) were reported to be in Edinburgh, Glenorchy to Carrick, 13 February 1566, *Campbell Letters*, 79.

[72] Memo, 8 May 1566, Argyll MSS Bundle 1074.

[73] 11 May 1566, *RPC*, I. 457, and 20 June 1566, AT, VI. 82.

[74] C. spring 1566, *Campbell Letters*, 78.

[75] Sidney to Cecil 9 June 1566 SP63/18 fo. 18r–v; *Letters and Memorials of State of Sir Henry Sidney* ed. A. Collins (2 vols., London, 1746), I. 11–12; Sidney told Cecil that Argyll would be with O'Neill in July, 24 June 1566, SP63/18 fo. 56v.

[76] 26 March 1566, quotation in Hill, *Fire and Sword*, 101; *Queen Elizabeth and her Times* ed. T. Wright (2 vols., London, 1838), I. 224–5.

his immediate downfall.[77] The new lord deputy, having come to Ireland at the beginning of the year, wanted assurances his expedition against O'Neill would be properly funded and followed up.[78] Sir Henry Sidney, well aware how crucial the 5th earl's attitude would be to his own success, had heard of Argyll's discussions of a marriage alliance with O'Neill.[79] Shane had been sufficiently committed to the negotiations to put away Katherine MacLean, whom he had married a few months earlier.[80]

Mary, Queen of Scots, seeing it as a method of pressurising Elizabeth, was delighted with the friendship between Shane and the 5th earl. Following his pardon for the Chase-about Raid in March 1566, she immediately sought his co-operation, asking him 'to interteny familiaritie with O'Neill in the best mane ye can'.[81] The 5th earl continued his negotiations, and it was reported the two chiefs had met, though this was unlikely.[82] In May, having introduced O'Neill's ambassador to the Scottish king, who gave him money to buy whisky, Argyll sent his own servant back with the Irishman.[83] Shane tried to make light of the embassy, claiming his man had gone to Scotland to demonstrate his hairstyle, 'the monstrus glib which he ware uppon his hedde'. Sidney was not impressed by this ingenious excuse.[84]

Despite Mary's attempt to exploit Argyll's dealings with O'Neill, the 5th earl had broken the automatic triangular link between Ulster politics and Anglo-Scottish relations. He was now concentrating his attention upon the plight of his dependants, the MacDonalds, especially the need to free Sorley Boy. The earl generously agreed to underwrite the expenses that Archibald,

---

[77] Elizabeth wanted 'the extirpation of him by open warre' and hoped 'such a cankrid dangerous rebell may be utterly extirpid', 28 March 1566, SP63/16 fo. 206r. For a general discussion of O'Neill's position, *Sidney State Papers, 1565–70* ed. T. O'Laidhin (Irish Manuscripts Commission, Dublin, 1962), 16–20; C. Brady, *Shane O'Neill* (Dundalk, 1996), 59–65.

[78] For example Sidney's letters to Cecil, 17 April 1566 SP63/17, fos. 37r–41v; Knollys' instructions (2 drafts), 18 April, SP63/17, fos. 47r–51v.

[79] Sidney thought the marriage would be between Shane and Lady Agnes, which seems unlikely, Sidney to Privy Council, 15 April 1566, SP63/17, fo. 31v. Earlier, Randolph had thought O'Neill's and MacDonald's sons and daughters were involved in a double marriage, 16 January 1566, *Illustrations of the Reign of Queen Mary*, 146–8.

[80] See above p. 130. In his postscript, Randolph told Cecil that he was enclosing a letter from a 'verie frende' whose hand Cecil knew, and added that if Cecil thought 'oughte shalbe done with Maccalyne, the commoditie now servethe well' (quite how the English were intending to use the MacLean chief was not clear): 26 April 1566, *CSPSc*, II. 276.

[81] 31 March 1566, *Letters to Argyll Family*, 5–6.

[82] Randolph to Cecil, 16 January and 7 February 1566, *Illustrations of the Reign of Queen Mary*, 146–8, 152–4 at p. 154. From Dublin Bagenall reported to Leicester, 'I do here saye that he [O'Neill] hath made a sure bande with Scotland and what harme he is then able to do, your honour best knowethe': February 1566, SP63/16 fo. 79v.

[83] Rogers to Cecil, 5 July 1566, *CSPSc*, II. 293–4.

[84] A glib was the long strand of hair hanging over the forehead. Sidney to Cecil 9 June SP63/18 fo. 18r–v; *Letters and Memorials of State of Sir Henry Sidney*, I. 11–12. Randolph to Cecil, 13 May, *CSPSc*, II. 278.

the eldest son of James and Agnes, might incur obtaining Sorley's freedom.[85] Together they sent over 1,000 men to Ireland to bargain from a position of strength with O'Neill, but no agreement was concluded.[86] Meanwhile, Alastair Og had stabilised the MacDonald holdings in Antrim.[87] Before anything further was achieved, Archibald died, leaving as successor his eighteen-year-old brother Angus, whom Argyll took into his protection and probably into his household.[88] With Angus and his mother, Lady Agnes, wanting revenge upon Shane more than Sorley's freedom, this harder attitude probably prevented the 5th earl from finalising a deal with O'Neill. Though Sorley was not released, there was a considerable improvement in his conditions of captivity.[89] It was a concession to win the help of the 5th earl and Alastair Og which Shane sent Patrick Dorelle, the precentor of Armagh, to request.[90] As a consequence of Dorelle's visit, Argyll reactivated his plan to visit Ulster, proposing a four-day trip in October accompanied by troops, including a hundred arquebusiers.[91] Even with the assurance that all the men would return with the earl, the Scottish queen worried that the visit would offend the English and, judging by their reaction, she was correct.[92] Occupied with the Jedburgh justice-ayre, the 5th earl sent his servant, Thomas Stevenson, to Ireland. Though changing his plans at Mary's request was a diplomatic concession to the English, Argyll also employed Stevenson to relay to them a threat concerning her succession claim.[93]

[85] 27 May 1566, AT, VI. 78.
[86] Killigrew to Cecil, 28 June and 4 July 1566, *CSPSc*, II. 290, 292.
[87] Alastair Og had written to Sidney to discover whether an offer of service to the English would produce better conditions. Sidney wanted to know 'in what sort I shall componde with them eyther to have them in actuall service or to kepe them with some promese from combyning with the rebell': Sidney to Privy Council, 9 and 14 September 1566, SP63/19 fo. 22r; *CSP Ireld*, I. 314 [11]; Hill, *Fire and Sword*, 107.
[88] Archibald must have died before 20 July, *RSS*, V, ii. 2990. Randolph to Cecil, 13 June, *CSPSc*, II. 284–5.
[89] Immediately after Glentaisie Shane threatened to starve Sorley to death if Dunluce Castle did not surrender: Hill, *Fire and Sword*, 94.
[90] Dorelle later made the excuse that he had only obeyed O'Neill because he was threatened with hanging, and that, once in Scotland, he did not follow Shane's commands but reported to the 5th earl and waited upon him: Terence Danyell or Donelly, dean of Armagh to Irish Privy Council, 10 December 1567, SP63/22 fo. 167.
[91] Master of Maxwell to Lord Scrope, 4 October 1566, *CSP For, 1566–8*, 136.
[92] Maitland to Cecil, 4 October 1566, *CSPSc*, II. 300–1. On 8 October the English Privy Council sent a letter to Forster on the border telling him to find out what was going on: *Acts of the Privy Council of England* ed. J. Dasent (46 vols., London, 1890–1964), 1558–70, II. 313–4, and probably sent a letter from Elizabeth to Mary complaining about Argyll aiding O'Neill. Forster stopped the letter because Melville had been sent on a mission to England, 13 October 1566 (not 1565 as in *CSP For, 1564–5*, 490), SP59/10, fo. 121r–v; 15 October 1566, *CSP For, 1566–8*, 139. Things were still confused when Cecil annotated the queen's instructions for Sidney sent with Edward Horsey, 20 October 1566, SP63/19 fo. 50r.
[93] Piers to Sidney, 15 December 1566, SP63/19 fo. 147r; and see below, p. 167.

As well as making strenuous efforts on their behalf in Ulster, the 5th earl propped up MacDonald power in the Highlands and Islands. He was following the tacit policy of his predecessors within the southern Hebrides, restricting the two major clans, the MacDonalds and the MacLeans, to separate parts of the Western Highlands and Islands. MacLean expansion was encouraged within Mull, Coll, Tiree, the mainland in Ardgour and to the north, but was not acceptable in the MacDonald-controlled south, especially the flashpoints of Islay and Gigha. Satisfying their conflicting ambitions and keeping both clans within his affinity was a permanent balancing act for Argyll, in 1565 made specially awkward by the weakening of the MacDonalds. Their terrible defeat in Ulster underscored the permanent problem they faced, because their attention and resources were divided between lands in Antrim and in Kintyre and Islay. Whenever they were embroiled in one area, the MacDonalds were vulnerable to attack in the other. The MacLeans, ever mindful of their feud over the Rhinns of Islay, found the temptation of MacDonald weakness too great to resist. Their immediate target was the island of Gigha just off the Kintyre coast, which formed part of Lady Agnes' jointure.[94] The raids proved a useful rallying point uniting all the MacLeans. In the latter part of 1566, the Duart and Coll branches, previously at loggerheads, joined together to raid Gigha. Initially distracted by his involvement in court politics, in spring 1567 a furious Argyll obtained a royal commission to discipline the MacLeans.[95] Though both kin groups were part of his affinity, Argyll appeared to favour the MacDonalds, as he had over the Islay dispute. Not surprisingly, the MacLeans complained that their loyal service was bringing loss, not gain. As compensation for the hard line he was taking over Gigha, the 5th earl favoured Duart and his tutee, Tormod MacLeod. However, he showed little sympathy for MacLean encroachments on MacDonald lands in Islay and Gigha, employing force to keep the rival clans apart and preserve MacDonald power.

The 5th earl had greater success maintaining order in the northern Hebrides. The final settlement of the MacLeod inheritance was agreed in February and March 1567. Argyll, endorsing the Gaelic view that a woman could not hold the chieftainship of a clan, decided that the heiress should be removed as a source of conflict. Consequently, Mary was married to Duncan

---

[94] Gigha had been held by the MacNeills, but in April 1554 Neil MacNeill had sold his land to James MacDonald and Agnes. However, Hector Allanson MacLean (the son of Ailean nan Sop) had been in actual control of Gigha and had received a crown charter to the island which he found annulled by MacNeill's sale. Although MacDonald's occupation was accepted in the 1550s, Gigha remained a potential flashpoint between the two clans whose dispute over Islay simmered on. 30 January 1552, *RSS*, IV. 1497; 23 June 1553, *RMS*, IV. 800; 1 April 1554, *RMS*, IV. 921; Maclean-Bristol, *Warriors and Priests*, 131, 150–1.

[95] 28 April 1567, AT, VI. 96; *HMC*, 4th, 488.

Campbell of Castle Sween, a younger son of the Laird of Auchinbreck.[96] Atypically, this union was not the prelude to a Campbell takeover, as had been the case with other marriages to prominent heiresses. Instead, it was a calculated piece of diplomacy, permitting a division of the MacLeod inheritance acceptable to all the parties. Argyll made a contract with Tormod MacLeod of Dunvegan, who provided a £1,000 dowry for Mary in return for a guarantee he would be granted her lands.[97] A few days later, having received the 5th earl's guarantee over the lands of Trotternish, Sleat and North Uist, which Tormod had previously claimed, Donald Gormeson MacDonald of Sleat renewed his bond of manrent, paying Argyll 1,000 merks, and contributing 500 merks towards Mary's dowry.[98] This settlement was devised and implemented by the earl without interference from the crown. By its interlocking arrangements, he prevented a serious crisis involving every major clan in the Hebrides and northern Highlands. In addition to those who signed the main agreements, the feud would have drawn in the MacDonalds of Dunivaig, the MacKenzies of Kintail, the MacLeans of Duart and the earl of Huntly, all of whom had connexions with the MacLeods. Instead, by the solution of this tricky inheritance dispute, peace was preserved throughout the Outer Hebrides and north-western coast. With royal acquiescence, Argyll's authority over the Highland region had been strengthened.

This concentration upon his Gaelic dependants brought a reassertion of traditional Campbell priorities. Within the localised politics of the Gaelic worlds, the earls of Argyll had paid closest attention to the core of their power in the Western Highlands and Islands. Not bordering directly upon Campbell territory and so located upon the clan's peripheries, the north of Ireland, and to a lesser extent the northern Highlands and Outer Hebrides, were of secondary concern. In both regions the 5th earl wanted to maintain his political influence, but, in this period, they were not regarded as potential areas for Campbell territorial expansion or colonisation. Within the confines of the Gaelic political world, Argyll's aims were limited and realistic. In particular, when circumstances were unfavourable, he was not prepared to risk military operations far from his home base. This pragmatic approach explains the 5th earl's more casual attitude to Calvagh O'Donnell's restoration to Donegal, when compared to the time and trouble he expended over his Highland clients. Knowing it would involve a full-scale attack upon O'Neill,

---

[96] The wedding took place around June 1570, when the 5th earl gave a charter of lands in Knapdale to Duncan and his future wife Mary: 6 June 1570, AT, VI. 48.

[97] 24 February and 15 September 1567, *Coll. de Rebus Alban*, 144–6, 149–51. I.F. Grant, *The MacLeods: The History of a Clan 1200–1956* (London, 1959), 125.

[98] 4 and 5 March 1567, *Coll. de Rebus Alban*, 147–9; AT, VI. 95; Wormald, *Lords and Men*, 197 [Arg 91].

Argyll had not planned military intervention on Calvagh's behalf, choosing instead to pester the English government for aid. In the very long run this worked, with O'Donnell restored to his lands in the wake of Sidney's successful Ulster campaign in 1566.[99] At the end of October, shortly after his restoration, Calvagh died, leaving as chief his brother Hugh, who was neither the 5th earl's personal friend nor dependant.[100]

In that 1566 campaign, his refusal to do battle with Sidney severely weakened Shane, though it did not defeat him. Though the lord deputy was advancing into his heartland, O'Neill remained confident of the support of the other Ulster chiefs, who were fearful of English colonisation. Aware the news would be passed to Argyll, Shane wrote explaining the situation to Cormac O'Connor, with the 5th earl in Edinburgh.[101] Having promised Mary, Queen of Scots not to assist O'Neill, the earl did not respond, sending the letter's Gaelic original to London accompanied by a Scots translation, including the bearer's verbal elaborations.[102] Shane's messenger had brought some incongruous gifts from his master and Katherine MacLean, who was back with O'Neill, but such blandishments did not sway the 5th earl.[103] In the spring of 1567, after he had been attacked and heavily defeated by Hugh O'Donnell at Farsetmore, Shane was forced to negotiate with the remaining power in Ulster, the MacDonalds.[104] Sorley Boy, still his captive, arranged a meeting at Cushendun with Alastair Og. After a couple of days hard negotiations, which failed to produce an agreement, Shane was killed at a private meeting with Alastair.[105]

[99] Agreements between Sidney and Calvagh, and Calvagh and his kinsmen, 20 October 1566, *Calendar of the Carew Manuscripts Preserved in the Archiepiscopal Library at Lambeth 1515–1624* ed. J. Brewer *et al.* (6 vols., London, 1867–73), I. 373–5.

[100] R. Bagwell, *Ireland under the Tudors* (3 vols., London, 1963; reprint of 1885–90 edn), II. 111; Sidney to Privy Council, 18 January 1567, *CSP Ireld*, I. 325 [13]; *The Annals of the Kingdom of Ireland by the Four Masters from the Earliest Period to the year 1616* ed. J. Donovan (7 vols., Dublin, 1851), 1566.

[101] O'Connor had returned to Scotland the previous year. As he explained to Elizabeth, even though he had her pardon he had been prevented from returning to his Irish lands, 9 July 1566, SP63/18 fo. 131; *CSP Ireld*, I. 309 [53].

[102] The Gaelic original, the Scots translation and the literal English translation, all dated 20 March 1567, which was probably when they reached London, *CSP Ireld*, I. 328 [Nos. 49–51]. All three are printed in 'Shane O'Neill's last letter' ed. R. Smith, *Journal of Celtic Studies*, 11 (1958), 131–3. O'Connor did not heed O'Neill's promises of help and instead travelled to the English Court, O'Connor to Elizabeth, 12 March 1567, *CSP Ireld*, I. 328 [45].

[103] Katherine sent a gold chain to her former step-son and Shane a set of garments, which his father had been given by Henry VIII. Drury to Cecil, 30 March 1567, *CSP For, 1566–8*, 198; Privy Council to Sidney, 3 April, *CSP Ireld*, I. 329 [60].

[104] 8 May, G.A. Hayes-McCoy, *Irish Battles: A Military History of Ireland* (Belfast, 1989; reprint of 1969 edn), 68–86.

[105] Fitzwilliam's letter of 11 June 1567 provides a more accurate version of a confused event than the story of the drunken brawl that was later circulated by the English and incorporated

The death of Shane O'Neill was greeted with huge delight by the English. Anxious to acquire a share of the glory, Captain Piers secured Shane's head and sent it 'pickled in a pipkin' to Dublin, where it was placed on a spike on the walls. In all their celebrations at the death of a man they labelled a great traitor, the English conveniently forgot they had not engineered O'Neill's downfall. It had been achieved by an O'Donnell victory and a MacDonald murder, neither of which were decisively assisted by the English. In their euphoria, the London and Dublin governments optimistically assumed that the eclipse of O'Neill power would end their Ulster troubles, allowing them to expel the Scots from the north of Ireland and to fortify the coasts to prevent their return.[106]

In Scotland, the news of O'Neill's death, conveyed by the returning Sorley Boy and Katherine MacLean, was overshadowed by the tumultuous events of Carberry Hill and Mary's abdication.[107] The 5th earl had little opportunity to react before Shane's successor made contact with him.[108] Turlough Luineach, the new O'Neill, was of a different mould than his cousin, Shane the Proud. As a worried Fitzwilliam explained, the willingness to negotiate seriously with the Scots made Turlough potentially more dangerous than Shane, 'who never of him self lycked the Scottes as by his deedes to them and their rewardes to him apeared'. With grim humour he warned that Turlough and Hugh O'Donnell were wanting Scottish wives in order to breed a new sort of rebel out of their loins.[109] Of greater concern was news that the MacDonalds were successfully re-establishing themselves in Antrim, having brought 700 men collected with Argyll's help.[110] The horrified Irish lord justice commented, 'of all people my nature abhorreth them [Scots] to be in Ireland'.[111] English hopes, raised by Shane's murder, of the imminent expulsion of the Scots, were quickly evaporating.

---

in the Act of Attainder against Shane, C. Brady, 'The Killing of Shane O'Neill: Some New Evidence', *Irish Sword*, 15 (1982–3), 116–23.

[106] Elizabeth to Sidney, 22 July 1567, *CSP Ireld*, I. 342–3 [65]; Dawson, 'Two Kingdoms or Three?', 87.

[107] See above, pp. 150–3. Katherine later married John Stewart of Appin, one of the earl's dependants, sometime between 1572 and 4 May 1576: *RPC*, II. 520–1.

[108] In the autumn of 1567 Turlough wrote to Argyll, but the first messenger was attacked by Rory Og MacQuillan. O'Neill told the English he had sent to Argyll because the 5th earl had stood surety for the MacDonalds, who had killed Shane, and Turlough was seeking an alliance with the 5th earl against the MacDonalds. Turlough to Irish Council, 24 November 1567, SP63/22 fo. 112. Bagenal to Irish Council, 5 February 1568 SP63/23 fo. 104.

[109] Fitzwilliam to Cecil, 27 November 1567, SP63/22 fo. 76. Fitzwilliam was exaggerating Shane's aversion to the Scots: Brady, *Shane O'Neill*, 64–5.

[110] Fitzwilliam to Piers and Malby and their reply, 21 October and 3 November, SP63/22 fos. 54, 70–1. Hill, *Fire and Sword*, 124–6.

[111] 27 November 1567, SP63/22 fo. 76.

Through his negotiations with Turlough, Argyll was creating a coalition uniting the three major Ulster powers of the MacDonalds, the O'Neills and the O'Donnells. This revolutionary realignment of Ulster politics was to be cemented through marriage alliances. The first move was made in November 1567 when Turlough sent two bards to negotiate such an alliance. They returned to Ireland in the middle of January 1568 with Argyll's presents for Turlough and a letter promising aid and encouraging O'Neill 'to be stoute in his dowinges'. Turlough willingly accepted the force of Campbell redshanks, who had been dispatched in case he needed them, but for some reason refused to keep the earl's gift of a 'taffete hat with a band sett with bewgles'.[112] To put the English off the scent, Turlough explained the mercenaries were to be used to fight the MacDonalds.[113] Sorley Boy contributed to the smoke screen by offering Dublin a truce in the hope that he could secure the long-sought-for recognition of his Antrim lands.[114] Hidden from the English, the real purpose of the negotiations was the Scottish–Irish marriages. As the 5th earl assured Turlough, Lady Agnes, James MacDonald's widow, would marry him and bring as many mercenaries as he wanted in her dowry. Viewing the O'Neill marriage as the best means of securing their Irish inheritance for her MacDonald sons, the forceful Lady Agnes chose the 5th earl to bargain for her and conclude the alliance, though Sorley's son had accompanied the Irish bards and his father was privy to the negotiations.[115] A second set of marriage negotiations were underway to bring the O'Donnells into the new coalition. Finola, or 'Inneen Dubh', the dark-haired daughter of Lady Agnes and James MacDonald, was to become Hugh O'Donnell's bride.[116] This alliance was quickly concluded and 400 Campbells sent to O'Donnell in early December 1567 as part of the dowry 'on account'.[117] Through his control over the supply of redshanks and over the marital destiny of his

---

[112] Bagenal to Irish Council, 5 February 1568, SP63/23 fo. 104; Danyell to Irish Council, 22 January 1568, SP63/23 fo. 69, spoke of 130 Campbells; Malby to Sidney, 13 February, SP63/23 fo. 128.

[113] Turlough to Carrickfergus Captains, and Marshall, 17 and 20 January 1568, *CSP Ireld*, I. 363 [32II and IV] where he wrote that he had employed the Scots of Veguibne or Meguib-hne, which was a form of Clan O'Duibne, one of the names for the Campbells; Danyell to Irish Council, 22 January 1567, SP63/23 fo. 69, *CSP Ireld*, I. 361 [20II].

[114] Sorley Boy to Piers and Malby, 16 and 23 December 1567, *CSP Ireld*, I. 358 [10II and 7V]; Hill, *Fire and Sword*, 125–6.

[115] Commission in north to council in Dublin, 29 November 1567 SP63/22 fo. 104; Bagenal to Lords Justices, 5 February 1568 SP63/23 fo. 104. Alastair Galt, Sorley's son, was one of the captains who returned with the Campbell mercenaries in February. Sorley Boy himself returned to Scotland in January 1568, Hill, *Fire and Sword*, 127–8. A list had been drawn up of all the Scots present in Ulster before the return of Sorley Boy, which totalled 750, 27 January 1568, SP63/23 fo. 50.

[116] Fitzwilliam passed the rumour to this effect onto Cecil, 27 November 1567, SP63/22 fo. 76.

[117] Danyell to Irish Council, 10 December 1567, Hill, *Fire and Sword*, 124–6.

kinswomen, the 5th earl had altered the complexion of politics in the north of Ireland.

Catching the English by surprise, the new alignment in Ulster left them struggling to find an adequate response. At the start of 1568, they were agitated by news of the first alliance between Argyll, O'Neill and the Mac-Donalds. By March, they were resigned to expecting the joint weddings and had stationed a pinnace in the North Channel in a vain attempt to intercept the Scottish party.[118] Reporting the acute English discomfort at the imminent marriages, the Spanish ambassador remarked that they would create a considerable disturbance, especially if the Scottish queen were to gain her freedom.[119] His observations were prophetic, for Mary's escape from Lochleven did indeed affect the Irish marriages, though not as he had predicted. With the 5th earl commanding the queen's forces, he had no choice but to postpone the weddings. Significantly, the two Irish chiefs did not complain about the delay and made no move to break the alliances. Knowing they needed Argyll, they were prepared to wait until he was free to provide the dowries of redshanks. The English remained fearful, dispatching John Douglas and prohibiting the export of timber from Wexford and Carrickfergus to Scotland in an ineffectual attempt to prevent Argyll building galleys to transport his redshanks.[120] Elizabeth employed her well-tried mixture of threats and promises, but he would not alter his plans without real concessions from the English queen.[121]

All was finally ready for the joint weddings in the summer of 1569. At the start of August, Lady Agnes and her daughter left Kintyre for Islay. From the Hebridean island thirty-two galleys and boats with around 4,000 men sailed to Rathlin, where O'Neill and O'Donnell awaited their brides.[122] Argyll and many of his Campbell kinsmen probably attended the wedding celebrations, though they did not stay for the entire fortnight of festivities.[123] The 5th earl

---

[118] Malby to Cecil, 19 March 1568, SP63/23 fo. 187; Danyell to Fitzwilliam, 29 March, SP63/24 fo. 29; T. Glasgow, 'The Elizabethan Navy in Ireland', *Irish Sword*, 7 (1974–5), 291–307.

[119] 1 May 1568, *CSP Sp, 1568–79*, 26–7.

[120] Sidney to Leicester and to Cecil, 8 August 1568, *Letters and Memorials of State of Sir Henry Sidney* ed. A. Collins, I. 34–6; 4 and 28 August 1568, SP63/25 fos. 150, 152.

[121] 14 August 1568, *Letters and Memorials of State of Sir Henry Sidney*, I. 36, and see below, pp. 168–9.

[122] Information from the merchant Leonard Sumpter of Bristol who was in Islay on 4 August, 13 August SP63/29 fo. 68; John Douglas to Cecil, 15 August, BL Cotton Calig. C 1 n. fo. 441 [No. 94]; *CSPSc*, II. 669; G. Hill, *An Historical Account of the MacDonnells of Antrim* (Belfast, 1978; reprint of 1873 edn), 151–2; Hayes-McCoy, *Scots Mercenary Forces*, 106.

[123] They were back in Dunoon for a clan council on 12 August: AT, VI. 136. Turlough promised the 5th earl about a hundred cattle and horses and the same to Sorley Boy: Turlough Brasselaugh O'Neill to Danyell, 27 August 1569, SP63/29 fo. 88.

had masterminded two marriages, which together re-aligned Ulster politics and whose consequences influenced the fate of the north of Ireland for the rest of the century.[124]

The experiences of 1565, especially the refusal by the English to answer calls for help from their Scottish friends and allies, destroyed the 5th earl's trust in Elizabeth and the governments in London and Dublin. Feeling personally betrayed and believing the special amity and vision of a united Protestant Britain and Ireland had been callously discarded, Argyll could not forgive English behaviour. Other Anglophiles, such as Moray and Morton, though they suffered the privations of exile, remained loyal to their pro-English views and their ideal of a united Protestant mainland. This divergence in attitude towards Anglo-Scottish relations began to distance the 5th earl from his close friend Moray and political allies, such as Morton, Maitland and Kirkcaldy of Grange. If Argyll had been naive and idealistic before 1565, thereafter he was suspicious and calculating in his dealings with the English. He assumed that, in future, bribery or threats were needed to bring English support for Scottish Protestantism or the Anglophile party.

In the two years after 1565, Anglo-Scottish relations were primarily reactions to the whirlwind of events that brought Mary's downfall. The Darnley marriage had moved Mary's claims to the succession to the centre of the British diplomatic stage, in turn increasing the tensions within English domestic politics.[125] Mary's marriage had been treated by Elizabeth as a hostile act, provoking a breakdown in diplomatic relations and bringing the countries to the brink of war. The Scottish queen had retaliated by employing threats to gain recognition as heir to the English throne. To frighten the English government, Mary used the spectre of a Roman Catholic league, which Protestant Europe was convinced had been formed at the Bayonne meeting in October 1565 between France and Spain. Thanks to the change in Argyll's position, for the first time Mary could employ a new weapon in her succession campaign, the threat of disruption in Ulster.

The first indication of Argyll's revised attitude in Anglo-Scottish relations was seen in May 1566 when he wrote to Randolph, who had been forced to retire to Berwick, explaining he was negotiating with O'Neill's messenger[126] The 5th earl offered to stop supporting Shane on condition Elizabeth softened

---

[124] For a full examination of the implications, see Hayes-McCoy, *Scots Mercenary Forces.*
[125] Alford, *Cecil*, ch. 6.
[126] Randolph was in diplomatic disgrace having been caught giving English money to the rebel lords during the Chase-about Raid.

her hard line towards the Scottish nobles involved in Riccio's murder.[127] Elizabeth was left in no doubt that, as a result of her previous policy, Argyll's good will had been withdrawn. Belatedly, she tried to retrieve the situation by offering the threadbare defence that there was no alternative in 1565, assuring the earl that Moray and Randolph would explain the difficulties she had faced at greater length.[128] Elizabeth and Cecil were seriously concerned by Argyll's attitude and its impact upon Irish affairs. They hoped Sidney's arrival in January 1566 would herald the subjugation of Ulster and the civilising of the entire kingdom, but the 5th earl's actions were crucial for these ambitious plans in the short, medium and long term. There were two huge obstacles to English success in Ulster. The first was Shane O'Neill, with whom Argyll was negotiating; the second was the MacDonalds, whom he was supporting. For O'Neill to be defeated and the Scots removed, a sustained military campaign had to be mounted. Then permanent garrisons had to be erected to hold the coast before English colonisation of the region could begin. Long before it was jettisoned by Argyll, the 1560 model of co-operation had been abandoned by Cecil and Sidney. They now proposed to exclude the 5th earl from Irish affairs and to stop or slow the mercenary trade. Future plans included the expulsion of the Ulster Scots, who, as Cecil reminded Sidney, were more dangerous than O'Neill, 'both because they are people of more valiantness and are increased by a foreign prince, and lastly because they posses the seacoast whereby they hold as it were the keys of her majesty's realm'.[129] Such a sentiment indicated more than a switch of tactics in Ireland; it was Cecil's rejection of the triangular British policy of Scottish assistance in Ulster.

In June 1566, the immediate problem was Shane O'Neill and the fear he was allied with the Scottish and French monarchs against England. With all O'Neill's Scottish links coming through Argyll, one strand of Sir Henry Killigrew's special mission to the Scottish court was to discover what the 5th earl was doing.[130] As his present negotiations with Shane had failed, Argyll could make reassuring noises to the English ambasssadors, repeating his conditions for help in Ireland, the restoration of the banished Scottish lords and the support of Scottish Protestantism.[131] Such bargaining upset his friends, Moray and Kirkcaldy, who pushed the 5th earl to become O'Neill's enemy, reminding him of the 1560 English intervention. They were unable

[127] Randolph to Cecil, 13 May 1566, *CSPSc*, II. 278.
[128] Elizabeth to Randolph, 23 May 1566, *Illustrations of the Reign of Queen Mary*, 161–3; *CSPSc*, II. 279.
[129] 11 March 1567, *CSP Ireld*, I. 328 [4] quotation from White, 'Tudor Plantations', II. 253.
[130] Instructions to Killigrew, 13–15 June 1566, *CSPSc*, II. 286–8.
[131] For example Killigrew to Cecil, 28 June 1566, *CSPSc*, II. 290.

to alter Argyll's new priority of caring first for his Gaelic dependants and only assisting the English if they reciprocated.[132] Embarrassed by his friend's unhelpful attitude, Moray apologised to Cecil for Argyll's actions, trying hard to excuse the links with O'Neill as the normal courtesies extended between well-acquainted Gaelic neighbours. He added that during the Chase-about Raid the 5th earl had to take his friends wherever they might be found. These mutually incompatible reasons illustrated the extent of Moray's discomfiture on finding that Argyll was no longer co-operating with the English.[133] The 5th earl was pressing hard for greater English assistance for the Riccio murderers. He had assured the exiled earl of Morton that, until he knew the exiles and Scottish Protestantism were safe, he would not travel abroad. By coupling the two things, Argyll was making an oblique offer to tour Europe instead of becoming further involved in Irish affairs. Morton, understanding the hint, suggested the English queen write to Argyll about Ireland.[134] In response, the earl did make a minor concession by rescheduling his visit to O'Neill from July to October 1566.

The 5th earl continued the game of veiled threats and occasional concessions while pursuing his own goals and allowing Mary to use the Irish card in her Anglo-Scottish diplomacy. By the autumn, the Scottish queen did not want to offend the English, so she persuaded Argyll not to visit Ireland in person.[135] However, she encouraged the 5th earl to employ his Irish connexion to convey a threat concerning the English succession. In December 1566, Captain Piers reported to Sidney that the 5th earl's messenger had told him 'that yff ther quyne were not mad ayere aparant to the krown thys parlement in Ingland that then the Lord off Argyle wowld be schortely in Irland to help Shan [O'Neill]'.[136] Argyll was reusing the triangular links against England. The birth of a healthy son in June 1566 had strengthened Mary's position and her claim to be recognised as Elizabeth's heir, but Darnley's murder the following February left her seriously weakened and needing Elizabeth's good will. Consequently, later that month she adopted a superficially tough line when O'Neill sent more messengers to Argyll. Her order to the earl to stop the flow of Scottish mercenaries and recall those already employed in Ulster, reassured Killigrew who had been dispatched north after Kirk o' Field.[137] However, O'Neill's own murder served to remind the English that, though the Scottish queen might issue commands

[132] Randolph to Cecil, 14 June 1566, BL Lansdowne 3 fo. 84; *CSPSc*, II. 285–6.
[133] Moray to Cecil, 11 July 1566, *CSPSc*, II. 294.
[134] Morton to Sir John Forster, July 1566, *CSPSc*, II. 296.
[135] See above, p. 158.   [136] 15 December 1566, SP63/19 fo. 147r.
[137] Cecil to Sidney 25 February 1567, SP63/20 fo. 78r–v. I am grateful to Dr Alford for this reference. Alford, *Cecil*, 159–61, 170; Hill, *Fire and Sword*, 113.

in Edinburgh, it was the actions of the MacDonalds and Argyll that really mattered in Ulster politics.

News of O'Neill's death held little interest for Mary, who was facing the confederate lords at Carberry. Her imprisonment and abdication threw Anglo-Scottish relations into confusion, undermining her claims to the English succession and even placing her life in danger. The English queen could not officially tolerate the deposition of a fellow monarch, despite being accomplished by her closest Scottish allies. Though Sir Nicholas Throckmorton was not permitted to visit Mary, Argyll urged the special English ambassador to work to save the queen's life.[138] Throckmorton remained suspicious of the 5th earl, having heard rumours about a Campbell marriage plan for Mary and fearing that Argyll and his redshanks threatened English interests.[139] With his independent line in Ulster, his split with Moray and his support for Mary, the earl had ceased to be England's friend and was reaping the consequences of his own change of attitude. Although publicly deploring the method, the English government was privately pleased with the solution of Moray as regent for the infant king. Events in Scotland had been a shock, as Cecil fervently exclaimed, 'God send us no mo such hard examplees as that land hath brought furth'.[140] In Edinburgh, Throckmorton had given tacit recognition to the King's party, indicating to the regent that he had the support of the English government. Realising English help would not be forthcoming to free Mary, the 5th earl bowed to the inevitable and settled with the regent. Whilst Mary was in prison in Scotland, Argyll did not have to consider the Anglo-Scottish dimensions of his Irish actions. His fragile and uneasy alliance with Moray meant the regent was not in a position to insist the 5th earl adopt a pro-English policy in Ireland. Argyll, free to base his decisions upon Gaelic priorities, negotiated the double Ulster marriages, which formed the core of the triple alliance between the MacDonalds, the O'Neills and the O'Donnells. If those three kindreds remained united, the English would be unable to implement their schemes for the conquest and colonisation of Ulster.

In the short term, the English were given a reprieve in Ulster by another turn of events within Scotland, illustrating how the shock waves of one cataclysmic event were felt within all the political worlds of sixteenth-century Britain. The marriages of Lady Agnes and her daughter Finola were

---

138 Argyll to Throckmorton and reply 11 and 14 July 1567, *Illustrations of the Reign of Queen Mary*, 196–7, 210–11. Throckmorton later claimed he had saved Mary's life: Wormald, *Mary, Queen of Scots*, 168.
139 Throckmorton to Elizabeth, 25 July 1567, Keith, *History*, II. 694–700; see above, p. 152.
140 Cecil to Sidney, 20 August 1567, SP63/21 fo. 183r. I owe this reference to Dr Alford. Alford, *Cecil*, 159–63.

postponed because Argyll was caught up in the events following Mary's escape from Lochleven. The queen's flight to England after Langside brought a new era within Anglo-Scottish diplomacy and dragged Argyll's Irish policies back into the arena of Anglo-Scottish relations. From 1568, the English and the 5th earl would both deploy Ulster politics as a bargaining counter in the negotiations over the future of Mary, Queen of Scots.

6

The withdrawal from British politics: 1569–1573

After Langside, Scotland slipped further into civil war, its national politics initially splitting into two opposing parties, respectively supporting the king and queen, and then slowly disintegrating into factions with little common focus. As the most powerful magnate in the Queen's Party, Argyll played an important role in these struggles, where regional, Scottish and British strands became tangled together. With the King's and Queen's Parties locked in an uneasy stalemate and political life fragmenting, especially after Moray's assassination in January 1570, he became increasingly pessimistic about the possibility of success. In 1571, with no prospect of Mary's release from her English prison and believing peace to be essential to counter English manipulation, the 5th earl abandoned the Queen's Party. Having made his settlement with the regent, he devoted his energies to reconstructing national political life by reconciling the different factions.

The arrival of the fugitive Scottish queen in England decisively shifted the balance of power within the British mainland, further weighted in favour of the southern kingdom. The revolution that had placed the infant James on the Scottish throne left the new regime heavily dependent upon English good will. With the Scottish queen in her custody, Elizabeth's influence north of the border was further strengthened, giving her the trump cards in Anglo-Scottish negotiations and a decisive voice in Scotland's domestic politics. By sending money and troops, England's intervention eventually broke the stalemate between the King's and Queen's Parties. An outraged Argyll came to regard English interference as the greatest danger threatening his country and a compelling reason to settle his differences with the regent. Scotland's evident weakness enabled English politicians to recover their taste for manipulating Scottish politics, which they continued to indulge for the remainder of the century. The harsh reality of the imbalance of power within the British mainland encouraged the English political élite to treat Scotland as a client state. By justifying their policy through theories of imperial superiority over the entire mainland, they fundamentally weakened any attempt to construct a British strategy resting upon co-operation between the two kingdoms. Yet these developments were not without dangers for the English government. Whilst holding Mary as a prisoner brought diplomatic advantages, it also produced internal complications. The context of the Scottish queen's claim to the succession shifted alarmingly: from being primarily an issue of international diplomacy, it became a permanent domestic crisis. While Mary lived, she was a security threat to Elizabeth and her kingdom. Even after her execution, the succession question and the inequality within Anglo-Scottish relations continued to define British mainland politics.

During the Scottish civil wars, the 5th earl adopted a strategy of damage limitation. Profoundly disillusioned, he withdrew from British politics, focusing upon the limited objectives of re-establishing political life within Scotland and upholding the interests of his house, clan and affinity. He was most at ease within the Gaelic political world where he enjoyed the greatest control, utilising it to support Clan Donald and bring stability to the Highlands and Islands. Within Ulster, his backing for Lady Agnes and her daughter strengthened the new political alignment created by their marriages. Though not pursuing an integrated British policy, Argyll's measures had significant British consequences by helping ensure the province remained outside English control until the end of Elizabeth's reign. In the 1590s, the O'Neill–O'Donnell coalition produced a united Ulster, which formed the core of Tyrone's rebellion. This Nine Years' War threatened the continued existence of the kingdom of Ireland, the unity of the Tudor state and the relationships between these islands. In the Irish context, the consequences of the 5th earl's final policies came full circle; instead of striving as in 1560 to produce a unified British Isles, they nearly broke them apart.

THE SCOTTISH CIVIL WARS

The speed of events in May 1568, with Mary's escape, the Langside defeat and her precipitate flight into England, presented her supporters with an insurmountable problem: they were a Queen's Party with no queen available for restoration. So long as she languished in an English prison, there was nothing they could achieve in Scotland that could guarantee her return. Whatever their Scottish strength or support, they were dependent upon Elizabeth to free Mary and had no option but to follow the timetable and agenda set by the English. One pamphlet succinctly mocked their powerlessness: 'For how can thai put hir in auctority that can not put hir in hir own chamber.'[1] Having engineered her downfall and given their allegiance to

[1] M. Loughlin, 'The Dialogue of the Twa Wyfeis: Maitland, Machiavelli and the Propaganda of the Scottish Civil War' in A. MacDonald *et al.*, eds., *The Renaissance in Scotland* (Leiden, 1994), 226–45 at pp. 239–40.

her son, Mary's restoration was anathema to the King's Party. Even a token restoration would only be accepted by the king's men if their weakness or defeat at home was coupled with pressure from their English allies to settle. For the Queen's Party, achieving their central positive objective of Mary's return was fraught with difficulties.

In the vacuum created by Mary's flight, her supporters were heavily dependent upon the power of the two great Highland magnates, Argyll and Huntly. Whilst their appointment as her lieutenants by the absent queen afforded them some constitutional standing, it was their deeply rooted regional power that made their authority effective. Based upon their own resources, the two earls offered the Queen's Party an alternative focus of central political authority. The King's Party possessed the decided advantage of having the boy king and being in control of the national institutions. But, with many regions ignoring their wishes, their writ did not run throughout the kingdom, and between 1570 and 1573 Huntly ran his own justice and administration in the north.[2] The lack of a single central authority recognised by all Scots was demonstrated in the succession of rival Parliaments held by each party in Edinburgh in 1570. This bifurcation had a corrosive effect upon Scottish national politics leading to further disintegration. In the confusing political struggles that followed, with alignments constantly changing, it became increasingly difficult to distinguish an ally from an enemy. Noble factions within the two main groupings threatened to reduce Scotland to a country torn apart by competing warlords, more intent upon their regional power struggles than national issues. Because of his well-known Protestant commitment, Argyll's leadership of the Queen's Party helped ensure that the conflicts which split Scotland between 1568 and 1573 did not follow the French example and degenerate into a war of religion. Despite attempts by the King's Party to introduce a confessional dimension into the conflict, by presenting themselves as the sole defenders of the Kirk, the divisions between the groups remained primarily political. Though all the Scottish Roman Catholics supported Mary or remained neutral, these were civil, rather than religious, wars.

Despite not being in a position to win the contest outright by placing Mary back upon her throne, those who rallied to the queen's cause had much to lose. They had joined the party for a range of motives and were held together as much by their opposition to the regents as by their common positive objective. On one level, the civil wars were a straightforward struggle for national political power amongst Scotland's higher nobility, especially intense during the confusion following Moray's assassination. The queen's men were seeking to replace their rivals or, at least, prevent the King's Party causing

---

[2] A. Murray, 'Huntly's Rebellion and the Administration of Justice in North-East Scotland, 1570–73', *Northern Scotland*, 4 (1981), 1–6.

serious damage to their powerbases. This drew many regional rivalries and disputes into the national conflict, such as the fight for dominance between the Hamiltons and the Lennox Stewarts in the West. Such a mixture of aims and motives helps explain the bewildering switches of allegiance between the parties and the difficulties encountered in achieving a lasting and comprehensive settlement. Secure in his Highland heartland, Argyll was under less pressure from regional confrontations than his main allies and could concentrate upon the national and international dimensions of the conflict. His virtually impregnable power gave him the luxury, not shared by other members of the Queen's Party, of being offered advantageous terms by the king's men in the assorted rounds of negotiations. Though the queen's men needed Argyll to coerce an equitable settlement from the King's Party, he did not need them. This unpalatable fact was revealed in 1569 and 1571 when the earl made agreements with the regents. In the latter case it added to the bitterness and sense of betrayal felt by his former allies.

The civil wars possessed another dimension. They were a struggle for control over the British mainland, which was being fought on Scottish soil. By good fortune as much as English policy, Scotland did not become the theatre for European intervention, allowing London to settle the mainland's affairs according to its own interests. The muddled and sometimes contradictory English policies were driven by the requirements of Elizabeth's and England's security, but their consequences were Scottish and British. English financial and military support propped up the king's men, preventing them from being dislodged permanently from the capital and allowing them to conduct successful campaigns against the Queen's Party in central and southern Scotland. This tipped the balance in the military contest in favour of the King's Party. Emerging triumphant at the close of the civil wars, Regent Morton found himself in charge of a much-weakened country. Like his predecessors in the regency, his Anglophile stance had become a necessity as much as a choice. This Scottish shift of emphasis was matched by a similar change in the English approach. Between 1568 and 1570, Elizabeth toyed with the idea of adopting a British solution to the problem posed by Mary, Queen of Scots: that of restoring her to her throne, though only under the strictest of conditions and restraints. The English queen finally abandoned that approach, opting to treat her fellow monarch solely as a troublesome domestic rival, to be kept securely confined. The wisdom of this decision seemed vindicated by the discovery of the Norfolk marriage scheme and the Ridolphi plot. By 1571, English politicians were ignoring Mary's claim to be ruler of Scotland and were concentrating upon her threat to Elizabeth. This compartmentalisation of the two mainland kingdoms altered the focus of British politics. By assuming Mary was an English, rather than a British, problem, they embarked upon the road leading to her execution in 1587.

Argyll's difficulties as a leader of the Queen's Party mostly stemmed from focusing upon such national and international dimensions rather than the regional objectives of his allies. This made his political decision making harder, especially when he finally settled with Regent Lennox in 1571. By that stage, the 5th earl was convinced English interference in Scotland was the overriding problem. The failure of the 1570 round of negotiations to secure Mary's release forced him to conclude that English manipulation of Scottish politics would only be reduced when peace was restored to the realm. To achieve this, Argyll was prepared to jettison the objectives of the Queen's Party. Other members of that party, treating his settlement with the regent as a betrayal, continued fighting, some until May 1573. The splits within the party, especially after 1570, and the accusations of bad faith which accompanied them reflected the fundamental confusion over what its members were fighting to achieve.

In the immediate aftermath of Langside, Mary's supporters had been scattered in defeat. The 5th earl returned to Argyll to recover from his illness, and there was little sign of activity for about a month after the battle.[3] Among those taken prisoner during the fighting was Matthew Campbell of Loudoun, sheriff of Ayr, who told his captors about the Irish discussions in Argyll's council.[4] Loudoun and the main Hamilton prisoners, though under sentence of death for treason, were pardoned.[5] Alongside the clemency, the Regent Moray sought to re-impose his authority. He captured Hamilton and Draffen castles and went into the south-west to crush resistance. Knowing he could not fight Argyll in the Highlands, Moray moved against the Lowland properties, at the end of June seizing the rents of Castle Campbell and the diocese of Brechin.[6] A Parliament was summoned for August with the express intention of forfeiting the Queen's Party.[7]

These aggressive actions spurred the regent's opponents into a response. By the beginning of July, the queen's men had regrouped under the leadership of Argyll and his uncle, John Hamilton, archbishop of St Andrews. Their first priority was to contact Mary, who began sending instructions from Carlisle.[8] Needing to gauge international reaction to Mary's plight, they wrote to Charles IX and the cardinal of Lorraine in France, and to the Spanish king and to his Netherlands governor, the duke of Alva.[9] What

---

[3] He signed a charter on 10 June 1568, AT, VI. 124 and had written to Mary by the beginning of June, Knollys to Cecil, 6 June 1568, *CSPSc*, II. 423–4.
[4] Elphinstone to Cecil, 21 May 1568, *CSPSc*, II. 411.   [5] Herries, *Memoirs*, 104.
[6] 25 and 26 June 1568, *TA*, XII. 133–4.
[7] Argyll to Crawford, 31 July 1568, Calderwood, *History*, II. 419–20.
[8] Mary, Queen of Scots to Argyll, 7 July 1568, *Letters to Argyll Family*, 6.
[9] To Charles IX, 6 July, NLS Adv. MSS 22.2.18, fos. 75r–76r; to cardinal of Lorraine, 24 August [?], BL Cotton Calig. B 9 n. fos. 317r–18r; to Alva, 30 July, *CSPSc*, II. 469;

mattered most was Elizabeth's attitude. An official letter was sent requesting Mary's return and English help to recover her throne.[10] In addition, the 5th earl wrote personally to the English queen.[11] Meanwhile, action was urgently needed to be taken in Scotland to counter the threat posed by the regent's Parliament. After a summit meeting at Largs on the Clyde coast, accessible to the queen's supporters from the west, south-west and Argyll, a proclamation was issued by the 5th earl, as Mary's lieutenant, for a general muster on 10 August.[12] Letters were sent to noble allies, urging them to ensure that no one attended Parliament, in the earl of Crawford's case to prevent representation from the burghs of Dundee, Montrose, Forfar and Brechin, lying within his region.[13] Argyll gathered Highland troops for an attack upon Glasgow, one of Lennox's strongholds. He commandeered the Clyde herring-boat fleet and sailed 2,000 redshanks up the river to join the forces assembled by his fellow lieutenant, Huntly.[14] The plan was to gather reinforcements along the march to Edinburgh, where the king's men were strong, and then stop the Parliament. The ambitious scheme failed because two contingents could not reach their rendezvous points. On their march south, Huntly's troops were blocked from crossing the River Tay by Lord Ruthven's forces and, in the west, Lord Herries was unable to bring his soldiers through hostile territory. Argyll was furious with his subordinate Herries, accusing him of delaying everything.[15]

To suit the English desire to act as brokers in the Scottish conflict, Mary ordered Argyll to cease hostilities and negotiate a truce with the King's Party.[16] Though he was in the middle of besieging Glasgow castle, he dispersed his forces and returned to Dumbarton where he wrote to Elizabeth.[17] As a postscript to her letter of thanks, Mary added in her idiosyncratic Scots

---

lost letter to Philip II mentioned in Argyll's letter to Crawford, 31 July 1568: Calderwood, *History*, II. 419–20.

[10] BL Cotton Calig. C 1 fo. 181; *CSPSc*, II. 466–8.

[11] Elizabeth to Argyll and reply, 14 and 24 August 1568, *Sidney State Papers, 1565–70* ed. T. O'Laidhin (Irish Manuscripts Commission, Dublin, 1962), I. 36–7; see below, pp. 193–4.

[12] Several copies in English hands, 28 July, BL Cotton Calig. B 9 n. fo. 322; Calig. C 1 n. fo. 183r–v; Royal 18 B 6 fo. 278; *CSPSc*, II. 463–4. A bond was signed by those present declaring their loyalty to the queen, mentioned in the list of six things decided at Largs, BL Cotton Calig. C 1 n. fo. 182; *CSPSc*, II. 464.

[13] Argyll to Crawford, 31 July, Calderwood, *History*, II. 419–20.

[14] Offences by Queen's Party, 4 October, *CSPSc*, II. 516.

[15] *Diurnal*, 134–5. Herries to archbishop of St Andrews, 13 August 1568, *Reg. Hon. de Mort*, I. 34–5. Herries to Argyll, 19 August 1568, *Letters to Argyll Family*, 7–8.

[16] *Diurnal*, 136–7. Mary's letter has not survived, but see Mary to Argyll, 31 August, *Letters to Argyll Family*, 10–11. She later admitted the decision had been a mistake.

[17] Argyll to Elizabeth, 24 August, BL Cotton Calig. C 1 n. fo. 209; printed in *Sidney State Papers, 1565–70*, I. 36–7; Queen's Party to Elizabeth, 24 August, BL Cotton Calig. C 1 n. fo. 210.

the warmest of appreciations of the earl: 'assur your self that ye havve dun yourself and al our frindes ne letle honour and gud in onli schauin your for-duartnes and obdiens to my. Y wil nocht spel tym in wourdes, but Y think mi so far adet to you that Y schal think on it al my lyf.'[18] The truce between the two Scottish parties was an uneasy affair. Moray held a Parliament and proceeded with the forfeitures of his enemies.[19] Local bouts of fighting con-tinued for the rest of the year, with old scores being settled, encouraging each side to complain that the other had violated the truce.[20] These events were mere shadow play: all attention was focused upon the 'first trial' of Mary, Queen of Scots taking place in England.[21] During the autumn and winter of 1568, the 5th earl retired to his region to deal with Gaelic politics and make ready for future campaigns.[22]

By the introduction of the 'Casket Letters' and the accusations of her complicity, Mary's trial returned Darnley's murder to the centre of debate in Scotland, as well as in England. When the York and Westminster proceed-ings were completed, Mary, wanting to reinvigorate the Scottish campaign, wrote to Argyll in mid-December. She ordered a full mobilisation and un-realistically suggested Moray be intercepted as he returned home.[23] The queen's supporters mounted a propaganda campaign in Scotland against the regent to refute the evidence he had produced at York.[24] Having been branded accomplices in Darnley's murder during the trial, Argyll and Huntly defended themselves with a personal protestation containing their version of events, especially concerning the Craigmillar conference, and challeng-ing Moray to a duel.[25] Mary's lieutenants moved on to the offensive, using public proclamations and letters accusing the regent of seeking the Scottish throne and betraying his country to the English in a secret deal.[26] Ignoring

---

[18] Mary to Argyll, 31 August 1568, *Letters to Argyll Family*, 10–11.

[19] Drury to Cecil, 21 August 1568, *CSPSc*, II. 484.

[20] For example the attack by Glencairn and Sempill against Fleming and archbishop of St Andrews: Argyll to Mure of Rowallan, 12 November 1568, NLS Adv. MS 54.1.7 fo. 27.

[21] For example 4 October 1568, *CSPSc*, II. 516–7. G. Donaldson, *The First Trial of Mary Queen of Scots* (London, 1969).

[22] The bond he made with the Fergussons was probably part of this process, 6 or 16 November 1568, GD112/1/174; GD111/4/4 (both badly damaged).

[23] Mary, Queen of Scots to Argyll, 16 December 1568, *Reg. Hon. de Mort*, I. 36–8; see also 'Answere to the Eeke[supplement]', 19 December 1568, Calderwood, *History*, II. 463–5; Mary to Huntly and Argyll, 5 January 1569, BL Cotton Calig. C 1 n. fo. 380.

[24] For example rhyme in defence of Mary, Queen of Scots, 9 December 1568, *CSPSc*, II. 573–4; Alford, *Cecil*, ch. 7; Donaldson, *First Trial of Mary Queen of Scots*, chs. 4–5.

[25] Aided by a draft prepared by Mary's adviser, John Leslie, bishop of Ross: Keith, *History*, III. 290–4; also see above p. 41.

[26] Proclamation, 9 January 1569, BL Cotton Calig. C 1 n. fo. 376; letter to Edinburgh Council, 11 January, *Reg. Hon. de Mort*, I. 40; proclamation, n.d., *The Warrender Papers* ed. A.I. Cameron (2 vols., SHS, 3rd ser. 18–19, Edinburgh, 1931–32), I. 57–60; letter accusing Elizabeth of deceit addressed to Queen's Party in Scotland, BL Cotton Calig. C 1 n. fo. 377.

their challenge, Moray replied with his own propaganda letter, backed by an English proclamation.[27] These bitter exchanges of personal accusations created an almost unbridgeable gap between the former friends, Argyll and Moray.

Within Scottish politics, the re-examination of Darnley's death had long-term implications. Although a rallying cry at Carberry and a slogan for the King's Party, it was not an issue either side genuinely wanted investigated. Too many Scottish aristocrats had skeletons in their cupboards, which they were reluctant to expose to public gaze. The charge of complicity in Darnley's death became a convenient excuse to attack a political opponent.[28] As a result of the 'first trial', the Queen's Party had no option but to seek to smear Moray's reputation, whatever the extent of his involvement. In an attempt to minimise the damage done by accusations of the queen's guilt and to re-establish some credibility for Mary, her supporters switched attention to the 'Craigmillar conference', thereby avoiding an account of events at Kirk o' Field. By leaving most stones unturned, they tried to prevent anything else crawling out to create further embarrassments.

With Mary's trial over, even though Elizabeth had refused to make a formal judgement, Moray returned to Scotland in February 1569. Military preparations had been under way on both sides, and fighting appeared imminent with the only question being where and when it would break out.[29] After his exile in France, the duke of Châtelherault's return to Scotland encouraged Moray to put additional military pressure upon the Hamiltons. His tactic of dividing the Queen's Party was successful, with a fearful duke not prepared to fight, but saying he could not compromise without Argyll's consent.[30] Though the 5th earl and Huntly initially persuaded Châtelherault to stand firm, an agreement between Moray and the Hamiltons was reached in April.[31] The loss of the Hamilton kindred signalled a low point in the fortunes of the Queen's Party. The revelations of the trial had weakened their cause and, with Mary more securely held in England, there seemed no clear objective. Moray was stabilising his regime, and his policy of divide and rule had succeeded

Their appeal to Kirkcaldy of Grange, holding Edinburgh Castle, got a frosty reception: Kirkcaldy to Huntly and Argyll, 14 January 1569, *CSPSc*, II. 607–8.

[27] Reply, 19 January 1569, Keith, *History*, III. 294–5. Elizabeth's proclamation, 22 January, *The Warrender Papers*, I. 60–1.

[28] After his switch of allegiance, Maitland was charged, see below, p. 178. In 1581, Morton was executed, allegedly for his part in Darnley's murder: G.R. Hewitt, *Scotland under Morton, 1572–80* (Edinburgh, 1982), ch. 10.

[29] Argyll to archbishop of St Andrews, 27 January 1569, *Reg. Hon. de Mort*, 41–2.

[30] Moray to Cecil, 25 February 1569, *CSPSc*, II. 625; Herries, *Memoirs*, 113; Calderwood, *History*, II. 477.

[31] Proclamation, 28 February, *CSPSc*, II. 626; negotiations 13 March, *CSPSc*, II. 631; *The Warrender Papers*, I. 61–2; *Diurnal*, 140–1.

in detaching the Hamiltons. He now turned his attention to Argyll and Huntly.

The 5th earl was under heavy pressure from within his own clan to settle with the regent in order to recoup his finances, ruined by the constant warfare. In the summer, his council proposed a tax to redeem the wadsets, or leases, encumbering his lands, on condition the earl made peace with the regent and only broke it 'be awise of his awne kin and freinds'.[32] Clan Campbell had had enough of civil war and the resulting withdrawal of the fruits of court patronage and exclusion from central institutions. Seeing no point to further opposition, they strongly encouraged the 5th earl to swallow his personal animosity against Moray and accept a compromise. Bowing to his kindred's wishes, he took an oath of loyalty to the infant king on 10 May.[33] The regent offered Argyll remarkably easy terms, ostensibly because he was Moray's kinsman and former friend. In addition, the earl had been credited with exercising restraint during the past campaign when, despite urgings by the Hamiltons, he refused to ravage the Lennox with his 1,500 Highlanders.[34] By contrast, much harder terms were offered to Huntly, who had inflicted as much damage as possible upon the king's supporters and whose feud with Moray dated from his father's defeat in 1562. Mary's other lieutenant did not accept them, and the civil strife continued.[35]

Tensions remained between Argyll and Moray, who were still not speaking despite having officially settled their differences. In a provocative gesture, the regent put his recent ally Maitland of Lethington on trial for being an accomplice in Darnley's murder. Ignoring their own proclamation of his guilt ten months earlier, Huntly and Argyll supported Maitland. They correctly interpreted the trial as a political attack and threatened to bring their troops for Maitland's 'day of law' on 21 November.[36] Though confrontation was avoided when the trial was postponed, feelings continued to run high throughout the autumn and winter of 1569. In a brilliant piece of anonymous political satire, Maitland's brother summed up the deep suspicions about Moray and the King's Party. The tract purported to be a letter sent by a friend at court to an unnamed kinsman of Argyll. The writer had supposedly overheard a secret council meeting between Moray and his six closest advisers, which had revealed their real intentions in ruling Scotland. In a wickedly observed portrayal, the tract presented an ambitious, but vacillating, regent

---

[32] 12 August, AT, VI. 136.

[33] He ignored or had not received the letter Mary had written on 28 April begging him not to accept conditions until she sent further word and signing herself 'your richt good sister and best frind foreuuer', *Letters to Argyll Family*, 11–12.

[34] Herries, *Memoirs*, 114.

[35] Calderwood, *History*, II. 487.

[36] Calderwood, *History*, II. 506–7; Herries, *Memoirs*, 120. For the offer to fight Maitland, see proclamation, Keith, *History*, III. 290–4, and above, p. 41.

surrounded by ruthless men, who would not scruple about killing James VI and destroying their opponents in their quest for absolute power.[37] The use of Argyll's kinsman as the supposed recipient of the letter suggests this jaundiced view of the regent and his allies was held among the Campbells. Though the 5th earl had acknowledged the boy king, there had been no personal reconciliation between him and Moray, and they had not spoken since the battle of Langside, eighteen months before. Shortly before Christmas, the earl of Mar, kinsman to both men, broke the deadlock by restoring relations between the regent and Argyll.[38] Though a king's man, Mar had largely remained aloof from the bitter factionalism of the civil wars, retaining the 5th earl's friendship and respect throughout the conflict.[39] By the end of 1569, some bridges had been built across the chasms separating Scottish national politics, but these fragile truces holding the regent's regime together were shattered by the regent's murder at the start of 1570.

The assassination of Moray on 28 January by James Hamilton of Bothwellhaugh was the critical turning point of the civil wars, changing their nature and lengthening their duration. The murder plunged Scottish politics into turmoil and confusion, with no one knowing friend from foe. Believing the regent was intent upon the total destruction of his kindred, Archbishop Hamilton had carefully planned Moray's death.[40] Even Hamilton allies were shocked by its cold-blooded nature and made every effort to distance themselves from the deed. On hearing the news, Argyll and Robert Lord Boyd wrote to Morton and Maitland, protesting they had nothing to do with the murder and offering to help catch those responsible.[41] The 5th earl went to meet with his jubilant Hamilton kinsmen at Dumbarton and Glasgow who, with Moray eliminated, were intent upon regaining their political influence.[42] Attempting to moderate their demands and mediate between them and the

---

[37] It was probably written by Thomas Maitland in the winter of 1569. Maitland might have been provoked to write it in retaliation against George Buchanan, chief propagandist of the King's Party, who had named him as the opposition spokesman in the dialogue, 'De iure regni', written in 1567. The 5th earl handed over the pamphlet to Mar who passed it to his brother, Alexander Erskine of Gogar. Erskine remarked that it was the most malicious set of lies that had ever been invented: Bannatyne, *Memorials*, 15. The manuscript version, BL Cotton Calig. B 9 n. fos. 390r–4v, was dated 10 October 1569, though Bannatyne, *Memorials*, 5–13 and Calderwood, *History*, II. 515–25 placed it immediately after Moray's assassination. For the different versions, see *The Bannatyne Miscellany I* eds. Sir W. Scott and D. Laing (Bannatyne Club, 19, Edinburgh, 1827), 33–50.

[38] *Diurnal*, 152–3; Drury to Cecil, 20 December 1569, *CSPSc*, III. 28–9.

[39] Mar and Argyll journeyed together from Edinburgh to Castle Campbell just before Christmas, *Diurnal*, 154.

[40] The Hamiltons believed Moray's real intentions followed the policies satirised in 'The copie of an advertisement', see n. 37.

[41] *Diurnal*, 157; Bannatyne, *Memorials*, 18; Herries, *Memoirs*, 123.

[42] Argyll *et al.* to Waus, 8 February 1570, *Correspondence of Sir Patrick Waus of Barnbarroch* ed. R.V. Agnew (2 vols., Ayrshire and Wigtonshire Archaeological Association, 14, Edinburgh, 1887), I. 66–7.

king's men, the earl dispatched his clansman Ardkinglas, 'ane hieland man in the fynest sort', to negotiate.[43]

Matters had been complicated by the arrival in Scotland of the English northern earls fleeing across the border after the collapse of their rebellion in 1569. Shortly before his death, Moray had captured the earl of Northumberland, provoking a storm of protest and the accusation he was an English puppet. Meanwhile, the earl of Westmoreland and Lord Dacre had linked up with the queen's men. Their presence in Scotland and their fate added further contentious issues to the delicate inter-party negotiations. Moray's death split the two main parties in the civil wars into different factions. Where before there had been rival groups loyal to the king's and queen's authorities, national politics now fragmented, leaving no clear centres of power, with the Scottish magnates operating separately or in loose alliances. During the next couple of years, the resulting decentralisation of political power shifted attention from national issues to local feuds and rivalries. By needing to reconcile these regional disputes and personal conflicts, a national settlement was harder to achieve.

Argyll, with his secure powerbase, faced fewer and less serious threats than other aristocrats, allowing him the luxury of making Scottish and British considerations his priorities, rather than regional ones. However, his concentration upon the fate of Mary, Queen of Scots left him reacting to English initiatives and unable to construct a coherent strategy of his own.[44] In addition, he signally failed to provide a decisive lead for his allies in the tangled national politics of 1570. Moray's assassination had made relations more poisonous between the Scottish nobility, leaving each faction fearful and suspicious, ready to misinterpret the actions and intentions of the others. With the magnates permanently accompanied by their armed dependants, violence was always close, and small incidents quickly flared into military confrontations. Argyll floundered in these tense situations, which demanded instant tactical decisions, at a loss to know when to negotiate, fight or withdraw. Hesitant and muddled about his objectives, he could not discern a clear path to follow. He turned to Robert Lord Boyd for advice, having become alienated from former friends and colleagues now in the King's Party. Boyd, a queen's man with impeccable Protestant credentials, had no policies to offer the earl, leaving them both prey to those adept politicians more clear-sighted and ruthless than themselves.

At the end of February, an important meeting brought Argyll, Boyd, Atholl and Maitland to discuss matters with Morton in his castle at Dalkeith. The agenda ranged from the British and Scottish issue of the possibility of Mary's return to Scotland to a regional settlement between Argyll and Atholl over the

[43] Bannatyne, *Memorials*, 18; *Diurnal*, 157, 160.   [44] See below pp. 196–8.

MacGregor feud.[45] Thomas Randolph, alerted to the meeting by Archibald Douglas, Morton's close adviser, hurried to Dalkeith. His presence so infuriated the 5th earl that the English ambassador was sent back to Edinburgh without being admitted to the discussions.[46] After Argyll had gone to Stirling to include Mar in their deliberations, this group of magnates decided to organise a conference of all the main factions for the first week of March.[47] The fragility of the situation and the ease with which it could be derailed by feuding nobles was demonstrated by the collapse of that conference. One section of the queen's supporters had agreed to meet in Linlithgow.[48] In early March, Argyll, Boyd and the Hamiltons arrived in the burgh with the English earls. However, when Boyd's man killed a Hamilton soldier, causing a fracas, the Hamiltons withdrew to Clydesdale. In the meantime, Huntly, Atholl and the other northern nobles of the Queen's Party were in Edinburgh, negotiating with Morton who was awaiting the arrival of Mar and other king's men. With Argyll's presence essential if the negotiations were to make progress, Huntly was sent to bring the 5th earl to Edinburgh. Unfortunately, by then Argyll had stormed out of Linlithgow because of an incident involving his friend the earl of Mar. Accompanied by Glencairn, Sempill and Lindsay, Mar had brought 300 horsemen to Linlithgow where, as part of a feud, they burnt Captain James Mure's house.[49] The angry 5th earl, treating this armed attack as a serious breach of faith, left the burgh affirming he would 'never creditit ane word that wes aither promittit or spokin be the King's Party thereafter'. When Huntly, Crawford and Ogilvy reached Linlithgow, they became angry in their turn, blaming Argyll for leaving at such a critical juncture and ruining the Edinburgh talks.[50] The whole muddled incident reflected the underlying distrust and violence infecting every faction in the civil wars, making co-operation and conciliation so difficult.

The rift between Huntly and Argyll was soon healed, bringing a sharp rise in the fortunes of the queen's men.[51] In April, their forces, including 300

[45] *Diurnal*, 160; agreement between Argyll and Atholl, 26 February 1570, GD112/1/181a.
[46] *Diurnal*, 161, and see below, p. 197. There was no personal animosity to Randolph: see Argyll's letter to him, 18 February 1570, *CSPSc*, III. 85.
[47] *Diurnal*, 162.
[48] Argyll to Waus, 20 and 22 February 1570, *Correspondence of Sir Patrick Waus of Barnbarroch*, 67–8.
[49] James Mure was the son of Alexander Mure of Ormesheuch in Ayrshire who was executed six months later after the fall of Brechin steeple to the King's Party, *RSS*, VI. 855, 981, and see below, p. 183. As a member of the Ayrshire Mures he had links with the 5th earl. See Mure of Rowallan's correspondence with Argyll in NLS Adv. MS 54.1.7.
[50] The confused events of 3–12 March have been reconstructed from a number of differing accounts: *Diurnal*, 163–4; Calderwood, *History*, II. 544–5; Bannatyne, *Memorials*, 18–20; Herries, *Memoirs*, 123.
[51] At Weem in Perthshire Huntly brokered a further agreement between Argyll and Atholl over the MacGregors and the lands of the abbey of Coupar Angus and the bishopric of Dunkeld, two separate agreements, 24 March 1570, AT, VI. 142; GD50/187/1; printed in *Chronicles*

of Argyll's Highlanders, entered Edinburgh in triumph, where they joined those who were holding the castle for Mary.[52] The new strength and cohesion of the queen's supporters produced an outpouring of propaganda from their opponents, much directed against Maitland, whose changes in allegiance earned him the nickname of Chameleon. He was portrayed as a Scottish Machiavelli, the evil genius who had persuaded William Kirkcaldy of Grange, captain of Edinburgh castle, to switch to the Queen's Party, and overawe the burgh beneath its walls.[53] The 5th earl was also attacked, in particular for his close relationship with Lord Boyd, who was later credited with being 'able to keep Argyll in tune'.[54] One pamphlet lampooned them as fools, the 'gook and hir titling', a saying describing inseparable and incongruous companions, one tall, like the 5th earl, and the other short.[55] By the spring of 1570, the newly consolidated Queen's Party could plausibly represent the majority of Scottish opinion. Instructions were drafted for their ambassadors in France and a mission sent to England.[56] On the domestic front, troops were gathered for a new military campaign, including an extra infantry company raised by Ogilvy with funds borrowed by Argyll.[57] With Huntly and the 5th earl in command, the army of the queen's supporters besieged Glasgow castle. Despite such a promising start, they were forced to lift the siege when English troops came to assist the King's Party.[58]

By preventing the queen's men from achieving a military victory, the arrival of the earl of Sussex with an English army broke the stalemate between the parties, signalling the beginning of the end of the civil wars. Sussex, the former lord lieutnant of Ireland, had lost none of his previous distrust of

---

of the Families of Atholl and Tullibardine ed. John, 7th duke of Atholl (5 vols., Edinburgh, 1908), I. 39; Wormald, *Lords and Men*, 289 [59].

[52] Calderwood, *History*, II. 553–5; *Diurnal*, 168–70; Bannatyne, *Memorials*, 32; Herries, *Memoirs*, 124.

[53] M. Loughlin, 'The Career of Maitland of Lethington c. 1526–1573' (University of Edinburgh PhD thesis, 1991), 226–45.

[54] Killigrew to Burghley, 14 March 1573, *CSPSc*, IV. 518.

[55] 'Dialogue of twa wyfeis', 30 April 1570, SP52/17/77 discussed by Loughlin, 'The Dialogue of the Twa Wyfeis' and Loughlin, 'The Career of Maitland of Lethington', ch. 8. The two nobles were also linked in Sempill's ballads, 'Regentis Tragedie' and 'The Spur to the Lordis', *Satirical Poems of the Time of the Reformation* ed. J. Cranston (2 vols., Scottish Text Society, Old ser. 20 and 24, Edinburgh, 1891–93), I. 103, lines 104–5; 157–8, lines 49–50, 73–80.

[56] Instructions for archbishop of Glasgow in France, April 1570, *The Warrender Papers*, I. 80–9; instructions to laird of Traboun for England, and letter to Elizabeth, 15 and 16 April 1570, *CSPSc*, III. 116–8, 122–3.

[57] *Diurnal*, 171. Argyll used his Forfarshire lands to fund Ogilvy, contract, 21 April 1570, NRA(S), 217, Box 1 No. 164; *Clan Campbell*, VI. 20; VIII. 62; charter, 9 May 1570, (sasine 18 July 1570), GD16/24/68; discharges, 21 and 24 April, GD16/42/18 and GD16/52/1.

[58] *Diurnal*, 174; Calderwood, *History*, II. 560–1, 563; Bannatyne, *Memorials*, 39; *RPC*, XIV [Add] 51 n.; Herries, *Memoirs*, 127; Lennox to Cecil, Sussex to Cecil, 17 and 18 May 1570, *CSPSc*, III. 178 and 182.

Argyll, and relations between the two men remained distant and formal. Despite their protestations of neutrality, the English destroyed the castles and residences in the Clyde valley of the Queen's Party, on the excuse they had assisted the rebel northern earls. Hamilton castle was so badly burnt that, as Atholl reported to Glenorchy, 'the nixt tyme that ye cum to Hammiltoun ye will nocht gette ane galerie to gang in'.[59] The Hamiltons' only consolation was the capture of their archenemy Robert Lord Sempill, who was imprisoned in Argyll.[60] The 5th earl found himself fighting on two fronts. Whilst an English army with an artillery train was devastating the region of his maternal kin, in the Central Highlands he faced an upsurge of activity in the MacGregor feud.[61] He called a clan council on 19/20 June to sort out the details of the Campbell force to aid Glenorchy against the MacGregors, but, with the national situation so confused, could not devote all his resources to the feud. English intervention allowed the King's Party to regroup and in July 1570 proclaim a new regent. The king's grandfather Lennox, a bitter regional rival of the Hamiltons and of Argyll, was chosen. He wasted no time pursuing the military campaign, sending troops into Angus against Huntly, who had been running a separate government in the north in the queen's name.[62] Lennox targeted Brechin, where Huntly's troops had retreated to the ancient steeple attached to the cathedral. When they were forced to surrender, all the captains and their thirty-four soldiers were executed, a deed that shocked the country, unused to such savagery.[63] At the end of August, Doune castle near Stirling fell, leaving Argyll's brother-in-law, James Stewart, to make the best of a hard bargain offered by the regent.[64] In most areas of armed conflict, the king's men, boosted by English intervention, were gaining the upper hand.

By the summer of 1570, there was considerable war weariness among the Scottish nobility. Many nobles had tried to remain on the fringes of the fighting and avoid firm commitments to either side. Together these men formed the core of a peace party who were 'reddy to ly still' and wanted 'quyatnes to be hed amangis ye hail nobilitie'. In his analysis, Sir William Stewart of Grandtully, Atholl's 'man of business', identified Lennox and his close supporters as the main stumbling block to a settlement because they

---

[59] 30 May 1570, *Campbell Letters*, 95.
[60] Calderwood, *History*, II. 565; *Diurnal*, 178; Bannatyne, *Memorials*, 43.
[61] Argyll to Glenorchy, 5 May 1570, *Campbell Letters*, 93 and the 'Glenlyon incident', 10 June, *Campbell Letters*, 99 and 101, and see above p. 42.
[62] Murray, 'Huntly's Rebellion'. The 5th earl had also been using his authority as justice-general, 23 June and 20 July 1570, GD112/56/7; GD112/2/117/3/43.
[63] Glenorchy to Argyll, 14 August 1570, *Campbell Letters*, 135; Maitland to John Leslie, *CSPSc*, III. 313.
[64] Ruthven to Katherine Ruthven, 21 September 1570; Stewart of Doune to Glenorchy, 25 September, *Campbell Letters*, 162 and 166.

were 'determinat to do furth thair purpois without ony myddis as God will leiff thame'.[65] With friendships and kinships continuing to function across the political divides, throughout the conflict it remained possible to restart negotiations.[66] Although coming to nothing, in July 1570 there was one such attempt at reconciliation. Argyll had planned to meet the king's men Mar and Morton at Sir William Murray of Tullibardine's house. Atholl and Grandtully were also involved along with Colin Campbell of Glenorchy, who was the contact point between Queen's and King's Parties through his cousin, Annabella Murray, the countess of Mar, and sister of Murray of Tullibardine.[67]

For Argyll and the queen's men, the political situation was confused by the conflicting signals emanating from Sussex, the English commander. On the one hand English troops were attacking them and, on the other, Sussex was sending messages offering to mediate. At the start of the summer, Argyll and the duke had written to Maitland asking if he understood what was happening.[68] To their relief, Maitland took over the task of the complex negotiations with Sussex, which dragged on for the remainder of the year.[69] Messengers were kept busy travelling between the different Scottish factions, Sussex, on the English border, and London. These negotiations provoked the grand conference of the Queen's Party at the beginning of September at the east end of Loch Tay to consider Sussex's proposals for a truce.[70] On behalf of their party, Argyll and Huntly, along with the duke, now little more than a cipher, gave their formal agreement.[71] Though Mary had hoped Argyll might travel south, Lord Livingston was sent to England to continue the negotiations.[72] Scotland settled into a tense truce whilst the focus of attention moved to London and Elizabeth's proposals for the Scottish queen's restoration. By the end of 1570, the 5th earl felt no progress had been made

[65] Grandtully named Atholl, Caithness, Methven, Errol, Rothes, Montgomery, Herries, Gray and Oliphant as well as himself as wanting peace: Grandtully to Glenorchy, 31 July 1570, GD112/39/8/23.
[66] For example Argyll's letter to Douglas of Lochleven, 22 July 1570, *Reg. Hon. de Mort*, I. 59, and see above, p. 36.
[67] 14 July 1570, *Campbell Letters*, 116, and Grandtully to Glenorchy, 28 July, *Campbell Letters*, 123.
[68] 12 June 1570, *CSPSc*, III. 228–9. The 5th earl had also written a personal letter to Maitland about the Glenlyon incident, 14 June 1570, *Campbell Letters*, 103.
[69] Loughlin, 'The Career of Maitland of Lethington', ch. 8.
[70] The conference was originally set for Dunkeld, but that was deemed too dangerous and so it was moved near Balloch Castle, despite Glenorchy's less than complete delight at the prospect: 20 and 21 August 1570, *Campbell Letters*, 141 and 144.
[71] 3 September 1570, *CSPSc*, III. 345–6; *Black Book of Taymouth* ed. C. Innes (Bannatyne Club, 100, Edinburgh, 1855), 136; Calderwood, *History*, III. 10–11; Bannatyne, *Memorials*, 52.
[72] Randolph to Sussex, 10 September, *CSPSc*, III. 340. Sussex to Maitland, 14 September 1570, GD112/39/10/2; *CSPSc*, III. 346.

on the negotiations, which had been dragging on for five months. With weary resignation, he reported the two queens were still in talks but 'quhat follis thairon either guid or ewill we will lait God be iuge thairto'.[73]

Any remaining possibility of Mary's restoration through English help disappeared with the discovery of the Norfolk marriage schemes followed by the Ridolphi plot in 1571. That banished the last realistic hope of putting the Scottish queen, at least nominally, back on her throne, and destroyed the common positive objective of the Queen's Party. Their position within Scotland had also deteriorated, especially after a daring raid in April had captured Dumbarton castle for the king's men. By its fall, the Queen's Party lost their port for supplies from abroad and a strategic, and supposedly impregnable, stronghold.[74] For the Hamiltons, it was a devastating blow, allowing the archbishop of St Andrews, their effective leader, to be captured and hung for Moray's murder.[75]

Having been sunk in a lethargic gloom at the end of 1570, these developments frightened Argyll into a frenzied round of triangular negotiations. The atmosphere had been so tense, with fighting always threatening to overtake the talking, that the 5th earl had worn his armour day and night. At the beginning of May, talks finally broke down without agreement. Argyll was depressed, directing his anger and frustration at the Castilians, holding Edinburgh castle for the queen, blaming them for refusing a reasonable compromise.[76] This experience probably finally convinced the earl to settle by himself, if necessary. Recriminations began immediately and, as Argyll gloomily warned Grey Colin, the country would soon be filled with bad rumours about him.[77] The breach with his former allies kept the 5th earl away from the Parliament held by the Queen's Party in June. By this stage, Argyll had given up hope that European aid for Mary's cause would materialise. As even the Scottish queen herself acknowledged, the 5th earl and Boyd were searching for the best way out of an impossible situation.[78]

The breakdown of Argyll's latest attempt to broker a compromise gave the King's Party an opening to draw him into a separate agreement. Morton travelled to Dunblane, where the 5th earl and Atholl had been putting the

---

[73] Argyll to Grey Colin, 16 December 1570, GD112/39/11/21.

[74] Argyll, Huntly and the duke had written to Charles IX trying to minimise the impact of the fall of Dumbarton, these letters were later intercepted, July 1571, *CSPSc*, III. 626.

[75] Calderwood, *History*, III. 54–9.

[76] Herries, *Memoirs*, 135; Calderwood, *History*, III. 74–5; 78; Bannatyne, *Memorials*, 120–1.

[77] 20 May 1571, GD112/39/13/3. Instructions for Captain Brickwell, 4 June 1571, *CSPSc*, III. 596. Argyll and Boyd had already been accused of playing on 'Dysartis pipe', which could produce any tune as the occasion required, *Satirical Poems of the Time of the Reformation*, I. 158, line 80.

[78] 28 June 1571, *Lettres et mémoires de Marie, reine d'escosse*, ed. A. Labanoff (7 vols., Paris, 1859), III. 304.

finishing touches to the settlement of the MacGregor feud.[79] In the subsequent discussions, Argyll was persuaded to treat directly with the regent, though Atholl chose to stay loyal to the Castilians and the rump of the Queen's Party.[80] The following week the earl consulted his kinsmen, gathered to celebrate a Campbell marriage.[81] Probably bolstered by their encouragement, he travelled secretly to Stirling to finalise terms with Mar and Morton. On 12 August, a settlement was reached between the King's Party and Argyll, who brought with him the queen's men from the south-west, the earls of Cassilis, Eglinton and Lord Boyd.[82] Indicating how much the regent was willing to concede to secure the 5th earl's support, the terms were generous, with Argyll given substantial rewards for changing sides. As well as escaping forfeiture at the forthcoming Parliament, he was immediately restored to the council and an active role in government in addition to receiving extra lands.[83]

The earl's decision to settle and the favourable terms he had been given brought a barrage of criticism and accusations of promise-breaking and inconstancy from the remnants of the Queen's Party.[84] The defection of Argyll and the south-western nobility had a demoralising impact upon their cause, inducing a number of others to make their peace with the regent. The rump of queen's men realised that, without the political weight provided by the 5th earl, their own chances of an equitable settlement were much reduced. Concluding the queen's men were doomed, the Edinburgh merchants withdrew their credit.[85] Argyll faced the awkward task of trying to justify his actions to his former allies. Seeking to occupy the high moral ground, he wrote immediately to his uncle the duke explaining he had abandoned the

---

[79] Bonds between Atholl and MacGregors, 15 July 1571, GD112/1/195–6; GD112/2/117/1/30; Ewin MacGregor to Glenorchy, c. 19 July 1571, *Campbell Letters*, 191, and see pp. 181–2 n. 51. Final agreement with Atholl, 24 July, GD112/1/197; MacGregor, 'MacGregors', 391–2.
[80] *The historie and cronicles of Scotland . . . by Robert Lindesay of Pitscottie* ed. A.J.G. Mackay (3 vols., Scottish Text Society, Old ser. 42–43, Edinburgh, 1899–1911), II. 258; *Diurnal*, 237–8; Drury to Burghley, 24 July 1571, *CSPSc*, III. 631.
[81] Argyll had negotiated the match between John Campbell, son of Ardkinglas, and Anna Campbell, daughter of Glenorchy: 23 July 1571, GD112/25/31–3; and *Campbell Letters*, 28–31.
[82] Drury to Burghley, 4 August 1571, *CSPSc*, III. 635; Herries, *Memoirs*, 138–9. Settlement, *CSPSc*, III. 642–3. The bond of 12 August 1571 (misdated 1572) printed in *Miscellany of the Abbotsford Club I* ed. J. Maidment (Abbotsford Club, 11, Edinburgh, 1837), I. 27–8; W. Fraser, *Memorials of the Montgomeries, Earls of Eglinton* (2 vols., Edinburgh, 1859), II. 207–8; Wormald, *Lords and Men*, 408 [27].
[83] Drury to Burghley, 24 August 1571, *CSPSc*, III. 664; parliament cancelled the escheat, *APS*, III. 63c17; Case to Drury, 2 September 1571, *CSPSc*, III. 677; grant of lands in the diocese of Dunkeld, 9 September 1571, *RSS*, VI. 1276.
[84] Drury reported to Burghley, Argyll was regarded as 'very inconstante and respekteth no promys', 4 September 1571, *CSPSc*, III. 677.
[85] Maitland and Anon. to Mary, 5 September 1571, *CSPSc*, III. 682–3, 683–4

fight for the queen because it appeared hopeless. He described the relative prospects for James VI and his mother, 'the Kingis coronatioun standing established in his estait, and he at hame amangis us, and that the Quenis grace his mother continewis under the power of the Quene of England, out of this realme, quhair she may not do nathing aither for this cuntrie or for hir self, but according to the pleasure of tham that now she is thrall unto'. His second and related reason was that, with Mary's cause lost, continuous civil warfare was causing too much damage to Scotland, forcing him to accept 'all gude meanis that may quiet the troublit state of our afflictit countrie, quhilk I am constrenit to think dear unto me, seing the present calamitie thairof sa great'. Argyll urged the duke to follow his example and offered to help in whatever way he could.[86]

The duke and Huntly replied to this plea by requesting a meeting and rehearsing the promises of foreign aid for Mary. Argyll, weary of broken promises and the external manipulation of Mary's plight, wrote sharply that he would 'nowise pass to put the title of the crown of Scotland under the judgement of any other Prince', adding that no one in Scotland had such authority.[87] The previous eighteen months had left the 5th earl disillusioned and depressed. Seeing Scotland torn apart by factional warfare and being helpless to prevent it, he had concluded that peace must be restored at all costs. As in 1569, his clan had probably been urging him to stop fighting and recover his losses. Believing the country had to be unified around a single centre of authority, he realised in 1571 that could only flow from the boy king, James VI, and not his mother. Argyll acknowledged Mary's cause was lost because the Scottish queen's fate was outside Scottish control, and to continue to strive for her restoration played into the hands of foreign powers. In his view, the English had used their custody of Mary as an excuse to manipulate Scotland's domestic politics. If the queen were restored by English power, or even by the unlikely aid of French or Spanish power, Mary would owe her crown to them, which would permanently undermine the authority of the monarchy and threaten Scotland's independence. He convinced himself that accepting the regent and swearing loyalty to the king was the sensible and patriotic option. The decision was made more palatable by the price the 5th earl could extract, being able to return to his place at the centre of government and receive substantial rewards of lands and offices for himself, his kin and affinity. Argyll's weariness, depression and desire to be free from the burden of political decision making might have been symptoms of declining health, which broke down the following month.

---

[86] Argyll to Châtelherault, 13 August 1571, *CSPSc*, III. 645.
[87] Argyll to Châtelherault and Huntly, 17 August 1571, *CSPSc*, III. 651.

To demonstrate their new allegiance, Argyll and the south-western lords remained in Stirling to attend the August Parliament. Ironically, this meant they were caught up in Huntly's raid, in which a number of men were killed, including two of Argyll's servants. During that skirmish, Regent Lennox was fatally wounded. His death provoked panic among those loyal to the young king, and there was a desperate desire to fill the vacancy immediately.[88] Within a couple of days, Mar had been chosen as the next regent.[89] Though his own name and that of Morton had been suggested as possible candidates, the 5th earl did not want the regency. He was disillusioned with politics, and his own health was bad. He had become ill just before Lennox's death, and an unpleasant journey to Dunoon in bad weather had not improved his condition. By 16 September he was too ill to travel, having to send his brother to an important meeting in Leith.[90] By the beginning of October, the 5th earl was reportedly close to death.[91] Once recovered from such a scare, Argyll felt compelled to reorganise his affairs. He settled the earldom and renewed his efforts to divorce his wife.[92] Henceforth, his half-brother and heir Colin was given a more prominent role in clan affairs and national politics.[93]

Colin's wedding to Annas Keith, the widow of Regent Moray, in January 1572 was used to symbolise the general spirit of reconciliation assiduously cultivated by the new regent.[94] The marriage restored the close friendship that had previously existed between the 5th earl and Moray. Regent Mar further rewarded Argyll with a grant restoring the Brechin lands taken from him by Moray.[95] The earl laboured hard to persuade his former allies to be reconciled to the new regent. Though it was simple to persuade the Islesmen to give their oaths of allegiance, Huntly was much more difficult to convince.[96] Initially, the 5th earl succeeded, though Huntly later reverted to supporting

[88] *Diurnal*, 247; Bannatyne, *Memorials*, 184; Calderwood, *History*, III. 139–41.
[89] Bannatyne, *Memorials*, 185–6; Anon. to Drury, 5 September 1571, *CSPSc*, III. 680.
[90] Argyll to Glenorchy, 16 September 1571, GD112/39/13/9.
[91] Drury to Burghley, 9 October 1571, *CSPSc*, IV. 4.   [92] See above pp. 32–3.
[93] For example Colin was included in the bond the 5th earl made with John Stewart of Bute, 16 December 1571, AT, VI. 170; Wormald, *Lords and Men*, 187 [46]. He went to Leith in place of the 5th earl at the time of the February parliament and was part of the Perth discussions, 13 April 1572, *CSPSc*, IV. 227.
[94] As the senior male relative of Moray's family, Mar acted for Annas Keith in the marriage negotiations, with Argyll acting for his brother: marriage alliance, 6 January 1572, AT, VI. 168; marriage banns, 13 January 1572, NRA(S), 217, Box 15 No. 344.
[95] 7 January 1572, *RSS*, VI. 1421.
[96] Advices from Scotland, 20 February 1572, *CSPSc*, IV, 135. Negotiations with Huntly, 17 January 1572, *Diurnal*, 257. As 'Lieutenant of our Sovereign Lady' Huntly granted a safe conduct to the honeymoon couple Annas Keith and Colin Campbell to travel to Moray to visit their estates: *Rose of Kilravock*, 259–60.

the Castilians.[97] Argyll was a good peacemaker, willing to grant reasonable conditions. Unlike the majority of the regent's supporters who had benefited greatly from the forfeitures and escheats of the queen's men, he was 'void of private quarrels' and largely unhindered by vested interests.[98] An exception to this impartiality was his dispute with Atholl over the diocese of Dunkeld, which nearly caused a breakdown in the Perth negotiations during April.[99] Despite this hiccup, the conciliatory methods of Mar and Argyll were slowly returning Scotland to more peaceful conditions. The outstanding problem was Edinburgh castle, especially the difficulty of granting a pardon to its occupants for their campaign of terror against the burgh.[100] In the autumn of 1572, a large-scale conference was planned to end the civil wars, but was disrupted by Mar's unexpected death on 28 October.[101]

Once again Scotland was in turmoil and seeking a regent. For the 5th earl it was a double blow: he had lost a political ally and a valued friend. Apart from the Linlithgow incident, he had not been at loggerheads with Mar during the wars. He expressed his great grief to Glenorchy, 'we haiff gret occasioun to lament the loss of sa tendir ane frend being sa ferventlie affectionat towartis our weill and the weill of our hous and freindis we can nocht bot patientlie abyd the pleasour of God'.[102] In response to the emergency situation, the 5th earl called a clan council, which might have discussed the suggestion he should become the next regent. Forgiving his earlier desertion of their cause, his candidature had the support of the Castilians. It was opposed by hard-liners in the King's Party who had never fully accepted him.[103] Despite the speculation, Argyll did not seek the regency. He stayed away from the Edinburgh convention, writing to Morton with the excuse that he could not leave his region.[104] In his letter, Argyll complained he had been occupied for

[97] 17 April 1572, *CSPSc*, IV. 231.
[98] Hunsdon to Elizabeth and to Burghley, 8 March 1572, *CSPSc*, IV. 155–8.
[99] Argyll and the Perthshire nobles met to settle an internal feud between Patrick 3rd Lord Drummond, and his mother, Lilias Ruthven, over Drummond's marriage, but also discussed the regional nobility's reconciliation with the regent: Drury to Burghley, 13 April 1572, *CSPSc*, IV. 227. Without his mother's consent, Drummond had married Elizabeth Lindsay, the daughter of the 9th earl of Crawford and his wife, Katherine Campbell, countess of Crawford. Argyll got the escheat of Dunkeld, 27 April 1572, *RSS*, VI. 1580.
[100] For example 19 April 1572, *CSPSc*, IV. 241.
[101] This was the forerunner of the meetings which led to the Pacification of Perth. Glenorchy was appointed to be one of the commissioners at the conference, which also included the English ambassadors: Ruthven to Glenorchy, 31 October 1572, GD112/39/14/6.
[102] 3 November 1572, GD112/39/14/8.
[103] They deemed Argyll unsuitable because he was not fully committed to the king's cause, had been involved in Darnley's death, was kin to the Hamiltons, was poor and based in the Highlands where he could do little to uphold justice: Killigrew to Smith and to Burghley, 6 and 11 November 1572, *CSPSc*, IV. 430–1, 432.
[104] Argyll to Morton, 8 November 1572, GD112/39/14/9.

so long in the Lowlands with national affairs that the neglect of Highland matters had reached the point that 'gif we laf thame now ye knaw quahat inconvenient may cum to us thairby'.[105] These messages read like a coded confirmation of an understanding, probably made before he left Stirling, that he would leave the field clear for Morton to become regent.[106]

Peace negotiations with Huntly and the other Castilians resumed under the new regent. In January 1573, Huntly turned to Argyll to ensure that the existing truce was extended.[107] By then, Morton had called a Parliament which passed an act granting immunity from prosecution to the 5th earl and his noble dependants for all their actions during the civil wars.[108] At the same time, Argyll was made chancellor, the highest ranking official in Scotland.[109] The 5th earl was being generously compensated by Morton for his support. As Sir Henry Killigrew, the English ambassador, reported, Argyll had become Morton's partner, with the regent always affording 'him the place of honour and the right hand both abroad and at home'.[110]

As chancellor, the 5th earl led the drive to bring a final settlement. Two groups remained unreconciled: the Castilians and Huntly, and the Hamiltons. Melville later recalled that Morton was willing to settle with either group but not both, because together they would outweigh his own power.[111] Whatever the truth of this recollection, the Pacification of Perth concluded by Argyll in February 1573 only covered the Hamiltons and Huntly.[112] Aided by English forces, a full-scale siege was mounted against Edinburgh castle, with the 5th earl bringing troops and sufficient artillery to cover an entire section of the encirclement.[113] The starving castle finally surrendered on 28 May.[114] Although most of its occupants departed in peace, the captain, Kirkcaldy of

---

[105] Note of certain heads committed to the laird of Glenorchy to be declared to the earl of Morton, c. 8–15 November 1572, GD112/1/224. Argyll settled his urgent business by 15 November: Argyll to Glenorchy, 15 November 1572, GD112/39/14/11.
[106] 15 November 1572, *CSPSc*, IV. 433.
[107] Huntly to Argyll, 20 January 1573, *CSPSc*, IV. 472. See also Hay to Killigrew, 17 January 1573, *CSPSc*, IV. 467–8.
[108] *APS*, III. 76; report on Parliament *CSPSc*, IV. 466. In the later April Parliament an act was passed which effectively guaranteed the 5th earl his divorce, see above, p. 33.
[109] Commission as chancellor, 17 January 1573, *RSS*, VI. 1820. He was also made chamberlain of the diocese of Dunkeld, 19 January 1573, AT, VI. 194. Atholl appears to have accepted his defeat over Dunkeld as he did not mention it in his letter to Argyll, 12 February 1573, Argyll MSS Bundle 46.
[110] Killigrew to Burghley, 14 April 1573, *CSPSc*, IV. 545.
[111] *The Memoirs of Sir James Melville of Halhill* ed. G. Donaldson (London, 1969), 97–9.
[112] Instructions from Morton to Argyll *et al.*, 12 February 1573, *The Warrender Papers*, I. 115–20. Terms of Pacification, 23 February 1573, Calderwood, *History*, III. 261–71; *RPC*, II. 193; *CSPSc*, IV. 495–8; Bannatyne, *Memorials*, 305–15.
[113] 12–14 May, *Diurnal*, 331–2.
[114] Calderwood, *History*, III. 281–3. The countess of Argyll was taken prisoner, see above, p. 33.

Grange, was convicted of treason and hanged, and, if he had not died on 9 July, Maitland of Lethington might have suffered the same fate.[115]

The fall of Edinburgh castle finally brought the civil wars to a close. The 5th earl enforced the terms of the Perth Pacification by forcibly recovering Paisley abbey from Lord Sempill and returning it to Lord Claud Hamilton.[116] With this mission completed and his divorce finalised, Argyll had leisure at the beginning of August to celebrate his second marriage at Castle Campbell. A couple of weeks later, he left for the Borders to accompany Morton on a law and order campaign.[117] On his return to Argyll, the 5th earl was taken ill and died suddenly on 12 September 1573.[118] Though not living long enough to enjoy it, Argyll had helped to bring peace back to Scotland and to start healing the divisions created by the civil wars. His early death has obscured his considerable contribution to the restoration of Scottish national politics after the fragmentation of the civil wars. Morton's regime has received the credit for the stability of the next decade. However, given the regent's later record for alienating his fellow magnates, it is unlikely that he could have achieved the pacifications of 1572–3 without Argyll's help. By that period, the 5th earl's political goals had shrunk to preserving the position of his house, clan and affinity. In his own mind, he had also been serving the cause of peace for his country and his king. But to his former allies among the queen's men, Argyll had betrayed them, leaving him with an abiding reputation for inconstancy and double-dealing.

THE CREATION OF A CLIENT STATE

Anglo-Scottish relations entered a new era on 16 May 1568, when Mary disembarked on the southern shore of the Solway. The queen seemed unaware of the extent of the difficulties she had created, naively believing her good cousin Elizabeth would help recover her throne.[119] For the remainder of her life, Mary remained an intractable problem for the English queen and for her government, which they solved nearly twenty years later by the drastic expedient of her execution. Within the immediate context of Anglo-Scottish relations, possession of the Scottish queen proved an immense advantage, permitting the English to intervene with impunity in the affairs of their northern neighbour. However, though not entirely shedding its international and

---

[115] Calderwood, *History*, III. 284–7.
[116] Killigrew to Burghley, 1, 13 and 20 June 1573, *CSPSc*, IV. 577, 586, 590; commission to Argyll, 10 June 1573, *RPC*, II. 241–2; summons to Mure of Rowallan, 10 June 1573, NLS Adv. MS 54.1.7 fo. 44.
[117] 25 August 1573, *Diurnal*, 337; and see above, p. 34.
[118] Brown to Burghley, 4 October 1573, *CSP For 1572–4*, 427; *Diurnal*, 337.
[119] J. Wormald, *Mary Queen of Scots: A Study in Failure* (London, 1988), 174.

British ramifications, Mary's presence became primarily a domestic issue for England. The overriding problem was Mary's claim to the succession or to the throne itself, and, whenever her fate was being considered, her restoration in Scotland was relegated to a subordinate position. The implications for English security dominated the discussions in the Privy Council about how to treat the Scottish queen immediately after her unexpected arrival. As Cecil pithily noted, this offered a choice of equally unattractive alternatives, 'neither her continuance here good, nor her departing hence quiet for us'.[120] In characteristic fashion, Cecil drew up a memo trying to discover a path for Elizabeth through this particular Scylla and Charybdis.[121] While the Scottish queen could not be permitted to travel to France, a suitable style of treating her within England was not easily found. On the one hand, she was a queen deposed by her subjects, an action Elizabeth could not condone. On the other, Mary's scandalous conduct in the last months of her personal reign provided some justification for her removal from the throne by England's friends. The relative success of Moray's regency during Mary's imprisonment and especially its enthusiastic support for the Scottish Kirk weighed considerably with Cecil. It was not in English interests to see the Anglophile Moray and his allies defeated. Added to these Scottish factors was the concern over the use Mary's English supporters would make of her arrival within the country.

However difficult to resolve, Mary's presence in England brought Cecil an opportunity to analyse this problem in British terms and formulate a policy encompassing all three kingdoms. Much had changed since 1560. English security and claims to superiority over Britain were at the heart of the 1568 policy. Cecil grasped the English claim to imperial rights over Scotland as the key to unravelling the diplomatic tangle of how to treat Mary, Queen of Scots.[122] He now exhibited in full view his concept of an imperial Britain, which, eight years earlier, had been safely kept for English consumption alone. Scottish sensibilities were no longer of major concern.

Cecil utilised the arguments asserting England's superiority over the entire British mainland to justify the creation of a quasi-judicial commission to investigate the charges against Mary. This clever device, with its strong emphasis upon the need for 'justice' for the Scottish queen, had two great advantages for Elizabeth. In the first place, by placing both Scottish parties in the role of supplicants it offered a mechanism for increasing English leverage within Scottish domestic politics. Secondly, it preserved Elizabeth's

---

[120] 13 July 1568, cited in Donaldson, *First Trial of Mary, Queen of Scots*, 77.
[121] About the end of May 1568, BL Cotton Calig. C 1 n. fos. 97r–100v; *CSPSc*, II. 418–9. For a full discussion of Cecil's views, see Alford, *Cecil*, ch. 7.
[122] Alford, *Cecil*, 162–3.

recognition of Mary's royal status, whilst denying her access to the English queen until the 'scandal' had been cleared from her name. The 'first trial' of Mary, as it has been aptly named, gave the English as much control as possible over the Scottish queen and her kingdom. Cecil's 1568 British policy sought to dictate a peaceful solution to Scotland's domestic crisis and impose a permanent friendship between the two countries underpinned by English imperial superiority. He remained committed to a united Protestant mainland, but it was to be achieved by completely different methods from those agreed in 1560. Equality between the kingdoms had been replaced by England's role as the dominant partner in the relationship, dictating a Scottish settlement best suited to England's interests and security. Ireland was not absent from Cecil's calculations, though the main aim was Scottish exclusion from that kingdom, reversing the co-operation envisaged in 1560. Having weathered the first decade of the reign, the Elizabethan regime was well established and more confident than it had been in 1560. Though the international situation was worrying, the French were embroiled in civil and religious war, and Philip II was coping with the revolt in the Netherlands and the Turks in the Mediterranean. With neither European power disposed to enter another conflict in the British Isles, England was left with a relatively free hand.

In the summer of 1568, Mary's Scottish supporters waited to discover how Elizabeth would react to her royal refugee. They had written to Elizabeth at the end of July formally asking her to assist Mary or, at the least, allow her to return home.[123] The response was not encouraging. Under English pressure, and though it damaged her party's cause, Mary ordered Argyll to halt his military campaign against Moray and agree a truce. At the same time, Elizabeth wrote 'plainly' to the 5th earl about the Irish mercenary trade and the Ulster marriages, including a thinly disguised threat that if Scots went to Ireland Elizabeth would 'make less account of your apparent good will'. The English queen had no need to spell out the implications.[124] Acknowledging the unwritten threat, Argyll offered a bargain: he would 'do quhatsoever mycht do your hienes plesour safer as lyin in my power in all thingis that is under my charge or all utheris that I may reasonabillie staye fra trubling of your hienes cuntre or liegis'. In return, he expected Elizabeth to set 'fordwerdis the Quenis Maiestie my soveran to hir authorite ryall and suppressing of hir unnaturall and disobedient subiectis conforme to your hienes promesses maid to hir grace'.[125] A second letter to Elizabeth from the entire Queen's Party

---

[123] 28 July 1568, *CSPSc*, II. 466–8.
[124] 14 August 1568 *CSPSc*, II. 477–8; printed in *Sidney State Papers, 1565–70*, I. 36.
[125] 24 August 1568, BL Cotton Calig. C 1 n. fo. 209; unsigned copy, Calig. B 9 n. fo. 310; printed in *Sidney State Papers, 1565–70*, I. 36–7.

complained they had accepted the truce she had requested, but Moray had broken its terms by forfeiting them in the Parliament.[126] Already there was resentment among Mary's supporters that England was pulling the strings in Scotland and their interference was benefiting the King's Party. Argyll with his Irish card was the only bargaining counter the Queen's Party had.

The commencement of Mary's 'first trial' switched attention to the proceedings at York and later at Westminster, and serious fighting in Scotland was suspended. The judicial process concentrated upon the murder at Kirk o' Field, with Moray and the King's commissioners producing the Casket letters as evidence of Mary's guilt. This was met by a range of counter-accusations from the queen's commissioners. The move to Westminster strengthened the impression of a criminal trial, with the English striving to wrap a cloak of legality around the proceedings. If they were to recognise Moray's regency, or force Mary into a settlement on their terms, they needed some proof of her guilt to give them leverage and a justification for European consumption.[127]

The Queen's Party in Scotland, remote from the trial and inactive for its duration, exerted little influence upon Mary's case. When it was concluded, Mary directed Argyll and Huntly to issue their proclamation to counter Moray's slanders.[128] The two earls, anxious to shift the spotlight from Darnley's murder, concentrated their propaganda offensive elsewhere. One obvious target was Elizabeth's behaviour. It was argued that, instead of protecting and restoring her fellow monarch as she had promised, the duplicitous English Queen had deceived Mary and put her on trial. One pamphlet indignantly declared, 'where is most truste, there is most treason. The Quene of Scottes puttythe her most truste in the Quene of Englande and she will most deceave her in the ende.'[129] However, the main focus of attack was Moray's subservience to English demands. The regent was depicted selling Scotland to her old enemy in return for personal power and support against his enemies. Moray was specifically accused of agreeing to hand over Edinburgh and Stirling castles to the English. The more sinister charge was made that he planned to send James VI into England, where he would 'be putt doun', allowing Moray to seize the throne. The final and most telling accusation was that the regent was willing to 'tak the realme of Scotland, to be haldin of the quene of England as tributar and in few, be the quhilk peace and peace sall draw the haill nobilitie and ancient blude thereof in miserable servitude and bondage and to be slaves siclike as we have to example in the Balliolles tyme'.[130]

[126] 24 August 1568, BL Cotton Calig. C 1 n. fo. 210.   [127] Alford, *Cecil*, 174–5.

[128] See above, pp. 176–7.

[129] A paper found circulating at Westminster, c. January 1569, BL Cotton Calig. C 1 n. fo. 377.

[130] Proclamation by Argyll, January 1569, *The Warrender Papers*, I. 57–60 at p. 58; Argyll to Edinburgh council, 11 January, *Reg. Hon. de Mort*, I. 40–1.

Argyll's appeal to anti-English sentiment, especially the memory of the Scottish independence struggle under Wallace and Bruce, was a far cry from the rhetoric of amity employed in 1560. It was in reaction to the imperial claims of superiority over Scotland which Cecil had employed to justify Elizabeth's right to hold the trial and pass judgement upon Mary. The feudal and quasi-historical arguments underpinning English superiority were challenged by the traditional Scottish rhetoric of defiance, asserting the sovereign independence of the kingdom. They provided a straightforward rejection of the specific claim that the English queen possessed the imperial right to act as 'umpere and principall arbitrer' in affairs throughout the British mainland, thereby enabling her to judge Mary's case.[131] The English government was sufficiently stung by these attacks to issue its own proclamation in Scotland, declaring its good intentions. The Queen's Party also confronted Cecil's broader agenda, using the trial as a means of imposing a solution upon all the Scottish parties. Part of any solution was a permanent alliance with England, on harsher terms than 1560. Instead of relying upon mutual interests, a common faith and an Anglophile party in Scotland, the English sought guarantees to bind the country irrevocably to its southern neighbour. Scotland was to be a satellite state, which could never again pose a threat to English security. As well as requests for James VI to be raised in England or the surrender of strategic fortifications, there were more subtle suggestions involving Scotland's government.

In the late summer of 1568, Cecil outlined his Scottish solution, and these proposals reappeared in assorted variations whenever Mary's fate was being negotiated during the next three years. Following his own views on conciliar government, Cecil sought to utilise Scotland's constitutional bodies, such as a regency, great council and Parliament to underpin any settlement with Mary. As well as providing a permanent political check upon the Scottish queen, they would create an avenue through which Elizabeth's role as the final arbiter in Scottish affairs could be institutionalised. However well meaning, these proposals were an attempt to remould Scottish government. Apart from undermining Scotland's independence, the scheme posed a threat to the political power of Argyll and his fellow peers. The propaganda assertions in the 5th earl's proclamations were founded upon a fear that the ancient nobility's role in Scottish government was being undermined by a conspiracy of English Privy Councillors and 'upstart' Scots, the traditional target of noble dissidents.[132]

---

[131] Cecil's memorial, August/September 1568, cited in Alford, *Cecil*, 168; full text printed in Alford, *Cecil*, 238–43.

[132] The threat to the Scottish nobility from those 'new stert up in honouris and nocht of the auncient nobilitie of this realme' was strongly emphasised, January 1569, *The Warrender Papers*, I. 59. This was a also major theme of the later satire, 'The copie of an advertisement',

For Cecil, a British solution to the problem of Mary, Queen of Scots included Ireland. His 1568 analysis of the triangular relationship between the kingdoms ran counter to his 1560 plans. In Cecil's opinion, an Anglo-Scottish alliance should guarantee the English a free hand in Ulster. Mary's predicament was a welcome opportunity to exclude Scottish influence from Ireland. Each of Cecil's proposals concerning Mary contained a clause preventing the passage of Scots across the North Channel, except with English permission. In one such article from May 1570, Mary promised she would 'suffer no Scottishman or any other of the owt Iles of Scotland to enter into any part of Irland, without licens of the Depute there'.[133] Six months later, it was suggested that a castle in Kintyre or Galloway be handed over to the English as a base from which to police the sea-lanes and transport their own troops to Ireland.[134] The Scottish queen happily accepted such clauses but, as all parties knew, only the 5th earl could make her promises good.

This awkward reality was underlined in a casual conversation when Nicholas White visited Mary in Tutbury Castle on his way to take up an Irish post. The Scottish queen politely commented that he was going 'into Irlande, which is a troublesome cuntry, to serve my sister there'. White made the sharp rejoinder, 'I do so, madame, and the chiefest trouble of Ireland proceeds from the north of Scotland, through the Earle of Argile's supportation'. Mary could find no suitable reply.[135] At this stage of his career, the 5th earl was pursuing an independent policy in Ireland which was neither under Mary's nor the Scottish regent's control. Though his strategy in Ulster was formulated outside the context of Anglo-Scottish relations, at times Argyll played the diplomatic game for all it was worth. In the winter of 1570, he boldly asserted that his brother's Irish expedition with 700 troops had not broken the terms of the truce with Sussex because the party had sailed before those terms had been agreed.[136]

Moray's assassination in January 1570 and the presence of the rebel northern earls redoubled English interest in Scottish affairs. Argyll had become so sensitive to England's interference that, when Randolph appeared during the secret Dalkeith meeting, he lost his temper. Since the Wars of the Congregation the English ambassador had played a major role in Scottish domestic politics, exerting an influence far beyond that of conventional diplomatic representatives. The earl had struck up a close friendship

discussed above, n. 37, and had a long pedigree in Scottish political thought, see R.A. Mason, *Kingship and the Commonweal: Political Thought in Renaissance and Reformation Scotland* (East Linton, 1998), ch.1.

133 7 May 1570, cited in Alford, *Cecil*, 170–1; *CSPSc*, III. 163.
134 27 October 1570, *Campbell Letters*, 183.
135 Cited in Hayes-McCoy, *Scots Mercenary Forces*, 105.
136 December 1570, *CSPSc*, III. 454 and see below, p. 203.

with Thomas Randolph, the resident ambassador, whom he regarded as a fellow promoter of the British goals of Anglo-Scottish amity and Protestantism. After the fracturing of that amity in 1565, the 5th earl's relations with the English ambassadors became more strained, although his personal links with Randolph remained. When Mary's fall brought a marked increase in intervention, Argyll identified the ambassadors as the main conduit of English manipulation of domestic politics. In particular, he assumed they had been instructed to keep Scotland weak by encouraging civil strife and stirring up the hatred poisoning national politics.

The 5th earl protested vehemently that the ambassador should not be permitted to remain at Dalkeith because he would be serving his country's interests by setting the Scottish nobility against one another 'to mak tumult and discord amingis the nobilitie of this realme, and to be the instrument to caus euerie ane of thame hait vtheris to the death, for the plesour of the quene of Ingland, and weilfare of hir realme: Bot it sould nocht ly in hir power to doe the same'. He then pleaded with his fellow nobles to unite and not listen to false English promises about Mary. He begged them in God's name 'that the said nobilitie wald nocht heir to hir fair wordis and feinzeat, bot wald aggrie all debaittis amang thameselfis'. He argued that, if they united, they would be strong enough together to 'procure the deliuerance of the quenis grace of Scotland, at the quene of Inglands handis with plesour; and gif sho wald not let hir depairt of Ingland with plesour, the said nobilitie suld obtene help, gif the samin wer to [be] fundin within the empyr, to caus the said quene of Scotland to be delyuerit, aginis the quene of Inglandis will'.[137] Despite his impassioned words, the 5th earl knew appealing to the emperor or any other European ruler was not going to free Mary, and there was little choice but to continue negotiating with the English. Already Argyll was realising that the best way to reduce English manipulation of Scottish politics was for the higher nobility to present a united front, even at the cost of deserting Mary, Queen of Scots.

Six months later, the 5th earl was losing hope that the Scottish queen would ever be free and started distancing himself from her cause. He revealed his opinion of English intentions and the likelihood of a final settlement in his answer to Mary's personal request to act as her ambassador to Elizabeth. Argyll replied 'that without he may be assured that by his coming she may have her free liberty, and be restored to her country, he would be loath to take that travail'.[138] When yet another round of talks was undertaken in

[137] *Diurnal*, 161.
[138] Randolph to Sussex, 10 September 1570, *CSPSc*, III. 340. Lord Livingston, Adam Gordon, bishop of Galloway and John Leslie, bishop of Ross were sent to Elizabeth, commission from Châtelherault, Argyll and Huntly, 10 and 15 September 1570, *CSPSc*, III. 342.

March 1571, Argyll made one final effort. He and the rest of the Queen's Party wrote in a conciliatory tone to Elizabeth, agreeing to provide hostages for good behaviour, one of whom would be Argyll's natural son.[139] Argyll's belief that Elizabeth was playing with Mary and using her plight to intervene in Scottish domestic politics and keep the country weak and divided helped persuade him to make his peace with Regent Lennox in August 1571. Having finally accepted the king's authority, the 5th earl felt he must support the alliance with England to which all the regents were committed. He did not oppose the alliance as such but wanted to remove English meddling in Scottish domestic politics, which would only be achieved once the fighting ended and the Scottish nobility reunited. A weakened Scotland had to accept a subservient relationship with its neighbour.

The revelations of the proposed marriage between Mary and the duke of Norfolk and the Ridolphi plot might have helped soften the 5th earl's view of the English. A year later, he was shocked by the events of St Bartholomew's eve.[140] The scale and extent of the French massacre brought home to all Britain's Protestants the fragility of their position within Europe and the importance of maintaining a Protestant bastion within the British mainland. For such reasons, the 5th earl resumed his co-operation with Elizabeth's government, including a return of the accurate information service on Irish matters he had provided up to 1565.[141] Though not committing himself to assisting the Dublin administration, he encouraged Donald Gormeson to offer Elizabeth 'his service with all his power as he shall be commanded' in Ireland.[142] Argyll was prepared to take a leading role in the joint Anglo-Scottish military effort mounted in the spring of 1573, besieging Edinburgh castle.

The clearest sign of the poor quality of the relationship between the two countries was the reintroduction of English pensions into Scotland. They had been employed during the Rough Wooing to create the 'assured Scots' who supported English unionist and imperialist policies. A similar, though less blatant, imperial strategy of control over Scotland came back into operation during the civil wars, when the King's Party received English 'loans'. Money was used to buy support as a guarantee for England's security. At the end of 1572, Sir Henry Killigrew had recommended that Argyll, the regent's right-hand man, be provided with a pension, which, as Cecil, now Lord Burghley, was well aware, would help matters in Ireland in addition to Scotland.[143]

---

[139] Queen's Party to Elizabeth, 3 March 1571, *CSPSc*, III. 489–91, 502, 505–8.
[140] Scottish Protestants, including Argyll's kin, kept a close eye on the progress of the French religious wars, eg. *Campbell Letters*, 113.
[141] Argyll reported upon his meeting with Lady Agnes and Con O'Donnell in Glasgow, Killigrew to Burghley, 14 April 1572, *CSPSc*, IV. 544–5.
[142] Advices from Scotland, 26 February 1572, *CSPSc*, IV. 136, and see below, p. 207.
[143] Killigrew to Burghley, 17 December 1572, *CSP For. 1572–4*, 217.

The 5th earl would accept £200 from the English, though France had offered 2,000 crowns.[144] It was a symbolic change from the enthusiastic idealism of Anglo-Scottish amity in 1560, when Argyll had freely offered his friendship and co-operation. By 1572, Scotland had become a client state whose loyalty needed to be bought. For the rest of the century, the influx of English gold had a corrosive effect upon English perceptions of the Scots and upon Scottish domestic politics, leaving a bitter legacy after 1603.[145]

RE-ESTABLISHING THE MACDONALDS

Argyll's willingness to arrange and support the marriages of Lady Agnes and Finola to O'Neill and O'Donnell in 1569 sent the Irish administration the unambiguous message that he was pursuing his own Gaelic interests in Ulster. From an English point of view, the 5th earl's strategy was at best independent, and at worst hostile, to their wishes. Dublin's central problem was to stop the flow of Scottish mercenaries, a trade largely under the control of the 5th earl. Various methods were adopted by the administration, either trying to block the mercenaries at source in Scotland or intercept them on their way to Ireland. The simplest approach was the inclusion of a clause in every negotiation with Mary, Queen of Scots or her party in Scotland, limiting Scottish access to Ireland. In practice, it would fall to Argyll to police the mercenary trade. As none of these agreements were finalised, this was never tested.[146] A variation on this theme was using the Scottish regents to put pressure upon the 5th earl, though, with virtually no leverage, they could achieve little. Another failed tactic was to try to employ a chief, such as Donald Gormeson MacDonald of Sleat, to create a diversion, thereby occupying the troops in the Highlands and preventing their release for Ulster. None of these methods worked because they could neither persuade nor pressurise the 5th earl. He was too powerful within the Highlands to be challenged and would not follow English bidding unless real concessions were made over Mary.

An alternative strategy was to patrol the North Channel, blocking mercenaries landing in Ulster. Despite having manoeuvrable pinnaces on station, their effectiveness was questionable, and a permanent naval blockade remained impractical. English squadrons were incapable of intercepting a large force sailing from the Hebrides to Rathlin Island or into Lough Foyle, as the

---

[144] Killigrew to Burghley, 14 March 1573, *CSPSc*, IV. 519. Killigrew was still sending reminders months later, Killigrew to Burghley, 1 June 1573, *CSPSc*, IV. 577.
[145] For a full discussion, see K.M. Brown, 'The Price of Friendship: The "Well-affected" and English Economic Clientage in Scotland before 1603' in R. Mason, ed., *Scotland and England 1286–1815* (Edinburgh, 1987), 139–62.
[146] See above, p. 196.

safe arrival of the MacDonald wedding flotilla proved.[147] A more promising proposal was the fortification of the entire north-eastern coast of Ireland. However, in April 1567, the abandonment of the garrison at Derry and the death of Captain Edward Randolph served as an unpleasant reminder to the English of the difficulties and crippling expense of such a scheme. Though English colonisation of part of Ulster had been considered for the previous ten years, the first attempts took place in the 1570s, sponsored by Sir Thomas Smith and the earl of Essex.[148] Neither was successful, demonstrating that the English could not secure a firm hold on the Ulster coast. The failure of such grandiose schemes underlined the chicken-and-egg nature of the problem facing the English. They could not colonise the area so long as the Irish Gaelic chiefs were supplied with redshanks. Without Argyll's co-operation, there was no viable policy for stopping the mercenaries. The two horns of this uncomfortable dilemma were hard for Dublin to acknowledge, and harder still to place before Elizabeth. It was easiest to ignore them or gloss over the difficulties, especially in the semi-fantasy world of proposals to subdue Ireland, which jostled for royal approval in the English court.[149]

The Dublin government's policy over Ulster and the mercenaries was reduced to a series of reactions. Unable to force or persuade Argyll to cease his operations or co-operate with them, the English had to cope as best they could. They tried to discover what Argyll was planning and counter his moves in whichever way possible. To gather intelligence, Dublin relied heavily upon the services of John Douglas, whose career had begun serving as a chaplain in Argyll's household.[150] Having spent the early 1560s in Ireland, he entered Archbishop Loftus' employ before moving into Lord Deputy Sidney's service. Though working for the English, Douglas kept his

---

[147] T. Glasgow, 'The Elizabethan Navy in Ireland, 1558–1603', *Irish Sword*, 7 (1974–5), 291–307.

[148] H. Morgan, 'The Colonial Venture of Sir Thomas Smith in Ulster, 1571–5', *Historical Journal*, 28 (1985), 261–78; R. Dunlop, 'Sixteenth-Century Schemes for the Plantation of Ulster', *SHR*, 22 (1924), 51–60, 115–26, 199–212.

[149] See Brady, *Chief Governors*.

[150] In 1557–8, see pp. 24–5. The ex-Carmelite friar was 'maimed' at the seige of Leith in the spring of 1560 which ended his clerical career. He went to Ireland where he was involved in a dispute with another Scotsman, William Leech, 7 December 1562, bishop of Kildare to Sussex, *CSP Ireld*, I. 211 [54]. In 1565 the archbishop of Armagh sent him with letters to Argyll and he sorted out the forgeries, see above, pp. 136, 141. In the summer of 1566 Sidney sent him to buy armour in Scotland, Sidney to Cecil, 9 June 1566, *Letters and Memorials of State of Sir Henry Sidney* ed. A. Collins (2 vols., London, 1746), I. 11–12. In 1567, probably with Argyll's knowledge and help, Douglas went to the MacDonalds, travelling with Alastair Og to Ulster. Douglas probably acted as the go-between for Captain Piers at Carrickfergus and Alastair Og in the shady dealings surrounding Shane's murder: see above, p. 161. Later Douglas was credited with bringing over the Scots who had killed O'Neill: Sidney to Leicester, 8 August 1568, *Letters and Memorials of Sir Henry Sidney*, I. 34–5; Douglas' own petition, April 1570, *CSP Ireld*, I. 430 [49].

Scottish friends and remained sufficiently in Argyll's favour to be recommended to the English queen in 1568 by the earl's kinsman, who was in London working for Mary's release.[151] Douglas' accurate information and his impressive range of Irish and Scottish contacts made him extremely useful to the English.[152] In the summer of 1568, he was the obvious choice to send north to discover the 5th earl's Irish plans, especially the worrying new Ulster alliances.[153] Douglas was briefed by Argyll on the current state of Highland politics and in particular what had happened at the earl's own council. He noted with alarm the 5th earl's closeness to Donald Gormeson of Sleat, offering a potential threat to English interests.[154] Discounting his assurances and assuming Argyll was playing a double game, Douglas hurried south to warn the English.[155] Cecil reacted immediately, persuading Elizabeth the situation was sufficiently serious for her to write personally to Argyll.[156] Carrying the queen's letter north, Douglas found the 5th earl at Glasgow on 22 August, received a prompt reply and travelled south again.[157]

The courier's shuttle diplomacy continued in late October when he brought Sidney's letters to Argyll and to Lady Agnes. The Ulster marriages had not taken place as planned in 1568, and the English were frantically trying to persuade the earl and Lady Agnes not to seal the alliance. During this visit the 5th earl discussed the situation frankly with Douglas. Tired of the subtleties of diplomacy, he sent a plain message to the English queen: unless she helped Mary, he would invade Ireland. Argyll added the revealing aside that he loved Douglas' master, Sidney, more than any other man whom he had never met, probably because of their shared Protestant convictions. On hearing from Douglas that Sidney was to be relieved of his Irish post, the earl joked that he hoped Sir Francis Knollys would be the replacement, because 'he is the

---

[151] John Hamilton, commendator of Arbroath, to Elizabeth, 24 February 1568, *CSPSc*, II. 401.

[152] Sidney felt able to commend Douglas to Cecil for his diligence and faithful and true reporting, even though he was a Scot, 8 August 1568, *Letters and Memorials of Sir Henry Sidney*, I. 35–6.

[153] The Carrickfergus commanders had reported optimistically that the Highland chiefs were so involved in domestic disputes that the marriages and mercenary influx would not take place: Piers and Malby to Elizabeth, 7 July 1568, SP63/25 fo. 42.

[154] John Willock to Cecil, 8 July 1568, *CSPSc*, II. 453–4.

[155] Douglas went via Galloway to meet Sidney in Shropshire and reported to Sir Francis Knollys at Bolton castle where the Scottish queen was being held, Knollys to Leicester, 1 August 1568, *HMC* Pepys (1911), 123–4; Knollys to Cecil, 18 August 1568, BL Cotton Calig. B 9 n. fo. 340. He reached Cecil on 10 August, Sidney to Leicester, 8 August 1568, *Letters and Memorials of Sir Henry Sidney*, I. 34–5; Sidney's secretary, Edward Waterhous to Lord Justices, from Chester, 4 August, SP63/25 fo. 152; *CSP Ireld*, I. 386 [70I]. Cecil to Sidney, 10 August 1568, SP63/23 fo. 137.

[156] 14 August 1568, *Letters and Memorials of Sir Henry Sidney*, I. 36 and see above, p. 193.

[157] Argyll to Elizabeth, 24 August 1568, *Letters and Memorials of Sir Henry Sidney*, I. 36–7 and see above, pp. 193–4. The 5th earl's letters to Sidney and Cecil have not survived.

greatest enemie that we have in England'. Using Douglas' recent contacts with Knollys, Argyll was able to confirm his previous suspicions about the anti-Marian views of the Elizabethan councillor.[158] Notwithstanding these frank exchanges, Douglas was unable to persuade the earl to modify his hostile stance towards the English.

Both Sidney and Douglas were caught off-guard by the celebration of the Ulster marriages. As the weddings had not taken place in the spring of 1569, they had relaxed. In the summer, Sidney was distracted by the serious Desmond rebellion, which took him away on campaign to Leinster and Munster. By the beginning of August, news filtered through to London and Dublin that something was afoot. Douglas was immediately dispatched to Scotland and, hearing Lady Agnes was about to depart, rushed to Kintyre to persuade her to wait, but arrived three days too late. All that could now be done was to try to minimise the damage by obtaining letters from Moray, seeking to reduce the number of mercenaries and the extent of Argyll's involvement. However, as Douglas commented, the Scottish regent was not powerful enough to command the 5th earl. Those great Anglophiles, Moray and Morton, earnestly wanted to help Elizabeth and Sidney, but could do nothing in Ireland without Argyll's co-operation.[159] With the marriages completed, Douglas' role as special English ambassador and spy upon Argyll was over.[160]

Douglas' perceptive reports and detailed information had been extremely valuable to Sidney and Cecil, who were kept better informed than they had been at any time since the 5th earl's shift to an anti-English strategy. However good their intelligence, neither the lord deputy nor the secretary could discover an effective method of altering the earl's policies within Ulster nor of cutting the supply of mercenaries to Ireland. The two men were being painfully taught the lesson that the only person capable of making the triangular British approach work was Argyll, and he was now employing it against them. As he frequently reminded the English, they could regain his co-operation provided major concessions were made over the Scottish queen. Though this would have brought undoubted benefits for Sidney in Ireland, it was not a course Elizabeth or Cecil were prepared to follow. Irish policy

---

[158] Sidney to Cecil, 12 November 1568, SP63/26 fo. 71, and see above, n. 155.

[159] Douglas to Cecil, 15 August 1569, BL Cotton Calig. C 1 n. fo. 441r–v.

[160] He probably made a final visit to Scotland in September 1570 seeking to subborn Donald Gormeson, see below, p. 207. Douglas sought some reward for his work and was eventually given an English pension, Douglas' petition to Cecil and Sidney's support, c. April 1570, *CSP Ireld*, I. 428, 430 [49]; Elizabeth to Sidney, 17 May 1570, *Sidney State Papers, 1565–70*, 75 [18], 130. Douglas acquired a mill on the Liffey near Dublin, which his brother claimed on his death, 26 November 1584, *CSP Ireld*, II. 538 [87]. He was back in Dublin holding a man who had information concerning Mary, Queen of Scots, August 1571, *HMC* Salisbury I. 516–8.

was never a high enough priority at Westminster to outweigh the needs of domestic politics. The rehabilitation of Mary, Queen of Scots was not a price Elizabeth and her advisers were willing to pay for success in Ireland. Domestic stability, England's security and the means of dominating Scotland were paramount considerations. The English Privy Council was prepared to examine the British dimension in its policy making, but not alter its priorities, which always placed the realm of England and its security within the British mainland above the needs of the Irish kingdom. The fundamental inequality within the Tudor state made it difficult to formulate an integrated three-kingdom policy for the Atlantic archipelago. It also doomed to failure Argyll's use of the triangular approach to create sufficient pressure in Ulster to wring concessions from London. He could seriously discomfort Dublin and disrupt English plans for the conquest and colonisation of the north of Ireland, but this did not translate into irresistible pressure upon Elizabeth.

After the completion of the Ulster marriages, the 5th earl stopped trying to disguise his involvement in the supply of redshanks. In 1570, his own half-brother John, the provost of Kilmun, openly led 700 men to Ulster.[161] The effect of the constant influx of mercenaries was painted in stark terms by Captain Piers at Carrickfergus. He warned Cecil that the north of Ireland was 'in danger to be utterly lost for the Scots be already in such numbers and fortifying upon her majesty's land and manuring the same, that if they be suffered they will shortly look into the English Pale . . . I am of the mind that until the north of Ireland be reformed, which is the only original of all rebellion, all the rest of the land will never be good'.[162] English officials within Ireland did not underestimate the military threat Argyll's strategy posed, realising it menaced the Pale itself. The Scottish mercenaries were fortifying the Gaelic chiefs of Ulster, making it virtually impossible for the lord deputy to subdue the O'Neills, the O'Donnells and the MacDonalds, and encouraging them to raid the south. As Piers prophetically explained, if the Ulster chiefs remained fiercely independent, they could continue to foment rebellion throughout the kingdom. Until the north was conquered, Ireland would not be a peaceful kingdom, a conclusion whose accuracy was proved by Tyrone's Rebellion.

As well as employing the redshanks as a tactic in British politics, the 5th earl used them to achieve important Gaelic objectives. Within Ulster, the build-up of Scottish mercenaries was organised by Lady Agnes and her daughter Finola. In his comprehensive report on the Scots' influence throughout Ireland, John Smith pinpointed the source of all English troubles. With

---

[161] Point 22 in Lennox's list of the Queen's Party's violations of the truce, 16 October 1570, GD149/266 fo. 71v (not listed in *CSPSc*, III. 395–6); December 1570, *CSPSc*, III. 454.
[162] Quotation from White, 'Tudor Plantations', II. 401; *CSP Irel*, I. 441–2 [41].

a grudging and slightly puzzled admiration he first acknowledged that 'these too woomen beying trayned up in the scotts courte...speake both frenche and inglyshe'. He had regrettably discovered that such civilised attributes did not make Agnes or Finola automatic allies of the English, who regarded themselves as the bringers of civilisation to Ireland. Instead, he lamented, the two women were 'trayners of all scotts into Ireland as allso conveighers of all commodities oute of the realme so that by these twoo woomen arriseth all mischief against thinglishe Pale'. In addition to supervising the trade in men and goods across the North Channel, the women were at the heart of Ulster politics, where their presence had upset the old equilibrium. The strong link between mother and daughter gradually eroded the traditional rivalry between the O'Donnells and the O'Neills, which had previously kept both kindreds in check. As Smith explained, 'by these meanes onell and odonill are specyall frends, what countennaunce soever odonill showeth to be a subiecte'.[163] The alliance made under Argyll's auspices between the three Ulster kindreds, the MacDonalds, O'Neills and O'Donnells, alarmed the English. They correctly surmised it would be turned against them, and a united and hostile Ulster would undermine the stability of the entire kingdom of Ireland.

For Lady Agnes, and to a lesser extent for her nephew, Argyll, the alliance served a different purpose. She regarded her marriage to Turlough Luineach as the means to secure her younger sons' future, by giving them lands and making them 'starke in Ireland'.[164] The strong-minded Agnes was more than a match for her weaker husband, and within a few months of the wedding there had been a serious quarrel, which Sidney fervently hoped would lead to a permanent split. Turlough had been accidentally shot by his own jester, and his injury, combined with his timidity, prevented him seizing the opportunity to attack the English whilst they were entangled with the Desmond rebellion and rising in Connaught. The great pool of Scottish mercenaries O'Neill had acquired through his wife were straining his resources to breaking point, and he was reported to be 'so wasted and eaten out as he is a verie beggar'. As a result, 'the Scots weary of him and he of them', with O'Neill's dependants sick of them both.[165] Such a lack of organisation did not impress Lady Agnes, who travelled home to Scotland. Her eldest surviving son, Angus, did not want his mother to return to Ireland.[166]

---

[163] 'John Smyth's Advice for the Realme of Ireland', c. 1569 printed in Hayes-McCoy, *Scots Mercenary Forces*, 346.

[164] Sidney to Privy Council, 17 March 1576, *Letters and Memorials of Sir Henry Sidney*, I. 164.

[165] Sidney to Privy Council, 27 December 1569, SP63/29 fo. 186v; Hayes-McCoy, *Scots Mercenary Forces*, 108.

[166] Malby to Cecil, 8 April 1570, *CSP Ireld*, I. 428 [37].

When Lady Agnes eventually rejoined Turlough, she persuaded him the best policy was to seek peace with the English, and with her help he concluded a treaty and disbanded his Scottish mercenaries.[167] Arguing his case, she wrote personally to Elizabeth and helped compose a more formal letter in Latin.[168] Using her Scottish connections, she wrote to Morton, then at Elizabeth's court, asking him to press their suit.[169] The English government in Ireland could not make up its mind about Lady Agnes. Sidney, though impressed by her sophistication and charm, worried that her influence over her husband would not always be used to further English interests.[170] Dublin knew that, through her daughter, she had an important voice in O'Donnell affairs and could counter any Anglophile advice O'Donnell might receive.[171] The Irish administration continued to be fearful of her strong Scottish connexions both with Argyll and the MacDonalds.[172] Whilst he lived, Lady Agnes frequently consulted the 5th earl and relied heavily upon his advice and influence.[173]

Agnes trusted the 5th earl because he was providing for her eldest surviving son, Angus. The first stage of this process was the resolution of the competing claims of the brothers and sons of James MacDonald. In return for his agreement over the Ulster marriages, Sorley Boy, the youngest brother, was recognised as having control over the Route and received payments from Lady Agnes' husband, Turlough O'Neill. Alastair Og, the elder brother, was content to remain in the traditional MacDonald lands of Islay and Kintyre, though a rift between him and Sorley Boy was rumoured.[174] Within Scotland, the main problem the MacDonalds faced was the continuing friction with the MacLeans. Argyll had called a great Highland convention in July 1568 to resolve the region's outstanding feuds, and it produced a MacDonald–MacLean agreement. When that collapsed, Argyll made both parties submit

---

[167] Irish Council to Elizabeth, 23 March 1571, *CSP Ireld*, I. 440 [33].

[168] Agnes Campbell to Elizabeth, 17 March 1571, *CSP Ireld*, I. 439 [25] printed in Hayes-McCoy, *Scots Mercenary Forces*, 116. Turlough to Elizabeth, 19 April 1571, *CSP Ireld*, I. 445 [11]; Bagenal to Fitzwilliam, 14 and 17 April, *CSP Ireld*, I. 445 [13I].

[169] Agnes Campbell to Morton, 17 March 1571, SP63/31 fo. 53, *CSP Ireld*, I. 439 [24]. Agnes wrote from the MacDonald territory of the Route.

[170] For example Sidney to Privy Council, 15 November 1575, *Letters and Memorials of Sir Henry Sidney*, I. 77–8. Generally, see Hayes-McCoy, *Scots Mercenary Forces*, chs. 3 and 4.

[171] For example Agnes blocked the earl of Kildare's attempts to stop a marriage proposal between the O'Neills and the O'Donnells, Fitzwilliam to Burghley, 14 March 1572, *CSP Ireld*, I. 467 [32].

[172] For example Captain Piers report and letter to Privy Council, 1574, *Calendar of the Carew Manuscripts Preserved in the Archiepiscopal Library at Lambeth 1515–1624* ed. J. Brewer et al. (6 vols., London, 1867–73), I. 490–2.

[173] For example the Glasgow meeting, 14 April 1573, Killigrew to Burghley, *CSPSc*, IV. 544–45.

[174] Waterhous to Lord Justices, 4 August 1568, SP63/25 fo. 152; Hill, *Fire and Sword*, 134.

to Campbell arbitration at Carnasserie castle.[175] The arbiters' decision over-
turned the Privy Council settlement of 1564 upholding MacDonald control of the Rhinns. In September 1570, the MacLeans of Duart agreed to
pay £4,000 Scots to Angus, the son of James MacDonald, for those Islay
lands.[176]

In the changed circumstances of 1570, Argyll and his advisers reversed the
Campbell policy of preserving separate MacDonald and MacLean zones of
influence. For a vast sum in Highland terms, the MacLeans had been allowed
to obtain the Rhinns. As well as the substantial financial compensation, the
5th earl provided alternative territorial expansion for the MacDonalds. He
granted Angus the substantial Ardnamurchan territories, previously held by
the MacIain branch of Clan Donald.[177] Argyll specifically tied the possession
of these lands to the MacLean agreement, ensuring Angus did not receive sasine until October 1570, after he had accepted the arbitration settlement.[178]
In addition, the 5th earl made provision that the Moidart branch of Clan
Donald would accept Angus as their new neighbour. In his own bond of
manrent with John of Moidart, captain of Clanranald, Argyll included a
clause licensing John to serve Angus.[179] As well as carefully settling Angus
into his mainland territory, Argyll smoothed the young chief's relations with
the Edinburgh government. In September 1571, the 5th earl helped arbitrate the large rent arrears due to the crown from the MacDonalds' Kintyre
lands.[180] Two Campbell merchants from Glasgow were provided to act as
Angus' surety to pay his debts to the comptroller.[181] The 5th earl had gone
to endless trouble to establish Angus, Lady Agnes' eldest surviving son and
James MacDonald's main heir. As well as assisting his forthright kinswoman,
Argyll was primarily concerned with stabilising the southern Hebrides and

---

[175] 15 September 1570, AT, VI. 150.
[176] The money was to be paid at a yearly rate of £400 from the rents of MacLean lands in
Islay, Jura, Luing and Mull, 22 June 1572, AT, VI. 193D.
[177] The eighty-mark lands of Mariota, the daughter of MacIain of Ardnarmurchan, had been
leased by 4th earl to James MacDonald (Angus' father) whose mother was Catherine
MacIain: 12 October 1550, NLS Ch 5759; AT, IV. 217–8; D.J. MacDonald, *Clan Donald*
(Loanhead, 1978), 186–7.
[178] Initial incomplete charter granting Ardnamurchan to Angus in 1568, signed by Argyll but
not by witnesses: GD176/97; AT, VI. 126. Second incomplete charter, 16 May 1569, NLS
Ch 5763; AT, VI. 136. Sometime in 1569 Angus paid £100 for relief and entry into the
Ardnamurchan lands, GD176/98; AT, VI. 134. Third charter, accompanied by sasine, 10
and 14 October 1570, NLS Ch 5764; AT, VI. 143.
[179] 23 November 1571, AT, VI. 166; *HMC* 6th, 625a; Wormald, *Lords and Men*, 110–111,
187 [Arg 45]. A similar provision was made in Clanranald's bond with Hugh Fraser, Lord
Lovat on 6 July 1572, GD 112/1/848; Wormald, *Lords and Men*, 277; printed in *SHR*, 24
(1927), 176–7.
[180] Regent Mar to Argyll, 9 September 1571, *Letters to Argyll Family*, 13.
[181] Bond dated 30 January 1572 mentioned in court case, 3 April 1573, *Clan Campbell*,
VI. 24.

removing the feud between two substantial clans within his affinity. Having concluded that the MacLeans would not be dislodged from the Rhinns of Islay, he tried to get their presence accepted by the MacDonalds. In the long run, neither the Islay settlement nor the Ardnamurchan expansion endured, though they did provide a peace that lasted long after the 5th earl's death.

The northern branch of Clan Donald also benefited from Argyll's attention. The 5th earl had already tied Donald Gormeson of Sleat to his affinity through the lucrative marriage to Jane, Campbell of Cawdor's daughter and the widow of Lord Lovat.[182] As John Douglas had warned, the new unity between the 5th earl and Donald Gormeson had serious implications for the English in Ireland.[183] Douglas also learnt that Donald Gormeson had raised 300 redshanks in the Outer Isles for the Irish-born MacGillespie from Antrim, head of a MacDonald cadet branch.[184] Donald's return to involvement in Ireland, where he had been active in Mary Tudor's reign, reawakened the possibility of using him to foment trouble for Argyll. In September 1570, a joint Anglo-Scottish delegation visited him, dangling the bribe of ecclesiastical lands, if he would act against the 5th earl.[185] Though the tempting offer was not accepted, even negotiating earned Argyll's displeasure. In April 1571, the earl renewed Donald Gormeson's bond of manrent, specifically pardoning a breach of their previous agreement and the offence of listening to the regent's offers. In token of the restoration of trust, Donald's foster son Colin, the 5th earl's illegitimate child, was returned to Skye.[186] The following year, Sleat was one of the Highland chiefs included in the general pacification when Argyll settled with Regent Lennox. As a trusted member of Argyll's entourage, he was rewarded with a large pension from the bishopric of Aberdeen.[187] At that point, the earl permitted Donald Gormeson to offer help to the English in Ireland.[188] As he had been pleased to discover,

---

[182] Lady Jane, widowed in 1557, was married to Donald Gormeson at the latest by 22 August 1573, *Clan Campbell*, VI. 25. In his report of c. March 1565, Captain Piers had alluded to the importance of the 5th earl's involvement in Donald Gormeson's marriage, see above, p. 134.

[183] Sidney to Leicester, 8 August 1568, *Letters and Memorials of Sir Henry Sidney*, I. 35; also 4 August, Waterhous letter, above n. 155.

[184] MacGillespie was the son of MacRanald Boy MacDonald of Lecale, Knollys to Cecil, 18 August 1568, BL Cotton Calig. B 9 n. fo. 340.

[185] Sleat was known to want a feu of the bishopric of Ross, Randolph to Sussex, 16 September 1570, *CSPSc*, III. 349; also *CSPSc*, IV. 135.

[186] 27 April 1571, AT, VI. 160–2; Wormald, *Lords and Men*, 186 [Arg 44].

[187] Donald stood surety for the behaviour of Rory MacLeod of Lewis, along with Argyll's other dependants, Hector Og MacLean of Duart and Dougal MacDougall of Dunollie, 27 February 1572, AT, VI. 175. The Aberdeen grant contained the highly unusual clause that Sleat's interests in the bishopric of Ross would also be considered, 20 February 1572, *RSS*, VI. 1491.

[188] 20 February 1572, *CSPSc*, IV. 135, see above, p. 198.

being loyal to the 5th earl had proved the most advantageous policy for a Hebridean chief.

In the last years of the 5th earl's life, his strategy within the Gaelic world was driven by regional objectives, though it did include an awareness of the British dimension. Argyll maintained tight control over his extensive affinity, and through it dominated the Western Highlands and Islands. This necessitated peace among his dependants, especially throughout the Hebrides. He therefore chose to support and enhance the northern and southern branches of Clan Donald and, to a lesser extent, the MacLeans. Ironically, it was his own clan, when at feud with the MacDonalds and the MacLeans in the seventeenth century, that came to rue Argyll's statesmanlike stabilisation of Highland politics between 1570 and 1572. The most dramatic consequences of the 5th earl's Gaelic policies were witnessed in Ulster. In the 1590s, Captain Piers' prophecy came true when the O'Neill and the O'Donnell combined to lead a rebellion that engulfed the kingdom of Ireland and produced the sternest challenge the Elizabethan regime ever faced.

CONCLUSION

The earl of Argyll and the nature of British politics in the age of the three kingdoms

Argyll's political career opens a window onto the 'British problem', reflecting in microcosm an image of the world of British politics.[1] It reveals many of the inherent tensions bedevilling the relationships between the three kingdoms, particularly after 1603. In particular, Argyll personified the choice facing Scottish and Irish Gaelic nobles between confrontation or harmonisation of the Anglophone and Gaelic cultures within the Atlantic archipelago. Before mature British politics had been created by the multiple monarchy, the 5th earl confronted the hurdle faced by future British politicians, especially those based in Scotland or Ireland, which was the fundamental conflict of attitudes towards the islands of Britain themselves.

Argyll's British policy contained two elements. The first was its British idiom: the ability to see the interconnections between the three kingdoms and, at the level of conceptual thinking, create a British strategy. The second was a corollary: the capacity to integrate national and regional objectives within a single scheme, unifying the elements in the service of a British goal. His own British perspective had grown out of his experience of moving between the separate political arenas of Gaeldom and Anglo-Scottish relations, where he operated in multiple cultural and conceptual worlds and found solutions to transect frontiers. By contrast, his contemporaries and most future politicians were tied to a single political world, with little understanding or appreciation of other viewpoints. Since the demise of England's first empire in the medieval period, thinking in a British idiom, rather than focusing upon one

---

[1] The 'British problem' has been defined as 'how to conceptualise the relationship between the kingdoms of England and Scotland and their relationship with the kingdom of Ireland and the Principality of Wales; to trace the development of a multiplex composite or triple monarchy with the accession of the Scottish House of Stewart to the thrones of England and Ireland in 1603; and to examine the reactions of the various peoples of the islands of Britain and Ireland to the growth of the English state...a study of state formation and the emergence of new nationalisms.': B. Bradshaw and J. Morrill, eds.,*The British Problem, c. 1534–1707: State Formation in the Atlantic Archipelago* (London, 1996), vii. Some discussion of 'British policies before a British state' with a slightly different perspective from my own can be found in Hiram Morgan's essay in chapter 3.

kingdom or bilateral problems, was rare. Even after 1603, when the three kingdoms shared one monarch, this remained an unusual attribute among the British political élite. The lack of experience or knowledge of other kingdoms, often resulting in an absence of a British perspective, handicapped Britain's statesmen during the seventeenth and eighteenth centuries.

In 1560, arriving at the same point from different directions and after contrasting journeys, Argyll's and Cecil's British policies coalesced. During the following years, that joint policy was lost.[2] In the changing circumstances the two men subsequently faced, their differing premises produced contradictory conclusions. Cecil and Argyll ended their careers in opposing camps. Similar clashes between an English viewpoint and that of the Scots or Irish recurred throughout the early modern period. Many aspects of the British problem derived from underlying London-centred assumptions, which flourished at the English court. As Argyll, and many later politicians discovered, such premises might be unacceptable to them, but they remained unalterable. Encountered en bloc, they presented an immovable barrier constraining the development of a supranational British politics of the kind envisaged by the 5th earl. A comparison of Cecil's and Argyll's viewpoints highlights potential conflict concerning four of the English minister's premises, each of which became enshrined within subsequent Anglo-British thinking. They were: beliefs in the overriding importance of English security, the 'imperial' claim to England's superiority over the Atlantic archipelago, the need to export English styles of governance, and a centralised and unitary definition of sovereignty.[3]

Much of Cecil's political career revolved around the first premise, the need to guard English security. In 1558, the fall of Calais transformed English thinking about the security of the islands of Britain. It brought the 'island mentality', the perception of England as separated and protected from Europe by the sea, placing the strategic emphasis upon the British mainland, the island of Ireland and its surrounding waters. It underlined the axiom that, for the mainland to be secure, Scotland must be in friendly hands and Ireland safely under control. These security imperatives led the English to treat the two kingdoms as potentially insecure outposts of the Tudor state. They were translated into a general perception of the Atlantic archipelago as possessing an essential core and insignificant peripheries. This category of strategic thinking produced the frequently repeated declaration that England was

---

[2] For a discussion of how easily Elizabethan policy could become paralysed within an Irish context, see C. Brady, 'Shane O'Neill Departs from the Court of Elizabeth: Irish, English and Scottish Perspectives and the Paralysis of Policy, July 1559 to April 1562' in S.J. Connelly, ed., *Kingdoms United?: Great Britain and Ireland since 1500* (Dublin, 1999), 13–28.

[3] For a discussion of the origins of such views see, R.A. Mason *Kingship and the Commonweal: Political Thought in Renaissance and Reformation Scotland* (East Linton, 1998), ch. 9.

an island. Despite being geographical nonsense, this unabashed statement indicated that in English minds the entire British mainland had been absorbed into a mentally enlarged Tudor kingdom. In English strategic calculations, with Wales incorporated and Scotland overlaid, British became English writ large. An overriding concern with the security of England spawned these presumptions about the British mainland. By implicitly denying the separate existence of the northern kingdom, they had a corrosive effect upon British policies, as was evident in the two turning points of Argyll's career. Solely on grounds of English security, Elizabeth I's Privy Council decided in 1560 to intervene in Scotland, removing the French and supporting the Scottish Protestants. The same reasoning in 1565 reversed that policy when the Privy Council decided to do nothing to assist its Scottish allies.[4] As Argyll came to realise, a British policy founded upon English security would, whenever necessary, jettison broader British goals.

The perceived needs of England's security brought a policy of exclusion, denying any foothold within the islands of Britain to the continental powers of France or Spain. The extension of English intervention throughout the Atlantic archipelago was used to prevent an internal threat developing within the other kingdoms. Actions by the English regime ranged from the overt manipulation of Scottish domestic politics between 1568 and 1573, which so infuriated the 5th earl, to Oliver Cromwell's military occupation of Scotland and Ireland to preserve the English Commonwealth in the middle of the seventeenth century. Because it was usually couched in security terms, England's main imperial aim during the early modern period was the extension of control rather than a drive for colonial expansion within the Atlantic archipelago.[5] Provided they retained a sufficiently secure grip over the kingdoms of Scotland and Ireland to extinguish any threat, the English remained indifferent to the configurations of Scottish or Irish politics. This explains their marked lack of interest throughout the period in adopting the grand schemes for British union or empire.[6] As experience had shown the 5th earl,

---

[4] For a fuller discussion of the Privy Council's discussions, see Dawson, 'Cecil', 214–15 and Dawson, 'Mary, Queen of Scots, Lord Darnley and Anglo-Scottish Relations in 1565', *International History Review*, 8 (1986), 1–24 at pp. 14–19; and Alford, *Cecil*, ch. 5.

[5] It is important to distinguish between official government policy and the colonial and conquistador attitudes displayed by the New English in Ireland. For a full discussion of the colonial drive and lack of it within the British state, see B.P. Lenman, *Colonial Wars and English Identities, c 1550–1688* (London, 2001). For a general discussion, see N. Canny ed. *Oxford History of the British Empire I: The Origins of Empire* (Oxford, 1998), especially the excellent chapter by J. Ohlmeyer, 124–47.

[6] In the sixteenth century, empire and imperial were primarily understood in terms of jurisdiction, as in the famous declaration in the English Act in Restraint of Appeals of 1533, and not in their modern sense of colonial expansion; for a lucid discusssion, see J. Guy, *Tudor England* (Oxford, 1988), 369–76. The different languages and concepts of empire are elucidated in D. Armitage, *The Ideological Origins of the British Empire* (Cambridge, 2000), chs. 1 and 2.

the English embraced a British strategy when they were afraid of other consequences, rarely otherwise. During the next two centuries, the adoption of
an integrated British policy, such as the 1643 Solemn League and Covenant
and the 1707 Treaty of Union itself, often sprang from the fear factor.

Forming his second premise, Cecil championed the 'imperial' claim, which
asserted English superiority over the entire Atlantic archipelago. It was a po-
tent mixture of historical myth-making combined with the achievements
of medieval expansion by the kings of England.[7] Building upon the conceptual framework of that first English empire, the Tudor state proclaimed
its dominance over Wales and Ireland. The Welsh Act of Union and the
creation of the kingdom of Ireland marked different methods of inclusion
within one polity, held together in the person of the English monarch. During the sixteenth century, the Welsh incorporation proved successful and,
to Elizabethan commentators, offered a working model for what should
have been happening in Ireland.[8] Such nostrums illustrated the immense gap
between constitutional theory and government practice within Ireland. The
limited extent of English control ensured that the kingdom's assimilation into
the Tudor state could not follow the relatively painless path it had taken in
Wales, subjected to successful conquest centuries before. Despite the endless
difficulties in its implementation, the English never doubted their right to
rule the whole island of Ireland. Ignoring the practicalities on the ground,
the theoretical assumption of English superiority throughout the Tudor state
remained intact.

The Stewart kingdom was in a different category, being an independent
monarchy over which the Tudor state had no political authority. This did
not hinder the articulation of a vigorous English claim to hold suzerainty
over the British mainland, justified by a collection of feudal and pseudo-
historical arguments.[9] Throughout the sixteenth century, the claim of juris-
dictional superiority remained a theoretical construct, an underlying refrain
within Anglo-Scottish relations lacking political or constitutional substance.
The attempt in the Rough Wooing to conquer Scotland and give a military

---

[7] R.R. Davies, ed., *The British Isles 1100–1500: Comparisons, Contrasts and Connections*
(Edinburgh, 1988); R.R. Davies, *The First English Empire: Power and Identities in the British
Isles, 1093–1343* (Oxford, 2000); R. Frame, *The Political Development of the British Isles,
1100–1400* (Oxford, 1990).

[8] For example *Croftus sive de hibernia liber by Sir William Herbert*, eds. A. Keavney and
J. Madden (Irish Manuscripts Commission, Dublin, 1992); C. Brady, 'Comparable Histories?:
Tudor Reform in Wales and Ireland' in S. Ellis and S. Barber, eds., *Conquest and Union:
Fashioning a British State, 1485–1725* (London, 1995); B. Bradshaw in Bradshaw and Morrill,
eds., *The British Problem, c. 1534–1707*, ch. 2.

[9] R.A. Mason, 'Scotching the Brut: Politics History and National Myth in Sixteenth-Century
Britain' in R.A. Mason, ed., *Scotland and England* (Edinburgh, 1987), 60–84; Mason,
Kingship and Commonweal, chs. 2 and 9. Cecil used these arguments, Alford, *Cecil*.

reality to the theory failed. Though relegated to the background, the imperial and unionist rhetoric endured, upholding the English belief in their permanent right to intervene within the vassal kingdom of Scotland. As the 5th earl was forced to recognise in 1570, this attitude towards Scottish independence threatened the kingdom as much as an invading army. Throughout the early modern period, the English tenaciously maintained their claims to dominance over Scotland and Ireland. Despite the avowedly equal constitutional frameworks of co-operation and co-existence following 1541 and 1603, the continued existence of such claims undermined Scottish and Irish independence and their status as separate kingdoms within a Greater Britain. The assertion of English imperial dominion compromised relationships that might develop between the three polities, for example, preventing the Irish crown from developing a discrete existence and undermining Scottish offers of alliance, partnership or even federal union.[10]

The third assumption made by Cecil and his English successors concerned the nature of governance. English institutions were deemed to be inherently superior and their export desirable. By the seventeenth century, this generalised conviction had produced as its offshoot the more precise attachment to 'the ancient constitution'.[11] Whenever uniformity was proposed, it was assumed the English model should prevail. In its simplest form this led to the shiring of Wales as the central dimension of its incorporation between 1536 and 1543. Though limited in their geographical effectiveness, the administrative structures within the new kingdom of Ireland continued to resemble those in England. Comforted by the sight of familiar-looking institutions such as the exchequer and council, Englishmen could believe that the Irish enjoyed the same governmental procedures as themselves.[12] Outwith the Tudor state, the export of England's methods of rule was more problematical. London's emphasis upon the formal institutional framework of governance, in particular conciliar rule and the centrality of parliamentary legislation, did not correspond to the variety of Scottish representative assemblies or to the more informal structures of its political world. When Cecil first attempted to introduce his conciliar model to Scotland in 1559–60, Argyll seems to have

[10] For the problems this created for Irish constitutional thought, see J. Ohlmeyer, ed., *Political Thought in Seventeenth-Century Ireland: Kingdom or Colony?* (Cambridge, 2000). For the Scottish perspective upon the union of the crowns, K.M. Brown, *Kingdom or Province?: Scotland and the Regal Union, 1603–1715* (London, 1992).
[11] For a summary of the debate about these ideas, see W. Klein, 'The Ancient Constitution Revisited' in N. Phillipson and Q. Skinner, eds., *Political Discourse in Early Modern Britain* (Cambridge, 1993), 23–44.
[12] The spread of English governance merged with the much broader mission of bringing 'civilisation' to the 'barbarian' Gaels. See B. Bradshaw, A. Hadfield and W. Maley, eds., *Representing Ireland: Literature and the Origins of Conflict 1534–1660* (Cambridge, 1993).

been more puzzled than offended. The language chosen to express the giving of counsel reflected their different approaches. Whilst concepts of citizenship and monarchical republicanism were familiar to Argyll, he instinctively employed the traditional language of kin and lordship.[13] The English and Scottish variations between the language, style and perception of government held by Cecil and Argyll prefigured a similar mismatch over words and meanings encountered by James VI when he wrestled with English politics and governmental institutions after 1603. Different English and Scottish views about patterns of organisation were more divisive when they related to matters of the church. Throughout the early modern period and beyond, debate raged in the British Isles as to the best form of ecclesiastical government. That raised the equally thorny question of whether ecclesiastical uniformity within the three kingdoms, which would have to be imposed, was either necessary or desirable.[14]

For Cecil, and most future English politicians, methods of governance were intimately bound up with the nature of sovereignty, the final premise. They held that the sovereign attributes of the imperial crown of England resided in its retention of complete and sole jurisdiction within the realm. By encapsulating and reinforcing this doctrine, the royal supremacy had created the unique English church-state amalgam. The ideal of the unitary realm of England had originally been encouraged by the unified structures of the medieval kingdom, and it was brought closer to reality by Thomas Cromwell's governmental reforms, abolishing other spheres of jurisdiction and shiring Wales. The belief that an essential component of sovereign power was a centralised authority vested in the crown became rooted deep within English political thinking.[15] When struggling to comprehend the position of the Gaelic chiefs, this doctrine of sovereignty hampered English officials.[16] Despite having worked alongside him, the English found it equally hard to comprehend Argyll's semi-sovereign status. Solutions that made perfect sense in Gaelic politics were meaningless to English ministers, as seen in

---

[13] Though Cecil had his distinctive blend of constitutional thinking, the Elizabethan political élite as a whole embraced a 'monarchical republicanism'; see P. Collinson, 'The Monarchical Republic of Queen Elizabeth' in P. Collinson, *Elizabethan Essays* (London, 1994), 31–57; for Argyll, see above, pp. 40–7.

[14] J. Morrill, 'A British Patriachy: Ecclesiastical Imperialism under the Early Stuarts' in A. Fletcher and P. Roberts, eds., *Religion, Culture and Society in Early Modern Britain* (Cambridge, 1994), 209–37.

[15] Sir Francis Walsingham enunciated this view when commenting unfavourably upon the authority James VI wielded in Scotland: 'Yt is almost impossyble for any prynce to be in suretye in a realme or kingdome where the regall authorytye is not merely deryved from the king', Walsingham to Thomas Fowler, 22 December 1588, *CSPSc*, IX. 651, cited in J. Goodare, *State and Society in Early Modern Scotland* (Oxford, 2000), 51.

[16] This basic dilemma was clearly revealed in the 1562 negotiations with Shane O'Neill, see C. Brady, *Shane O'Neill* (Dundalk, 1996), 38–47, 66–8.

Lady Agnes' proposal, coming so naturally to a Campbell, that her husband, Turlough Luineach O'Neill, become a loyal servant of Elizabeth whilst still retaining his sovereign powers in Tyrone. Its rejection by the English as a complete contradiction in terms had little impact upon Turlough. However, the denial of that same possibility to his successor, Hugh O'Neill, earl of Tyrone, helped propel him into rebellion in the Nine Years' War.[17]

During the early modern period, the Anglo-British perspectives of English politicians, such as Cecil, were often at odds with those of their Scottish and Irish counterparts, like Argyll. Usually, though by no means exclusively, Scottish and Irish politicians were more committed to a British approach and more enthusiastic advocates of British strategies. To a significant extent, this reflected the imbalance of political power within the islands of Britain. The British perspective and an integrated policy were frequently chosen as the best method by which Scotland or Ireland could compensate for their lack of political weight. Not wanting to adopt an Anglo-British perspective or follow a British policy framed in English terms, the Scots and Irish sought to persuade or cajole their powerful neighbour to modify its Anglo-British perspective. Even when falling on deaf ears, an appeal to an idealistic common British objective might be employed as a defensive measure, with the rhetoric of equality between the three kingdoms erected as a barrier against increased English domination. For the less powerful kingdoms, a determinedly British approach sometimes appeared the only viable political option. There was no such imperative for the English. Rather than a necessity, the Anglo-British perspective was usually an additional extra in English policy making, with the disadvantages of an integrated policy often appearing to outweigh any advantages England might secure. English politicians reached for British policies when there was a direct threat to English security but otherwise were deeply suspicious of them. They much preferred to continue to treat British as a synonym for English.

Argyll's difficulties with Cecil's four assumptions about the Atlantic archipelago provide a signpost to those areas of conflict and tension created by an Anglo-British approach that would afflict British politics for the next two hundred years. Operating before the full emergence of British politics, far less a British state, nevertheless he faced the quintessential British problems. He encountered the unsettling combination of an English assertion of imperial dominion throughout the British Isles accompanied by a lack of interest in matters not deemed relevant to that kingdom's security. The resulting hot-and-cold policies undermined the stability of the relationships between the three kingdoms. In addition, the 5th earl collided with the view that Britain

[17] See above, p. 51, and H. Morgan, *Tyronne's Rebellion* (Woodbridge, Suffolk, 1999; reprint of 1993 edn).

was essentially England with additional peripheries and, therefore, English and British could be treated as synonyms. When British policies strayed beyond English interests, they were abandoned. By placing the English political system and its concerns at the core, this stunted the development of supranational British politics or institutions. Finally, Argyll faced a total misunderstanding of his own semi-sovereign authority and a condemnation of his manner and style of rule as inferior. The English definition of a unitary, centralised sovereignty became the standard throughout the islands of Britain.

However prophetic of future problems, in the 1560s Argyll's British approach and strategy were a political failure. The joint policy agreed with Cecil in 1560 was first quietly reversed in Irish affairs by the English secretary and then abandoned by Argyll after 1565. Though the 5th earl revised his objectives and eventually withdrew from British politics, the existence of his original integrated policy and the consequences of his subsequent strategies were of immense importance for the early modern Atlantic archipelago. By working between the political worlds and adopting a British policy to link them, Argyll helped carve out the space in which British politics could exist and grow. That policy did not bring the results the 5th earl hoped, but his strategies produced three major consequences. They had far-reaching implications for the struggle over the future shape of mainland Britain and of Ireland, thereby altering the course of British history. In the first place, by fighting to establish Protestantism throughout the British mainland and assisting in the diplomatic revolution bringing the Anglo-Scottish alliance, Argyll helped determine Britain's confessional allegiance and constitutional future. Secondly, his policies in Ireland from 1565, by delaying the completion of the Tudor conquest until the end of the century, prepared the way for the Ulster plantation, which itself propelled Irish and British history down a new track. Finally, he introduced a consciousness of the British dimension to the Gaelic world, pushing Gaeldom into the arena of British politics and removing the likelihood of a separate Gaelic state.

In 1573, if he had contemplated the heady days of 1560 which had promised the fulfilment of his hopes, the 5th earl would have been struck by his lack of success as a British politician. What had been destroyed in the interim was his idealistic belief that all three kingdoms could be transformed into a united Protestant British Isles through an amicable partnership with like-minded Englishmen, such as Cecil. His pursuit of a joint British policy had led to frustrations in Ireland and betrayal in Scotland. After 1565, Argyll separated his deep commitment to the Protestant cause from his attitude towards England. Whilst retaining a British perspective in his thinking, he abandoned a British strategy based upon amity and a common Protestant faith. Rather than serving these British goals, his Irish activities were used as a bargaining counter in Anglo-Scottish relations.

Shorn of its idealistic vision, much of Argyll's audacious British policy had been accomplished. Of all his goals, Argyll's religious programme came closest to full realisation. Despite his fears in 1565 of a Roman Catholic resurgence in Scotland, the Reformation achieved in 1559–60 was permanent. The Scottish church had become unequivocally Protestant, and 'the face of ane perfyt reformed kyrk' was beginning to be seen in Scotland.[18] Within the Highlands, a Gaelic form of Protestantism was taking root, thanks to his own and Carswell's efforts. If granted the benefit of hindsight, his religious achievements would probably have afforded him the greatest satisfaction. During the second half of the sixteenth century, their shared faith was helping to bind England and Wales to Scotland, and the existence of a secure Protestant mainland brought a fundamental cultural convergence of enduring importance.[19] This was a pale imitation of the deep confessional friendship and alliance Argyll thought he had entered in 1560 and which he believed was destroyed five years later. The events of 1565 made him realise that the defence of Scotland's Protestantism was not an essential component within Anglo-Scottish amity because the English understood the alliance's primary purpose as upholding their security. The disastrous end to Mary's personal rule in 1566–8 and her foolish decision to flee to England offered Elizabeth a risk-free and inexpensive opportunity to manipulate her northern neighbour. English imperial claims to superiority over Scotland, hidden in 1560, resurfaced, threatening Scottish independence by creating a client state. The Anglo-Scottish alliance was turned into a commercial transaction, seeking to purchase the friendship hitherto given freely. By employing inducements as a method of control, the English created the image of the rapacious Scot intent upon seizing English wealth that haunted British politics for the next two centuries. However, in a reduced and tarnished form, both the Anglo-Scottish alliance and the Protestant mainland had survived from their inception in the British policy of 1560 to become the foundations for the union of the crowns of 1603. Viewed from that vantage point, the struggle for the religious and constitutional alignment of the British mainland had been won, with the victory of Cecil and Argyll in 1560 proving the decisive turning point.

---

[18] *Register of the Minister, Elders and Deacons of the Christian Congregation of St Andrews . . . 1559–1600* ed. D. Hay Fleming (2 vols., SHS, 1st ser. 4 and 7, Edinburgh, 1889–90); J.E.A. Dawson, ' "The Face of Ane Perfyt Reformed Kyrk": St Andrews and the Early Scottish Reformation' in J. Kirk, ed., *Humanism and Reform: The Church in Europe, England and Scotland, 1400–1642* (Studies in Church History, Subsidia 8, Oxford, 1991), 413–35, and see above, pp. 43–4, 80–1.

[19] J.E.A. Dawson, 'Anglo-Scottish Protestant Culture and the Integration of Sixteenth-Century Britain' in S. Ellis and S. Barber, eds., *Conquest and Union: Fashioning a British State, 1485–1725* (London, 1995), 87–114.

The struggle over the fate of the kingdom of Ireland had a different outcome and one far removed from the idealistic vision of a Protestant country forming part of a united British Isles. Nothing could be salvaged from Argyll's 1560 scheme to solve the Ulster problem, and it was Irish policy that suffered most from the failure to pursue the joint British strategy.[20] The chief governors and the Irish administration had not been prepared to implement it, and eventually Cecil had adopted their anti-Scottish viewpoint. For the rest of the century, England moved away from integration and conciliation and fitfully towards conquest and colonisation. Consequently, the kingdom of Ireland was eventually brought under English rule through destructive, and expensive, military methods. The hardening of attitudes this produced destroyed all hope of an Irish Gaelic Reformation, similar to that sponsored by Argyll in the Highlands, and crippled the spread of Protestantism throughout Ireland.[21] Ironically, the long-term religious casualty of the abandoned British policy was not, as the earl had feared in 1565, the suppression of Scotland's Kirk, but the premature demise of Ireland's Reformation.

After 1565, the 5th earl, reversing the joint approach in Ulster, sought to stabilise the Gaelic political world on both sides of the North Channel. This was achieved by the double marriages of Lady Agnes and Finola, realigning the three Ulster powers of the MacDonalds, the O'Neills and the O'Donnells and ensuring a flourishing mercenary trade with the Western Isles. For the remainder of the century, this kept the Gaelic north of Ireland strong and independent, enabling Ulster to become Tyrone's base for the Nine Years' War in which Elizabeth nearly lost the kingdom of Ireland.[22] Within the West Highlands and Islands, when the two clans later became enemies, Argyll's reconstruction of MacDonald power brought endless difficulties for his Campbell successors. As well as dominating Highland history during the seventeenth century, this Campbell–MacDonald feud became entangled in the mid-century wars, thereby affecting the fate of all three kingdoms.[23] Such involvement reflected the way in which the Gaelic world had absorbed

---

[20] For a fuller discussion see Dawson, 'Two Kingdoms or Three?'.

[21] S.A. Meigs, *The Reformation in Ireland: Tradition and Confessionalism 1400–1690* (London, 1997); A. Ford, *The Protestant Reformation in Ireland* (Frankfurt, 1985; Dublin edn, 1999).

[22] In the dark days of 1598, Elizabeth linked the disasters in Ireland with her sister Mary's loss of Calais. The Queen was reported to have said, 'for my sister losed her lyffe for displeasour at the loss of a toun, I can not tell quhat I may do at the losse of a kingdome'. Memo of news from David Foulis, NRA(S), 217, 43 No. 242. I am grateful to Linda Dunbar for this reference.

[23] J. Ohlmeyer, *Civil War and Restoration in the Three Stuart Kingdoms: The Career of Randal MacDonnell, Marquis of Antrim, 1609–1683* (Cambridge, 1993); D. Stevenson, *Alastair MacColla and the Highland Problem* (Edinburgh 1980); A.I. Macinnes, *Clanship, Commerce and the House of Stuart, 1603–1788* (Edinburgh, 1996), ch. 4.

the British dimension introduced by Argyll and become an integral part of British politics.

One of the 5th earl's most enduring legacies was within his own clan. His kinsmen and successors adopted his British dimension in their thinking and formulated their own British strategies. The marquis of Argyll in the mid-seventeenth and the dukes of Argyll in the eighteenth century conducted their careers on the British stage, at times dominating Britain's political world. Like the 5th earl, they drew their initial strength from the massive Campbell powerbase without which they could not have become British politicians. It fitted with the 5th earl's own appreciation of his priorities and achievements that his own house continued to uphold the leitmotivs of his career, his Protestantism and his British policy.

CHRONOLOGY, 1558–1573

Date (year/month)	Scottish	Anglo-Scottish	Gaelic	French/ European
1558/11	Protestant petition to Parliament	Elizabeth's accession	Argyll succeeds to earldom	Mary adopts English arms
1558/12				Dauphin to receive Scottish crown matrimonial
1559/01	Beggars' Summons			
1559/02			Argyll council, tax for French trip	
1559/03	Provincial church council			
1559/04		Elizabethan Reformation Parliament		Treaty of Câteau-Cambrésis
1559/05	Perth iconoclasm starts Wars of the Congregation			
1559/06	Congregation takes Edinburgh	Congregation negotiates with English		Death of Henry II
1559/07	5th earl's marriage in trouble			
1559/08	Congregation reorganises in its regions		Argyll's council in Lorn, Islesmen support Congregation	Arran escapes from France
1559/10	Regent deposed by Congregation			
1559/11	Congregation retreats from Edinburgh Regent starts treason proceedings	Congregation sends Maitland to London		

Date (year/month)	Scottish	Anglo-Scottish	Gaelic	French/ European
1559/12		Privy Council debates intervention		
1560/01		English fleet sent north		
1560/02		Treaty of Berwick		
1560/03			Argyll's treaty with Calvagh O'Donnell He marries Katherine MacLean	Tumult of Amboise
1560/04		English army lays siege to Leith	Cecil memo on Ireland	
1560/06	Death of regent	Cecil to Edinburgh	Sussex returns to Ireland	
1560/07	'Concessions' to Scots in treaty	Cecil negotiates Treaty of Edinburgh	Argyll's Ulster proposals	French sign Treaty of Edinburgh
1560/08	Reformation Parliament Scottish Confession of Faith	English army leaves Arran marriage proposal	O'Neill offers alliance to 5th earl	French troops withdraw
1560/09			5th earl waits for news from Ireland	
1560/12	1st General Assembly of Kirk	Elizabeth rejects Arran marriage	Argyll returns to Edinburgh	Death of Francis II
1561/01	1st Book of Discipline presented to convention of estates		Negotiations between MacDonalds and Irish administration	
1561/03				Lord James visits Mary
1561/04			Sussex sends Hutchison to 5th earl	
1561/05			Sussex returns to Ireland O'Neill captures O'Donnell	
1561/06			Sussex campaigns against O'Neill	
1561/08	Mary returns to her kingdom Proclamation concerning religion			
1561/09	Triumvirate confirmed in power			

Date (year/month)	Scottish	Anglo-Scottish	Gaelic	French/ European
1561/12	Feud between the earls of Bothwell and Arran			
1562/01		Proposal for two queens to meet	O'Neill submits to Elizabeth in London Argyll council re Islay feud	Final session of Council of Trent begins
1562/03				Massacre of Vassy
1562/06		Meeting between queens called off	MacGregor raid starts feud with Campbells	
1562/07				French religious wars start English alliance with Huguenots
1562/08	Mary's northern progress Justice-ayre in Aberdeen		MacDonalds v. MacLeans raiding	
1562/10	Huntly defeated at Corrichie	Elizabeth close to death with smallpox		English occupy Le Havre
1563/01		English Parliament discusses succession	Capt. Piers sent to negotiate with James MacDonald	
1563/02				Duke of Guise assassinated
1563/03				Peace of Amboise
1563/04			MacDonald signs agreement with English Sussex campaigns against O'Neill	
1563/05	Parliament forfeits Gordons Trial of prelates			
1563/07			Mary on progress in Argyll	English lose Le Havre
1563/10			5th earl's commission of fire and sword against MacGregors	

Date (year/month)	Scottish	Anglo-Scottish	Gaelic	French/ European
1564/03		Dudley (Leicester) proposed as Mary's suitor		
1564/04				Anglo-French Peace of Troyes
1564/05			Sussex leaves Ireland	
1564/06			MacGregors to Ireland	
1564/09	Lennox returns to Scotland			
1564/10	Lennox restored to lands			
1564/12	Parliament reverses Lennox's banishment		Scottish Council tries to settle Islay feud	
1565/02	Darnley returns to Scotland			
1565/03	Mary decides to marry Darnley	Elizabeth letter to Mary re succession	MacGregor feud flares up	
1565/04	Palm Sunday riot in Edinburgh		Sir Henry Sidney negotiates in London re lord deputyship	
1565/05	Bothwell's treason trial Stirling Convention agrees to Darnley marriage		O'Neill defeats MacDonalds at Glentaisie	
1565/06			Debate in London on Irish policy	Meeting of French and Spanish at Bayonne
1565/07	Mary proclaims Darnley king and marries him		James MacDonald dies of wounds	
1565/08	Chase-about Raid		Argyll attacks Atholl and the Lennox Forged letter sent to Argyll	

Date (year/month)	Scottish	Anglo-Scottish	Gaelic	French/ European
1565/09	Rebel lords at Dumfries	Privy Council rejects intervention in Scotland	Temporary settlement of MacGregor feud Forged letter sent to Loftus	
1565/10		Scottish rebels cross border In London Elizabeth rebukes Moray	Pincer attack on Argyll fails O'Neill offers Argyll help	Protestants suspect Catholic league
1565/11			Argyll seeks aid from Loftus	
1565/12	Hamiltons settle with Mary Argyll in secret negotiations			
1566/01	Glenorchy submits in Edinburgh		Lord Deputy Sidney arrives in Ireland	
1566/02			Argyll and O'Neill negotiate	
1566/03	Riccio murdered	Riccio's murderers flee to England		
1566/04	Argyll and Moray back on council	English Parliament discusses succession		
1566/05			MacLean of Duart and Stewart of Appin apologise to Argyll	
1566/06	Birth of Prince James	Sir Henry Killigrew's mission to Scotland	O'Neill's ambassador sent to 5th earl	
1566/08				'Iconoclastic fury' in Netherlands
1566/09		English Parliament reopens, succession debated		

Date (year/month)	Scottish	Anglo-Scottish	Gaelic	French/ European
1566/10	Justice-ayre at Jedburgh		Sidney restores O'Donnell to Donegal O'Donnell's death Argyll postpones personal visit to O'Neill	
1566/11	Mary's illness, recovers at Craigmillar		MacLeans raid MacDonalds	
1566/12	Craigmillar conference James' baptism Riccio murderers pardoned			
1567/02	Darnley murdered	Sir Henry Killigrew sent to Scotland	Settlement of MacLeod inheritance	
1567/04	Bothwell acquitted of Darnley's murder Parliament Ainslie Tavern bond Mary abducted by Bothwell		John Carswell's Gaelic *Book of Common Order* published English garrison at Derry abandoned	
1567/05	Mary marries Bothwell		O'Donnell defeats O'Neill at Farsetmore	
1567/06	Mary taken prisoner at Carberry, sent to Loch Leven Argyll leaves confederates and signs Dumbarton bond for queen		O'Neill killed at Cushendun by MacDonalds	
1567/07	Mary abdicates James VI crowned	Sir Nicholas Throckmorton's mission to Scotland	Argyll Council re Isles	
1567/08	Moray takes regency Hamilton bond of queen's men		5th earl remains in Highlands	Alba and his army arrive in Brussels

Date (year/month)	Scottish	Anglo-Scottish	Gaelic	French/European
1567/09	Queen's men take oath to king			
1567/11			Turlough O'Neill negotiates with Argyll	Renewed fighting in French religious wars
1567/12	1st Parliament of regency			
1568/03	Justice-ayre in Glasgow		Negotiations for Ulster marriages	Peace of Longjumeau
1568/05	Mary escapes Queen's forces defeated at Langside	Mary flees to England	Argyll Council	
1568/07	Queen's men meet at Largs		Argyll council re Islay feud John Douglas sent to 5th earl re Ulster marriages	
1568/08	Argyll's troops attack Glasgow		Irish Privy Council bans timber exports to Argyll	
1568/09	Truce between king's and queen's men			
1568/10		Mary's trial at York		
1568/12	Queen's supporters return home from trial	Trial ends inconclusively at Westminster		English seizure of Spanish bullion provokes crisis
1569/01	Argyll and Huntly proclamation re Darnley's murder	Elizabeth pronounces re Mary at Hampton Court		
1569/02	Regent Moray returns to Scotland	Mary moved from Bolton to Tutbury castle		
1569/03			Irish Parliament attaints Shane O'Neill	Huguenot defeat at Jarnac

Date (year/month)	Scottish	Anglo-Scottish	Gaelic	French/ European
1569/04	Hamiltons settle with regent			
1569/05	Argyll settles with regent			
1569/06	Regent on progress to north Maitland splits with Moray			
1569/07			Sidney campaigns in Leinster and Munster	
1569/08			John Douglas sent to Argyll Joint weddings on Rathlin Island Argyll Council agrees tax	
1569/10		Scheme to marry Norfolk to Mary revealed		
1569/11		Rebellion of northern earls		
1569/12	Argyll and Moray resume speaking	Northern earls flee to Scotland		
1570/01	Moray assassinated			
1570/02	Meeting at Dalkeith re Moray's murder			Papal bull exommuni- cates Elizabeth
1570/03	Negotiations at Edinburgh, fracas at Linlithgow			
1570/05		English army sent to Scotland		Cecil memo re Anjou marriage
1570/06			Argyll council re MacGregor feud Campbell of Glenlyon ambushed	
1570/07	Lennox proclaimed regent			

Date (year/month)	Scottish	Anglo-Scottish	Gaelic	French/ European
1570/08	Brechin steeple captured, all queen's troops executed			
1570/09	Queen's men meet by Loch Tay	Sussex and Cecil negotiate with both Scottish parties and Mary	Carnasserie arbitration of Islay feud	
1570/10			Angus MacDonald receives Ardnamurchan Kilmun takes troops to Ulster Failed attempt to subborn MacDonald of Sleat	
1570/12			Settlement of Campbell-MacGregor feud	
1571/02				Anglo-French negotiations re Anjou marriage
1571/03			Lady Agnes petitions Elizabeth for husband, O'Neill	
1571/04	Dumbarton castle captured by king's men Archbishop Hamilton hanged		5th earl renews bond with MacDonald of Sleat	
1571/05	Negotiations between factions break down			
1571/07			Atholl settles with MacGregors	
1571/08	Argyll settles with Regent Lennox			
1571/09	Lennox killed Mar becomes regent	Ridolphi plot exposed	MacDonald arrears re Kintyre settled	

Date (year/month)	Scottish	Anglo-Scottish	Gaelic	French/ European
1571/10			Argyll close to death	Defeat of Turks at Lepanto
1572/01	Wedding of Colin Campbell and Annas Keith	Norfolk executed for treason		
1572/02			Argyll makes brother Colin his heir	
1572/04				Sea-beggars take Brill Anglo-French Treaty of Blois
1572/05		English Parliament opens, discusses Mary		
1572/08			Sir Thomas Smith and colonists land in Ulster	St Bartholomew's eve massacre
1572/10	Death of Regent Mar			
1572/11	Morton becomes regent		Argyll council at Inveraray	
1573/01	Parliament 5th earl made chancellor			
1573/02	Pacification of Perth			
1573/05	Edinburgh castle surrenders	English troops help in castle's siege		
1573/06	Argyll gets divorce			Peace of La Rochelle
1573/08	Argyll marries Jean Cunningham		Earl of Essex arrives at Carrickfergus	
1573/09			Argyll dies at Barbreck	

BIBLIOGRAPHY

MANUSCRIPT SOURCES

In the footnotes, the Argyll Transcripts were generally cited in preference to the Argyll Manuscripts themselves because they are readily available to scholars. Whilst at Inveraray, I checked a considerable number of Duke Niall's transcripts and generally found them accurate and reliable. The other main Campbell archive is the very substantial Breadalbane Collection (GD112) housed in the National Archives of Scotland which is now fully catalogued.

BODLEIAN LIBRARY, OXFORD

Carte MS No. 530

BRITISH LIBRARY, LONDON

Additional MS 19,401
Additional MS 23,109
Additional MS 32,091
Additional MS 33,591
Additional MS 35,830
Cotton Caligula B 9
Cotton Caligula B 10
Cotton Caligula C 1
Cotton Caligula C 4
Cotton Titus B 13
Egerton 1818
Landsdowne 3
Landsdowne 102
Royal 18 B 6
Sloane 3199

INVERARAY CASTLE, ARGYLL

Argyll MSS

Bundles 21; 28–35; 41; 46; 48, 56; 62; 83; 95; 135; 715; 731; 1073–84; 1090; 1093–6; 1099; 1101; 1177

Argyll Transcripts

Vols. 1–7 (1257–1600) made from records concerning the earls of Argyll by Niall
Campbell, 10th duke of Argyll. (Also available in the Scottish History Department,
University of Glasgow.)

NATIONAL LIBRARY OF SCOTLAND, EDINBURGH

Ch 902
Ch 5759
Ch 5763–4
MS 73
MS 3157
MS 3657
Advocates MS 22.2.18
Advocates MS 31.4.2
Advocates MS 33.1.1
Advocates MS 54.1.7
Advocates MS 72.2.2

PUBLIC RECORD OFFICE, LONDON

SP51, State Papers, Scotland, Mary
SP52 State Papers, Scotland, Elizabeth I
SP59 State Papers, Borders, Elizabeth I
SP62 State Papers, Ireland, Mary
SP63 State Papers, Ireland, Elizabeth I
SP70 State Papers, Foreign, Elizabeth I

NATIONAL ARCHIVES OF SCOTLAND, EDINBURGH

B16 Dumbarton Protocol Books
CC8/2/5–6 Acts and decreets of Edinburgh Commissary Court
CC8/8/4 Wills and testaments (Edinburgh)
CS7 Acts and decreets of the Court of Session
CS15 Extracted and unextracted processes of the Court of Session
JC 1/11 and 12 court books of High Court of Justiciary

GD8 Boyd papers
GD15 Cardross writs
GD16 Airlie muniments
GD18 Clerk of Penicuik muniments
GD24 Abercairny muniments
GD26 Leven and Melville muniments
GD50 John Macgregor collection
GD103 Society of Antiquaries collection
GD111 Curle collection

GD112 Breadalbane Papers

GD112/1 Land documents
GD112/2 Land documents by estate
GD112/3 Family papers
GD112/5 Charter collection
GD112/17 Court books and judicial records
GD112/23 and 24 Bonds
GD112/25 Marriage documents
GD112/39 Correspondence
GD112/56 Ecclesiastical papers
GD112/75–7 Additional papers

GD149 Cunningham of Caprington muniments
GD160 Drummond Castle muniments
GD170 Campbell of Barcaldine muniments
GD176 Mackintosh muniments

RD1 Register of deeds
RH13/2 Oliver Colt's Legal Style Book

NATIONAL REGISTER OF ARCHIVES, SCOTLAND

NRA(S) 217 Moray Papers

PRIMARY AND REFERENCE SOURCES

Accounts of the Collectors of Thirds of Benefices, 1561–1572 ed. G. Donaldson
    (SHS, 3rd ser. 42, Edinburgh, 1949).
Accounts of the Lord High Treasurer of Scotland eds. T. Dickson *et al.* (12 vols.,
    Edinburgh, 1877–1970).
Acta curiae admirallatus scotiae, 1557–61 ed. T.C. Wade (Stair Society, 2, Edinburgh,
    1937).
Acts of the Lords of the Isles, 1336–1493 eds. J. Munro and R.W. Munro (SHS, 4th
    ser. 22, Edinburgh, 1986).
Acts of the Parliaments of Scotland eds. T. Thomson and C. Innes (12 vols.,
    Edinburgh, 1814–42).
Acts of the Privy Council of England ed. J. Dasent (46 vols., London, 1890–1964).
Ancient Criminal Trials in Scotland ed. R. Pitcairn (3 vols., Bannatyne Club, 42,
    Edinburgh, 1833).
*The Annals of the Kingdom of Ireland by the Four Masters from the Earliest Period
    to the Year 1616* ed. J. Donovan (7 vols., Dublin, 1851).
Argyll, An Inventory of the Ancient Monuments (7 vols., RCAHMS, Edinburgh,
    1971–92).
Atlas of Scottish History to 1707 eds. P. McNeill and H.L. MacQueen (Scottish
    Medievalists, Edinburgh, 1996).
Ayr Burgh Accounts, 1534–1624 ed. G.S. Pryde (SHS, 3rd ser. 28, Edinburgh, 1937).
Bamff Charters and Papers, 1232–1703 ed. J. Ramsay (Oxford, 1915).
The Bannatyne Miscellany I eds. Sir W. Scott and D. Laing (Bannatyne Club, 19,
    Edinburgh, 1827).

The Bannatyne Miscellany III ed. D. Laing (Bannatyne Club, 19, Edinburgh, 1855).

Bàrdachd Albannach: Scottish Verse from the Book of the Dean of Lismore ed. J.W. Watson (Scottish Gaelic Texts Society, 1, Edinburgh, 1937).

Bàrdachd Ghàidhlig: Gaelic Poetry 1550–1900 ed. W. Watson (3rd edn, Inverness, 1976).

The Bighouse Papers ed. D. Wimberley (Inverness, 1904).

Black Book of Taymouth ed. C. Innes (Bannatyne Club, 100, Edinburgh, 1855).

The Book of the Thanes of Cawdor ed. C. Innes (Spalding Club, 30, Edinburgh, 1859).

'*The Booke of the Universall Kirk of Scotland*': Acts and Proceedings of the General Assemblies of the Kirk of Scotland ed. T. Thomson (3 vols., Bannatyne Club, 81, Edinburgh, 1839-45).

The Books of Assumption of the Thirds of Benefices: Scottish Ecclesiastical Rentals at the Reformation ed. J. Kirk (Records of Social and Economic History, New ser. 21, Oxford, 1995).

The Buik of the Canagait, 1564–7 ed. A. Calderwood (Scottish Record Society, Old ser. 90, Edinburgh, 1961).

Calderwood, D., *The History of the Kirk of Scotland* ed. T. Thomson (8 vols., Wodrow Society, Edinburgh, 1842–9).

Calendar of the Carew Manuscripts Preserved in the Archiepiscopal Library at Lambeth 1515–1624 ed. J. Brewer et al. (6 vols., London, 1867–73).

The Calendar of Fearn ed. R. Adam (SHS, 5th ser. 4, Edinburgh, 1991).

Calendar of Laing Charters, 847–1837 ed. J. Anderson (2 vols., Edinburgh, 1899).

Calendar of State Papers, Foreign Series, Edward, Mary and Elizabeth eds. J. Stevenson et al (25 vols., London, 1861–1950).

Calendar of State Papers relating to Ireland eds. H.C. Hamilton et al. (24 vols., London, 1860–1911).

Calendar of State Papers relating to Scotland and Mary, Queen of Scots, 1547–1603 eds. J. Bain et al. (13 vols., Edinburgh, 1898–1969).

Calendar of State Papers, Spanish eds. R. Tyler et al. (13 vols., London, 1862–54).

Campbell Letters, 1559–1583 ed. J.E.A. Dawson (SHS, 5th ser. 10, Edinburgh, 1997).

Campbell, N., 'The Castle Campbell Inventory (1595)', *SHR*, 10 (1913), 299–315.

Campbell, N., 'Two Papers from the Argyll Charter Chest', *SHR*, 21 (1923–4), 142–3.

Catalogue of Gaelic Manuscripts ed. J. MacKechnie (Boston, MA, 1973).

Chronicles of the Families of Atholl and Tullibardine ed. John, 7th duke of Atholl (5 vols., Edinburgh, 1908).

The Clan Campbell eds. D. Campbell and H. Paton (8 vols., Edinburgh, 1913–22).

Collectanea de rebus albanicis (Iona Club, Edinburgh, 1847).

Collection of state papers... left by William Cecil, Lord Burghley eds. S. Hayes and W. Murdin (2 vols., London, 1740–59).

Correspondence of Sir Patrick Waus of Barnbarroch ed. R.V. Agnew (2 vols., Ayrshire and Wigtonshire Archaeological Association, 14, Edinburgh, 1887).

Croftus sive de hibernia liber by Sir William Herbert, eds., A. Keavney and J. Madden (Irish Manuscripts Commission, Dublin, 1992).

Davidson, John, 'A Memorial of the Life of Two Worthye Christians, Robert Campbel, of the Kinyeancleuch, and his Wife, Elizabeth Campbel' in C. Rogers, ed., *Three Scottish Reformers* (Grampian Club, 9, London, 1986), 100–31.

A diurnal of remarkable occurrents that have passed within the country of Scotland since the death of King James the Fourth till the year MDLXXV ed. T. Thomson (Bannatyne Club, 43, Edinburgh, 1833).
Early Records of the University of St Andrews ed. J. Anderson (SHS, 3rd ser. 9, Edinburgh, 1926).
Estimate of the Scottish Nobility ed. C. Rogers (Grampian Club, 6, London, 1873).
Fasti ecclesiasae scotiae ed. H. Scott (8 vols., Edinburgh, 1915–50).
The First Book of Discipline ed. J.K. Cameron (Edinburgh, 1972).
Foirm Na N-Urrnuidheadh: John Carswell's Gaelic Translation of the Book of Common Order ed. R.L. Thomson (Scottish Gaelic Text Society, Edinburgh, 1970).
Fraser, W., *Memorials of the Montgomeries, Earls of Eglinton* (2 vols., Edinburgh, 1859).
The Lennox (2 vols., Edinburgh, 1874).
Memorials of the Family of Wemyss of Wemyss (2 vols., Edinburgh, 1888).
The Melvilles, Earls of Melville and the Leslies, Earls of Leven (3 vols., Edinburgh, 1890).
A Genealogical Deduction of the Family of Rose of Kilravock ed. C. Innes (Spalding Club, 18, Edinburgh, 1848).
Hamilton Papers ed. J. Bain (2 vols., Edinburgh, 1890).
Harvey Johnston, G., *The Heraldry of the Campbells* (2 vols., Inveraray, 1977; reprint of 1920 edn).
Highland Papers ed. J. Macphail (4 vols., SHS, 2nd ser. 5, 12, 20; 3rd ser. 22, Edinburgh, 1914–34).
Historical Manuscripts Commission 4th Report (Argyll Manuscripts, London, 1874).
Historical Manuscripts Commission 6th Report (Argyll Manuscripts, London, 1877).
Historical Manuscripts Commission Salisbury (Cecil) 9th Report (London, 1883–1976).
Historical Manuscripts Commission Pepys 70th Report (London, 1911).
Historical Memoirs of the Reign of Mary, Queen of Scots by Lord Herries ed. R. Pitcairn (Abbotsford Club, 6, Edinburgh, 1836).
The historie and cronicles of Scotland . . . by Robert Lindesay of Pitscottie ed. A.J.G. Mackay (3 vols., Scottish Text Society, Old ser. 42–43, Edinburgh, 1899–1911).
'A Historie of the Estate of Scotland from July 1558 to April 1560' in D. Laing, ed., *Miscellany of Wodrow Society I* (Wodrow Society, 11, Edinburgh, 1844).
The History of Scotland by George Buchanan ed. J. Aikman (4 vols., Edinburgh, 1827).
The History of the Church of Scotland. By John Spottiswood, Archbishop of St Andrews eds. M. Napier and M. Russell (3 vols., Bannatyne Club, Edinburgh, 1850).
Irish History from Contemporary Sources, 1509–1610 ed. C. Maxwell (London, 1923).
Johnston, John, *Heroes ex omni historia scotica lectissimi* (Leiden, 1603).
The Justiciary Records of Argyll and the Isles, 1664–1742 eds. J. Cameron and J. Imrie (2 vols., Stair Society, 12 and 25, Edinburgh, 1949 and 1969).
Keith, R., *History of the Affairs of Church and State in Scotland, from the Beginning of the Reformation to the Year 1568* eds. J.P. Lawson and C.J. Lyon (3 vols., Spottiswoode Society, 1, Edinburgh, 1844–50).
Knox, J., *The Works of John Knox* ed. D Laing (6 vols., Edinburgh 1846–64).
Knox, J., *The History of the Reformation in Scotland* ed. W.C. Dickinson (2 vols., London, 1949).

Letters to the Argyll Family ed. A. MacDonald (Maitland Club, 50, Edinburgh, 1839).

Letters and Memorials of State of Sir Henry Sidney ed. A. Collins (2 vols., London, 1746).

The Letters and Papers of Sir Ralph Sadler ed. A. Clifford (3 vols., Edinburgh, 1809).

Lettres et mémoires de Marie, reine d'escosse ed. A. Labanoff (7 vols., Paris, 1859).

Liber officialis sancti Andree ed. J.H. Forbes, Lord Medwyn (Abbotsford Club, 25, Edinburgh, 1845).

MacFarlane's Geographical Collections eds. A. Mitchell and J. Clark (3 vols., SHS, 1st ser. 51, 52 and 55, Edinburgh, 1906–8).

'The Manuscript History of Craignish' in H. Campbell, ed., *Miscellany of the Scottish History Society, IV* (SHS, 3rd ser. 9, Edinburgh, 1926).

Martin, Martin, *A Description of the Western Islands of Scotland, c 1695* (Edinburgh, 1994; reprint of 1934 edn).

Memoirs of John Napier of Merchiston ed. Mark Napier (Edinburgh, 1834).

The Memoirs of Sir James Melville of Halhill ed. G. Donaldson (London, 1969).

Memorials of Transactions in Scotland 1569–72 by Richard Bannatyne ed. R. Pitcairn (Bannatyne Club, 51, Edinburgh, 1836).

Miscellany of the Abbotsford Club I ed. J. Maidment (Abbotsford Club, 11, Edinburgh, 1837).

Miscellany of the Maitland Club IV ed. J. Robertson (Maitland Club, 67, Edinburgh 1847).

Muniments of the Royal Burgh of Irvine (2 vols., Ayrshire and Wigtonshire Archaeological Association, 15, Edinburgh, 1890–91).

Munro's Western Isles of Scotland and Genealogies of the Clans, 1549 ed. R.W. Munro (London, 1961).

Norvell, Robert, *The Meroure of an Christiane* (Edinburgh, 1561).

Papal Negotiations with Mary, Queen of Scots during her Reign in Scotland 1561–7 ed. J.H. Pollen (SHS, 1st ser. 37, Edinburgh, 1901).

Papiers d'etat relatifs a l'histoire de l'écosse au 16ᵉ siècle ed. A. Teulet (3 vols., Bannatyne Club, 107, Edinburgh, 1852–60).

Queen Elizabeth and her Times ed. T. Wright (2 vols., London, 1838).

Records of Argyll ed. Lord Archibald Campbell (Edinburgh, 1885).

Red Book of Grandtully ed. W. Fraser (2 vols., Edinburgh, 1868).

Red and White Book of Menzies ed. D.P. Menzies (Glasgow, 1897).

Register of the Minister, Elders and Deacons of the Christian Congregation of Saint Andrews...1559–1600 ed. D. Hay Fleming (2 vols., SHS, 1st ser. 4 and 7, Edinburgh, 1889–90).

Register of the Privy Council of Scotland eds. J. Burton *et al.* (HMSO, 1st ser., 14 vols., Edinburgh, 1877–98).

Registrum honoris de Morton eds. T. Thomson *et al.* (2 vols., Bannatyne Club, 94, Edinburgh, 1853).

Registrum magni sigilii regum scotorum, Register of the Great Seal of Scotland eds. J. Thomson *et al.* (11 vols., Edinburgh, 1882–1914).

Registrum secreti sigilli regum scotorum, Register of the Privy Seal of Scotland eds. M. Livingstone *et al.* (8 vols., Edinburgh, 1908–82).

Rental Book of the Cistercian Abbey of Cupar Angus ed. C. Rogers (2 vols., Grampian Club, 17, London, 1879–80).

236 *Bibliography*

'Report by de la Brosse and d'Oysel on Conditions in Scotland, 1559–60' ed. G. Dickinson in *Miscellany of the Scottish History Society, IX* (SHS, 3rd ser. 50, Edinburgh, 1958).
The River Clyde and the Clyde Burghs ed. J.D. Marwick (Scottish Burgh Records Society, 20, Edinburgh 1909).
Satirical Poems of the Time of the Reformation ed. J. Cranston (2 vols., Scottish Text Society, Old ser. 20 and 24, Edinburgh, 1891–93).
Scotland before 1700 from Contemporary Documents ed. P. Hume Brown (Edinburgh, 1893).
The Scots Peerage ed. J.B. Paul (8 vols., Edinburgh, 1904–14).
The Scottish Correspondence of Mary of Lorraine, 1542/3–60 ed. A.I. Cameron (SHS, 3rd ser. 10, Edinburgh, 1927).
Selections from unpublished manuscripts . . . illustrating the reign of Queen Mary ed. J. Stevenson (Maitland Club, 41, Edinburgh, 1837).
'Shane O'Neill's Last Letter' ed. R. Smith, *Journal of Celtic Studies*, 11 (1958), 131–3.
Sidney State Papers, 1565–70 ed. T. O'Laidhin (Irish Manuscripts Commission, Dublin, 1962).
Statutes of the Scottish Church ed. D. Patrick (SHS, 1st ser. 54, Edinburgh, 1907).
Two Missions of Jacques de la Brosse ed. G. Dickinson (SHS, 3rd ser. 36, Edinburgh, 1942).
The Warrender Papers ed. A.I. Cameron (2 vols., SHS, 3rd ser. 18–19, Edinburgh, 1931–32).

SECONDARY SOURCES

Alford, S., *The Early Elizabethan Polity: William Cecil and the British Succession Crisis, 1558–1569* (Cambridge, 1998).
'Knox, Cecil and the British Dimension of the Scottish Reformation' in R. Mason, ed., *John Knox and the British Reformations* (Aldershot, 1999), 201–19.
Allan, D., *Philosophy and Politics in Later Stuart Scotland: Neo-Stoicism, Culture and Ideology in an Age of Crisis* (East Linton, 2000).
Anderson, P., *Robert Stewart Earl of Orkney, 1533–93* (Edinburgh, 1982).
Armitage, D., *The Ideological Origins of the British Empire* (Cambridge, 2000).
Asch, R., ed., *Three Nations: a Common History?* (Bochum, 1992).
Bagwell, R., *Ireland under the Tudors* (3 vols., London, 1963; reprint of 1885–90 edn).
Bannerman, J.W., 'Two Early Post-Reformation Inscriptions in Argyll', *PSAS*, 105 (1972–4), 307–12.
'The Lordship of the Isles' in J. Brown, ed., *Scottish Society in the Fifteenth Century* (London, 1977), 209–40.
'The MacLachlans of Kilbride and their Manuscripts', *Scottish Studies*, 21 (1977), 1–34.
'Literacy in the Highlands' in I. Cowan and D. Shaw, eds., *The Renaissance and Reformation in Scotland* (Edinburgh, 1982), 214–35.
The Beatons: A Medical Kindred in the Classical Gaelic Tradition (Edinburgh, 1986).
Barber, P., 'A Tudor Mystery: Laurence Nowell's Map of England and Ireland', *Map Collector*, 22 (1983), 16–21.

'England II: Monarchs, Ministers and Maps, 1550–1625' in D. Buisseret, ed., *Monarchs, Ministers and Maps* (Chicago, 1992), 57–98.

Bardgett, F.D., *Scotland Reformed: The Reformation in Angus and the Mearns* (Edinburgh, 1989).

Barty, A., *History of Dunblane Cathedral* (Stirling, 1995).

Blanning, T.C.W. and D. Cannadine, eds., *History and Biography: Essays in Honour of Derek Beales* (Cambridge, 1996).

Boardman, S., 'The Medieval Origin Legends of Clan Campbell', *Journal of the Clan Campbell Society (UK)*, 27 (2000), 5–7.

Bradshaw, B., *The Irish Constitutional Revolution in the Sixteenth Century* (Cambridge, 1979).

'Manus "the Magnificent": O'Donnell as Renaissance Prince' in A. Cosgrove and D. MacCartney, eds., *Studies in Irish History Presented to R. Dudley Edwards* (Dublin, 1979), 15–36.

Bradshaw, B., A. Hadfield and W. Maley, eds., *Representing Ireland: Literature and the Origins of Conflict 1534–1660* (Cambridge, 1993).

Bradshaw, B. and J. Morrill, eds., *The British Problem, c. 1534–1707: State Formation in the Atlantic Archipelago* (London, 1996).

Bradshaw, B. and P. Roberts, eds., *British Consciousness and Identity: The Making of Britain, 1533–1707* (Cambridge, 1998).

Brady, C., 'The Killing of Shane O'Neill: Some New Evidence', *Irish Sword*, 15 (1982–4), 116–23.

The Chief Governors: The Rise and Fall of Reform Government in Tudor Ireland, 1536–1588 (Cambridge, 1994).

'Comparable Histories?: Tudor Reform in Wales and Ireland' in S. Ellis and S. Barber, eds., *Conquest and Union: Fashioning a British State, 1485–1725* (London, 1995).

Shane O'Neill (Dundalk, 1996).

'Shane O'Neill Departs from the Court of Elizabeth: Irish, English and Scottish Perspectives and the Paralysis of Policy, July 1559 to April 1562' in S.J. Connelly, ed., *Kingdoms United?: Great Britain and Ireland since 1500* (Dublin, 1999), 13–28.

Brown, K.M., *Bloodfeud in Scotland, 1573–1625* (Edinburgh, 1986).

'The Price of Friendship: The "Well-affected" and English Economic Clientage in Scotland before 1603' in R. Mason, ed., *Scotland and England 1286–1815* (Edinburgh, 1987), 139–62.

Kingdom or Province?: Scotland and the Regal Union, 1603–1715 (London, 1992).

Noble Society in Scotland: Wealth, Family and Culture from Reformation to Revolution (Edinburgh, 2000).

Burns, J.H., *The True Law of Kingship: Concepts of Monarchy in Early Modern Scotland* (Oxford, 1996).

Caldwell, D., 'The Battle of Pinkie' in N. Macdougall, ed., *Scotland and War AD79–1918* (Edinburgh, 1991), 61–94.

Cameron, J., *James V* (East Linton, 1998).

Campbell, Lord Archibald, *Argyllshire Galleys* (London, 1906).

Campbell of Airds, A., *The Life and Troubled Time of Sir Donald Campbell of Ardnamurchan* (Society of West Highland and Island Historical Research, Inverness, 1991).

A History of Clan Campbell I: From Origins to Flodden (Edinburgh, 2000).

Campbell of Airds, A. and D. McWhannell, 'The MacGillechonnells – A Family of Hereditary Boatbuilders', *West Highland Notes and Queries*, ser. 2, 14 (July 1995), 3–9.

Canny, N., *The Elizabethan Conquest of Ireland: A Pattern Established 1565–76* (Hassocks, Sussex, 1976).

Canny, N., ed., *Oxford History of the British Empire I: The Origins of Empire* (Oxford, 1998).

Clark, W., 'Tides in the Water of Moyle', *The Kintyre Antiquarian and Natural History Magazine*, 43 (Spring 1998), 9–11.

Collinson, P., 'The Monarchical Republic of Queen Elizabeth' in P. Collinson, *Elizabethan Essays* (London, 1994), 31–57.

Cowan, E.J., 'The Angus Campbells and the Origin of the Campbell-Ogilvie Feud', *Scottish Studies*, 25 (1981), 25–38.

'"Fishers in drumlie waters": Clanship and Campbell Expansion in the Time of Gilleasbuig Grumach', *TGSI*, 4 (1984–6), 269–312.

Cruden, S., *Castle Campbell* (HMSO, Edinburgh, 1984).

Davies, R.R., *The First English Empire: Power and Identities in the British Isles, 1093–1343* (Oxford, 2000).

Davies, R.R., ed., *The British Isles 1100–1500: Comparisons, Contrasts and Connections* (Edinburgh, 1988).

Dawson, J.E.A., 'Mary, Queen of Scots, Lord Darnley and Anglo-Scottish Relations in 1565', *International History Review*, 8 (1986), 1–24.

'Two Kingdoms or Three?: Ireland in Anglo-Scottish Relations in the Middle of the Sixteenth Century' in R. Mason, ed., *Scotland and England, 1286–1815* (Edinburgh, 1987), 113–38.

'The Fifth Earl of Argyle, Gaelic Lordship and Political Power in Sixteenth-Century Scotland', *SHR*, 67 (1988), 1–27.

'William Cecil and the British Dimension of Early Elizabethan Foreign Policy', *History*, 74 (1989), 196–216.

'"The Face of Ane Perfyt Reformed Kyrk": St Andrews and the Early Scottish Reformation' in J. Kirk, ed., *Humanism and Reform: The Church in Europe, England and Scotland, 1400–1642* (Studies in Church History, Subsidia 8, Oxford, 1991), 413–35.

'The Origins of the "Road to the Isles": Trade, Communications and Campbell Power in Early Modern Scotland' in R.A. Mason and N. Macdougall, eds., *People and Power in Scotland: Essays in Honour of T.C. Smout* (Edinburgh, 1992), 74–103.

'Calvinism in the Gaidhealtachd in Scotland' in A. Pettegree, A. Duke and G. Lewis, eds., *Calvinism in Europe, 1540–1620* (Cambridge, 1994), 231–53.

'Argyll: The Enduring Heartland', *SHR*, 74 (1995), 75–98.

'Anglo-Scottish Protestant Culture and the Integration of Sixteenth-Century Britain' in S. Ellis and S. Barber, eds., *Conquest and Union: Fashioning a British State, 1485–1725* (London, 1995), 87–114.

'The Gaidhealtachd and the Emergence of the Scottish Highlands' in B. Bradshaw and P. Roberts, eds., *British Identity and Consciousness* (Cambridge, 1998), 259–300.

'Clan, Kin and Kirk: The Campbells and the Scottish Reformation' in N.S. Amos, A. Pettegree and H. van Nierop, eds., *The Education of a Christian Society* (Aldershot, 1999), 211–42.

'The Protestant Earl and Godly Gael: The Fifth Earl of Argyll (c. 1538–73) and the Scottish Reformation' in D. Wood, ed., *Life and Thought in the Northern Church, c. 1100–c. 1700: Essays in Honour of Claire Cross* (Studies in Church History, Subsidia, 12, Woodbridge, Suffolk, 1999), 337–63.

Dodghson, R.A., 'West Highland Chiefdoms: A Study of Redistributive Exchange' in R. Mitchison and P. Roebuck, eds., *Scotland and Ireland* (Edinburgh, 1988), 27–37.

'"Pretense of blude and place of thair dwelling": The Nature of Highland Clans, 1500–1745' in R.A. Houston and I.D. Whyte, eds., *Scottish Society 1500–1800* (Cambridge, 1989).

From Chiefs to Landlords: Social and Economic Change in the Western Highlands and Islands c. 1493–1830 (Edinburgh, 1998).

Donaldson, G., 'Flitting Friday, The Beggars' Summons and Knox's Sermon at Perth', *SHR*, 39 (1960), 175–6.

The First Trial of Mary, Queen of Scots (London, 1969).

Scotland: James V–James VII (Edinburgh, 1978; reprint of 1965 edn).

All the Queen's Men: Power and Politics in Mary Stewart's Scotland (London, 1983).

'Foundations of Anglo-Scottish Union' in G. Donaldson, *Scottish Church History* (Edinburgh, 1985), 137–63.

Dunlop, R., 'Sixteenth-Century Schemes for the Plantation of Ulster', *SHR*, 22 (1924), 51–60; 115–26; 199–212.

Durkan, J., 'James 3rd Earl of Arran: The Hidden Years', *SHR*, 65 (1986), 154–66.

'Heresy in Scotland, the Second Phase 1546–58', *RSCHS*, 24 (1992), 320–65.

Ellis, S.G., *Tudor Frontiers and Noble Power: The Making of the British State* (Oxford, 1995).

Ireland in the Age of the Tudors, 1447–1603 (London, 1998).

Ellis, S. and S. Barber, eds., *Conquest and Union: Fashioning of a British State 1485–1720* (London, 1995).

Falls, C., *Elizabeth's Irish Wars* (London, 1950).

Finlay, J., *Men of Law in Pre-Reformation Scotland* (East Linton, 2000).

Finnie, E., 'The House of Hamilton: Patronage, Politics and the Church in the Reformation Period', *The Innes Review*, 36 (1985), 3–28.

Fittis, R. S., *Ecclesiastical Annals of Perth* (Edinburgh, 1885).

Ford, A., *The Protestant Reformation in Ireland* (Frankfurt, 1985; Dublin edn, 1999).

Frame, R., *The Political Development of the British Isles, 1100–1400* (Oxford, 1990).

Furgol, E., 'The Scottish Itinerary of Mary, Queen of Scots, 1542–8, 1561–8', *PSAS*, 117 (1987), 219–31.

Gibbs, G., R. Oresko and H.M. Scott, eds., *Royal and Republican Sovereignty in Early Modern Europe* (Cambridge, 1997).

Gillies, W., 'Some Aspects of Campbell History', *TGSI*, 50 (1976–8), 256–95.

'The Invention of Tradition, Highland-Style' in A. MacDonald, M. Lynch and I. Cowan, eds., *The Renaissance in Scotland* (Leiden, 1994), 144–56.

'The "British" Genealogy of the Campbells', *Celtica*, 23 (1999), 82–95.

Glasgow, T. 'The Navy in the First Elizabethan Undeclared War', *Mariners Mirror*, 54 (1968), 23–37.

'The Elizabethan Navy in Ireland, 1558–1603', *Irish Sword*, 7 (1974–5), 291–307.

Goodare, J., 'Queen Mary's Catholic Interlude' in M. Lynch, ed., *Mary Stewart: Queen in Three Kingdoms* (Oxford, 1988), 154–70.

'The Scottish Parliamentary Records, 1560–1603', *Historical Records*, 72 (1999), 248–55.

State and Society in Early Modern Scotland (Oxford, 2000).

Grant, A. and K. Stringer, eds., *Uniting the Kingdom?: The Making of British History* (London, 1995).

Grant, I.F., *The MacLeods: The History of a Clan 1200–1956* (London, 1959).

Gregory, D., *History of the Western Highlands and Isles of Scotland* (London, 1881).

Guy, J., *Tudor England* (Oxford, 1988).

Hay Fleming, D., *The Reformation in Scotland* (London, 1910).

Hayes-McCoy, G.A., 'The Early History of the Gun in Ireland', *Journal of the Galway Archaeological and Historical Society*, 18 (1938–9), 43–65.

Irish Battles: A Military History of Ireland (Belfast, 1989; reprint of 1969 edn).

Scots Mercenary Forces in Ireland, 1565–1603 (Dublin, 1996; reprint of 1937 edn).

Hazlitt, W.I.P., 'The Scots Confession 1560: Context, Complexion and Critique', *Archiv für Reformationsgeschichte*, 78 (1987), 287–320.

Hewitt, G.R., *Scotland under Morton, 1572–80* (Edinburgh, 1982).

Hill, G., *An Historical Account of the MacDonnells of Antrim* (Belfast, 1978; reprint of 1873 edn).

Hill, J. Michael, *Fire and Sword: Sorley Boy MacDonnell and the Rise of Clan Ian Mor 1538–90* (London, 1993).

Hodson, S., '*Princes étrangers* at the French Court in the Seventeenth Century', *The Court Historian*, 3.1 (1998), 24–8.

Hogan, J., 'Shane O'Neill Comes to the Court of Elizabeth' in S. Pender, ed., *Essays and Studies Presented to Professor Tadhg Ua Domnachadha (Torna)* (Cork, 1947), 154–70.

James, M., 'English Politics and the Concept of Honour' in M. James, *Society, Politics and Culture* (Cambridge, 1986), 308–415.

Kirk, J., *Patterns of Reform* (Edinburgh, 1989).

Kirk, J., ed., *The Church in the Highlands* (Edinburgh, 1998).

Klein, W., 'The Ancient Constitution Revisited' in N. Phillipson and Q. Skinner, eds., *Political Discourse in Early Modern Britain* (Cambridge, 1993), 23–44.

Knecht, R., *Catherine de' Medici* (London, 1998).

Lamont, W.D., *The Early History of Islay* (Dundee, 1970; reprint of 1966 edn).

Lawson, J., *The Book of Perth* (Edinburgh, 1847).

Lee, M., *James Stewart, Earl of Moray* (Westport, CT, 1953).

Leneman, L., *Alienated Affections: The Scottish Experience of Divorce and Separation, 1684–1830* (Edinburgh, 1998).

Lenman, B.P., *Colonial Wars and English Identities, c 1550–1688* (London, 2001).

Lennon, C., *Sixteenth-Century Ireland: The Incomplete Conquest* (Dublin, 1994).

Lindsay, I. and M. Cosh, *Inveraray and the Dukes of Argyll* (Edinburgh, 1977).

Loughlin, M., 'The Dialogue of the Twa Wyfeis: Maitland, Machiavelli and the Propaganda of the Scottish Civil War' in A. MacDonald *et al.*, eds., *The Renaissance in Scotland* (Leiden, 1994), 226–45.

Lynch, M., *Edinburgh and the Reformation* (Edinburgh, 1981).

'Queen Mary's Triumph: the Baptismal Celebrations at Stirling in December 1566', *SHR*, 69 (1990), 1–21.

Lynch, M., ed., *Mary Stewart: Queen in Three Kingdoms* (Oxford, 1988).

MacCulloch, D., *Archbishop Cranmer* (New Haven, CT, 1996).
MacDonald, C.M., *The History of Argyll up to the Beginning of the Sixteenth Century* (Glasgow, 1950).
MacDonald, D.J., *Clan Donald* (Loanhead, 1978).
Macinnes A.I., *Clanship, Commerce and the House of Stuart, 1603–1788* (East Linton, 1996).
MacInnes J., 'West Highland Sea Power', *TGSI*, 48 (1972–4), 518–56.
'The Panegyric Code in Gaelic Poetry and its Historical Background', *TGSI*, 50 (1976–8), 435–98.
Mackechnie, J., 'Treaty between Argyll and O'Donnell', *Scottish Gaelic Studies*, 7 (1953), 94–102.
MacLean-Bristol, N., *Warriors and Priests: The History of Clan MacLean, 1300–1570* (East Linton, 1995).
Murder under Trust: The Crimes and Death of Sir Lachlan Mor Maclean of Duart, 1558–1598 (East Linton, 1999).
MacLeod, F., ed. *Togail Tir: Marking Time, The Map of the Western Isles* (Stornoway, 1989).
McRoberts, D., *Essays on the Scottish Reformation 1513–1625* (Glasgow, 1962).
McWhannell, D., 'Ship Service and Indigenous Sea Power in the West of Scotland', *West Highland Notes and Queries*, ser. 3, 1 (2000), 3–18.
Mason, R.A., 'Covenant and Commonweal: The Language of Politics in Reformation Scotland' in N. Macdougall, ed., *Church, Politics and Society: Scotland, 1408–1929* (Edinburgh, 1983), 97–126.
'Scotching the Brut: Politics History and National Myth in Sixteenth-Century Britain' in R.A. Mason, ed., *Scotland and England* (Edinburgh, 1987), 60–84.
Kingship and the Commonweal: Political Thought in Renaissance and Reformation Scotland (East Linton, 1998).
Mason, R.A., ed., *John Knox and the British Reformations* (Aldershot, 1998).
Meek, D. 'The Scots-Gaelic Scribes of Late Medieval Perthshire: An Overview of the Orthography and Contents of the Book of the Dean of Lismore' in J. McClure and M. Spiller, eds., *Brycht Lanterns: Essays on the Language and Literature of Medieval and Renaissance Scotland* (Aberdeen, 1989), 387–404.
'The Reformation and Gaelic Culture' in J. Kirk, ed., *The Church in the Highlands* (Edinburgh, 1998), 37–62.
Meigs, S.A., *The Reformation in Ireland: Tradition and Confessionalism 1400–1690* (London, 1997).
Merriman, M., *The Rough Wooings: Mary, Queen of Scots, 1542–1551* (East Linton, 2000).
Moody, T.W., F.X. Martin and F.J. Byrne, eds., *A New History of Ireland III* (Oxford, 1978).
Morgan, H., 'The Colonial Venture of Sir Thomas Smith in Ulster, 1571–5', *Historical Journal*, 28 (1985), 261–78.
Tyronne's Rebellion (Woodbridge, Suffolk, 1999; reprint of 1993 edn).
Morrill, J., 'A British Patriachy: Ecclesiastical Imperialism under the early Stuarts' in A. Fletcher and P. Roberts, eds., *Religion, Culture and Society in Early Modern Britain* (Cambridge, 1994), 209–37.
'The British Problem, c. 1534–1707' in B. Bradshaw and J. Morrill, eds., *The British Problem, c. 1534–1707: State Formation in the Atlantic Archipelago* (London, 1996), 1–38.

Murray, A., 'The Procedure of the Scottish Exchequer in the Early Sixteenth Century', *SHR*, 11 (1961), 89–117.
'Huntly's Rebellion and the Administration of Justice in North-East Scotland, 1570–73', *Northern Scotland*, 4 (1981), 1–6.
Nicholls, M., *The History of the Modern British Isles, 1529–1603* (London, 1999).
O'Cuiv, B., *The Irish Bardic Duanaire or Poem-Book* (Dublin, 1973).
Ohlmeyer, J., *Civil War and Restoration in the Three Stuart Kingdoms: The Career of Randal MacDonnell, Marquis of Antrim, 1609–1683* (Cambridge, 1993).
Ohlmeyer, J., ed., *Political Thought in Seventeenth-Century Ireland: Kingdom or Colony?* (Cambridge, 2000).
Paton, G.C.H., ed., *An Introduction to Scottish Legal History* (Stair Society, 20, Edinburgh, 1958).
Pettegree, A., A. Duke and G. Lewis, eds., *Calvinism in Europe, 1540–1620* (Cambridge, 1994).
Phillips, G., *The Anglo-Scots Wars, 1513–50* (Woodbridge, Suffolk, 1999).
Pocock, J.G.A., 'British History: A Plea for a New Subject', *Journal of Modern History*, 4 (1975), 601–28.
'The Limits and Divisions of British History', *American Historical Review*, 87 (1982), 311–86.
Potter, D., 'French Intrigue in Ireland during the reign of Henri II, 1547–1559', *International History Review*, 5 (1983), 159–80.
Riddell, J., *Inquiry into the Law and Practice in Scottish Peerages* (Edinburgh, 1842).
Rixson, D., *The West Highland Galley* (East Linton, 1998).
Rodríguez-Salgado, M.J., *The Changing Face of Empire: Charles V, Philip II and Habsburg Authority, 1551–9* (Cambridge, 1988).
Sanderson, M.H.B., *Scottish Rural Society in the Sixteenth Century* (Edinburgh, 1982).
Mary Stewart's People: Life in Mary Stewart's Scotland (Edinburgh, 1987).
Ayrshire and the Reformation: People and Change, 1490–1600 (East Linton, 1997).
Sellar, W.D.H., 'The Earliest Campbells: Norman Briton or Gael?', *Scottish Studies*, 17 (1973), 109–25.
'Marriage, Divorce and Concubinage in Gaelic Scotland', *TGSI*, 51 (1978–80), 464–93.
'Highland Family Origins – Pedigree Making and Pedigree Faking' in L. Maclean, ed., *The Middle Ages in the Highlands* (Inverness Field Club, Inverness, 1981), 103–16.
'Marriage, Divorce and the Forbidden Degrees: Canon Law and Scots Law' in W.M. Osborough, ed., *Explorations in Law and History: Irish Legal History Society Discourses, 1988–1994* (Dublin, 1995), 59–82.
Sellar, W.D.H., ed., *Stair Society Miscellany II* (Stair Society, 35, Edinburgh, 1984).
Simms, K., 'Warfare in the Medieval Gaelic Lordships', *Irish Sword*, 12 (1975–6), 98–108.
'Guesting and Feasting in Gaelic Ireland', *Journal of the Royal Society of Antiquaries of Ireland*, 108 (1978), 67–100.
From Kings to Warlords (Woodbridge, Suffolk, 1987).
Small, J., 'Queen Mary at Jedburgh in 1566', *PSAS*, 3 (1881), 210–33.
Small, T.A., 'Queen Mary in the Counties of Dumbarton and Argyll', *SHR*, 25 (1927), 13–19.
Smith, D., 'The Spiritual Jurisdiction, 1560–64', *RSCHS*, 25 (1993), 1–18.

Steer, K. and J. Bannerman, *Late Medieval Monumental Sculpture in the West Highlands* (RCAHMS, Edinburgh, 1977).
Stevenson, D., *Alastair MacColla and the Highland Problem* (Edinburgh 1980).
Thomas, A., ' "Dragonis baith and dowis ay in double forme": Women at the Court of James V, 1513–42' in E. Ewan and M. Meikle, eds., *Women in Scotland, c 1100–c 1750* (East Linton, 1999), 83–94.
Thomson, D., 'Gaelic Learned Orders and Literati in Medieval Scotland', *Scottish Studies*, 12 (1968), 57–78.
  An Introduction to Gaelic Poetry (Edinburgh, 1990; reprint of 1974 edn).
Tranter, N., *The Fortified House in Scotland* (5 vols., Edinburgh, 1962–70).
Verschuur, M.B., 'The Outbreak of the Scottish Reformation at Perth, 11 May 1559', *Scotia* (1987), 41–53.
Watson, W.J., 'Classic Gaelic Poetry of Panegyric in Scotland', *TGSI*, 29 (1914–19), 194–234.
  'Unpublished Gaelic poetry', *Scottish Gaelic Studies*, 3 (1931), 139–59.
Wernham, R.B., 'The British Question, 1559–69' in R.B. Wernham, ed., *New Cambridge Modern History III: The Counter Reformation and Price Revolution 1559–1610* (Cambridge, 1968), 209–33.
Wood, D., ed., *Life and Thought in the Northern Church, c. 1100–c. 1700: Essays in Honour of Claire Cross* (Studies in Church History, Subsidia 12, Woodbridge, Suffolk, 1999).
Wormald, J., 'Bloodfeud, Kindred and Government in Early Modern Scotland', *Past and Present*, 87 (1980), 54–97.
  Lords and Men in Scotland: Bonds of Manrent, 1442–1603 (Edinburgh, 1985).
  Mary Queen of Scots: A Study in Failure (London, 1988).

UNPUBLISHED THESES

Flett, I., 'The Conflict of the Reformation and Democracy in the Geneva of Scotland' (University of St Andrews MPhil thesis, 1981).
Loughlin, M., 'The Career of Maitland of Lethington c. 1526–1573' (University of Edinburgh PhD thesis, 1991).
Macdonald, F., 'Ireland and Scotland: Historical Perspectives on the Gaelic Dimension, 1560–1760' (2 vols., University of Glasgow PhD thesis, 1994).
MacGregor, M., 'A Political History of the MacGregors before 1571' (University of Edinburgh PhD thesis, 1989).
Stewart, J.H., 'Highland Settlement Evolution in West Perthshire' (University of Newcastle-upon-Tyne PhD thesis, 1986).
Ritchie, P., 'Dynasticism and Diplomacy: The Political Career of Marie de Guise in Scotland, 1548–60' (University of St Andrews PhD thesis, 1999).
Verschuur, M.B., 'Perth and Reformation' (2 vols., University of Glasgow PhD thesis, 1985).
White, D.G., 'The Tudor Plantations in Ireland before 1571' (2 vols., Trinity College, Dublin, PhD thesis, 1967).

INDEX

Single entries and passing mentions of places or persons are not generally indexed. Personal and place names follow modern spellings and forms, except in the territorial designation of nobles. Individuals are indexed under their family names with cross-references given to the titles of peers and ecclesiastics.

244

O'Neill of Tyrone, Hugh, earl of Tyrone,
208, 215, 218, *see also* Nine Years' War
  Shane, 8, 53, 82, 105–9, 111–12, 125
    n. 60, 127–30, 133–6, 139, 142, 146,
    150, 156–8, 160–2, 165–8, 214
    n. 16
  Turlough Luineach, 16, 62 n. 81, 81,
    108 n. 118, 143, 162–5, 199, 203–5,
    215, 218

Panholls, 72 n. 126, 79 n. 163
Parliament, Scottish, 87–8, 90, 95, 103–4,
    112, 118, 121, 145, 149, 150 n. 36,
    154, 172, 174–6, 185–6, 188, 190,
    194–5
Percy, Thomas, earl of Northumberland,
    96 n. 55, 180–1, 183, 196
Perth, 79, 89–94, 109
  Pacification of, 188 n. 93, 189–91
Perthshire, 65, 92–3, 122–3, 126, 181 n. 51,
    189 n. 99
Philip II, king of Spain, 2, 174, 193
Piers, William, Captain of Carrickfergus,
    133–4, 138, 162, 167, 200 n. 150, 203,
    205 n. 122, 208
Pinkie, battle of, 52, 100 n. 78
Privy council, Scottish, 84, 114, 116 n. 20,
    118, 120, 131–2, 146–7, 156, 186, 195,
    206

Queen's Party, 25, 32, 37–8, 44, 53, 153–5,
    170–91, 193–4, 199, 203 n. 161

Radcliffe, Thomas, earl of Sussex, 5–6, 8,
    102, 106–9, 127–30, 133, 135,
    136 n. 134, 139, 182–4, 196
Randolph, Thomas, 35 n. 113, 99, 103, 117,
    119, 124, 127–8, 130, 133, 135, 138,
    139 n. 147, 140–1, 142 nn. 156 and
    158, 157 nn. 79 and 80, 165–6, 181,
    196–7
Rathlin island, 131 n. 99, 199
Rhinns of Islay, 131, 159, 206–7
Riccio murder, 27 n. 66, 37, 118, 122 n. 45,
    143, 145–8, 156, 166–7
Ridolphi plot, 173, 185, 198
Robertson of Tullgavane, Patrick, 82 n. 172,
    83
Rose of Kilravock, Hugh, 83 n. 180, 109
Ross, diocese of, 207 nn. 185 and 187
  bishop of, *see* Leslie, John
Rough Wooing, 3–4, 119, 198, 212
Route [Antrim], 6, 106, 129, 205 n. 169,
    captain of, *see* MacDonald of Antrim,
    Sorley Boy

Russell, Francis, earl of Bedford, 141,
    146 n. 9
Ruthven, Katherine, Lady Glenorchy, 35
    n. 109, 39–40, 62, 79 n. 159, 90 n. 18
  Patrick, 3rd Lord Ruthven, 89–92, 93
    n. 34, 94 n. 43, 95 n. 51, 100, 101
    n. 84, 122, 124, 145–6

St Andrews, 92–3, 99–100
  archbishop of, *see* Hamilton, John
  priory, 71 n. 120, commendator prior of,
    see Stewart, Lord James
St John, Lord, *see* Sandilands, James
Sandilands, James, Lord St John, 87 n. 5,
    112 n. 1
Sempill, Robert, 3rd Lord Sempill, 91,
    176 n. 20, 181, 183, 191
Sidney, Sir Henry, 134, 136, 149 n. 34,
    156–7, 158 n. 78, 161, 166–7, 200–2,
    205
Sinclair, George, 4th earl of Caithness,
    58 n. 57, 184 n. 65
Skye, 59 n. 62, 207
Smith, John, 203–4
Spain, 2–3, 50, 142, 164–5, 174, 187, 211
Spottiswood, John, superintendent of
    Lothian, 32 n. 93, 124, n. 56
Stewart of Appin, John, 57 n. 47, 82, 156,
    162 n. 107
Stewart of Atholl, John, 4th earl of Atholl,
    26 n. 58, 31–2, 38, 42, 69 n. 113,
    81–2, 109, 116, 122, 125, 144, 146,
    150, 156, 180–1, 183–5, 189,
    190 n. 109
Stewart of Bute, John, 79, 188 n. 93
Stewart of Doune, James, 16, 122, 146,
    152, 183
Stewart of Grandtully, William, 90 n. 18,
    183–4
Stewart of Lennox, 120–3, 149, 173
  Henry, Lord Darnley, 37–8, 49, 111,
    121–3, 125, 140, 149–50, 156–7, 165,
    murder of, 58 n. 53, 143–51, 154, 167,
    176–8, 189 n. 103, 194
  Matthew, earl of Lennox, 119–21, 125,
    140, 146 n. 13, 147, 149, 170, 174–5,
    183, 186–8, 198, 203 n. 161, 207
Stewart of Ochiltree, Andrew, 2nd Lord
    Ochiltree, 92 n. 29, 116
Stewart, Lord James, commendator prior of
    St Andrews, earl of Moray, 20, 23, 29,
    30 n. 38, 36, 38–9, 41, 49, 81, 84,
    88–104, 109, 111–26, 137–8, 140–4,
    146, 148–9, 153–5, 165–8, 174–80,
    188, 192–4, 202

Cambridge Studies in Early Modern British History

Titles in the series